The Year of Living Biblically

A. J. Jacobs is the *New York Times* best-selling author of *The Know-It-All: One Man's Humble Quest to Become the Smartest Person in the World*. He is the editor at large at *Esquire* magazine, for which he wrote the article 'My Outsourced Life.' He has also written for the *New York Times*, *The Washington Post*, and *Entertainment Weekly*. He lives in New York City. You can visit his website at ajjacobs.com.

ALSO BY A. J. JACOBS
The Know-It-All

Praise for THE YEAR OF LIVING BIBLICALLY by A. J. Jacobs

"A. J. Jacobs has written about the Bible in a manner that is brilliantly funny but unerringly respectful, learned but goofy, deeply personal yet highly relevant. I am covetous and wish him smited."

—Mary Roach,
Bestselling author of *Spook* and *Stiff*

"A book that is at one and the same time delightfully readable and profoundly memorable is a wonder! *The Year of Living Biblically* is exactly that. A. J. Jacobs has perceived the distinction between the wisdom of the Bible and its absurdities. It is a shame that so many of both our clergy and our politicians seem incapable of making that distinction."

—John Shelby Spong,
Author of *Jesus for the Non-Religious*
and former Episcopal bishop

"As a man incapable of developing any facial hair aside from a really amazingly cruddy moustache, I would have bought this book for the astonishing big beard chronicle alone. That *The Year of Living Biblically* grows, beardlike, into a long, hilarious, tangled, and ultimately moving story of spiritual growth is all the more astonishing. But why should I continue to be surprised at what springs from A. J.'s head? He is a brilliantly hilarious writer who truly lives up to that oft-misused adverb/adjective combination and then some. Plus: HE IS GOING TO HEAVEN. So how can you not afford to tithe your salary to his cause and buy this book?"

—John Hodgman
Daily Show correspondent and author of
Areas of My Expertise

"Seeing that most people violate at least three of the ten commandments on their way to work—even people who work from home—says a lot about the scale of A. J.'s feat. The fact that you need to buy six copies of this book to unlock the code to save all humanity . . . well, that's just pure genius."

—Ben Karlin,
cocreator of *The Colbert Report*
and coauthor of *America: The Book*

"Setting out to explore the consequences of strict adherence to biblical laws, A. J. Jacobs encounters a series of experiences that are as hilarious as they are thought-provoking. Along the way he teaches us both the fallacies of modern day religious fundamentalism and the joys of discovering the transcendent and timeless truths of faith."

—Francis S. Collins, M.D., Ph.D.,
director, Human Genome Project, author of *The Language of God: A Scientist Presents Evidence for Belief*

"Throughout his journey, Jacobs comes across as a generous and thoughtful (and yes, slightly neurotic) participant observer, lacing his story with absurdly funny cultural commentary as well as nuanced insights into the impossible task of biblical literalism."

—*Publishers Weekly* (Starred)

"Impressive and often tremendously amusing. . . . The author's determination despite constant complications from his modern secular life (wife, job, family, NYC) underscores both the absurdity of his plight and its profundity. While debunking biblical literalism—with dinner party–ready scriptural quotes—Jacobs simultaneously finds his spirituality renewed. . . . A biblical travelogue—and far funnier than your standard King James."

—Kirkus Reviews

The Year *of* Living Biblically

One Man's Humble Quest
to Follow the Bible
as Literally as
Possible

A. J. Jacobs

WILLIAM HEINEMANN: LONDON

Published by William Heinemann, 2008

2 4 6 8 10 9 7 5 3 1

First published in the United States in 2007 by Simon & Schuster
First published in Great Britain in 2008 by William Heinemann

Random House, 20 Vauxhall Bridge Road,
London SW1V 2SA

www.rbooks.co.uk

Addresses for companies within The Random House Group Limited can be
found at: www.randomhouse.co.uk/offices.htm

The Random House Group Limited Reg. No. 954009

A CIP catalogue record for this book
is available from the British Library

ISBN: 9780434017119

The Random House Group Limited makes every effort to ensure that the
papers used in its books are made from trees that have been legally sourced
from well-managed and credibly certified forests. Our paper procurement
policy can be found at: www.rbooks.co.uk/environment

Mixed Sources
Product group from well-managed
forests and other controlled sources
www.fsc.org Cert no. TT-COC-2139
© 1996 Forest Stewardship Council
FSC

Printed and bound in Great Britain by
CPI Mackays, Chatham, ME5 8TD

To Julie

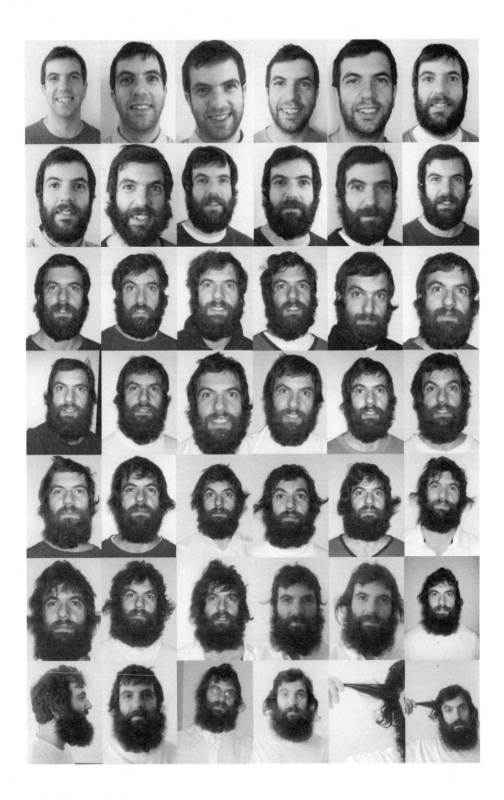

The Year *of* Living
Biblically

Introduction

As I write this, I have a beard that makes me resemble Moses. Or Abe Lincoln. Or Ted Kaczynski. I've been called all three.

It's not a well-manicured, socially acceptable beard. It's an untamed mass that creeps up toward my eyeballs and drapes below my neckline.

I've never allowed my facial hair to grow before, and it's been an odd and enlightening experience. I've been inducted into a secret fraternity of bearded guys—we nod at each other as we pass on the street, giving a knowing quarter smile. Strangers have come up to me and petted my beard, like it's a Labrador retriever puppy or a pregnant woman's stomach.

I've suffered for my beard. It's been caught in jacket zippers and been tugged on by my surprisingly strong two-year-old son. I've spent a lot of time answering questions at airport security.

I've been asked if I'm named Smith and sell cough drops with my brother. ZZ Top is mentioned at least three times a week. Passersby have shouted "Yo, Gandalf!" Someone called me Steven Seagal, which I found curious, since he doesn't have a beard.

I've battled itch and heat. I've spent a week's salary on balms, powders, ointments, and conditioners. My beard has been a temporary home to cappuccino foam and lentil soup. And it's upset people. Thus far, two little girls have burst into tears, and one boy has hidden behind his mother.

But I mean no harm. The facial hair is simply the most noticeable physical manifestation of a spiritual journey I began a year ago.

My quest has been this: to live the ultimate biblical life. Or more precisely, to follow the Bible as literally as possible. To obey the Ten Commandments. To be fruitful and multiply. To love my neighbor. To

tithe my income. But also to abide by the oft-neglected rules: to avoid
wearing clothes made of mixed fibers. To stone adulterers. And, naturally, to leave the edges of my beard unshaven (Leviticus 19:27). I am
trying to obey the entire Bible, without picking and choosing.

To back up: I grew up in an extremely secular home in New York
City. I am officially Jewish, but I'm Jewish in the same way the Olive
Garden is an Italian restaurant. Which is to say: not very. I attended no
Hebrew school, ate no matzoh. The closest my family came to observing
Judaism was that paradoxical classic of assimilation: a Star of David on
top of our Christmas tree.

It's not that my parents badmouthed religion. It's just that religion
wasn't for us. We lived in the twentieth century, for crying out loud. In
our house, spirituality was almost a taboo subject, much like my father's
salary or my sister's clove-cigarette habit.

My only brushes with the Bible were brief and superficial. We had a
next-door neighbor, Reverend Schulze, a kindly Lutheran minister who
looked remarkably like Thomas Jefferson. (By the way, Reverend
Schulze's son became an actor and, oddly enough, went on to play the
part of the creepy priest on *The Sopranos*.) Reverend Schulze told great
stories about college sit-ins during the sixties, but whenever he started
talking about God, it just sounded like a foreign language to me.

I attended a handful of bar mitzvahs where I zoned out during services and spent the time trying to guess who had bald spots under their
yarmulkes. I went to my paternal grandfather's funeral, which was, to
my surprise, presided over by a rabbi. How could the rabbi eulogize a
man he'd never met? It was disconcerting.

And as far as childhood religion, that was about it.

I was agnostic before I even knew what the word meant. Partly, it
was the problem of the existence of evil. If there is a God, why would He
allow war, disease, and my fourth-grade teacher Ms. Barker, who forced
us to have a sugar-free bake sale? But mostly, the idea of God seemed su-
perfluous. Why do we need an invisible, inaudible deity? Maybe He exists, but we'll never know in this life.

College didn't help my spiritual development. I went to a secular
university where you were more likely to study the semiotics of Wicca
rituals than the Judeo-Christian tradition. And when we did read the

Bible, it was as literature, as a fusty, ancient book with the same truth quotient as *The Faerie Queene*.

We did, of course, study the history of religion. How the Bible has been the force behind many of humankind's greatest achievements: the civil rights movement, charitable giving, the abolition of slavery. And how, of course, it's been used to justify our worst: war, genocide, and the subjugation of others.

For a long time, I thought that religion, for all the good it does, seemed too risky for our modern world. The potential for abuse too high. I figured it would slowly fade away like other archaic things. Science was on the march. Someday soon we'd all be living in a neo-Enlightenment paradise where every decision was made with steely Spock-like logic.

As you might have noticed, I was spectacularly mistaken. The influence of the Bible—and religion as a whole—remains a mighty force, perhaps even stronger than it was when I was a kid. So in the last few years, religion has become my fixation. Is half of the world suffering from a massive delusion? Or is my blindness to spirituality a huge defect in my personality? What if I'm missing out on part of being human, like a guy who goes through life without ever hearing Beethoven or falling in love? And most important, I now have a young son—if my lack of religion is a flaw, I don't want to pass it on to him.

So I knew I wanted to explore religion. I just needed to figure out how.

The germ of the idea came from my own family: my uncle Gil. Or ex-uncle, to be exact. Gil married my aunt and divorced her a few years later, but he remains the most controversial member of our family. If the rest of my relatives are ultrasecular, Gil makes up for it by being, quite possibly, the most religious man in the world. He's a spiritual omnivore. He started his life as a Jew, became a Hindu, appointed himself a guru, sat for eight months on a Manhattan park bench without speaking, founded a hippie cult in upstate New York, turned into a born-again Christian, and, in his latest incarnation, is an ultra–Orthodox Jew in Jerusalem. I may have missed a phase—I think he was into Shinto for a bit. But you get the idea.

At some point along his spiritual path, Gil decided to take the Bible literally. Completely literally. The Bible says to bind money to your hand (Deuteronomy 14:25), so Gil withdrew three hundred dollars from the bank and tied the bills to his palm with a thread. The Bible says to wear fringes on the corners of your garment (Numbers 15:38), so Gil bought yarn from a knitting shop, made a bunch of tassels, and attached them to his shirt collar and the ends of his sleeves. The Bible says to give money to widows and orphans, so he walked the streets asking people if they were widows or orphans so he could hand them cash.

About a year and a half ago, I was telling my friend Paul about Gil's bizarre life over lunch at a sandwich shop, and I had my epiphany. *That's it.* I needed to follow the Bible literally myself. I needed to do it for several reasons.

First, since the Bible requires me to tell the truth (Proverbs 26:28), I must confess that part of the reason is to write this book. A couple of years ago, I came out with a book about reading the *Encyclopaedia Britannica*, all of it, from A to Z—or more specific, from a–ak (East Asian music) to Żywiec (a town in southern Poland known for its beer). What could I do next? The only intellectual adventure that seemed a worthy follow-up was to explore the most influential book in the world, the all-time best seller, the Bible.

Second, this project would be my visa to a spiritual world. I wouldn't just be studying religion. I'd be living it. If I had what they call a God-shaped hole in my heart, this quest would allow me to fill it. If I had a hidden mystical side, this year would bring it out of the closet. If I wanted to understand my forefathers, this year would let me live like they did, but with less leprosy.

And third, this project would be a way to explore the huge and fascinating topic of biblical literalism. Millions of Americans say they take the Bible literally. According to a 2005 Gallup poll, the number hovers near 33 percent; a 2004 *Newsweek* poll put it at 55 percent. A literal interpretation of the Bible—both Jewish and Christian—shapes American policies on the Middle East, homosexuality, stem cell research, education, abortion—right on down to rules about buying beer on Sunday.

But my suspicion was that almost everyone's literalism consisted of picking and choosing. People plucked out the parts that fit their agenda, whether that agenda was to the right or left. Not me. I thought, with some naïveté, I would peel away the layers of interpretation and find the true Bible underneath. I would do this by being the ultimate fundamentalist. I'd be fearless. I would do exactly what the Bible said, and in so doing, I'd discover what's great and timeless in the Bible and what is outdated.

I told my wife, Julie, my idea, and warned her it might affect our life in a not-so-minor way. She didn't gnash her teeth or tear out her hair. She just emitted a little sigh. "I was kind of hoping your next book would be a biography of Eleanor Roosevelt or something."

Everyone—family, friends, coworkers—had the same concern: that I'd go native. That I'd end up as a beekeeper at a monastery, or I'd move into my ex-uncle Gil's spare room in his Jerusalem apartment.

In a sense, they were right to worry. It's impossible to immerse yourself in religion for twelve months and emerge unaffected. At least it was for me. Put it this way: If my former self and my current self met for coffee, they'd get along OK, but they'd both probably walk out of the Starbucks shaking their heads and saying to themselves, "That guy is kinda delusional."

As with most biblical journeys, my year has taken me on detours I could never have predicted. I didn't expect to herd sheep in Israel. Or fondle a pigeon egg. Or find solace in prayer. Or hear Amish jokes from the Amish. I didn't expect to confront just how absurdly flawed I am. I didn't expect to discover such strangeness in the Bible. And I didn't expect to, as the Psalmist says, take refuge in the Bible and rejoice in it.

The Preparation

And he shall read in it all the days of his life . . .

—DEUTERONOMY 17:19

On the admittedly random day of July 7, 2005, I begin my preparations. I pull out a Bible that is tucked away in the corner of my bookshelf. I don't even remember where I got it, but it looks like the Platonic ideal of a Bible. Like a Bible they'd use in a fifties Western to stop a bullet from piercing the hero's chest. On the front, it says "Holy Bible" in faded gold embossing. The tissue-thin pages remind me of my beloved encyclopedia. The black leather cover smells exactly like my parents' 1976 Plymouth Valiant. It feels good, comforting.

I crack open the Bible. The title page says, "This Bible is presented to . . ." and then, in handwritten bubble letters, the name of my exgirlfriend. Huh. Somehow I had inadvertently pilfered my ex-girlfriend's childhood Bible. I hope inadvertently. It's been a decade since we broke up, and I can't remember. Regardless, that's not a good sign. At the very least, I need to return it when I'm done.

I've read bits and pieces of the Bible before, but never the whole thing, never straight through from Genesis to Revelation. So that's what I do for four weeks, five hours a day. Luckily, I'm used to marathon reading from my *Britannica* project, so it felt pleasantly nostalgic.

As I read, I type into my PowerBook every rule, every guideline, every suggestion, every nugget of advice I find in the Bible. When I finish, I have a very long list. It runs seventy-two pages. More than seven hundred rules. The scope is astounding. All aspects of my life will be affected—the way I talk, walk, eat, bathe, dress, and hug my wife.

Many of the rules will be good for me and will, I hope, make me a better person by the end of the year. I'm thinking of: No lying. No coveting. No stealing. Love your neighbor. Honor your parents. Dozens of them. I'll be the Gandhi of the Upper West Side.

But plenty of other rules don't seem like they'll make me more righteous at all. Just more strange, more obsessive, more likely to alienate friends and family: Bathe after sex. Don't eat fruit from a tree planted less than five years ago. Pay the wages of a worker every day.

And a good number of the rules aren't just baffling, but federally outlawed. As in: Destroy idols. Kill magicians. Sacrifice oxen.

This is going to be a monster project. I need a plan of attack. I need to make some decisions.

1. Which version of the Bible should I use?

The Bible I pulled from my bookshelf is called the Revised Standard Version, which it turns out is a well-respected translation, an offspring of the famed King James Version from 1611, but stripped of most of the "thee"s and "thou"s.

It's a good start. But it's just one of many, many versions—an estimated *three thousand* of them in English alone. One of my goals is to find out what the Bible really says, so I decide I can't rely on any single translation. I want to compare and contrast at least some of those three thousand.

I go to a Bible bookstore in midtown Manhattan. It's a huge Wal-Mart-sized store with fluorescent lighting and a long counter of cash registers at the front. My salesman is named Chris, a soft-spoken guy with the body of an Olympic power lifter. He shows me tables covered with Bibles of all shapes, sizes, and linguistic slants—from the plain-spoken English of the Good News Bible to the majestic cadence of the Jerusalem Bible.

He points out one Bible I might want. It's designed to look exactly like a *Seventeen* magazine: An attractive (if long-sleeved) model graces the front, next to cover lines like "What's Your Spiritual IQ?" Open it up and you'll find sidebars such as "Rebecca the Control Freak."

"This one's good if you're on the subway and are too embarrassed to be seen reading the Bible," says Chris. "Because no one will ever know it's a Bible." It's an odd and poignant selling point. You know you're in a secular city when it's considered more acceptable for a grown man to read a teen girl's magazine than the Bible.

I leave the store with two shopping bags packed with Scripture. But my buying spree isn't over. When I get home, I click on Amazon.com and get several Jewish translations of the Bible, and a half-dozen Bible commentaries. To be safe, I order *The Bible for Dummies* and *The Complete Idiot's Guide to the Bible*—anything aimed at those with a sub-80 IQ.

That's not to mention the Bibles sent to me by friends. One gave me the waterproof Outdoor Bible so that I could study the Scripture even during floods and other Old Testament weather patterns. Another sent me a hip-hop version, where the Twenty-third Psalm reads "The Lord is all that." (The more traditional translation is "The Lord is my shepherd.")

In short, I've got the proverbial stack of Bibles, almost waist high.

2. What does it mean to follow the Bible literally?

To follow the Bible literally—at face value, at its word, according to its plain meaning—isn't just a daunting proposition. It's a dangerous one.

Consider: In the third century, the scholar Origen is said to have interpreted literally Matthew 19:12—"There are eunuchs who have made themselves eunuchs for the sake of the kingdom of heaven"—and castrated himself. Origen later became a preeminent theologian of his age—and an advocate of figurative interpretation.

Another example: In the mid-1800s, when anesthesia was first introduced for women in labor, there was an uproar. Many felt it violated God's pronouncement in Genesis 3:16: "I will greatly multiply your pain in childbearing; in pain you shall bring forth children." If Julie and I ever have another child, would I dare get between her and the epidural needle? Not a chance.

It's a good bet that, at some time or other in history, every single passage in the Bible has been taken as literal. I've decided I can't do that. That'd be misleading, unnecessarily flip, and would result in missing body parts. No, instead my plan is this: I will try to find the original intent of the biblical rule or teaching and follow that to the letter. If the passage is unquestionably figurative—and I'm going to say the eunuch one is—then I won't obey it literally. But if there's any doubt whatsoever—and most often there is—I will err on the side of being literal. When it says don't tell lies, I'll try not to tell any lies. When it says to stone blasphemers, I'll pick up rocks.

3. Should I obey the Old Testament, the New Testament, or both?

Many, perhaps most, of the teachings in the two testaments are similar, but some are significantly different. So I've decided to split up my quest.

I will devote most of my year—eight months or so—to the Old Testament, since that's where you'll find the bulk of the Bible's rules. The Old Testament consists of thirty-nine books that mix narrative, genealogy, poetry, and lots and lots of laws. The first five books alone—the books of Moses—have hundreds of decrees, including the crucial Ten Commandments, as well as some of the more seemingly atavistic ones about executing homosexuals. That's not to mention divinely inspired advice in later Old Testament books. The Proverbs—a collection of King Solomon's wisdom—offer guidance on child rearing and marriage. The Psalms tell you how to worship. I'll be abiding by everything. Or trying to.

Being officially Jewish, I feel much more comfortable living and writing about the Old Testament. (Or, as many Jews prefer to call it, the Hebrew Bible, since *old* implies "outdated," and *new* implies "improved"). But in the final four months of my year, I want to explore—in at least some way—the teachings of the Christian Bible, the New Testament.

To ignore the New Testament would be to ignore half of the story. The evangelical movement and its literal interpretation of the Bible hold enormous sway, both for the good (they were powerful advocates for aiding Darfur) and, to my secular mind, the not-so-good (far-right fundamentalists are driving the creationism movement).

Naturally, there's the most famous of all Christian literalists—the conservatives in the Jerry Falwell/Pat Robertson mold. I plan to meet them later this year. But I also want to look at evangelical groups such as the "Red-letter Christians," which focus on what they see as literal adherence to Jesus's teachings about compassion, nonviolence, and the redistribution of wealth.

It's debatable whether the New Testament even has a legal code—it depends on your definition of "law"—but it has many teachings that have been followed with varying degrees of literalness, from Jesus's "turn the other cheek" and "love your enemy" to the Apostle Paul's decree that men should have short hair. Frankly, I haven't hammered out all the details of my New Testament plan but hope to figure it out once I get my spiritual footing.

4. Should I have guides?
The Bible says, "It is not good for the man to be alone." Plus, I'm flying blind here. So over the course of a couple of weeks, I assemble a board of spiritual advisers: rabbis, ministers, and priests, some of them conservative, some of them one four-letter word away from excommunication. Some are friends of friends, some are names I stumbled upon in Bible commentary books. I'll be talking to them as much as possible.

Plus, I make a pledge to get out of the house. I'll visit a bunch of groups that take the Bible literally in their own way: the ultra-Orthodox Jews, the ancient sect of Samaritans, and the Amish, among others.

My guides will give me advice and context. But they won't be the final word. The Bible will. I don't want to follow any single tradition exclusively. As naïve or misguided as it may be, I want to discover the Bible for myself, even if it entails trekking down some circuitous paths. "DIY religion," as my friend calls it. Perhaps I'll find the beauty of a particular tradition fits me best. Or perhaps I'll start my own sect of Judeo-Christianity. I don't know.

As I expected, not everyone thinks my project is a great idea. My aunt Kate—who has remained an Orthodox Jew even after her divorce from the controversial Gil—told me I was, as our people say, meshuga.

I first floated the idea by Kate in early August. We were at my grandfather's house sitting around his big dining room table. Kate had just finished changing after a dip in the pool. (She won't wear a bathing suit for modesty reasons, so she plunged in with her long, black billowy dress, which impressed me. The thing looked heavy enough to sink a lifeguard.) When I explained the premise of my book, her eyebrows shot up to her hairline. "Really?" she said.

Then she laughed. I think part of her was happy that someone in our godless family was showing some interest in religion.

After which she got concerned: "It's misguided. You need the oral law. You can't just obey the written law. It doesn't make sense without the oral law."

The traditional Jewish position is this: The Bible—known as the written law—was composed in shorthand. It's so condensed, it's almost in code. Which is where the oral law comes in. The rabbis have unraveled the Bible for us in books such as the Talmud, which are based on the oral teachings of the elders. When the Bible says to "rest" on the Sabbath, you need the rabbis to tell you what "rest" means. Can you exercise? Can you cook? Can you log on to drugstore.com?

Without the rabbis, I'm like the protagonist of the early eighties TV show *The Greatest American Hero*—he found a bright red suit that gave him all these superpowers, but he lost the instruction manual, so he was always flying into walls.

Some conservative Christians were also baffled by my undertaking. They said I couldn't truly understand the Bible without accepting the divinity of Christ. They said that many of these laws—like the ones about animal sacrifice—were nullified by Jesus's death.

And I did start to have doubts. These were good points. I felt torn, anxious about my approach, my monumental ignorance, my lack of preparation, about all the inevitable blunders I'd make. And the more I read, the more I absorbed the fact that the Bible isn't just another book. It's the book of books, as one of my Bible commentaries calls it. I love my encyclopedia, but the encyclopedia hasn't spawned thousands of communities based on its words. It hasn't shaped the actions, values, deaths, love lives, warfare, and fashion sense of millions of people over three millennia. No one has been executed for translating the encyclopedia into another language, as was William Tyndale when he published the first widely distributed English-language edition of the Bible. No president has been sworn in with the encyclopedia. It's intimidating, to say the least.

Fortunately, I got a couple of pep talks from two of my favorite advisers. The first was Reverend Elton Richards, my friend David's father, who just retired as minister of his Lutheran congregation in Des Moines, Iowa. He calls himself a "pastor out to pasture." I told him about the doubters.

"You just have to tell them that you have a hunger and a thirst. And you may not sit at the same banquet table as them, but you have a hunger and thirst. So they shouldn't judge you."

I love the way he talks. By the end, perhaps I'll be able to speak in majestic food metaphors like Reverend Richards.

I also had breakfast with Rabbi Andy Bachman, a brilliant man who heads up one of Brooklyn's largest synagogues, Congregation Beth Elohim. He told me a *midrash*—a story or legend that is not in the Bible proper, but which deals with biblical events. This midrash is about the parting of the Red Sea.

"We all think of the scene in *The Ten Commandments* movie with Charlton Heston, where Moses lifted up his rod, and the waters rolled back. But this midrash says that's not how it happened. Moses lifted up his rod, and the sea did not part. The Egyptians were closing in, and the sea wasn't moving. So a Hebrew named Nachshon just walked into the water. He waded up to his ankles, then his knees, then his waist, then his shoulders. And right when water was about to get up to his nostrils, the sea parted. The point is, sometimes miracles occur only when you jump in."

So I did. And here is what happened.

Month One: September

Fear God and keep his commandments; for this is the whole duty of man.
—Ecclesiastes 12:13

It's the first day, and I already feel like the water is three feet over my head.

I have chosen September 1 to start my project, and from the moment I wake up, the Bible consumes my life. I can't do anything without fearing I'm breaking a biblical law. Before I so much as inhale or exhale, I have to run through a long mental checklist of the rules.

It begins when I open my closet to get dressed. The Bible forbids men to wear women's clothing (Deuteronomy 22:5), so that comfortable Dickinson College sweatshirt is off-limits. It was originally my wife's.

The Bible says to avoid wearing clothes made of mixed fibers (Leviticus 19:19), so I have to mothball my poly-cotton *Esquire* magazine T-shirt.

And loafers? Am I allowed to wear leather? I go to the living room, click on my PowerBook and open my Biblical Rules file. I scroll down to the ones about animals. Pigskin and snakeskin are questionable, but it looks like regular old cow leather is permissible.

But wait—am I even allowed to use the computer? The Bible, as you might have guessed, doesn't address the issue specifically, so I give it a tentative yes. Maybe sometime down the road, I could try stone tablets.

And then I stumble. Within a half hour of waking, I check the Amazon.com sales ranking of my last book. How many sins does that comprise? Pride? Envy? Greed? I can't even count.

I don't do much better on my errand to Mail Boxes Etc. I want to xerox a half dozen copies of the Ten Commandments so I can Scotch tape them up all over the apartment, figuring it'd be a good memory aid.

The Bible says, those with good sense are "slow to anger" (Proverbs 19:11). So when I get there at the same time as this wiry fortyish woman, and she practically sprints to the counter to beat me in line, I try not to be annoyed.

And when she tells the Mail Boxes Etc. employee to copy something on the one and only functioning Xerox machine, I try to shrug it off. And when she pulls out a stack of pages that looks like the collected works of J. K. Rowling and plunks it on the counter, I say to myself: "Slow to anger, slow to anger."

After which she asks some complicated question involving paper stock . . .

I remind myself: Remember what happened when the Israelites were waiting for Moses while he was up on the mountaintop for forty days? They got impatient, lost faith, and were struck with a plague.

Oh, and she pays by check. And asks for a receipt. And asks to get the receipt initialed. The Proverbs—a collection of wisdom in the Old Testament—say that smiling makes you happy. Which is actually backed up by psychological studies. So I stand there with a flight attendant–like grin frozen on my face. But inside, I am full of wrath.

I don't have time for this. I have a seventy-two-page-list of other biblical tasks to do.

I finally make it to the counter and give the cashier a dollar. She scoops my thirty-eight cents of change from the register and holds it out for me to take.

"Could you, uh, put the change on the counter?" I ask.

She glares at me. I'm not supposed to touch women—more on that later—so I am simply trying to avoid unnecessary finger-to-finger contact.

"I have a cold," I say. "I don't want to give it to you."

A complete lie. In trying to avoid one sin, I committed another.

I walk home. I pass by a billboard that features two well-toned naked people clutching hungrily at each other's bodies. It's an ad for a gym. The Bible's teachings on sexuality are complicated, and I haven't figured them out yet. But to be safe, I figure I should avoid lust for now. I keep my eyes on the ground for the rest of the walk home.

When I get back to my apartment, I decide to cross Numbers 15:38

off my list: Attach tassels to the corners of my garment. Inspired by my ex-uncle Gil, I had purchased some tassels from a website called "Tassels without Hassles." They look like the kind of tassels on the corners of my grandmother's needlepoint pillows. I spend ten minutes safety pinning them to my shirtsleeves and hem.

By the evening, I'm bushed. I barely have the energy to listen to Julie talk about the U.S. Open—and even that conversation is fraught. I have to be sure to avoid mentioning Venus Williams, since she's named for the Roman goddess of love, and it would violate Exodus 23:13 (make no mention of other gods).

As I go to bed, I wonder whether or not I took a step toward enlightenment today. Probably not. I was so busy obsessing over the rules—a lot of which still seem thoroughly insane—that I didn't have time to think. Maybe I'm like a student driver who spends every moment checking the blinkers and speedometer, too nervous to contemplate the scenery. But it's just the first day.

"Be fruitful and multiply . . ."

—Genesis 1:28

Day 2. My beard grows fast. I'm already starting to look a little seedy, somewhere between a Brooklyn hipster and a guy who loiters at the OTB all day. Which is fine by me. I'm enjoying the hiatus from shaving. I may be spending all sorts of time on biblical duties, but at least I'm not wasting three minutes each morning in front of the mirror.

For breakfast, I grab an orange from the refrigerator. Food is going to be tricky this year. The Bible bans many things: pork, shrimp, rabbit, eagle, and osprey, among others. But citrus is fine. Plus, oranges have been around since biblical times—one of my books even says that the forbidden fruit in the Garden of Eden was an orange. It certainly wasn't an apple, since there were no apples in the Middle East of Adam's day.

I sit down at the kitchen table. Julie is flipping through the Arts & Leisure section of the *New York Times* trying to decide on a movie for Saturday night.

"Should we see *The Aristocrats*?" Julie asks.

Huh. *The Aristocrats* is the documentary about the dirtiest joke ever. It contains at least a half dozen sex acts specifically banned by the Book of Leviticus. Julie could not come up with a worse suggestion for an evening activity. Is she testing me? She's got to be.

"I don't think I can. It doesn't sound very biblical."

"You serious?"

I nod.

"Fine. We'll see something else."

"I don't know if I should be seeing movies at all. I have to think about that."

Julie lowers her gaze and looks at me over the top of her glasses.

"No movies? For a year?"

I'm going to have to choose my battles these next twelve months. I decide I'll bend on this one for now—I'll phase out movies slowly, giving Julie a little grace period.

Things, after all, are kind of tense in our house right now. Julie had a hard time getting pregnant with our first child, as I mentioned in my last book. We did eventually succeed (we have a son named Jasper), but apparently, practice did not make perfect, because the second time around is just as much of an ordeal.

In the last year, I've been—as the Bible says—uncovering Julie's nakedness. A lot. Too much. Not that I dislike it, but enough is enough, you know? It gets tiring. Plus, Julie's getting increasingly frustrated with me because she thinks I'm micromanaging—always quizzing her about ovulation times and basal temperatures and her five-day forecast.

"You're stressing me out, and it's really counterproductive," she told me the other day.

"I'm just trying to stay involved."

"You know what? The more stressed out I am, the less chance there is that I'll get pregnant."

I tell her I want our son, Jasper, to have a little sibling.

"Then please stop talking about it."

So we're in this weird elephant-in-the-room phase where we're both thinking about having a second child, but studiously avoiding the topic.

This is especially hard for someone who spends as much time as I do reading and pondering the Bible. Fertility is one of the most dominant themes in the Bible—probably *the* dominant theme of Genesis. If you believe some of the more modern biblical scholars, Genesis reflects a nature/fertility stage of monotheism, an influence of the pagan sects. In fact, the very first command that God gives to Adam is "Be fruitful and multiply." It's the Alpha Rule of the Bible.

Now, if I were taking the Bible absolutely literally, I could be "fruitful" by loading up on peaches at Whole Foods Market and "multiply" by helping my niece with her algebra homework. I could scratch this commandment off my list in twenty minutes flat.

This hammers home a simple but profound lesson: When it comes to the Bible, there is always—but always—some level of interpretation, even on the most seemingly basic rules. In this case, I'm pretty sure that the Bible was talking about fertility, not math, so that's what I'll continue to pursue.

Conception was a huge preoccupation of the ancients. If you think about it, many of the Bible's most famous stories center on the quest to get pregnant. Abraham and Sarah probably had the hardest time conceiving of anyone in the Bible, if not history. At one point, the seemingly barren Sarah became so distraught, she lent her Egyptian handmaiden to Abraham as a concubine. That union produced Ishmael, the forefather of Islam. A few verses later, God and two angels visited Abraham and Sarah's tent and announced that Sarah would soon be pregnant. Sarah's reaction? She laughed, presumably with skepticism. In her defense, she was ninety years old. But God fulfilled his promise, and the nonagenarian matriarch gave birth to Isaac—Hebrew for "he will laugh."

And then there's Rachel. Rachel and her older sister Leah were both married to the clever shepherd (and my namesake) Jacob. Leah was a procreation machine—giving birth to no fewer than six sons and a daughter. But Rachel remained childless and heartbroken. At one point she said to Jacob, "Give me children or I shall die!" Another time, Rachel bought some mandrakes from her sister—mandrakes are a Mediterranean herb once thought to be an infertility cure. But it was to no avail. Finally God "opened Rachel's womb," and she gave birth to Joseph, he of the multicolored coat.

There is an upside to the Bible's infertility motif: The harder it was for a woman to get pregnant, the greater was the resulting child. Joseph.

Isaac. Samuel (whose mother pledged her son to God as thanks for the conception). These are some of the giants of the Hebrew Scriptures.

Yesterday I broke Julie's gag rule to inform her that if we do have another kid, he or she could be one for the ages. Which made her smile.

"I think that's true," she said. "Good things come to those who wait." Which sounds like a biblical proverb but is actually from Henry Wadsworth Longfellow.

You shall have no other gods before me.

—Exodus 20:3

Back to day 2. Julie has a meeting, so I'm left alone with my breakfast orange, my list of rules, and my stack of Bibles. I've got a half hour before our son, Jasper, wakes up. Now seems a good time to embark on the more spiritual part of my quest: prayer.

As I said, I've always been agnostic. In college I studied all the traditional arguments for the existence of God: the design argument (just as a watch must have a watchmaker, so the universe must have a God), the first-cause argument (everything has a cause; God is the cause of the universe). Many were dazzling and brilliant, but in the end, none of them swayed me.

Nor did a new line of reasoning I heard from my cousin Levi a couple of weeks ago. Levi—the son-in-law of my Orthodox aunt Kate—told me he believes in God for this reason: The Bible is so strange, so utterly bizarre, no human brain could have come up with it.

I like Levi's argument. It's original and unsanctimonious. And I agree that the Bible can be strange—the command to break a cow's neck at the site of an unsolved murder comes to mind (Deuteronomy 21:4). Still, I wasn't convinced. Humans have come up with some astoundingly bizarre stuff ourselves: biathlons, turducken, and my son's Chicken Dance Elmo, to name a few.

In short, I don't think I can be debated into believing in God. Which presents a problem, because the Bible commands you not only to believe in God but to love Him. It commands this over and over again. So how do I follow that? Can I turn on a belief as if it flows out of a spiritual spigot?

Here's my plan: In college I also learned about the theory of cognitive dissonance. This says, in part, if you behave in a certain way, your beliefs will eventually change to conform to your behavior. So that's what I'm trying to do. If I act like I'm faithful and God loving for several months, then maybe I'll become faithful and God loving. If I pray every day, then maybe I'll start to believe in the Being to whom I'm praying.

So now, I'm going to pray. Even though I'm not exactly sure how to pray. I've never prayed before in my life, not counting the few perfunctory uplifted gazes when my mom was sick.

For starters, what do I do with my body? The Bible describes a multitude of positions: People kneel, sit, bow their heads, lift their eyes skyward, put their heads between their knees, raise up their hands, beat their breasts. There's no single method.

Sitting is tempting, but it seems too easy. I'm of the no-pain, no-gain mind-set. So I settle on holding my arms outstretched like a holy antenna, hoping to catch God's signal.

As for what to say, I'm not sure. I don't feel confident enough to improvise yet, so I've memorized a few of my favorite prayers from the Bible. I walk into our living room, stand in front of our brown sectional couch, hold out my arms, bow my head, and, in a low but clear voice, recite this passage from the Book of Job: "Naked I came from my mother's womb, and naked shall I return. The Lord gave, and the Lord has taken away; blessed be the name of the Lord."

It's a beautiful passage, but I feel odd uttering it. I've rarely said the word *Lord,* unless it's followed by *of the Rings.* I don't often say *God* without preceding it with *Oh my.*

The whole experience is making me uncomfortable. My palms are sweaty. I'm trying to speak with earnest intent, but it feels like I'm transgressing on two separate levels. First, I feel like I'm violating some sort of taboo issued by the agnostic high priests. Worse, what if I'm breaking the Third Commandment? If I don't believe the holy words I'm saying, isn't that taking the Lord's name in vain?

I glance at the clock. I've been praying only for a minute. I've promised myself I'd try to pray for at least ten minutes three times a day.

So I get back to work. I squint my eyes and try to visualize Him. It's a fiasco. My mind goes to a series of clichés: the Universe, aka the view from inside the Hayden Planetarium; a fog-shrouded Middle Eastern mountain; something akin to the multicolored special effects from Stanley Kubrick's *2001: A Space Odyssey,* when the spaceship went into hyperspace. Pretty much everything but the guy in the flowing white robe and the basso profundo voice.

All I can say is, I hope I get better.

And it is possible I will. When I was in high school, I had a handful of what might qualify as quasimystical experiences. Surprisingly, none involved a bong. They would happen unexpectedly, and they would last only for a moment, about as long as a sneeze, but they were memorable.

The only way to describe them makes me sound like I'm leading an est seminar, but so be it: I felt at one with the universe. I felt the boundary between my brain and the rest of the world suddenly dissolve. It wasn't that I intellectually comprehended that everything and everyone is connected, I felt it the way one might feel cold or carsick. The epiphanies would descend on me without warning: One came while I was lying on a blanket in Central Park's Great Lawn, another while I was riding the bullet train on a family trip in Japan. They were at once utterly humbling (my life so piddling and insignificant) and totally energizing (but it's also part of something so huge). The glow from these mental orgasms would last several days, making me, at least temporarily, more serene and Buddha-like.

For no reason I can think of, my epiphanies suddenly stopped around senior year of high school. Perhaps this year will give me the map to find them again. Or else make me conclude my brain was playing two-bit mind tricks on me.

Nor shall there come upon you a garment of cloth made of two kinds of stuff.
—Leviticus 19:19

Day 5. I've made a list of the Top Five Most Perplexing Rules in the Bible. I plan to tackle all five this year, but I figured I'd start with one that requires neither violence nor pilgrimages. Namely: the ban on wearing clothes made of mixed fibers. It's such an odd proscription, I figured there was zero chance that anyone else in America was trying to follow it.

Of course, I was flat wrong.

My friend Eddy Portnoy—who teaches history at New York's Jewish Theological Seminary—told me he recently spotted a flyer in Washington Heights advertising a *shatnez* tester. *Shatnez,* he informed me, is the Hebrew word for "mixed fibers." A tester will come to your home and inspect your shirts, pants, sweaters, and suits to make sure you have no hidden mixed fibers.

So today I dial the number, and a man named Mr. Berkowitz agrees to make a house call. Mr. Berkowitz arrives right on time. He has a gray beard that descends below his collar, large glasses, and a black tie tucked into the top of his pants, which sit a good six inches above his navel. His yarmulke is slightly askew.

Mr. Berkowitz clicks open his black American Tourister rolling suitcase. Inside, his tools: a microscope, an old canister with the faded label "vegetable flakes," and various instruments that look like my mother's sewing kit after a genetic mutation. He spreads them out on my living room table. Mr. Berkowitz reminds me of an Orthodox CSI. God's wardrobe detective.

He gives me a shatnez primer. Shatnez is not just any mixed fiber. Poly-cotton blends and Lycra-spandex blends—those are fine. The problem is mixing wool and linen. That's the forbidden combination, according to Deuteronomy 22:11 (the Bible's only other verse that talks about mixed fibers).

"How do you tell when something is shatnez?" I ask.

Well, you can't trust the clothing labels, explains Mr. Berkowitz. They're often inaccurate. "You have to look at the fibers yourself. All the fibers look different under the microscope," he says.

He draws me a diagram: Linen looks like a piece of bamboo. Wool is like a bunch of stacked cups. Cotton resembles twisted streamers. And polyester is smooth, like a straw.

I bring out a pile of sweaters, and he goes to work. He snips some threads off a black V-necked sweater and puts them under the microscope.

"See if you can tell," he says. I squint into the microscope.

"It's polyester," I say.

"No. Look. The stacked cups? It's wool."

He seems disappointed. Clearly I'm not a shatnez inspector protégé.

Mr. Berkowitz is kind, gentle, but persistently frazzled. And I wasn't helping matters.

Mr. Berkowitz makes some notes on a sheet that looks like a hospital chart. The sweater is kosher, he tells me. So is the next one I bring out.

"Look," he says, motioning to the microscope.

"Wool?" I say.

"No. Cotton."

Damn!

I bring out my wedding suit. This could be trouble, he says: Wool suits often have linen hiding somewhere in them, especially Italian suits, which this is.

Mr. Berkowitz gets out a tool that resembles a fondue fork and begins digging into various parts of my suit—the collar, the pockets, the sleeves—with something approaching ferocity. This suit is the only suit I own, and it cost me about one-third of my salary. I'm a little alarmed. I'm glad Julie's not here to see this.

"Is it shatnez?" I ask.

He doesn't answer for a minute. He's too busy with the microscope. His beard is squashed around the eyepiece.

"I have a strong suspicion this is linen," he says. The alleged culprit is some white canvas that was hiding under the suit's collar.

Mr. Berkowitz spins the fabric with his fingers.

"I'm sending it to the laboratory to make sure, but I am almost convinced it is linen." He tells me I'll have to put my only suit into storage, or get it de-linened by a tailor.

Mr. Berkowitz seems suddenly unfrazzled. He is relieved.

"It's joyous," he says. "If I save someone from breaking a commandment, it gives me a little high." He pumps his fist. "I never took drugs, but I imagine this is what it feels like."

His joy is infectious. I feel momentarily happy too, but then return to my baseline bewilderment.

"It's really that important not to wear linen and wool?" I ask.

"Absolutely."

"Are some commandments in the Bible more important than others?"

"All equal," he says. Then pauses. "Well, I can't say that. Not murdering is at a very high level. So are adultery and not worshipping idols."

He seems torn. On the one hand, all the rules are from the same place. The Orthodox Jews follow a list of 613 rules originally compiled by the great medieval rabbi Maimonides from the first five books of the Bible. On the other hand, Mr. Berkowitz also has to admit that homicide is worse than wearing an unkosher blazer.

Before Mr. Berkowitz leaves, I ask him the obvious staring-us-in-the-face question: Why? Why would God care if we wore mixed fibers?

The answer is: We don't know.

There are theories. Some say it was to train the ancient Hebrews to keep things separate so they'd be less inclined to intermarry. Some say it's an allusion to Cain and Abel's sacrifice—Cain offered flax to God, and Abel offered sheep. Some say that the heathens once wore the combination, and the Hebrews were trying to distinguish themselves from the pagans in any way they could.

Bottom line, though: We have no idea.

"This is a law that God gave us. We have to trust Him. He's all-powerful. We're like children. Sometimes parents have laws children don't understand. Like when you tell a child not to touch fire, he doesn't understand why, but it is good for him."

In Judaism, the biblical laws that come without explanation—and there are many—are called *chukim*. This is such a law. The point is, you can never know what is important in the long term. God might have a different measuring scale than us. In fact, some say it's *more* crucial to follow the inexplicable ones, because it shows you're committed, that you have great faith.

The notion of obeying laws that have no rational explanation is a jarring one. For most of my life, I've been working under the paradigm that my behavior should, ideally, have a logical basis. But if you live biblically, this is not true. I have to adjust my brain to this.

> *You shall not covet.*
>
> —Exodus 20:17

Day 6. After a day devoted to the obscure, I'm craving some good old-fashioned Ten Commandments to bring me back into the mainstream.

Since I break this commandment every day, I decide "You shall not covet" is most in need of immediate attention. This commandment is the final one of the ten, and the only one to regulate a state of mind, not behavior. It's also arguably the hardest, especially in modern-day New York. This is a city that runs on coveting.

It's 2:00 p.m., and here's the list of things I've coveted since I woke up:

- Jonathan Safran Foer's speaking fee (someone told me he gets fifteen thousand dollars per lecture).
- the Treo 700 PDA.
- the mental calm of the guy at the Bible bookstore who said he had no fear because he walked with God.
- our friend Elizabeth's sprawling suburban front yard.
- the George Clooney level of fame that allows you to say whatever you feel like, moronic or not.
- the brilliant screenplay for the 1999 movie *Office Space*. (I sometimes have a weird fantasy that I could go back to 1997 with a videotape, transcribe the dialogue, and beat writer Mike Judge to the punch.)

Plus, ever since I became a father, I've been introduced to a whole new level of coveting. I'm not just coveting for myself, I'm coveting for my son. I'm trying to keep up with the Jones's kid.

Like with Jasper's vocabulary. I love the guy, but he's distressingly behind the curve in the speaking department. He communicates mostly by using eight different types of grunts, each one with its own meaning. I feel like the ethnographer who had to decipher the nuances of the twenty-three Eskimo words for snow. A medium-pitched grunt means "yes." A lower-pitched grunt means "no." A brief chimplike grunt means "come here now!" Jasper's a great walker and ball thrower, but words—those things I'm supposed to arrange for a living—they're not so interesting to him.

Meanwhile, his friend Shayna—three months his junior—knows words like *helicopter* and *cabinet*. She's practically got her own blog. I covet Shayna's vocabulary for Jasper.

To sum up, I expend a lot of mental energy breaking this commandment. And I'm not even including "coveting" in the sexual sense—though I certainly did that with the woman in purple flip-flops on the street. Or the woman with the low-riding Calvins. Or . . . I'll return to that topic later, since it deserves its own chapter.

The full anticoveting commandment reads like this: "You shall not covet your neighbor's house; you shall not covet your neighbor's wife, or his manservant, or his maidservant, or his ox, or his ass, or anything that is your neighbor's."

The ox and the ass aren't a problem in postagrarian Manhattan. But the phrase "anything that is your neighbor's"—that pretty much covers it all. No wiggle room.

But how do you stop yourself from coveting?

The word *covet* is a translation of the Hebrew root *hamad,* roughly equivalent to "desire" or "want." There are two schools of thought on what the commandment is preventing.

Some interpreters say that coveting in itself isn't forbidden. It's not always bad to yearn. It's coveting your *neighbor's* stuff that's forbidden. As one rabbi puts it, it's OK to covet a Jaguar—but you shouldn't covet your neighbor's Jaguar. In other words, if your desire might lead you to harm your neighbor, then it's wrong.

But others say that coveting *any* Jaguar is wrong, whether it's your neighbor's or the one at the dealership. A moderate interest in cars is OK. However, coveting means that you are overly desirous of the Jaguar, you are distracted by material goods, you have veered from the path of being thankful for what God provides. You have, no doubt, fallen victim to advertising, the Tenth Commandment's arch-nemesis.

To play it safe, I'm trying to avoid both types of coveting.

Julie rejects one of my strategies—I asked her to censor the newspapers and magazines by ripping out all the ads for iPods and Jamaican vacations and such. Instead I've been forced to cut down my magazine consumption to a trickle.

But coveting material goods in ads isn't the big hurdle for me. My real weakness is jealousy of others. The relentless comparison to my peers. Am I more successful than Julie's ex-boyfriend who invented a lighting gadget that fits over the page of a book so you can read it at night? It's been featured on the cover of the Levenger catalog, as my mother-in-law reminds me often.

If it's not the ex-boyfriend, it's someone else. And this type of coveting will never be assuaged. If by some crazy quirk or twist of fate or ac-counting error, I were to get J. S. Foer's speaking fee, then I'd move right on to coveting Madeleine Albright's speaking fee. The Bible is right. Jealousy is a useless, time-wasting emotion that's eating me alive. I should focus on my family and, nowadays, God.

Of course, stopping an emotion is not easy. The prevailing paradigm is that we can't control our passions. As Woody Allen said when his af-fair with Soon-Yi Previn was discovered, "The heart wants what it wants." But I can't just give up—I need a new point of view. So I consult my spiritual advisory board.

One recommended method is to tell yourself that the coveted car/job/house/speaking fee/donkey is just not a possibility. A medieval rabbi—Abraham ibn Ezra—uses this example (he's talking about the sexual sense of covet, but you can apply it more broadly): When you see a pretty woman married to another man, you have to put her in the same class as your mother. She's off-limits. The very notion of her as a sex partner is repulsive, unthinkable, except to perverts and/or those who have read too much Freud. Or else, think of the woman as a peasant would a princess. She's pretty, but she's so far out of your realm, your admiration is abstract, not lascivious.

I try to do this with J. S. Foer's speaking fee. It's outside of my realm, I say. The strategy runs counter to you-can-do-anything-you-set-your-mind-to ambition, but maybe it's better for my mental health.

And then there's this tactic: If you're intently focused on following the rules of the Bible, you don't have time to covet. Not as much, any-way. You're just too busy. A couple of weeks ago, my daily coveting list would have taken up one-third of this book. Now I've trimmed it down to half a page. Progress, I think.

You shall rejoice before the Lord your God seven days.

—Leviticus 23:40

Day 7. It's been a week. My spiritual state: still agnostic. My beard state: itchy and uneven—I've got these bald patches that look like crop circles made by tiny UFOs. My wardrobe state: I've traded my usual T-shirts and jeans for khakis and Oxfords because it feels somehow more respectful. My emotional state: strung out.

The learning curve remains crushingly steep. I continue to second-guess everything I do and say. I've noticed my speech has slowed down, as if I'm speaking English as a second language. This is because I mentally check every word before allowing myself to utter it. Is it a lie? Is it a boast? Is it a curse? Is it gossip? What about exaggeration? Does the Bible allow me to say "My friend Mark's been working at *Esquire* since 1904?" (He's been there a mere seventeen years). I censor about 20 percent of my sentences before they leave my mouth. The Bible's language laws are rigorous.

I'm poring over religious study books, desperately trying to get a handle on this topic and every other. My reading list grows exponentially. Every time I read a book, it'll mention three other books I feel I have to read. It's like a particularly relentless series of pop-up ads.

I still read the Bible itself, taking it with me wherever I go. That Bible salesman was right—I should have gotten that version of the Scriptures that's camouflaged as a teen magazine. When I read my Bible on the subway, I can feel the hostility emanating from the secular commuters. They look at me with their lips taut and faces tense, like they expect me to tackle them at any moment and forcibly baptize them.

In addition to the Bible, I also carry around a stapled printout of my rules, which I scan frequently. My original plan had been to pay equal attention to all the rules every day. This turned out to be impossible. That's like trying to juggle seven-hundred-plus balls. The brain can't handle it. I was too scattered.

So my revised plan is this: I will still attempt to follow all the rules simultaneously. But on a given day, I'll home in on a particular rule and devote much of my energy to that rule, while keeping the others in my peripheral vision.

How to choose the right time to focus on a particular rule? It's not a science. I've opted instead to go where the spirit takes me. I imagine a lot of factors will come into play: life's curveballs, my whims, logistics, my day job (I write for *Esquire* magazine, which I know will force me to confront the lust rules soon enough). And variety. I want to alternate obscure with mainstream, physical with mental, hard with easy. I need variety. I don't have the stamina to spend a month focused solely on the forty-five rules of idolatry.

> *With the humble is wisdom.*
>
> —PROVERBS 11:2

Day 11. I'm going to take a bunch of biblically themed road trips this year, and today is my first: Amish country. It seems a good place to start. Not only are the Amish tied with the Hasidic Jews for the title of most easily spotted Bible followers, but they are also interesting in this sense: They strictly adhere to rules in both the Old Testament and the New Testament. For instance:

- Their famous facial hair is the result of the Old Testament's ban on trimming the beard. (The Amish do, however, shave their moustaches, because the moustache was thought to have military associations.)
- They refuse to pose for or take photos, since it would violate the Old Testament's Second Commandment: "You shall not make . . . any likeness of anything that is in heaven above, or that is in the earth beneath." This is why, if you click on an Amish website, you'll often see photos of the backs of their heads. (And yes, the Amish have websites; go ahead and chuckle if you must. To be fair, the Amish don't run the sites themselves. It's a third party promoting their woodworks and quilts.)
- Amish women wear bonnets in keeping with the New Testament's 1 Corinthians 11:5, which states that women's heads must be covered while praying.
- The Amish perform a foot-washing ritual in accordance with the New Testament's John 13:14–15, which says, "If I then, your Lord and Teacher, have washed your feet, you also ought to wash one another's feet. For I have given you an example . . ."

The Amish version of biblical living is combined with what's called the Ordnung—the traditions that have built up since the Amish origins in sixteenth-century Switzerland. The Ordnung is what dictates the Amish dress code and their ban on electricity.

Julie and I rent a car and drive down to Lancaster County, Pennsylvania. Julie may not be a huge fan of my project, but she figures she can at least take advantage of a road trip or two. Our destination is called Smucker's Farm Guest House. It's one of the few bed-and-breakfasts actually owned and operated by an Amish family. Most inns just offer some sort of vague proximity to Amish people. This is the real thing.

The trip takes four hours. Incidentally, I'm proud to say that I had absolutely no urge to make a double entendre when we passed Intercourse, Pennsylvania, which I see as a moral victory.

We pull into the driveway, and the first thing I lay eyes on is a woman in full Amish regalia—ankle-length blue dress and a white bonnet—wielding a gas-powered leaf blower. This isn't an image I expected to see. She doesn't have a video iPod, but still. It punctures my Amish stereotypes right up front.

The woman—Anna—brings us to meet her father, Amos, the head of the household. Amos Smucker is tall, thin, and slope shouldered. He's dressed exactly as you'd imagine: black suspenders, straw hat, pants pulled high above his waist. His snow-white hair is shaped in the traditional Amish style: a modified bowl cut that curves over the ears and then angles down, becoming just a bit longer in the back.

I introduce myself. He nods, gives me a quiet "Hello," and walks us to our room.

Amos talks slowly and carefully, like he only has a few dozen sentences allotted for the weekend, and he doesn't want to waste them at the start. I read later in the Amish book *Rules of a Godly Life* that you should "let your words be thoughtful, few, and true." By adopting minimalism, Amos has mastered those speech laws I'm struggling with.

I tell Amos that I'd love to talk to him about the Amish. He obliges. I wonder how sick he is of answering the same annoying questions from curious outsiders. At least I pledged to myself not to bring up *Witness* or that Randy Quaid movie about the one-armed Amish bowler.

We sit in Amos's kitchen—sparse, of course, with a wooden table and a three-ring binder that says "A Journal of By-gone Years: The Smuckers."

"When did your family come over?" I ask.

"My ancestor Christian Smucker came over from Switzerland in the eighteenth century."

And yes, Amos is a distant cousin of the strawberry-jam Smuckers, though that branch is no longer Amish.

"How many brothers and sisters do you have?"

"There were seventeen of us," says Amos.

"Seventeen?"

He nods.

"And where were you in the order?"

"I was the baby," Amos says. "Once my mother got me, she said, 'I'm done. I got what I wanted.'"

Did he just make a joke? I think so. Amos allows himself just the slightest, faintest wisp of a smile.

I explain the premise of my book to Amos. He stares over my left shoulder in silence. No reaction. From my brief visit with the Amish, I got the feeling that they are not enamored of talking about theology, at least not with the English, at least not with me. Best stick to more practical topics.

"Are you working now?"

"I used to be a dairy farmer, but I don't do so much anymore. I'm not retired. I'm just tired."

I think Amos just made another joke. You haven't seen deadpan delivery till you've seen the Amish.

"What's your schedule?" I ask.

"I go to sleep at eight-thirty or so, and wake up at four-thirty. I can't sleep after five. I was a dairy farmer, and that's the way my computer is programmed."

An interesting metaphor for a man who doesn't use electricity, I think to myself.

Amos drums his fingers on the table. He has amazing hands. Knotty, but somehow elegant, with thumbs that curve around like candy canes and practically brush up against his wrist.

We sit silently.

Finally, Julie asks if maybe he could show us the property. He nods. Our first stop is the garage. Amos owns three black buggies, all of them lined up against the wall, their red fluorescent triangles facing outward. His daughter Anna is polishing the middle one.

The garage opens into the stables, where Amos keeps his horses. He has two of them—they're beautiful and chocolate brown, and they trot over to greet Amos.

"They used to be racehorses," says Amos, patting one on the neck. "Ninety percent of the horses the Amish have were once racehorses."

This is the only time during the weekend that Amos approached being prideful. Humility is absolutely central to the Amish way of life, and it's one of the most beautiful things about the community. But if you're going to be proud of anything, I figure these horses are a pretty good choice.

Amos grew up in this house, he tells us.

"What was your childhood like?"

"It was cold. There was no insulation, so it got to be two below in our room."

"Wow," I say.

"Two below the covers."

This time he can't suppress the corners of his mouth from turning slightly upward. That was definitely a gag.

Back in the kitchen, I ask about his kids. He has seven, all of them still Amish, many of them living nearby or even across the street. Before coming, I had read that the Amish population in America—now at almost two hundred thousand—had doubled in the last twenty years. They are in no danger of fading away.

"Are there a lot of conversions to the Amish faith?"

"Very few." Amos pauses, then says: "Do you want to hear an Amish joke?"

"Sure."

This is great. The Amish have been an easy go-to punch line for far too long. In fact, I almost didn't come to Amish country because I didn't want to fall into the trap. So it'll be a delight to hear an Amish joke from an actual Amish person.

"What happened when the Mennonite man married the Amish woman?"

Julie and I don't know.

"She drove him buggy."

We laugh. It's not Chris Rock, but you have to remember: Amos is working with some pretty stringent preconditions.

"*Ba-dum-bum,*" says Julie.

I wonder if the rim-shot reference made any sense to him, or if he just thought Julie makes odd sounds.

I try to bring up spirituality once more. I tell him that the Book of Amos is one of my favorite parts in the Bible. Again, silence. For a long thirty seconds.

"Do you know 'Amazing Grace'?" he finally says.

We nod.

"Help us out then."

Amos fishes a harmonica out of his pocket, takes a deep breath, and starts playing the most astounding version of the hymn I've ever heard. He was working that harmonica, his hand flapping, playing notes on both the inhale and the exhale.

Julie and I fumble the words a bit in the middle, but we end strong: "I once was lost, but now am found. Was blind, but now I see."

"Do you play at church?" I ask when he stops.

"No, we don't play instruments," he says. "It might encourage pride. You might get some thoughts. Try to show off for other people."

Amos holds up his harmonica. "This is just for home use."

A pause. "Well, I best get moving," says Amos. "Supper is at five-thirty."

And with that, Amos disappears into his dining room.

Julie and I drive to a local tourist-trap restaurant that serves butter-soaked vegetables and shoofly pie. On the way, we see another startling sight, right up there with the leaf blower: It is an Amish teen, his hands behind his back, Rollerblading leisurely down a country road.

I found out later that some of the Amish allow Rollerblades. Rubber tires are forbidden, so bikes are out, but Rollerblade wheels are made of plastic. Likewise, though electricity is banned, tools using batteries, solar power, or gas are sometimes OK. Hence the leaf blower.

The lesson from my weekend with the Amish is this: You cannot stop religion from evolving. Even here, where customs and dress were supposedly frozen in the sixteenth century, they will still find a way. It makes my quest to rewind my life to biblical times that much more daunting. Can I really scrape off all those millennia of accumulated tradition?

Before we arrive at the restaurant, Julie and I spot a cluster of about thirty buggies. We pull over to see what's happening. We have stumbled onto an Amish baseball game. Amos tells us that many Amish—him included—discourage competitive sports.

But here are eighteen Amish teenage boys, their sleeves rolled up, their shirts and suspenders dark with sweat. Julie and I watch for a long time. These kids are good, but something is off about the game. I realize after a few minutes what it is: This is the quietest baseball game I've ever seen. No trash talk. No cheering from the parents in the stands. Near silence, except for the occasional crack of the bat. It is eerie and peaceful and beautiful.

> *Do not now be stiff-necked as your fathers were,*
> *but yield yourselves to the Lord . . .*
>
> —2 Chronicles 30:8

Day 13. Back in New York, the Bible is keeping me overscheduled. The mornings are particularly crammed. I have to attach my tassels. Say my prayers. Tie a Xeroxed copy of the Ten Commandments to my forehead and hand in accordance with Exodus 13:9 (more on that later). The rest of the day is consumed with Bible study, midday prayer, perhaps a good deed, biblical shopping (today I plan to buy a wooden staff), a few hours devoted to secular *Esquire* matters, a scripturally approved dinner, then prayers at night.

Oh, and my spiritual advisory board. I try to meet or talk with at least one sage per day. Today is a doubleheader. It starts with breakfast with my friend Roger Bennett.

Roger is a Liverpudlian who ends all conversations with "Rock on." He has about eight jobs—writer, documentarian, foundation head, and so on—most of which have at least a vague connection to religion.

Roger doesn't mind that my morning rituals made me ten minutes late, but he does want to tell me something: "You're going into this thinking that it's like studying the sumo wrestlers in Japan," Roger says. "You're saying to yourself, 'I won't really become one. I'll maintain my distance.'"

I start to protest. Roger continues.

"You're dealing with explosive stuff. People a lot smarter than you have devoted their lives to this. So you have to admit there is a possibility that you will be profoundly changed by the end."

He could be right. And it scares me. I hate losing control. I like to be in command of everything. My emotions, for instance. If I'm watching a love story, and I start to get too weepy, I'll say to myself: "OK, there's a boom mike right over Audrey Hepburn's head; see if you can spot its shadow," and that'll snap me out of the movie, and I'll regain my composure. I also spend a lot of time trying to control my health, mostly by fixating on germs. I have a mild case of obsessive-compulsive disorder (a disease that has, I'm afraid, become a bit trendy, thanks to Larry David, et al.). My medicine cabinet is packed with a dozen bottles of Purell at all times. I haven't touched a subway pole with my bare hands in a decade—I usually just plant my feet wide apart in the subway car and pretend I'm a surfer.

The problem is, a lot of religion is about surrendering control and being open to radical change. I wish I could stow my secular worldview in a locker at the Port Authority Bus Terminal and retrieve it at the end of the year.

After breakfast with Roger, I take a subway downtown to have lunch with the Brooklyn rabbi Andy Bachman at a diner. It's back-to-back mentoring today. Andy's easy to relate to. He also grew up in a secular home, though that home was in Wisconsin (Jews there are known as the "frozen chosen," by the way). He was drawn to religion when he first saw the beautiful typography of the Talmud. He's youngish, forty-two, and insists I call him Andy, which seems disrespectful, but I try.

"How's it going?" asks Andy.

I tell Andy about Mr. Berkowitz and the mixed-fiber inspection.

"I was riveted," I say. Maybe too riveted, actually. I know myself. I'm drawn to the weird. In my last book, on the encyclopedia, I made seven references to philosopher René Descartes's fetish for cross-eyed women, which I think and hope is a record.

"I'm worried I could spend the whole year on the strange parts of the Bible and neglect the parts about goodness and justice," I say.

Andy thinks about it for a half minute. He takes a sip of coffee.

"My advice is: Don't forget the prophets."

The prophets, he explains, are twenty extraordinary men and women found in the Hebrew Scriptures. They come onto the scene several hundred years after the age of Moses. By then, the Israelites were living in the Promised Land, but they'd botched it all up. They'd gotten corrupt and lazy. They were oppressing the poor just like their former masters in Egypt. The prophets were the Martin Luther Kings of their day, railing against the crooked system. Not so coincidentally, MLK liked to quote them—including Amos's amazing words: "Let justice roll down like waters and righteousness like a mighty stream!"

"Try to make everything you do measure up to the moral standards of the prophets," Andy told me. "Remember what Micah said. He said that the animal sacrifices weren't important. The important thing is to 'Do justice. And to love mercy. And to walk humbly with your God.'"

. . . and he gave him a tenth of all.

—Genesis 14:20 (JPS)

Day 14. Andy's correct, of course. I have to be more moral. I have to do something that would please the prophets. The next morning, I flip through my list of rules and find an excellent candidate on page twenty-eight: Give away 10 percent of your income.

"I'm going to tithe," I announce to Julie over breakfast.

She seems concerned. In general, she's much more magnanimous than I am. She's a sucker for those charities that send you free sheets of return-address labels with little cartoons of a Rollerblading Ziggy, along with a heartbreaking brochure about lymphoma. I tell her it's emotional blackmail. She ignores me and mails them checks.

But even for Julie 10 percent is high, especially with Jasper and, we hope, another kid to come. She asks me whether I can count my literary agent's fee as a tithe. She's only half-joking.

Unfortunately, I doubt even the most brilliant rabbi could figure out a way to classify International Creative Management as "the poor" (especially after the agents raised their commission to 15 percent a few years ago).

"Can you at least do 10 percent after taxes?" she says.

That night, I call my spiritual advisory board to ask. I reach Elton Richards, the pastor out to pasture.

"You shouldn't get too legalistic with it," says Elton. "Give what you can afford. And then give some more. It should feel like a sacrifice."

I study my Bible for insight. It seems that in the time of ancient Israel—before the Romans took over—no one paid taxes per se. The tithes *were* the taxes. And the tithing system was as complicated as any 1040 form. You gave portions to the priests, the temple keepers, the temple itself, the poor, the widows, and the orphans. So, I suppose, at least for now, after-tax tithing is probably OK.

I calculate 10 percent of my projected salary. It's not a huge number—but that's precisely the problem. If I were making $10 million a year and had to give away one million, that'd be easier.

That night I spend three hours browsing a website called Charity Navigator. It's sort of a Zagat guide to aid organizations. (Even this leads to coveting—they list the salaries of these charity CEOs, and some break $500,000.)

I settle on several organizations—Feed the Children and Save Darfur among them—and donate about 2 percent of my income. That's as much as I can do in one shot.

When the confirmation emails ping in, I feel good. There's a haunting line from the film *Chariots of Fire*. It's spoken by Eric Liddell, the most religious runner, the one who carries a Bible with him during his sprint. He says: "When I run, I feel His pleasure." And as I gave away money, I think I might have felt God's pleasure. I know: I'm agnostic. But still—I feel His pleasure. It's a warm ember that starts at the back of my neck and spreads through my skull. I feel like I am doing something I should have been doing all my life.

On the other hand, like a hard sprint, the pleasure is mixed with pain. I have just carved off 2 percent of my salary, and I've got 8 percent left to go. So here's the mental strategy I've adopted: If it weren't for the Bible, I wouldn't be living a biblical year. I wouldn't have a book deal. No Bible, no income. So it's only fair to give 10 percent to God's people. It's the most righteous finder's fee around.

> *He who spares the rod hates his son, but he who loves him*
> *is diligent to discipline him.*
>
> —Proverbs 13:24

Day 23. As I mentioned, one of my motivations for this experiment is my recent entrance into fatherhood. I'm constantly worried about my son's ethical education. I don't want him to swim in this muddy soup of moral relativism. I don't trust it. I have such a worldview, and though I have yet to commit a major felony, it seems dangerous. Especially nowadays. Within a couple of years, Jasper will be able to download Tijuana donkey shows on YouTube while ordering OxyContin from an offshore pharmacy.

So I want to instill some rock-solid, absolute morals in my son. Would it be so bad if he lived by the Ten Commandments? Not at all. But how do I get him there?

This morning, it's clearer than ever that I need help. I'm exhausted, a direct result of the fact that I'm the worst disciplinarian in America.

At about 2:00 a.m. Jasper woke up, so I let him climb into bed with me and Julie—already a sucker move. Instead of lulling him to sleep, this gave him lots of new activities. For instance, grabbing my sleep mask, pulling it away from my eyes till the elastic band is fully extended—a length of about two feet—then releasing it. The mask would shoot back onto my face with alarming force, producing an eye-watering snap. (Note: Contrary to what you might think, my sleep mask does not violate the Bible's prohibition against wearing women's clothes. It came in a box featuring a photo of a very masculine and well-rested man sleeping next to his attractive wife.)

I told Jasper to stop, but my tone was about as menacing as Fred Rogers. So he did it again and again.

This is probably unbiblical. At the very least, my leniency is a violation of the Proverbs. The Proverbs are the Bible's collection of wisdom attributed to King Solomon, and they come down clearly on the side of disciplining kids. As in corporal punishment.

> Proverbs 22:15: "Folly is bound up in the heart of a child; but the rod of discipline drives it far from him."
> Proverbs 23:14: "Thou shalt beat him with the rod, and shalt deliver his soul from hell." (KJV)
> Proverbs 23:13: "Do not withhold discipline from a child; if you beat him with a rod, he will not die."

Some Americans hew to these proverbs literally. Until 2005 you could buy "The Rod," a twenty-two-inch nylon whipping stick that sold for five dollars. It was the creation of an Oklahoma-based Southern Baptist named Clyde Bullock, who advertised it with the motto "Spoons are for cooking, belts are for holding up pants, hands are for loving, and rods are for chastening." He shut down the business partly because of an outcry from more liberal Christians and partly because he couldn't buy its cushioned grips anymore.

Other not-quite-as-literal literalists say paddles are an acceptable alternative. James Dobson—founder of Focus on the Family, the ultraconservative Christian group—recommends paddling, especially if you want to keep your hand as "an object of love."

I don't own a rod or a paddle. In fact, corporal punishment of any sort is deeply counter to my parenting philosophy. I've always considered walloping your kid the H-bomb of childcare—it's in the arsenal but shouldn't be deployed.

Even for Project Bible, I can't deploy it. At least not yet. I've reached my first limit. So what to do? I decided this is one of those times when I should fulfill the letter of the law, if not the spirit. It's better than fulfilling nothing at all.

A few days ago I Googled "flexible rod" and "soft rod," and, after sifting through several biblically questionable ads, I ended up ordering a very unmenacing Nerf bat. I try it today on Jasper. After dinner, he grabs a handful of nickels off the dresser and chucks them across the room.

So I take the Nerf bat and smack Jasper's butt with it. I've never spanked him before, despite several temptations to do otherwise. When I swing my bat—even though it's spongy and harmless—I break some sort of barrier. I have now punished my son physically. It's an unsettling feeling. It drives home just how lopsided the relationship is: Parents have God-like physical dominance over their kids, at least when those kids have yet to hit puberty.

Jasper seems undisturbed by all this. He responds by laughing hysterically, grabbing his Wiffle bat, and attempting to smack me back. So I'm basically sanctioning violence here.

The rod is a fiasco. But here's the thing: I agree with the gist of Proverbs. I need to discipline my son more. I need to give Jasper some tough love, dispense more time-outs, or risk having him turn into a three-foot-tall monster. Julie has become the family disciplinarian, which is causing tension in our marriage, as she's not fond of being the bad cop. I've got to get stricter.

Look at the example set by God. The God of the Bible treats his children—the human race—with both justice and mercy. Right now, I'm out of whack; I'm 10 percent justice and 90 percent mercy. If I had been in charge of the Garden of Eden, Adam and Eve would have gotten three strikes, then a fourth, then a stern warning, then had their bedtime moved up twenty minutes. God, as you know, kicked them out. As a sign of His compassion, he clothed them in animal skins before the eviction, but He still kicked them out.

> *Make me understand the way of thy precepts, and I will*
> *meditate on thy wondrous works.*
>
> —PSALMS 119:27

Day 30. It's the end of month one. Physically I feel okay. The beard's itchiness has receded, and, at least for the moment, it looks more comparative-literature-professor than guy-who-stopped-taking-his-meds.

As for my spiritual life, the word that comes to mind is *disconnected*. I've been playing the role of the Bible Man for a month, but that's what it still feels like: a role. A character. Like the time at summer camp when I was twelve, and, for reasons I no longer remember, I adopted a deep

Southern accent—a real Foghorn Leghorn twang—and spoke it exclusively for a month.

This biblical alter ego of mine is such a separate being, I've taken to calling him a different name: Jacob. It seemed the most natural choice; close but not identical. I've been observing this Jacob guy, studying him.

And here's what I've found: He, too, has a split personality. On the one hand, Jacob is much more moral than I am. He attempts to fulfill Leviticus 19:18—"Love your neighbor as yourself." Which means he's doing things like holding the elevator door for slow-moving passengers. Or giving a buck to the homeless guy outside the Museum of Natural History who says he's seeking donations for the "United Negro Pizza Fund."

He pays attention to the hundreds of small, almost unnoticeable moral decisions we make every day. He turns off the lights when leaving the room. He refrains from gawking at odd-looking passersby—the four-hundred-pound man, the guy with the banana-colored pants, the woman who's eight inches taller than her boyfriend—something that I, as a lifelong people watcher, would love to do. Jacob stares straight ahead like a Buckingham Palace guard.

He's not getting short-listed for the Nobel yet, but he's a better man than my secular self.

On the other hand, my alter ego Jacob is engaging in some deeply strange behavior. He says, "Maybe we could have lunch on the fourth day of the workweek," since "Thursday" is forbidden. It comes from the Norse god Thor.

He rubs a dab of olive oil in his hair each morning, as instructed by Ecclesiastes 9:8 ("let not oil be lacking on your head"), which leaves these unfortunate green stains on all my baseball hats.

And he's developed this byzantine method of paying our babysitter Des. The Bible says the "wages of a hired servant shall not remain with you all night until the morning," (Leviticus 19:13) so Jacob gives her cash every night. But my secular self needs to pay her by weekly check so that she can properly file for taxes. Which means that I have to ask that she bring all the cash back at the end of the week and exchange it for a check. I'm not sure this is helping anyone. Des has already started trying to slip out at night without saying good-bye to me/Jacob.

My alter ego's behavior points to one of the biggest mysteries of the Bible. How can these ethically advanced rules and these bizarre decrees be found in the same book? And not just the same book. Sometimes the same page. The prohibition against mixing wool and linen comes right after the command to love your neighbor. It's not like the Bible has a section called "And Now for Some Crazy Laws." They're all jumbled up like a chopped salad.

Maybe all will become clear by the end of the year. Maybe.

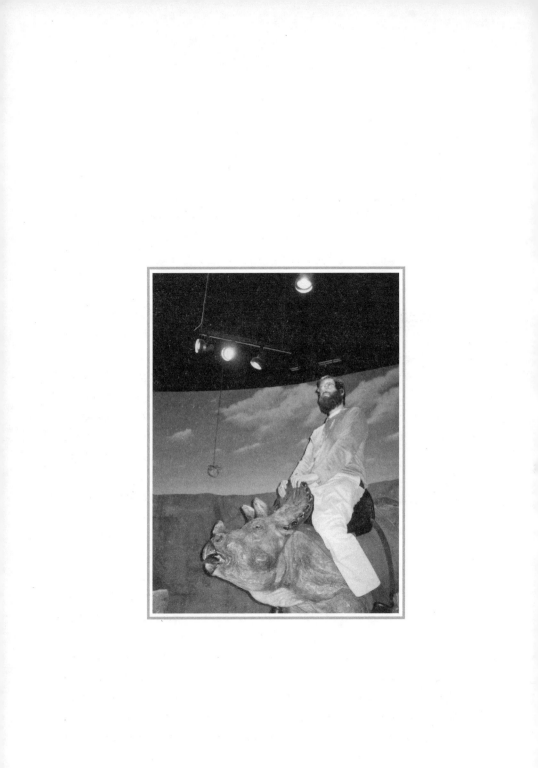

Month Two: October

Three times a year you shall celebrate a pilgrim feast to me.
—Exodus 23:14 (NAB)

Day 31, morning. I spend a half hour checking airfares to Israel. I need to go this year. I can't devote twelve months to living biblically without making a pilgrimage to the birthplace of the holy book itself.

I've been once before. When I was fourteen, my parents wanted to take us to Israel and Egypt, so we signed up for a tour group whose members consisted of my family, a couple of dozen retired orthodontists, and an unmarried twenty-seven-year-old woman who had been led to believe this would be a singles tour, which it was, if you count the high percentage of widows and widowers.

I don't remember much about the tour. I remember the long bus rides, with the Israeli tour guide asking, "Does anyone want to stop at the smile room?" That was Israeli tour guide slang for the bathroom, since "everyone smiles when they walk out of the smile room." I remember preferring the Egyptian portion of the trip; I'd always been fascinated by the pyramids and had some knowledge of the Nile culture, or had at least memorized the lyrics to Steve Martin's "King Tut" song.

But Israel itself made little impression at all on my secular mind. At the time, I was going through an ill-thought-out Marxist phase. Religion was the opium of the people. And not just that: I was sure the opium pushers—the rabbis, the bishops, the ministers—were in on the con and were only trying to pay for their Mercedes Benzes. Israel was the center of the corrupt system.

By default, this trip has to be more meaningful. Plus, it will give me a chance to meet my ex-uncle Gil. Yes, as in meet him for the first time.

Here's the weird thing: He was married to my aunt for years, but I've never seen him face to face. The family considered him such an unstable character, such a fraud, that no one wanted him around at reunions or birthday parties. They didn't see him as a harmless eccentric. He was dangerous. There were rumors of his Svengali-like, abusive techniques when he was a cult leader.

The main strategy was to pretend that he didn't exist. In her semimonthly family newsletter, my grandmother couldn't even bring herself to type Gil's name. She referred to him only as "He." As in "He and Kate will be visiting in March," which I always found an ironic echo of the Orthodox refusal to write the name God (usually written *G-d.*) The only time I remember my grandmother mentioning Gil was when she talked about a disturbing conversation she'd had with Kate. "She told me she'd be happy to stare into his eyes all day," said my grandmother. "That's not how a marriage should be. You should be side by side, facing the world, not looking into each other's eyes all day." So Gil has always been this mysterious, forbidden, slightly scary figure to me.

Gil met Kate in 1982, and she became Orthodox soon after. I don't remember much about her from her pre-Gil life. I remember her waist-length hair (now tucked under a headdress), her creepy UFO-expert boyfriend, and her gift of a whoopee cushion she brought back from France, which I guess was way more sophisticated than any whoopee cushion that we yokel Americans could make.

I remember her giggling a lot. And she still does; Orthodox Judaism hasn't erased her sense of humor. She has a great, loud, whooping laugh. But her passion nowadays is for two things: her four children and the Torah.

It's a tricky and guilt-inducing proposition, meeting Gil. The truth is, I'm rebelling against my family. No one wants me to meet him. Early on, my mom asked point blank: "You're not going to talk to Gil, are you?" I didn't answer.

She thinks that if I meet Gil, it'll give him some sort of legitimacy he doesn't deserve. I don't know about that. I don't think I'm in the position to bestow legitimacy on anyone. Regardless, I can't resist the chance to visit him. The man helped with the genesis of this quest. For better or worse, he could be a pivotal figure in my struggle to understand religion. At the end, I'll beg my family's forgiveness.

Blow the trumpet at the new moon . . .

—Psalms 81:3

Day 31, afternoon. The Bible commands me—or Jacob, or whoever I am—to blow a trumpet at the start of every month. (To be safe, I'm also blowing a trumpet at the start of every Hebrew month.)

I find a ram's horn at the Jewish community center gift shop. It's a small shofar—thirty dollars will only get you so much—about three times the size of a kazoo and shaped like an elbow macaroni.

There's no doubt it's from a ram, though. It smells like a barn that hasn't been cleaned for days. I stand in my living room and blow. No sound. Just loudly exhaled air. These ram's horns are surprisingly hard to play. I'm still working under the assumption that the Bible didn't ban computers, so I spend half an hour on the internet picking up tips:

- Separate the lips as if you were making a raspberry.
- Keep your jaw in the position you would if you were spitting a watermelon seed.
- Wet your lips—
- —but not too much.
- If you do wet them too much, spittle is best removed from the shofar by a coffee brush or an aquarium brush.
- Put the shofar in the corner of your mouth, not in the center.

I sip a glass of water, part my lips, jut out my jaw, and blow the shofar again. It sounds like a dying fax machine. But, I remind myself, I still have eleven more months.

I did a little research, and, as I suspected, I'm not alone. There are a handful of twenty-first-century people who also blow a trumpet to kick off each month. But they are admittedly on the religious fringe. Mainstream Judaism and Christianity have both discontinued the practice, along with the observance of hundreds of other obscure biblical rules. The reason?

Christians believe that Jesus was the ultimate sacrifice. His crucifixion made animal sacrifice unnecessary. And not just animal sacrifice, but many of the ceremonial laws of the ancient Hebrews. This is why Christians can eat bacon and shave their beards with impunity. And why they don't need to blow a trumpet to the new month.

Most—but not all—Christians draw a distinction between "moral laws" and "ritual laws." They still adhere to the Old Testament's moral laws, such as the Ten Commandments (and, sometimes, the ban on homosexuality), but they scrap many of the ritual laws. Of course, there's a good amount of debate in Christianity over which should be considered moral laws and which ritual. Is the Sabbath a moral law? Or ritual? What about the ban on tattoos? I read a long tirade by one Christian against so-called Christian tattoo parlors.

There are dozens of rules that Jews no longer follow as well. The reason is different, though. According to Judaism, animal sacrifice can take place only at the Temple in Jerusalem. The Romans destroyed the Second Temple in 70 CE. And when the temple was gone, so was the relevance of more than two hundred sacrifice-related rules. (Including blowing a trumpet to the new moon, which was originally done along with a sacrifice.) Plus, Americans are off the hook with regard to another forty-five laws that they believe apply only in the land of Israel—many of them dealing with agriculture.

When I started this project, I vowed to try to follow all the Bible's rules—ritual, moral, agricultural, and sacrificial—and see where it takes me. But, to use a food metaphor in honor of my adviser Pastor Richards, I think I've bitten off more than I can chew.

> *When a woman has a discharge of blood, which is her regular discharge*
> *from her body, she shall be in her impurity for seven days, and*
> *whoever touches her shall be unclean until the evening.*
>
> —LEVITICUS 15:19

Day 34. In case you were wondering, Julie got her period yesterday—which is bad news in two senses. First, it means that our attempt to be fruitful and multiply has failed yet again. Second, it ratchets up the biblical living to a whole new level of awkwardness.

The Hebrew Bible discourages the faithful from touching a woman for the week after the start of her period. So far in my year, adhering to this rule has been only mildly uncomfortable, nothing worse. In fact, it's got an upside: It dovetails quite nicely with my lifelong obsessive-compulsive disorder and germaphobia, so it's turned out to be a brilliantly convenient excuse to avoid touching 51 percent of the human population.

A female friend will come in for a cheek kiss, and I'll dart my head out of the way like Oscar de la Hoya. A colleague will try to shake my hand, and I'll step backward to safety.

"I'm sorry, I'm not allowed to."

"Oh. Um. OK."

Usually that's the end of it. Usually but not always. Consider this conversation I had with Julie's Australian friend Rachel, whom we met in Central Park last week.

"You're not allowed to? What do you mean?"

"Well, you might be . . . impure."

"What do you mean 'impure'?"

"You know. In your cycle."

I paused. She looked perplexed. I decided this was a good time to avoid eye contact and study the pavement.

"Oh, you mean I might be menstruating? Don't worry, I menstruated last week."

At which point she hugged me. No escaping it.

Oddly, Rachel is not alone. A small but surprisingly vocal minority of Julie's friends have volunteered detailed information about their biological cycles. The photo editor at *Esquire* took the considerate step of emailing me her schedule. Did I perhaps want an Excel chart as well, she wondered?

I even managed to flatter this one woman I met at my sister-in-law's party. When I explained to her why I couldn't shake her hand, she told me, "Well, that's the nicest compliment I've heard in a long time." I looked at her again: gray hair, crow's feet, sixtysomething—yes, probably long past needing to worry about unplanned pregnancies.

Julie, however, is not flattered at all. She finds the whole ritual offensive. I'm not loving it either. It's one thing to avoid handshakes during flu season. But to give up all physical contact with your wife for seven days a month? It's actually quite exhausting, painful, and lonely. You have to be constantly on guard—no sex, of course, but also no hand holding, no shoulder tapping, no hair tousling, no good-night kissing. When I give her the apartment keys, I drop them into her hand from a safe height of six inches.

"This is absurd," she tells me, as she unlocks the door. "It's like cooties from seventh grade. It's theological cooties."

I tell Julie that I can't pick and choose what I follow in the Bible. That'd negate the whole point of my experiment. If I'm trying to get into the mind-set of the ancient Israelites, I can't ignore even the most inconvenient or obscure rule. I also point out that I didn't send her to a red tent.

She's not amused. "I feel like a leper."

"Actually, leprosy in the Bible is a mistranslation. It's more likely a generic name for skin disease. Some even claim it's syphilis."

This is the wrong response. It's a vestigial reflex from my days as an encyclopedia-reading know-it-all: Whenever I run out of things to say, I crowbar random facts into the argument.

Julie walks out of the room. When she's annoyed, she walks with heavy, stomping footsteps. I felt magnitude-five tremors throughout the apartment.

Since I understand Julie's objection and kind of agree with it, I figure it'd be good to get some historic and cultural context. I consult my spiritual advisory board and read up on the literature. As with all of the baffling Bible rules, there is a wealth of positive spin.

First, if done properly, the no-touching ban isn't bad for your marriage. Quite the opposite. Orthodox Jews still follow a version of the original menstruation laws, and many told me they enjoy the enforced sex hiatus. "It's like we get to have honeymoon sex every month," said an Orthodox woman I met one day in Central Park. "It's like makeup sex. You only appreciate what you have when you don't have it."

Second, avoiding your wife at this time of month is not misogynistic. It actually has to do with a reverence for life. When a woman has her period, it's like a little death. A potential life has vanished. This is a way of paying respect, like sitting shivah.

In fact, words like *impurity* and *unclean* are mistranslations. Some Orthodox Jews find such terms offensive. The Hebrew word is *tumah*, a state of spiritual impurity that doesn't have the same negative connotations.

(By the way, the history of impurity laws is fascinating but complex. Let me try to cram an hourlong talk I had with a rabbi into eight lines: The purity laws date from the Jerusalem temples. Back then, you had to be pure to make a sacrifice. When the Second Temple was destroyed, many of the purity laws fell out of use. Many, but not all. Jewish men still steer clear of their wives during menstruation. But they cite a different motivation: Touching might lead to sex, and sex during that time of the month—temple or no temple—is forbidden by another law, Leviticus 20:18. Also, to be extrasafe, the no-touching ban has been extended from a week to about twelve days. OK, finished.)

None of this positive spin appeases Julie, especially since I've decided to abide by another law that makes the no-touching-impure-women rule seem like a breeze. It's found in Leviticus 15:20: "everything upon which she lies during her impurity shall be unclean; everything also upon which she sits shall be unclean." In other words, you shouldn't lie on a bed where a menstruating woman has lain, and you can't sit on a chair where she has sat.

It's a rule that no one follows to the letter anymore. But, again, I want the ultimate ancient-Israelite experience. And it can't hurt to be pure, right?

As for not lying on unclean beds, I'm off the hook. Julie and I don't share a bed. Apparently, when I sleep, I thrash around like a beached marlin, so Julie has opted for two twin beds pushed together, a disturbing echo of my parents and early sixties sitcoms.

The no-sitting-on-impure-seats presents more of a challenge. I came home this afternoon and was about to plop down on my official seat, the gray pleather armchair in our living room.

"I wouldn't do that," says Julie.

"Why?"

"It's unclean. I sat on it." She doesn't even look up from her TiVo'd episode of *Lost*.

OK. Fine. Point taken. She still doesn't appreciate these impurity laws. I move to another chair, a black plastic one.

"Sat in that one, too," says Julie. "And the ones in the kitchen. And the couch in the office."

In preparation for my homecoming, she sat in every chair in the apartment, which I found annoying but also impressive. It seemed in the biblical tradition of enterprising women—like Judith, who seduced the evil general Holofernes, only to behead him when he was drunk.

I finally settle on Jasper's six-inch-high wooden bench, which she had overlooked, where I tap out emails on my PowerBook with my knees up to my chin.

The next day I do a web search and find a thirty-dollar solution to the chair problem: the Handy Seat. This is an aluminum cane that unfolds into a three-legged miniature chair. It's marketed to the elderly, as well as "individuals who suffer from asthma, arthritis, hip or leg surgery, fibromyalgia, back injury," and various other ailments.

My Handy Seat arrives a few days later, and man, do I adore it. I've started bringing it everywhere. First, it's a cane, which is sort of like a staff, which feels very biblical to me. Plus, if you think about it, every subway seat, every bus seat, every restaurant seat—almost certainly impure. The Handy Seat is the foolproof solution. It's not overly comfortable (the plastic part for sitting is only about the size of a Frisbee, and I've got minor back pain from the hunching posture it causes). And there's the inevitable problem of raised eyebrows from passersby and scolding from lobby security guys. ("What are you doing?" asked the guard at the Time Warner Center. "Just sitting, waiting for my friend." "Well, you can't sit here. Get up.") But the Handy Seat is my little island of cleanliness. There's something safe and comforting about it.

O God, thou art my God, I seek thee . . .
—Psalms 63:1

Day 36. A spiritual update: I'm still agnostic. I am feeling a little more comfortable saying the word *God*—thanks to sheer repetition, it no longer makes me sweat. But the anxiety has been replaced by frustration. And frankly, boredom.

The God of the Bible is an amazingly interactive deity. He's not aloof—He talks to people all the time. God spends forty days with Moses on a mountaintop telling him the commandments. God instructs Ezekiel to make bread, and even gives him a recipe of wheat, lentils, and spelt. God wrestles—physically wrestles—with Jacob on a patch of desert called Penuel. Jacob comes out of the fight with a broken hip and a new name: Israel, which means "one who was struggled with God." (Incidentally, some say it wasn't God Himself who struggled, but one of God's angels; the point is, there was contact with the divine.)

I don't expect the level of interaction that the patriarchs had. I don't think God is going to put me in a quarter nelson. But I'm having trouble even sensing the presence of God.

I'm praying three times a day. In the Bible, to my surprise, there's no agreed-upon per-day prayer quota, but morning, afternoon, and night seems a safe, traditional schedule. I'm still praying with the prefabricated prayers provided by the Bible. Today I use a moving passage from Psalms 63:1.

> O God, thou art my God, I seek thee,
> my soul thirsts for thee;
> my flesh faints for thee,
> as in a dry and weary land where no water is.

It's a beautiful prayer. It's got two powerful metaphors at work: first, thirsting for God, and second, loving God like a man loves his wife. And yet, despite the prayer's power, my mind wanders as I read it. "I have to remember to charge my cell phone. . . . We need more quarters for the laundry room."

> *A righteous man hateth lying . . .*
>
> —Proverbs 13:5 (KJV)

Day 37. Man, do I lie a lot. I knew I lied, but when I started to keep track, the quantity was alarming. As with coveting, I try to catalog my daily violations.

A sample from today:

- I lied to Julie about how much internet access at Starbucks costs. I told her eight dollars instead of ten, so she'd be 20 percent less annoyed.

- I gave a fake email address to a religious magazine called *Sojourn-ers* because I didn't want to be swamped by junk email.
- I told a friend who writes children's books that my son loved her book about cookies, even though we've never even cracked open said book about cookies.
- And I lied to kindly Mr. Berkowitz, the man who tested my clothes for mixed fibers. This I do at least once a week. Mr. Berkowitz calls—usually at eight in the morning when Julie is still asleep—and asks if he can come over to my apartment to pray with me. If I said yes every time, he'd practically be a roommate. So I lie. "Can't today, Mr. Berkowitz. An important business meeting." "Sorry Mr. Berkowitz, I'm sick today. A throat ache, a headache, the whole thing."

I don't tell huge lies. My lies aren't of the "I don't remember that meeting, Senator" variety, or even the "I spent time in jail with my friend Leonard" variety. They're little lies. White lies. Half-truths. Sugarcoating.

I'm such an experienced liar, I once edited an article for *Esquire* on the art of the "noncommittal compliment." When your friend makes a movie that is just dreadful, what do you say? I gave a bunch of options, like "You've done it again!" or "I loved the credits!"

I've always thought that this sort of truth hedging was necessary in human relations. Without little lies, chaos would erupt. Marriages would crumble, workers would be fired, egos would be shattered. I've seen *Liar Liar* with Jim Carrey. I know how it works.

But if you take the Bible strictly, it says to avoid lying on all occasions. It says this several times. (A relevant detour: Some scholars argue that the commandment "You shall not bear false witness" should be interpreted more narrowly—it originally applied only to lying under oath. Unfortunately for liars, there are heaps of other passages banning deceit of any kind, including Proverbs 6:17, which calls "the lying tongue" an "abomination.")

In his book *Why the Ten Commandments Matter,* conservative Florida minister D. James Kennedy says my little white lies are, in fact, sins. Think of it this way: You have a date with a friend, but you just want to stay home and watch TV. You don't want to hurt her feelings, so you say you're sick. The friend comes over with a pot of chicken soup and finds you healthy. She can never trust you again. Just tell her the truth in the first place, says Dr. Kennedy.

So at the very least, I should cut back on lying. I decide to do this in stages. My first mission is to stop telling lies to my son, then move on from there. I lie to Jasper all the time, especially at meals. One classic is this: "Just one more bite," I'll say. He'll take a bite. Then I'll say "OK, just one more bite." And so on.

Mind you, he's equally as deceitful. He's allowed to watch TV only when eating, so he'll try to stretch the dinner out for hours. He'll put a string bean halfway into his mouth and just dangle it there like a Marlboro Light.

I'll say "Eat, Jasper."

And then he'll gum it for a bit before stopping and getting back to the business of watching Dora explore.

My question is: Does the parent-child relationship have to be one of dishonesty? Perhaps there's something to transparent parenting.

I start it this morning. Jasper wants a bagel for breakfast. So I ask Julie where she put the bagels.

"We're out," she says. "Just give him an English muffin and tell him that it's a bagel."

Julie says she did it yesterday, and he didn't know the difference.

So I give him a whole wheat Thomas' English muffin.

"Bagel?" he asks, pointing to the English muffin.

"Actually, it's not a bagel. It's an English muffin."

He looks confused.

"It's still very good. But it's not a bagel."

As it registers that he isn't getting a bagel, his expression turns from confusion to anger to rage. He looks like someone has just circumcised him again.

"Bagel! Bagel!"

"We don't have bagels. We'll get bagels tomorrow."

Within about a minute, this has escalated into a full-blown tantrum. I'm still amazed that kids can live out clichés quite as precisely as they do. When throwing tantrums, Jasper will get down on his stomach and pound the floor with his fists and feet like he's a character in a *Peanuts* cartoon.

"What's going on here?" asks Julie. As you might have guessed, I had to tell the truth.

There are probably long-term advantages to being completely honest with your kid (he'll know he can't have his way all the time, for one thing. He'll trust you for another). But there are severe short-term disadvantages.

> *In the beginning God created the heavens and the earth.*
> —Genesis 1:1

Day 40. When I told my friend Ivan—a good Catholic—that I was considering visiting a creationist museum, he let out a loud groan. "Those people give Christianity a bad name."

I understand what he's saying. It's the way many Jews feel when we see a billboard proclaiming Rabbi Menachem Mendel Schneerson as the Messiah. Or the way many gay men feel when they see Rip Taylor tossing a handful of confetti. It's kind of embarrassing. Like Ivan, I've always taken evolution to be a cold, hard truth. As indisputable as the fact that the sun is hot or that Charles Darwin married his first cousin (the latter of which I learned in the encyclopedia and can't get out of my head).

But creationism is biblical literalism at its purest, so I need to check it out. I researched various creationist hot spots—both Jewish and Christian—and found a handful of possibilities. But nothing came close to a huge structure perched on a gentle Kentucky hill. There lies the Creation Museum, the Louvre for those who believe God made Adam less than six thousand years ago from dust. Its founders are an evangelical group called Answers in Genesis. (A note on timing: I'll be talking more with evangelicals—both conservative and liberal—in month nine when my New Testament portion begins; but since creationism is so tied to the Old Testament's Genesis, I'm doing it early.)

The Creation Museum is still under construction—it's slated to open after my year ends—which is fine by me. There's something appropriate about seeing the creation of a creationist museum. So I fly down to Cincinnati, a few miles from the site.

At the airport, I realize once again how deeply biblical symbolism has seeped into every nook in my brain. As I exit, I see a strange FAA sign that warns ominously: "Don't Look Back." It doesn't say how you'd be punished if you do—I'm guessing body-cavity search, not getting turned to a pillar of salt—but I still find it a bizarre echo of God's warning to Lot as he fled the destruction of Sodom: "Do not look back."

A half hour later, I pull up to the museum—a low building fronted by thick yellow columns. In the parking lot, I spot a bumper sticker of a Jesus fish gobbling up a Darwin fish.

I'm greeted by publicist Mark Looy, a gray-haired man with a gentle schoolteacher voice, who guides me to a door that lets us into the lobby. The lobby is, in a word, awesome.

The museum is still a work in progress. Hard hats everywhere, the smell of sawdust, the whine of drills. But even in its unfinished state, you can tell this is going to send the media into a Michael Jackson–trial-like frenzy.

The first thing I see is a life-size diorama of an Eden-like scene. There's a waterfall, a stream, and cypress trees. An animatronic caramel-skinned cave girl giggles and cocks her head to look straight at me, which is odd and impressive and disturbing all at once. She's playing awfully close to a fierce-looking razor-toothed T. rex. Don't worry, Mark tells me. In the beginning, humans and dinosaurs lived together in harmony. The T. Rex's scary incisors are for coconuts and fruit, just like pandas' teeth.

When the museum opens, the Answers in Genesis folks expect thousands of visitors. And it'll probably get them—polls say that as many as 45 percent of Americans believe in creationism. Not intelligent design. We're talking strict the-earth-is-less-than-ten-thousand-years-old creationism. (The creationists I met scoffed at intelligent design, the theory that the world was designed by a superior being, but not necessarily in seven literal days. The creationists think of this as some sort of nebulous theological mumbo jumbo.)

Mark introduces me to Ken Ham, the founder of Answers in Genesis. Ken is a wiry and energetic fifty-six-year-old with a gray Vandyke beard. Ken quizzes me about my last book, the one about reading the encyclopedia, and I end up telling him about my ill-fated appearance on *Who Wants to Be a Millionaire*. I was stumped by the question "What is an erythrocyte?"

"It's a red blood cell," says Ken.

He's right. I'm thrown off guard. A creationist who trumps me in science knowledge—that's unexpected and unsettling.

Ken was born to religious parents in Queensland, Australia, and still has a thick Aussie accent despite his twenty years in America. We start walking through the rooms. "The guy who designed the museum also designed the *Jaws* attraction at the Universal theme park," Ken says. And it shows. The place is professional. We stroll past more than a dozen robotic dinosaurs. A statue of Eve, with her flowing hair placed conveniently over her pert breasts. A partly built ark. A room with a circular slope like New York's Guggenheim Museum, a subtle reminder of man's fall from paradise. A theater with sprinklers to simulate the flood. A huge crocodile (a prop from the secular movie *Crocodile Dundee*). The future home of a talking Saint Paul robot. A medieval castle–themed bookstore. Medieval? Because the dragons of medieval times were actually still-living dinosaurs.

As we pass by the statue of a Roman centurion and the currently headless giraffe, I ask Ken the questions he's been asked a thousand times.

If Adam and Eve gave birth to two boys, Cain and Abel, how did Cain and Abel have kids?

"That's an easy one. Adam and Eve didn't just have Cain and Abel. It says in Genesis 5:4 that Adam had 'other sons and daughters.'"

When it says "day," does that mean a literal twenty-four-hour day?

"Yes. You've got to go back to the original word in Hebrew, which is *yom*. It's the same word that's used for a twenty-four-hour day. If you don't take that to mean 'day,' it's a slippery slope."

What about scientific dating that says the world is millions of years old?

"Ninety percent of age-dating methods are faulty."

Which version of the Bible do you use?

"Usually the King James. But you have to be careful with translations."

Ken explains that, for instance, many versions say the rabbit "chews its cud" (Leviticus 11:6). "The skeptics say the rabbit doesn't chew its cud. But you look at the original language, it says 'the rabbit re-eats its food.' And look at what a rabbit does. It excretes rabbit pellets and then eats the pellets. The Bible is correct."

We walk into a room with a brick wall covered with menacing-looking graffiti. This room is devoted to modern ills, among them drugs and racism. "There is only one race, the human race," says Ken.

The creationists I meet are surprisingly liberal on race matters. Racial intermarriage is considered just fine. In fact, they think that Darwin's theory can lead to racism because minorities are sometimes seen as lower forms of Homo sapiens on the evolutionary scale. They are also progressive on Darfur. On other topics—including abortion and gay marriage—they are down-the-line conservatives.

We pass a dinosaur with a saddle on it. This display was mocked by my own magazine—*Esquire*—which called it a dressage dinosaur because of the English saddle. Ken downplays it. "It's just a novelty. Just something for the kids." He ushers me through. "This way, A. J." (That's one thing I notice: They say "A. J." here a lot. It seems common among certain types of very religious people to say your name all the time. It makes me think of God's first words to Moses, which were "Moses, Moses!" but it's probably unrelated.)

Speaking of dinosaurs, if they really were on the ark, as creationists claim, how did Noah squeeze them all in?

"He put them in when they were younger and smaller. The equivalent of teenagers."

I later bought a paperback at the museum bookstore called *Noah's Ark: A Feasibility Study,* which spends three hundred pages outlining the brilliant engineering that made the boat possible. There are chapters on the ark's ventilation system, methods of onboard exercise for the animals, and the myth of explosive manure gases.

The book is beautifully argued—and I don't believe a syllable of it. Which I know is counter to my quest. I had told Mark the publicist that I was coming in with an open mind, but while down here, I realize my mind won't open that far. I can understand being open to the existence of God and the beauty of rituals and the benefits of prayer. But the existence of a juvenile brontosaurus on the ark? And an earth that's barely older than Gene Hackman? I have to go with 99 percent of scientists on this one.

Of course, the creationists cite plenty of scientific evidence of their own. Or more precisely, they interpret the same evidence as being proof of creationism. Mark told me about a T. rex bone in Montana that broke open and had blood vessels. No way that could be millions of years old, he said.

The article *Esquire* ran was called "Greetings from Idiot America," and it was very funny. But I have to disagree with the headline. The Answers in Genesis folks aren't idiots. And despite a British news show that scored its segment with *Deliverance*-style banjo music, they aren't hillbillies. Everyone I met had a full set of well-orthodontured teeth and blinked at regular intervals. I can't prove it, but I'd wager there's no difference in the average IQ of creationists and evolutionists.

The thing is, their faith in the literal Bible is so strong, they will squeeze and distort all data to fit the Genesis account. In fact, you have to be quite sharp to be a leading creationist. The mental gymnastics can be astonishing.

Consider AiG's resident astrophysicist, Jason Lisle. Mark introduced me to him proudly. "A real, live PhD who believes in creationism. Here he is, in 3-D."

Jason has meticulously parted hair, looks a bit like Paul Reubens, and is sweet in an unforced way. He tells me it wasn't easy being a creationist PhD student. He had to stay closeted about his beliefs and write for the AiG magazine under a pseudonym.

Now here's the interesting part: Like mainstream scientists, he thinks the universe is billions of light years big. But if it's that big, and only six thousand years old, the light rays from distant stars wouldn't have time to travel to the earth. Shouldn't the night sky be black?

"That's a tough one," he says. "But it's not a killer." There are several possibilities.

1. The speed of light may not have always been 186,000 miles per second. Perhaps it was faster when the universe began.

2. The time-zone analogy. You can leave Kentucky at 5:00 p.m. and

arrive in Missouri at 4:00 p.m. In the same way, there may be something to continuous time zones in space.

3. Something called gravitational time dilation. I didn't quite understand it, but it had to do with our galaxy having a special place in the universe.

After Jason the astrophysicist, I'm brought across the hall to meet another creationist named Carl Kerby. Carl is a big guy—turns out his dad was a pro wrestler. He's wearing a Hawaiian shirt and gives off a casual, feet-on-the-desk vibe. His specialty: He is the Creation Museum's resident expert on pop culture. Carl monitors movies and TV shows for subtle, or not-so-subtle, pro-evolution content so that he can alert fellow creationists to the danger.

On his list: *Finding Nemo* (namely, the line "Give it up old man, you can't fight evolution, I was built for speed"). And *Gilligan's Island* (they used the word *prehistoric* twice in one episode; "there's no such thing as prehistoric," Carl says). Other violators include *Bugs Bunny, Lilo & Stitch, Bob the Builder*, and *The Incredible Mr. Limpet*.

"It used to be my favorite movie," he says of *Limpet*. "And then I played it for my family, and thirteen minutes in, there was a nerdy science guy who pulls down a chart and starts talking about how fish were our ancestors. I had to stop the movie and talk to my family and explain."

Of course, when it comes to secular entertainment, creationism's enemy number one is *Inherit the Wind,* about the famous Scopes "monkey trial." It debuted as a play in 1955 and was later turned into a Spencer Tracy movie. And Carl—along with all his colleagues—insists that it's wildly unfair to Christians.

When I got home, I rented the movie and compared it to the actual court transcripts. And I have to say . . . the movie is wildly unfair to Christians. Or at least to this strain of Christianity.

William Jennings Bryan—a deeply religious three-time Democratic presidential nominee who was the prosecuting attorney for the anti-evolution folks—was turned into a total buffoon named Matthew Harrison Brady, played by Fredric March. Brady is a potbellied glutton prone to burping and smacking his lips. In one scene, he's gorging on fried chicken out of a basket—in the courtroom.

The film re-creates the famous showdown over the Bible between Bryan and the brilliant Chicago lawyer Clarence Darrow. It's a good scene. But if you read the court transcript, it was actually a more interesting and subtle confrontation. For instance, here's the dialogue from the movie:

> Darrow: Do you believe every word of the Bible is true?
> Bryan: Yes. Every word is literally true.

And here's the corresponding real exchange:

> Darrow: Do you claim that everything in the Bible should be literally interpreted?
> Bryan: I believe everything in the Bible should be accepted as it is given there. Some of the Bible is given illustratively; for instance, "Ye are the salt of the earth." I would not insist that man was actually salt, or that he had flesh of salt, but it is used in the sense of salt as saving God's people.

Like creationists today, he admits that there is some figurative language in the Bible, even if most of it should be taken as literally true.

And he had wit: "I believe [the Bible] was inspired by the Almighty, and He may have used language that could be understood at that time, instead of using language that could not be understood until Darrow was born." [Laughter and applause.]

Not bad, you know?

As I said, I still believe in evolution. There's nothing that will change that, even if they found Noah's Year-at-a-Glance calendar on a pristinely preserved ark. And, yes, I know there's artistic license and all that. But it does seem odd to me that this movie—which is supposed to be a champion for the truth—distorted the truth so much. Why do that? Especially when you have reality on your side.

I spend my last half hour at the museum bookshop. I flip through dinosaur books for kids, a *Far Side*–like cartoon book about the fallen world, biology books, and theology books. I spend several minutes skimming an astronomy book called *Dismantling the Big Bang*, which aims to expose the philosophical weaknesses of said theory.

It makes me think of AiG's resident astrophysicist, Jason. Before I left, he wanted to make clear to me that he's not geocentric—he doesn't believe the earth is the center of the universe. "Does anyone anymore?" I asked. He said, yes, there is a group called "biblical astronomers"—they believe the earth is stationary because the Bible says the earth "shall never be moved" (Psalms 93:1). Jason considers them an embarrassment.

That was something I hadn't expected: moderate creationists who view other creationists as too extreme. But it will turn out to be one of this year's big lessons: *Moderation* is a relative term.

In the seventh year there shall be a Sabbath of solemn rest for the land . . .

—LEVITICUS 25:4

Day 42. On my flight back to New York, I sink into a minidepression about the museum. All that creativity and enthusiasm—it seems like such misplaced energy.

I feel the need to compensate, to do justice to the Bible itself. So I vow to spend the next few days finding biblical literalism at its most noble. And today I may have found it while reading a book about faith-based ethics called *The Quiet Hand of God*. Namely, the movement by faithful Christians and Jews to apply the Bible's financial laws to the world's poverty crises. Here the Bible has saved thousands, maybe millions, of lives.

Here's how it works: The Bible says that years—like days of the week—belong in a cycle of seven. The seventh year is called the Sabbath year, and big things happen.

First, that entire year, you must stop working. No farming is allowed. This is so the land can rest, and the needy can come and eat all they want from the vines and olive trees. Second, you must forgive your neighbor's debts. All IOUs are erased.

After seven consecutive Sabbath cycles—forty-nine years—something even more radical happens: the Jubilee year. During the Jubilee year, you must return all property to its original owner (Leviticus 25:10).

Scholars aren't sure how strictly the Jubilee law was practiced in

ancient Israel. It's possible it was practiced only by a devout sprinkling
of farmers. And naturally, as my banker friend Ivan points out, if we
followed these today, it would throw the financial markets into utter
chaos.

Even on a personal level, I've found it a challenge to practice. Consider the not-working part. I've worked for sixteen years straight, so I'm
long overdue for a yearlong hiatus. The problem is, I've got a deadline
for this book and a kid who is obsessed with offensively pricey Thomas
the Tank Engine toys.

As for forgiving debts, I try two things:

1) Since bonds are debts, I try to forgive a bond I have owned for
   nine years. It was issued by the New York State Dormitory
   Authority.

   "We've never had a request like this before," says the fourth
   guy I was sent to. He finally suggests that I donate some money
   to my favorite State University of New York school.

2) To my recollection, the only other outstanding debt that stretches
   more than seven years is the one owed by my sophomore-year
   college roommate. He owed me at least twenty dollars. The weasel would buy yogurt with the communal house money, then hide
   it from the rest of us in paper bags labeled "Photo Equipment—
   Do Not Touch." I've always held a grudge. I let it go.

But there is something practical I can do. And that's through an organization called Jubilee USA Network.

Back in the 1990s, two British evangelists named Martin Dent and
Bill Peters had an epiphany: They made the connection between the Bible's Jubilee concept and the third-world debt crises. Dent and Peters
had both worked in Africa for the British equivalent of the peace corps.
Dent, in fact, had been appointed an honorary chief of a Nigerian tribe.
He had seen poverty firsthand. He argued that the developed nations
should forgive third-world debt. Often these IOUs were left over from
corrupt regimes. The Bible says that everyone deserves a fresh start.

The Jubilee movement they started has resulted in massive cancella-
tions of debt by England, France, the U.S., and others. They got a huge

publicity boost when Bono and his sunglasses joined the cause. Here's what he said about Jubilee in his speech at the National Prayer Breakfast in 2006:

"It is such an important idea, Jubilee, that Jesus begins his ministry with this. Jesus is a young man, he's met with the rabbis, impressed everyone, people are talking. The elders say he's a clever guy, this Jesus, but he hasn't done much—yet. He hasn't spoken in public before . . .

"When he does, his first words are from Isaiah: 'The Spirit of the Lord is upon me,' he says, 'because He has anointed me to preach good news to the poor.' And Jesus proclaims the year of the Lord's favor, the year of Jubilee (Luke 4:18).

"What he was really talking about was an era of grace—and we're still in it."

I joined a group called Jubilee USA as a volunteer and have been sending out postcards to congressmen and senators about debt relief.

I know. Call Oslo and alert the Peace Prize committee. But it's better than watching *Entourage* and eating Fruit Roll Ups. Plus, I scored some points with my socially conscious wife, who joined me for several hours of address writing and stamp affixing. Whenever Julie collaborates with me on my biblical quest, I get a Mr. Berkowitz-like high.

If you can read the writing and make known to me its interpretation,
you shall be clothed with purple . . .

—DANIEL 5:16

Day 44. In an effort to cut down on temptation, I've been rationing my news intake, especially when the news concerns Hollywood actresses running off with Pilates instructors. But I spotted one news story that seemed worthwhile. It was about Supreme Court justice Antonin Scalia.

Scalia apparently made a speech in Puerto Rico to a student group. He said that those who believe the Constitution should evolve with society are "idiots." Wrong, he says. We should stick to the original intent of the Founding Fathers. As Scalia put it, "Scalia does have a philosophy; it's called originalism." (By the way, referring to yourself in the third person may not be biblically forbidden, but should be. Unless you have a biblical alter ego named Jacob, of course.)

This is helpful. I've been trying to focus my mission. Here is my answer: I'll do the Scalia technique on the Bible. I'll try to find the original intent. I want to live the original religion.

A lot of people tell me that such a quest is a fantasy. The Bible was written thousands of years ago by people with profoundly different worldviews. And I agree, it's hard. Much harder than finding the original intent of the Constitution, which was at least written in some form of English, even if the *S*s and *F*s look alike. The Bible was originally written in Hebrew, Aramaic, and Greek. Its journey into other languages has been famously bumpy; the Bible could be the most mistranslated text in history.

The Red Sea is a mistranslation of the "Sea of Reeds." The idea that Moses (and his descendents) had horns comes from a mistranslation of the Hebrew word *qaran*. It actually means that Moses's face was shining, or emitted beams of light.

I've been doing my best. Since I've been told that reading the Bible in translation is like watching TV in black and white, I'm trying to compensate any way I can. I flip between different versions. I have this fancy Bible software with an ancient-language dictionary. I have my advisory board. I've bought books on teaching yourself Hebrew and ancient Greek—which is overly optimistic, given my time frame.

But even if I assume a proper translation, then there's the not-so-trivial matter of changes in the text over time. Most modern scholars (at least those of a secular bent) don't believe the medieval scribes were flawless Xerox machines. They made tweaks both intentional and accidental. Similarly, the Hebrew Bible has been stable for centuries, but you can see small variations if you compare it to, for instance, the Dead Sea Scrolls.

But I don't want to give up just because it's hard. Especially since the Scalia method of "original intent" continues to be a major force in biblical interpretation, both in Christianity and—rather differently—in Judaism.

A thirty-second history: For centuries, most believed the Bible was a true account of what happened. It was nonfiction, plain and simple.

Most people were, as religious scholar Marcus Borg calls them, "natural literalists"—they had no strong evidence to believe otherwise.

But more and more, science began to butt up against the literal biblical story. How to reconcile Galileo's universe with Joshua stopping the sun in the sky? Or Darwin's theory of evolution with Noah's ark? You saw several reactions. Two of the major ones that have dominated for a century are:

1. Modernism. This says that science and religion are separate. As Stephen Jay Gould put it, they are "nonoverlapping magisteria." The Bible is packed with figurative language and poetry. The creation story, powerful as it may be, is a myth. But religion and the Bible still have a place, because science can't answer questions about faith, purpose, and the meaning of life.

2. Fundamentalism. This view continues to assert that the Bible is 100 percent inerrant, both in morals and historical accuracy. Joshua really did make the sun stand still. Noah really did pile the animals onto a big boat made of gopher wood. They admit there is some nonliteral language in the Bible—when Isaiah says the "trees clapped," it's obviously a metaphor. Same with Jesus's parables. But unless a phrase is clearly figurative, the Bible should be taken at face value.

Like sixties White House advisers, fundamentalists have their own domino theory. If one part of the Bible is proved wrong, why should we believe any of it? It's a good point. And as an agnostic, I had this view from the other side. Why should I follow a book that seems to condone slavery and hand chopping? The question helped inspire my quest.

The Christian literal movement is, of course, famous for its conservative politics. To oppose homosexuality, for instance, its adherents cite Leviticus 18:22: "You shall not lie with a male as with a woman; it is an abomination."

But not all Christian literalists are conservative; there's a growing progressive movement. One branch calls itself Red-letter Christians—after the color of the text of Jesus's sayings in old Bibles. The Red-letter Christians—such as reverends Tony Campolo and Jim Wallis—focus not on homosexuality or abortion, but instead on the literal adherence to Jesus's teachings about poverty and peace. When I start exploring the New Testament, I'll be consulting both sides.

Jewish biblical interpretation has taken a slightly different path. I got a crash course in this from a frighteningly smart rabbi named Robbie Harris. Robbie—who talks so quickly that my fingers ache from typing notes—is a professor of the Bible at the Jewish Theological Seminary in Upper Manhattan.

When I first met him, Robbie was on his cell phone with a publicist from the Knitting Factory, the hipster downtown music club.

"OK," he said. "Great. I'll call you later."

He was playing there next week, he told me. His band is called Shake, Rabbis and Roll (SR2, for short).

"What kind of music is it?" I asked.

"Rock and roll. Do you like rock and roll?"

"Who doesn't?"

Robbie played me a couple of songs from his first album, which "went aluminum." I liked them, especially the one about the snobby New York girl. ("She looks at Central Park as the Great Divide/And now she thinks she's slumming on the Upper West Side.")

He's an observant Jew, but one to whom I can relate, since—unlike the totally religious Mr. Berkowitz—he straddles the secular and Jewish worlds.

Here's what Robbie taught me: In Judaism there's the literal meaning of the biblical passage, and then there's the interpretation of the rabbis in books like the Talmud.

Sometimes these two line up. When the Bible says don't mix wool and linen, that's what it means: Don't mix wool and linen. Here the rabbis just elaborate on what kind of wool (sheep's) and how far apart it must be from the linen.

But other times, the literal meaning is light years from the rabbis' interpretation. For instance, the famous line in Leviticus "an eye for an eye" doesn't really mean pluck out the other guy's eye. It's much more civilized than that. The tradition says it means this: "cash for an eye." The attacker has to pay the victim the monetary value of the eye.

Or consider this passage: "You are not to boil a young goat in the milk of its mother" (Exodus 23:19, NASB).

If you take this literally, as I'm trying to do, this is relatively easy. I think—with a little willpower and a safe distance from farms—I can make it for a year without boiling a baby goat in its mother's milk. My friend John suggested that, worse comes to worst, I could boil the baby goat in its aunt's milk. Thanks, John.

But the rabbis have a far more elaborate interpretation: Exodus 23:19 actually means to separate milk and meat. Which is where you get the kosher rules banning cheeseburgers. Along with the myriad rules about how long you must wait between a meat course and a dairy course (from one hour to six hours, depending on local tradition) and whether you should separate dairy utensils and meat utensils in a dishwasher (yes).

Strict Orthodox Jews believe that God gave these amplifications—the "oral laws"—to Moses on the mountaintop. That's why he was up there for forty days. Moses passed on the oral laws to the Israelites, who told them to their sons, and so on until they were eventually written down. Traditionally, the laws from the all-important five books of Moses—the Torah—come to a total of 613. (My list of rules is slightly longer because I included advice from other parts of the Old Testament, such as Proverbs and Psalms.) Other Jews believe that the oral laws have developed over thousands of years but are sacred nonetheless.

There is one sect of Judaism that rejects oral law altogether. Its followers are called Karaites, and they are theological minimalists, adhering only to the Bible. This can result in some ultrastrict behavior. On the Sabbath, many turn off the heat so as not to engage in commerce with the electric company, which could be considered work. "I just wear a lot of layers," one Karaite I interviewed told me. "It's not so bad." The Karaites had their golden age in medieval times—an estimated 10 percent of Jews were once Karaite. They have since dwindled in number to about fifty thousand, mostly in Israel and, oddly enough, Daly City, California.

On this journey, I plan to be mindful of the oral law. But I'm not going to follow it exclusively. I feel I have to try to puzzle out for myself what the Bible means, even if it means I take some wrong turns.

All this makes me realize: In a sense, my project is steeped in Judaism, since I'm spending a lot of time on the Hebrew Scriptures. But in some ways, it's actually more influenced by the Protestant idea that you can interpret the Bible yourself, without mediation. *Sola scriptura,* as it's called.

Martin Luther advocated sola scriptura in reaction to the Catholic Church. At the risk of muddying matters, Catholicism is somewhere between Judaism and Protestantism in terms of biblical interpretation. Like Judaism, there's a middle step between you and the Bible—namely the church doctrine. But the Catholic church's mandates are generally slightly less elaborate and complex than those of the rabbis.

In some ways, going literal is turning out to be easier than rabbinic Judaism. Do I need to wear a yarmulke? No, the Bible doesn't mandate it. That came from the rabbis. But in some ways, it's infinitely harder. I'm trying to follow the word. When the Bible says, "an eye for an eye," I don't want to soften it to the rabbinically approved "some money for an eye." When it says smash idols, I want to smash idols. Plus, I'm already feeling guilty—which is how I know I'm actually Jewish. I feel like I'm disappointing my forefathers. I imagine my distant ancestor the Vilna Gaon—a famous rabbi in Eastern Europe—shaking his head somewhere, sighing, emitting an *Oy-yi-yi-yi-yi.*

Give strong drink to him who is perishing, and wine to those in bitter distress.

—PROVERBS 31:6

Day 44, afternoon. My *Esquire* colleague David broke up with his girl-friend. He has sciatica—which I had always thought was restricted to people who drive Ford Crown Victorias and get half-off movie tickets. Also, he wrote a very funny movie script about elaborate Christmas displays—and then had someone sell the exact same idea two days before he sent it out.

Next time I'm at *Esquire,* I stop by his office with a bottle of Kendall-Jackson red wine.

"Here," I say, handing it to him over his desk.

"What's this?"

"It's because you're depressed. The Bible says to bring wine to the heavy of heart."

"The Bible says that?"

"Yes. It also says that you shouldn't sing to people with a heavy heart. That'd be like rubbing vinegar in the wound."

"So you're not going to sing to me?"

"No."

David seems grateful for the wine, and no doubt the lack of singing as well. I love it when the Bible gives Emily Post–like tips that are both wise and easy to follow.

Remember the sabbath day, to keep it holy.

—EXODUS 20:8

Day 45. It's the seventh Sabbath of my biblical year. Well, actually, it's the day after the seventh Sabbath. I couldn't type this entry on the Sabbath itself because the Bible tells me not to work. (A friend of mine said that even observing the Sabbath might be breaking the Sabbath, since my job is to follow the Bible. That gave me a two-hour headache.)

Before my biblical year, I was among the biggest Sabbath violators in America. I'm a workaholic. It's a trait I got from my father, who scribbles away on his law books without ceasing—on the beach, on the train, while "watching" old Katharine Hepburn movies on DVD (which means an occasional glance at the screen to make sure the picture is still moving). If the Apocalypse comes, there's no doubt he'd work right on through, looking up to take note of the rising rivers of blood before returning to his case study. I'd probably do the same.

We'd have a lot of company. In the post-BlackBerry age, is there really a boundary between the weekday and the weekend, between work hours and overtime? We work on Saturday, the Jewish Shabbat. We work on Sunday, the Christian Sabbath. We put in more hours than the God of Genesis himself.

It wasn't always so in America. As *New York Times* writer Judith Shulevitz points out, the Puritans left England in large part for the freedom to follow the fourth commandment. The Puritans took the Sabbath seriously: no sports, no dancing, no smoking, no visiting. You must attend church, but the Puritans "punished anyone who got there with unseemly haste or on too showy a horse." The Sabbath in America survived even after the Puritans faded away. As recently as eighty years ago, writes Shulevitz, "football was considered too vulgar to be played on Sunday."

You can see traces of the Puritan influence today—just try buying liquor on Sunday morning in Manhattan. And the hardcore Sabbath is making a comeback in some evangelical circles. The Florida-based megapastor D. James Kennedy tells his parishioners not to eat at a restaurant on Sunday, because that's encouraging waiters to work, thus breaking God's law.

The strictest Sabbath keepers today are probably the Orthodox Jews. In postbiblical times, the rabbis wrote down a complex list of forbidden behavior. It's got thirty-nine types of work, including cooking, combing, and washing. You can't plant, so gardening is off-limits. You can't tear anything, so toilet paper must be pre-ripped earlier in the week. You can't make words, so Scrabble is often considered off-limits (though at least one rabbi allows Deluxe Scrabble, since the squares have ridges, which provides enough separation between letters so that they don't actually form words).

I got a firsthand taste of the Orthodox Shabbat when my aunt Kate was visiting my parents' house. Kate's very cute, very observant thirteen-year-old daughter, Rivka, was over. She'd eaten part of an ice cream sundae and wanted to store it in the freezer for later. But it was Friday, and sundown was coming fast. (The Jewish Sabbath lasts from before sundown Friday to after sundown Saturday.)

She couldn't open the freezer after sundown because that would turn on a freezer light, which was illegal.

"Can you unscrew the freezer lightbulb?" she asked my mom.

My mom tried to unscrew it, but couldn't reach the bulb without removing every last Eggo and Ben & Jerry's from the freezer drawer.

"I'll tell you what," said my mom. "I'll open the freezer for you."

"You can't. You're Jewish," said Rivka.

"Then I'll ask Joelle to do it." (Joelle is my Catholic great-aunt.)

"You can't ask her. She just has to volunteer to do it."

At which point, my mom gave up. I'm guessing that the poor kosher sundae is still in there today.

At first glance, the Sabbath and all of its rules seemed outlandish. And yet I've opted to reserve judgment till I experience the Sabbath myself.

Or at least the explicitly biblical version of the Sabbath. Unlike the rabbis, the Bible itself gives few detailed instructions on how exactly to refrain from work. And the ones it does give apply only to farmers and reality-show contestants: no kindling of fire, no gathering sticks, no plowing or harvesting.

So I have to figure this one out myself. Since my work is writing, I decide I need to abstain from writing, of course. But also researching, phoning colleagues, and scouting the newspaper for ideas. The thing is, going cold turkey terrifies me. I want to wade into this ocean cautiously, like a Sarasota retiree.

The first week, I told myself: no checking of email. I lasted all of an hour, after which I told myself, well, I won't open the emails themselves. I'll just scan the subject headers. That doesn't count as working. So I clicked on the mail. Hmm. An email from my mom. The Bible does say to respect your parents. And maybe it's urgent. Plus, I have another fifty-one Sabbaths to get it right. I clicked on it. It's a joke about five blondes and a blind man in a bar.

Week number two, I tried it again. I shall open no email from sun-down on Friday to sundown on Saturday. I made it past Friday night, but then broke down on Saturday morning and stole a peek again. Well, I told myself, I've still got fifty Sabbaths left. Unfortunately, I didn't im-prove with Sabbaths three to six.

This week I vowed to make it all the way. I felt optimistic. At 6:00 p.m. on Friday night, the sun officially dipped below the New York ho-rizon. I snapped shut my computer, shoved all my books in the corner, silenced the electronic cowbell on my cell phone that I've been meaning to change anyway—and did a little Berkowitz-like fist pump. Something clicked in my brain. It was a school's-out-for-summer feeling. A wave of relief and freedom. No matter how much I want to, I cannot work. I have no choice.

It was a beautiful moment. And short lived. An hour later, my brain clicked back, and I started to suffer pangs of withdrawal every time I walked past my idle PowerBook. What emails are piling up in my in-box? What if the editor of *The New Yorker* sent me a surprise job offer? On Saturday at noon, I broke down. I checked. Who's going to know?

I was too embarrassed to tell Julie. Julie loves that I'm trying to break the seven-day work cycle—the Sabbath is her favorite part of my experiment. So I keep my failure a secret.

Worse, I then use the Sabbath to weasel out of household tasks.

"Can you put the papers in the recycling bin?"

"I really shouldn't. I'm not allowed to carry a burden outside of my house."

As she took out the papers herself, I could hear her footsteps thump down the hallway corridor.

You shall not wrong a stranger or oppress him . . .
—Exodus 22:21

Day 46. Tonight I invited a Jehovah's Witness into my home. I realize that this fact already puts me in an extreme minority.

And, mind you, I didn't just idly answer the door and let a Jehovah's Witness inside. I aggressively pursued the Jehovah's Witnesses. I phoned the headquarters and requested that a Jehovah's Witness be sent to my apartment. After three calls and not a little confusion on their part—it's not a common inquiry—I finally got my wish.

Yes, I'm aware that it doesn't make much sense. It's like volunteering for jury duty or paying to see a Vin Diesel movie.

OK, enough! The poor Jehovah's Witnesses. Their zeal for ringing doorbells have made them one of America's favorite religious punch lines. So I promise: No more cheap Jehovah's Witness jokes.

But I do want to know more about the Jehovah's Witnesses and what they really stand for. Because they are perhaps the fastest-growing biblical literalists in the world. Their current membership stands at more than 6.6 million, with about 300,000 new converts a year. They're also interesting to me because they are usually classified as Christian, but, like the Amish, they lean heavily on the Hebrew Scriptures.

My Jehovah's Witness is named Michael, and he arrives right on the dot, at 7:30 p.m. He wears a brown suit, brown shoes, brown tie, and carries a brown leather case holding a Bible and a pamphlet. He looks somewhat like the actor Gary Busey, if Gary Busey had his hair parted in the middle.

Michael is warm and likeable. He has a deep voice, but it is more soothing than booming, more shrink than football coach.

And he is grateful. So grateful it's almost heartbreaking. He thanks me for having him over. "There are so many misconceptions about Jehovah's Witnesses. I'm just so glad you're talking to me to find out the truth."

He sits on the living room couch, leaning forward, his hands in the "fish-was-this-big" posture. "People say ours is a primitive Christianity—and we take that as a compliment." The Witnesses believe they're getting back to the original meaning of the Bible—the booklet Michael gives me is called "What Does the Bible *Really* Teach?"

Michael, who works in computers at the massive Jehovah's Witness headquarters in Brooklyn, gives me a crash course in his faith. Here, some of the highlights of the belief (vastly oversimplified, of course):

- God should be called Jehovah, because that's what the Bible calls him. "You can call a person 'man,' or you can call him by his name, 'Bob.' God has a name: 'Jehovah.'"
- Humans should take literally Jesus's pacifist words. "You won't find any Jehovah's Witnesses in Iraq," Michael says. "Jesus said, 'He who lives by the sword, dies by the sword.'"
- They don't believe in the Trinity. Jesus is not God, but instead God's first creation. (This belief is why they are sometimes seen as belonging outside of Christianity.)
- Armageddon is coming soon—and believers will be resurrected and live in paradise. But most righteous people won't live in heaven. Almost everyone will live in a paradise here on earth. Heaven will be reserved for 144,000 pious souls who will reign with Jehovah as divine administrators.
- The Witnesses don't celebrate Christmas or Easter, as neither holiday is mentioned in the Bible. Birthdays are also out: The only two birthdays celebrated in the Bible were those of evil people—one a Pharaoh and one a pro-Roman Jewish king. Michael's fine

with the ban, especially now. "As I get older, I don't want to be reminded of my birthday."
- There is no hell. The Witnesses believe *hell* is a mistranslation of
  Gehenna, which was an ancient garbage dump. They say that
  nonbelievers simply die at Armageddon, rather than being thrown
  into an inferno. "How can you have a kind and loving God who
  also roasts people?" he asks.

I am surprised by the Jehovah's Witness theology, especially this
last point. I had always heard that they were a fire-and-brimstone sect,
but here's Michael telling me they reject the notion of hell. The belief
is probably heretical by mainstream standards, but it has a gentleness
to it.

It has been an hour and a half, and Michael is glancing at his watch
every few minutes now.

"You just tell me when you want me to go," says Michael. "I'm from
the Midwest, so I'm conscious of overstaying my welcome."

"No, I'm fine," I say. It's true. I could keep going for hours. I doubt
Michael will convert me, but I love discussing the Bible. Can't get enough
of it.

I ask him what's the most controversial part of his faith.

"The blood transfusion issue," he says. "People think we're kooks. But
we absolutely use the medical system." (Was this a subtle dig at the Christian Scientists, I wondered?) "We just don't take blood transfusions."

The reason is the literal translation of several verses, among them
Acts 15:29, Genesis 9:4, and Leviticus 7:26—the last of which reads, "Ye
shall eat no manner of blood" (KJV).

The Witnesses make an unusual argument here. They say that the
word *eat* should really be translated as "consume," and that transfusion
qualifies as consumption.

As Michael points out, this is seriously controversial. Critics say that
the ban has caused numerous deaths, and the Witnesses have been the
subject of several lawsuits. In recent years, the church elders have scaled
back a bit. Now, elements of blood—such as hemoglobin—can be trans-
fused. But still, the ban on transfusing whole blood remains.

To me, it boils down to this question: Should you obey the Bible's rules even if doing so endangers your life? I've looked in the Bible to see what guidance it gives. As I suspected, there's no clear-cut yes or no.

On the one hand, the Bible is filled with martyrs and near-martyrs to their faith. In the Book of Daniel, the evil King Nebuchadnezzar commands three Hebrews to bow down before a golden idol or else get thrown in a fire. The men refuse to bow. Nebuchadnezzar stokes the fire—making it seven times hotter—and tosses the rebels in. But God protects his faithful, and they emerge unscorched.

On the other hand, there are plenty of times when life takes precedence over obeying rules. Jesus lashes out at the Pharisees who criticize his followers for gathering grain on the Sabbath. Likewise, in modern Judaism, life trumps all. Even the most kosher rabbi would allow his followers to get pigs' valves put in their hearts if necessary (despite a misleading *Grey's Anatomy* plotline to the contrary).

As you might have guessed, I'd make a horrible Jehovah's Witness. Even in my biblical year, if I needed a blood transfusion, I'd be rolling up my sleeve before the doctor finished his sentence. I'm just not faithful/ brave/foolhardy enough to do otherwise. The Bible, in fact, has made me more reverent of life.

Finally, at ten-thirty—three hours after he arrived—Michael says politely that he should let me get to sleep. I'm about to say no, I could keep going, when his Palm Treo rings. It's his wife.

"Yes, we're just finishing up here. I'm about to leave."

Michael stands up to shake my hand.

And then it hits me: I have just done something few human beings have ever achieved. I have out-Bible-talked a Jehovah's Witness.

You shall keep the feast of booths seven days . . .
—Deuteronomy 16:13

Day 47. The Bible gives explicit instructions on how to build Noah's ark—300 by 50 by 30 cubits, with a roof and three decks of gopher wood. Later there's an impressive eight pages on how to construct the Tabernacle, the tent where the Ten Commandments were stored, right on down to its blue and purple curtains.

Luckily, I'm exempt from both these projects. They were one time only.

But the Bible does command me to build something else: a hut. Once a year, we're supposed to build a hut and dwell in it for a week so that we may be reminded of the huts used by the ancient Hebrews when they wandered the desert for forty years. It's a major biblical holiday called the Feast of Ingathering—or *Sukkoth*—and is still practiced by religious Jews. It starts today. (October, incidentally, is a huge month for biblical holidays. I've also observed Yom Kippur and Rosh Hashanah—but let me return to those later.)

Frankly, the idea of building a large three-dimensional structure gives me a stomachache. I'm no handyman. Put it this way: When I watch *Bob the Builder* with Jasper, I always learn something new (oh, so *that's* what a strut is).

I try to console myself that the hut will be a nice change from all the negative commands, the "thou shalt nots." Here, a clear "thou shalt." So I dive in and tackle the first issue: Where to put up my hut? The roof seems logical. I call our building's manager and explain my plan.

"I can't let that happen," he says. "Liability issues."

"What about the courtyard?"

"The courtyard isn't accessible to anyone except one apartment."

"Which apartment?"

"It's not going to work. You can't build a hut in the courtyard."

So I go to my backup plan: building the hut in our living room. This is not ideal for two reasons. The first reason is that it's a hut in our living room.

The second is that my hut—called a *sukkah,* in Hebrew—wouldn't pass muster with even the most laid-back go-with-the-flow rabbi in America. The rabbis say huts must be built outside, and conform to dozens of other rules as well. This time of year, approved sukkahs sprout up all over West Side roofs.

"Wouldn't it be easier just to use the sukkah on the roof of the Jewish community center?" Julie asks.

"Maybe," I say. "But I'd feel like I was cheating."

I explain to Julie that I'm on a solo mission to find the core of the Bible. I am a lone adventurer. I must blaze my own path.

"OK, but it sounds like you're making work for yourself."

She's got a point. My day starts with a trek down to a store called Metropolitan Lumber to pick up a dozen two-by-fours, a handful of cinder blocks, and some canvas. I begin to feel better about the project. There's something satisfying about buying lumber. It makes me feel like a guy who builds porches and rec rooms and uses words like *drywall*.

Next I sling my duffel bag over my shoulder and hike off to Riverside Park. I need some more materials. The Bible instructs us to get "the fruit of goodly trees, branches of palm trees, and boughs of leafy trees, and willows of the brook." (In biblical times, these might have been used to build the huts, though the longstanding Jewish tradition is to wave them in the air.)

As I walk through New York's version of nature, I stuff my bag full of leafy boughs and willows. I buy a palm plant the size of a volleyball and a Middle Eastern lemonlike fruit called an etrog (traditionally thought to be the fruit in question). It feels good. I'm accomplishing stuff. I'm sweating.

At 11:00 a.m., back in my apartment, I begin hammering crossbeams and holding nails in my mouth and sweating a lot more. Three hours later, thanks to the simpleton's blueprint I downloaded off the internet, I actually have the skeleton of a bona fide hut. Which promptly collapses like it's in a Buster Keaton movie and smashes into the wall. I start again, and this time add extra struts, and this time it stays up.

"Oh my God," Julie says when she arrives home.

I ask her if she's annoyed.

"A little. But more stunned that you actually built something. It's enormous."

Julie inspects my hut. It's got four wooden poles topped by a big sheet of white canvas that just grazes our apartment's ceiling. The interior is spare but decorated with boughs of leafy trees and willows of the brook. She squeezes between the hut and the radiator to get another view. She eyes the cinder blocks, making sure that they didn't scratch the floor.

The Bible says to dwell in the hut, so I plan to dwell as much as possible—eat my meals in my hut, read my books there, sleep there. I invite Julie along, but she says she'll let me "fly solo on this one."

So that night, at eleven-thirty, I spread three blankets out on the wood floor. I lie down, put my hands behind my head, stare at the draped canvas, breathe in the citrus and willows (which smell like something they'd rub into you during a massage at Bliss Spa), and try to figure out what I'm feeling.

First, I realize, I'm still on a high from building the hut. I put the thing up myself. Bertrand Russell—the famously agnostic philosopher—said there are two kinds of work in this world: altering the position of matter on earth, and telling other people to alter the position of matter on earth. I like doing the former. I like breaking the stereotype of the physically inept Jew, at least for a day.

My elation is tainted with guilt, though. This sukkah is way too comfortable. This is supposed to remind me of the ancient huts in the desert, but here I am in a climate-controlled apartment—no sand, no wind, and no lack of food. I don't have to worry about the freezing nights or blistering days or plagues, which killed forty thousand of the six hundred thousand Israelites.

But that guilt, in turn, is relieved by this epiphany: This holiday is all about living biblically. God, if He exists, is ordering everyone—not just those with a book contract—to travel back in time and try to experience the world of the ancient Middle East. God created "immersion journalism," as my friend calls it. Maybe God approves of my project after all.

He who is slow to anger has great understanding,
but he who has a hasty temper exalts folly.

—PROVERBS 14:29

Day 50. I've noticed that a lot of biblical living is about constant reminders. That's the purpose of the tassels I've safety pinned to my shirt—the Bible says they are to remind me of the commandments, like a biblical version of the string around the finger.

In the spirit of reminders, I've taped a list to my bathroom mirror.

It's my Most Violated List. We'll see if it helps; it's worth a try. The list includes the following classics:

- Lying. Most recent violation: I told my friend I'd return his book about prayer very soon, when in fact I'd lost it.
- Vanity. I check my temples every day for signs of hair loss.
- Gossip. Julie and I talked about how her brother Doug still wears these loud, multicolored sweaters right out of *The Cosby Show*.
- Coveting. I did a signing at a book fair a few days ago, and at the next table was Anthony Bourdain, the rakish celebrity chef/author. My table got such visitors as: my mother, my father, my wife, my son. Meanwhile the line in front of Bourdain's table resembled opening night of *The Phantom Menace*, though without as many Darth Maul costumes.
- Touching impure things. Handy Seat aside, it's just too hard to avoid.
- Anger. I gave the finger to an ATM.

You see, the ATM charged me a $1.75 fee for withdrawal. A dollar seventy-five? That's bananas. So I flipped off the screen. As Julie tells me, when you start making rude gestures to inanimate objects, it's time to work on your anger issues.

Mine is not the shouting, pulsing-vein-in-the-forehead rage. Like my dad, I rarely raise my voice (again, I like to be emotionally in control at all times). My anger problem is more one of long-lasting resentment. It's a heap of real or perceived slights that eventually build up into a mountain of bitterness.

Did I really need to get so angry at the juggler at the street fair who stopped juggling to take a cell phone call? And then talked for, like, fifteen minutes while Jasper looked on all eager and hopeful? Yes, it's annoying, but worse things have happened.

Or what about the guy in Starbucks who monopolized the bathroom for forty-five minutes? (In my defense, he was also wearing a black beret; this was 2006 Manhattan, not 1948 La Rive Gauche.) I was fuming.

And what about the incident at the soup kitchen?

I've been volunteering at Holy Apostles Soup Kitchen in Chelsea. It's an incredible place, the largest soup kitchen in New York, the second-biggest in the country; they serve more than 1,100 meals a day. The man who runs it is a charismatic tough-love leader who I could see commanding a rebellion against the Roman centurions.

And usually, I get a little ethical head rush from working at the soup kitchen. This, I tell myself, is biblical living at its best. I'm following the inspiring words in Deuteronomy 15:7: "If there is among you a poor man, one of your brethren . . . you shall not harden your heart or shut your hand against your poor brother."

And yet . . . even at the soup kitchen, I'm able to find slights.

On my most recent visit, I get assigned to kitchen duty—then immediately demoted. They tell me it's because of my beard. I understand. No one wants an unpleasant surprise in his rice pilaf. I am fine with it, until I spot some other volunteer working in the kitchen—despite having his face covered with a big bushy beard of his own.

Why the discrepancy?

"Oh, I'm shaving my beard tomorrow," explains my rival volunteer.

Which makes exactly no sense. Does gravity somehow stop working the day before you shave?

I get reassigned to garbage duty. My job is to take the plastic trays from those who have finished lunch, remove the cutlery, bang the trays forcefully against the side of the garbage can—clearing off all the mashed potatoes and string beans—and then hand them to the stacker. I think I am doing a pretty decent job, which is confirmed by the garbage team captain, a guy in a Jets T-shirt who tells me, "Good job." I am feeling pumped.

Then, after an hour and a half, I'm the victim of a soup kitchen power play. This older guy named Max—he has a droopy face and a permanent scowl—comes up to me, hands me an iced tea in a particularly aggressive manner, and says: "Drink this. Then go away."

I don't want iced tea, and I don't want to go away. I just stare at him.

"Drink this. Then go away," he repeats, glowering.

As far as I can tell, he is no higher on the volunteer food chain than I am; for reasons unknown, he just wants my garbage duty spot.

The Bible says to respect your elders and do not quarrel. So I leave. But I stew about it for a good two days. Drink this. Then go away. What a bastard.

I've been battling my anger since this project started. I want to let go of my resentment. I know it's healthier, a better way to live. But how to do this when faced with a real-life soup kitchen Nazi? The best biblical inspiration I've found is in the book of Jonah. A quick recap for those (like me three months ago) who know only the whale part:

God calls on Jonah to preach to the evil city of Nineveh (now in Iraq). Jonah refuses. He tries to flee God by boarding a ship. This doesn't work: God creates a mighty tempest, and the frightened sailors throw Jonah overboard. God then sends a whale that swallows Jonah (actually, the Bible says "big fish," not whale) and spits him safely out onto land.

Chastened, Jonah agrees to go to Nineveh. Jonah preaches there, and it works. More than 120,000 men, women, and children repent. God forgives them.

You'd think Jonah would be happy with God's forgiveness, but he's actually angry. He wanted the evil ones smote. He wanted fire and brimstone. He gets so furious at God, he no longer wants to live. God says, "Do you do well to be angry?"

Jonah doesn't answer but goes off to the outskirts of Nineveh to sulk. So God decides to teach Jonah a lesson: God grows a plant that shields the prophet from the harsh desert sun. Jonah is exceedingly glad. But the very next day, God causes a worm to kill the plant. Once again, Jonah is exposed to the harsh sun and gets very angry. Again, God asks Jonah: "Do you do well to be angry?"

God then drives home his point: Jonah lost his temper over a plant for which he "did not labor" and which lasted but a day. God says, "And should I not be concerned about Nineveh, that great city, in which there are more than a hundred and twenty thousand persons who do not know their right hand from their left, and also many animals." In other words, get some perspective.

So that's what I try to do. I ask myself the question God asked Jonah. "Do you do well to be angry?" I ask it out loud to myself. No, I don't, I answer. So I got elbowed aside by a strangely competitive soup kitchen volunteer. The world will not end.

I should remember the modern-day Ninevehs where thousands of lives are in danger—the crowd of homeless out the door at Holy Apostles, for instance, or pretty much anywhere in East Africa.

There is such a thing as biblically acceptable anger—righteous indignation. Moses gets angry at the Israelites for worshipping a false idol. Jesus gets angry at the money changers for profaning the Temple. The key is to pump up your righteous anger and mute your petty resentment. I'll be happy if I can get that balance to fifty-fifty.

David danced before the Lord with all his might . . .
—2 SAMUEL 6:14

Day 55. It's the night of October 25, and I'm at the loudest, rowdiest, most drunken party of my life. Me and several hundred Hasidic men.

I came for the dancing. There's a part in the Bible where King David celebrates the arrival of the Ark of the Covenant to Jerusalem. This was an older David, years after he slew Goliath with a rock and sling. He has defeated his increasingly paranoid mentor Saul to become king of Israel. And he brings home the ark, a sacred box containing the Ten Commandments. He celebrates by dancing. And, man, does he dance. He dances with such abandon, with such joy, that he doesn't notice that his robe is flying up, exposing his nakedness to the young handmaidens in the kingdom.

His uptight wife, Michal, is appalled. She makes the mistake of scolding King David, and, as a result, is cursed with childlessness.

The unhappy ending seems unduly harsh. But I do love the image of the king doing a wild holy jig. The joy of religion; that's what David was feeling, and that's something I underestimated—or pretty much ignored—in my secular life. I want to feel what David felt, so I took a subway to Crown Heights, Brooklyn, on a Tuesday evening.

The occasion is a Jewish holiday called Simchas Torah, the last night before the sukkah is taken down. It's not in the Bible proper, but it does celebrate something biblical: the end to the annual reading of the five books of Moses. And it sounded too interesting to miss.

My guide, Gershon, is a friend of a friend. He's a kind, bespectacled, newlywed Hasid whose outgoing voice-mail message says: "Your next action could change the world, so make it a good one."

As we walk, I get to see a side of ultra-Orthodox Jews that I'd never seen before. They always look so somber on the subway, so purposeful. But here they are, well, wasted. They're weaving down the sidewalks, some holding bottles of Crown Royal whiskey, some singing loudly in Hebrew.

On this holiday, it's not just OK to drink, it's pretty much mandatory. Gershon and I go to his parents' house and pound a few shots of vodka in their front-yard sukkah. It's raining, and the raindrops fall through the gaps in the sukkah roof and splash into our glasses.

When Gershon says the prayers in Hebrew before drinking, I sneak a peek at him. His eyes are half-closed, his eyelids fluttering, his eyeballs rolled toward the back of his head. Will I ever come close to that spiritual state? Will I get my longed-for epiphany? I'm worried that I won't.

After our vodka shots, we head over to the party's headquarters—the huge building known as 770 Eastern Parkway, the nerve center of this branch of Hasidism. (The sect is called Lubavitchers, and its members are the least insular of the Hasidic Jews, committed to bringing unaffiliated Jews into the fold.)

I'm wearing black pants and a black sweater to better blend in with the Hasidim. I forgot to bring the crucial yarmulke, but Gershon lends me one of his.

"We dance for our animal nature," says Gershon, as we step across the puddles. "The Torah is for both sides of the nature. The reading is for the divine side, and the dancing is for the animal side."

As we approach within a few yards of 770—as it's called—Gershon asks me:

"You ever been bungee jumping?"

"No."

"Well, I have. The instructors say to just jump, don't think about it. That's what you have to do here."

I see what he means. Just getting inside is going to be an extreme sport. The doors are glutted with dozens of revelers in their black coats—all men, no women (the Hasidim aren't much for gender mixing). We have to elbow our way through.

A fat, red-bearded guy comes up to Gershon and hugs him. Red Beard goes off on a drunken I-love-you-man, you-are-the-greatest-guy-I-know rant that lasts a good two minutes.

Gershon finally extracts himself.

"Who was that?" I ask.

"Never met him before in my life."

We squeeze our way inside. And there, an ocean of undulating black hats. Hundreds, maybe thousands of them in a hall the size of a large gymnasium. It's as loud as any concert I've ever been to. But instead of drums and guitar, it's a village of men singing *Ay yi yi yi*.

The floor is exactly like a Seattle mosh pit circa 1992. Everyone's bumping, smacking, thumping into one another. One guy barrels into me so hard that he sends me stumbling. "Hey you with the beard!" he says. Everyone looks up. He unleashes a deep laugh.

We are making a slow, huge circle, sort of a Holy Roller derby. If you look up, you can see the occasional Hasid bouncing up in the air like a pogo stick. When there is a patch of free space on the floor—which isn't often—a reveler will do a somersault. Two men are swapping their black hats repeatedly as if they were reenacting a Laurel and Hardy scene.

I tell you, I've never seen such pure joy. It is thick, atmospheric, like someone had released a huge canister of nitrous oxide into the room. Here we are, hundreds of dancing King Davids. Even for a control freak like me, there's no choice but to go along with it. You are overwhelmed. You follow the sweaty, bouncing, shouting, *ay-yi-yi*-ing hordes, or you are trampled.

I swing from emotion to emotion: terror that I'll be crushed, fascination that humans act this way, paranoia that they'll deal with the interloper in a manner I'd never forget (think *Deliverance* meets *Yentl*). But occasionally I swing to delirious happiness. I don't know if I feel God. And it isn't as intense as the epiphanies I had as a kid. But a couple of times that night, I feel something transcendent, something that melts away the future and the past and the deadlines and the MasterCard bills and puts me squarely in the moment. At least for a few seconds, there is no difference between me and Jacob, my biblical alter ego.

After three hours of dancing—at one in the morning—I tell Gershon that I'm going to go, even though the hardcore dancers stay on till six. He walks me out. "Remember," he says to me as we shake hands good-bye on the street corner, "sometimes you have to look beyond the weirdness. It's like the temple in ancient Jerusalem. If you went there, you'd see oxen being slaughtered and all sorts of things. But look beyond the weirdness, to what it means."

As I ride the subway home, with the *Ay-yi-yi*-ing still echoing in my ears, I try to think of the meaning beyond the weirdness. Here's what I decide: Underneath my repression, maybe I have a closeted mystical side. Maybe I'm a rational Presbyterian on the outside, but an emotional Baptist on the inside. Given the right circumstances, maybe everyone is, even Henry Kissinger.

The next morning, I tell Julie about my wild night of dancing with Hasidic men and how I got a taste of pure joy.

"And where were the women during this thing?"

"Well, they were watching. They have these observation windows."

"Observation windows?" Julie looks pissed.

It's strange. Naturally, I noticed the gender segregation—but there were so many odd and overwhelming things about the night that I didn't laser in on that one. It's the obliviousness that comes with being in the majority.

"Yeah," I say. "Well, I was trying not to be judgmental."

"Well, seems like they're being judgmental of women."

I can sense Julie becoming more and more skeptical of religion, or at least hardcore religion.

Before my project, Julie was the mildly proreligion one in the family. She believed in a God of some sort, or at least a universe that wasn't morally apathetic. "Things happen for a reason," she was always telling me when I'd moan about some career setback. She loves the rituals of Hanukkah and Passover. She's already started coming up with themes for Jasper's bar mitzvah (soccer! The Academy Awards!).

But now, I feel her drawing away—even as I start to warm to some aspects of religious life. It's the difference between living the Bible and living with someone who is living the Bible.

> . . . He had done so, walking naked and barefoot.
>
> —Isaiah 20:2

Day 61. I'm typing this right after midnight. The Psalms urge us to rise at midnight and praise God, so I've been doing that for a week. I promised Julie I'd do it only for a week, since I've had to set an alarm for 11:58 p.m., two hours into her sleep cycle.

It's the end of my experiment's second month, and here's what I'm feeling: exhilarated, confused, overwhelmed, underqualified, fascinated, and scared. Also, embarrassed.

My biblical alter ego Jacob is starting to look freakish. I've got tassels hanging from my garments. I take this purity-insuring Handy Seat everywhere. My beard has gone beyond shaggy. It now hangs a good two inches below my chin, and it's starting to make curlicues and shoot off in unexpected directions. (Julie wanted to go to Halloween with me as Tom Hanks from *Cast Away* and her as the volleyball, but I can't do Halloween because it's a pagan holiday.)

Yes, of course, part of me likes the attention. I write memoirs for a living, for Pete's sake. And, yes, I know I brought this on myself—no one's forcing me to follow the Bible at knifepoint. But the constant stares and quizzical looks—it'd be enough to make anyone, even me, self-conscious. A bit paranoid, even.

Luckily, I've found inspiration in the Bible. As the Brooklyn rabbi Andy Bachman suggested, I've been rereading the Prophets. He's right. They are amazing.

I love their message of social justice—especially Amos, Micah, and Isaiah. Again and again, they berate the hard-hearted rich who lie on beds of ivory and sip wine contentedly and "trample the heads of the poor into the dust of the earth." Their days are numbered.

But I also love the way they delivered that message. You see, the prophets didn't just utter their prophecies. They staged what are known as "prophetic acts"—wild, attention-grabbing, God-inspired pieces of performance art. The prophets were the inventors of street theater, as scholar Marcus Borg points out in his book *Reading the Bible Again for the First Time*. They were ancient David Blaines, but with orders from God, not a network executive.

Consider Hosea, who married a prostitute and named his children "Not pitied" and "Not my people." The names were a warning: Israel must repent for its idolatrous ways, or God will continue to have no pity and cut them off.

Even more radical was Isaiah, who walked naked and barefoot for three years among the people of Jerusalem. (This was symbolic of what would happen if Judah allied itself with Egypt and Ethiopia; they would be conquered, and everyone would end up naked captives.) Another prophet, Jeremiah, did wear clothes but walked the streets with a wooden yoke around his neck to signify the yoke of Babylonian rule.

But eclipsing them all was Ezekiel. He was the master. I knew from reading the encyclopedia that Ezekiel had eaten a scroll to symbolize his appropriation of its message. And yet that was tame compared to his other performances. One time, for instance, God told Ezekiel to carve a model of Jerusalem into a brick, then lie down beside the model on his left side. He continued lying there. For 390 days. Then Ezekiel turned to his right side to lie another forty days. These days were to symbolize the years that Israel and Judah would be in exile after the Babylonian conquering.

During his 430-day feat, Ezekiel was to eat a meager diet of bread— cooked over human dung. Ezekiel pleaded with God, and God agreed to let him use cow dung as fuel instead.

As I enter my third month, Ezekiel and his fellow prophets have become my heroes. They were fearless. They literalized metaphors. They turned their lives into protest pieces. They proved that, in the name of truth, sometimes you can't be afraid to take a left turn from polite society and look absurd.

Maybe my alter ego Jacob is in the prophetic tradition of Ezekiel. I hope so. On the other hand, he could be way off. I imagine that for every Ezekiel, there were a couple hundred false prophets walking around Jerusalem with, say, loincloths on their heads and eating clumps of dirt.

I blow my shofar. It still sounds like a fax machine, but a healthy one.

Month Three: November

They shall be stoned with stones, their blood shall be upon them.
—LEVITICUS 20:27

Day 62. It's been more than a month since my mixed-fiber adventure. Time for me to tackle the second item on my list of Most Perplexing Laws: capital punishment.

The Hebrew scriptures prescribe a tremendous amount of capital punishment. Think Saudi Arabia, multiply by Texas, then triple that. It wasn't just for murder. You could also be executed for adultery, blasphemy, breaking the Sabbath, perjury, incest, bestiality, and witchcraft, among others. A rebellious son could be sentenced to death. As could a son who is a persistent drunkard and glutton.

The most commonly mentioned punishment method in the Hebrew Bible is stoning. So I figure, at the very least, I should try to stone. But how?

I can't tell you the number of people who have suggested that I get adulterers and blasphemers stoned in the cannabis sense. Which is an interesting idea. But I haven't smoked pot since I was at Brown University, when I wrote a paper for my anthropology class on the hidden symbolism of bong hits. (Brown was the type of college where this paper actually earned a B+.)

Instead I figured my loophole would be this: The Bible doesn't specify the size of the stones. So . . . pebbles.

A few days ago, I gathered a handful of small white pebbles from Central Park, which I stuffed in my back pants pocket. Now all I needed were some victims. I decided to start with Sabbath breakers. That's easy enough to find in this workaholic city. I noticed that a potbellied guy at the Avis down our block had worked on both Saturday and Sunday. So no matter what, he's a Sabbath breaker.

Here's the thing, though: Even with pebbles, it is surprisingly hard to stone people.

My plan had been to walk nonchalantly past the Sabbath violator and chuck the pebbles at the small of his back. But after a couple of failed passes, I realized it was a bad idea. A chucked pebble, no matter how small, does not go unnoticed.

My revised plan: I would pretend to be clumsy and drop the pebble on his shoe. So I did.

And in this way I stoned. But it was probably the most polite stoning in history—I said, "I'm sorry," and then leaned down to pick up the pebble. And he leaned down at the same time, and we almost butted heads, and then he apologized, then I apologized again.

Highly unsatisfying.

Today I get another chance. I am resting in a small public park on the Upper West Side, the kind where you see retirees eating tuna sandwiches on benches.

"Hey, you're dressed queer."

I look over. The speaker is an elderly man, mid-seventies, I'd guess. He is tall and thin and is wearing one of those caps that cabbies wore in movies from the forties.

"You're dressed queer," he snarls. "Why you dressed so queer?"

I have on my usual tassels, and, for good measure, have worn some sandals and am carrying a knotty maple walking stick I'd bought on the internet for twenty-five dollars.

"I'm trying to live by the rules of the Bible. The Ten Commandments, stoning adulterers . . ."

"You're stoning adulterers?"

"Yeah, I'm stoning adulterers."

"I'm an adulterer."

"You're currently an adulterer?"

"Yeah. Tonight, tomorrow, yesterday, two weeks from now. You gonna stone me?"

"If I could, yes, that'd be great."

"I'll punch you in the face. I'll send you to the cemetery."

He is serious. This isn't a cutesy grumpy old man. This is an angry old man. This is a man with seven decades of hostility behind him.

I fish out my pebbles from my back pocket.

"I wouldn't stone you with big stones," I say. "Just these little guys."

I open my palm to show him the pebbles. He lunges at me, grabbing one out of my hand, then flinging it at my face. It whizzes by my cheek.

I am stunned for a second. I hadn't expected this grizzled old man to make the first move. But now there is nothing stopping me from retaliating. An eye for an eye.

I take one of the remaining pebbles and whip it at his chest. It bounces off.

"I'll punch you right in the kisser," he says.

"Well, you really shouldn't commit adultery," I say.

We stare at each other. My pulse has doubled.

Yes, he is a septuagenarian. Yes, he had just threatened me using corny *Honeymooners* dialogue. But you could tell: This man has a strong dark side.

Our glaring contest lasts ten seconds, then he walks away, brushing by me as he leaves.

When I was a kid, I saw an episode of *All in the Family* in which Meathead—Rob Reiner's wussy peacenik character—socked some guy in the jaw. Meathead was very upset about this. But he wasn't upset that he committed violence; he was upset because it felt so *good* to commit violence.

I can relate. Even though mine was a stoning lite, barely fulfilling the letter of the law, I can't deny: It felt good to chuck a rock at this nasty old man. It felt primal. It felt like I was getting vengeance on him. This guy wasn't just an adulterer, he was a bully. I wanted him to feel the pain he'd inflicted on others, even if that pain was a tap on the chest.

Like Meathead, I also knew that this was a morally stunted way to feel. Stoning is about as indefensible as you can get. It comes back to the old question: How can the Bible be so wise in some places and so barbaric in others? And why should we put any faith in a book that includes such brutality? Later that week, I ask my spiritual adviser Yossi about stoning. Yossi was born in Minnesota and calls himself a "Jewtheran"— Jewish guilt and Lutheran repression mesh nicely, he told me. He's an ordained Orthodox rabbi but never practiced, instead opting for the *shmata* trade—he sold scarves to, among others, the Amish. He's tall and broad shouldered with a neatly trimmed beard. In his spare time, Yossi writes wry essays about Jewish life, including a lament about how his favorite snack, Twinkies, recently became nonkosher. I met him through Aish HaTorah, an Orthodox outreach group.

He isn't fazed by my question at all.

We don't stone people today because you need a biblical theocracy to enforce the stoning, he explains. No such society exists today. But even in ancient times, stoning wasn't barbaric.

"First of all, you didn't just heave stones," says Yossi. "The idea was to minimize the suffering. What we call 'stoning' was actually pushing the person off the cliff so they would die immediately upon impact. The Talmud actually has specifications on how high the cliff must be. Also, the person getting executed was given strong drink to dull the pain."

Plus, the stonings were a rare thing. Some rabbis say executions occurred only once every seven years, others say even less often. There had to be two witnesses to the crime. And the adulterer had to be tried by a council of seventy elders. And, weirdly, the verdict of those seventy elders could not be unanimous—that might be a sign of corruption or brainwashing. And so on.

I half-expected Yossi to say they gave the adulterer a massage and a gift bag. He made a compelling case. And yet, I'm not totally sold. Were biblical times really so merciful? I suspect there might be some white-washing going on. As my year progresses, I'll need to delve deeper.

And you shall eat and be full, and you shall bless the Lord your God for the good land He has given you.

—DEUTERONOMY 8:10

Day 64. A spiritual update: I'm still agnostic, but I do have some progress to report on the prayer front. I no longer dread prayer. And sometimes I'm even liking it. I've gone so far as to take the training wheels off and am testing out some of my own prayers instead of just repeating passages from the Bible.

Elton Richards—the pastor out to pasture—broke down prayer for me into four types. It's a handy mnemonic: ACTS. *A* for adoration (praising God). *C* for confession (telling God your sins). *T* for thanksgiving (being grateful to God for what you have). *S* for supplication (asking God to help you).

Right now, the one that's working for me best is *T,* thanksgiving. Adoration feels awkward to me. Confession feels forced. As for supplication, I'm doing it, but I feel greedy asking God to help my career. Should I really be cluttering His in-box by asking for better placement of *The Know-It-All* at airport bookstores?

But thanksgiving, that I'm getting into. In Deuteronomy, the Bible says that we should thank the Lord when we've eaten our fill—grace after meals, it's called. Christians moved grace to the beginning of the meal, preappetizer. To be safe, I'm praying both before and after.

Today, before tasting my lunch of hummus and pita bread, I stand up from my seat at the kitchen table, close my eyes, and say in a hushed tone:

"I'd like to thank God for the land that he provided so that this food might be grown."

Technically, that's enough. That fulfills the Bible's commandment. But while in thanksgiving mode, I decide to spread the gratitude around:

"I'd like to thank the farmer who grew the chickpeas for this hummus. And the workers who picked the chickpeas. And the truckers who drove them to the store. And the old Italian lady who sold the hummus to me at Zingone's deli and told me 'Lots of love.' Thank you."

Now that I type it, it sounds like an overly earnest Oscar speech for best supporting Middle Eastern spread. But saying it feels good.

Here's the thing: I'm still having trouble conceptualizing an infinite being, so I'm working on the questionable theory that a large quantity is at least closer to infinity. Hence the overabundance of thank-yous. Sometimes I'll get on a roll, thanking people for a couple of minutes straight— the people who designed the packaging, and the guys who loaded the cartons onto the conveyor belt. Julie has usually started in on her food by this point.

The prayers are helpful. They remind me that the food didn't spontaneously generate in my fridge. They make me feel more connected,

more grateful, more grounded, more aware of my place in this complicated hummus cycle. They remind me to *taste* the hummus instead of
shoveling it into my maw like it's a nutrition pill. And they remind me
that I'm lucky to have food at all. Basically, they help me get outside of
my self-obsessed cranium.

I'm not sure this is what the Bible intended, but it feels like a step
forward.

> *The fool says in his heart, "There is no God."*
>
> —Psalms 14:1

Day 67. The ancient Israelites were surrounded by unbelievers. This is
clear from the amount of space the Bible devotes to condemning idolatry,
paganism, and false gods. An impressive 46 of the 613 Jewish laws deal
with the topic (give or take a few, depending on how you classify them).
It is, I think, one of the main similarities between ancient Israel and
twenty-first-century New York—we live amidst a sea of unbelievers.

I feel tempted all the time—not so much by a cult to Baal, but by the
lure of secular humanism. To face my demons, I decide to go deep into
the heart of unbelief: the weekly New York City Atheists meeting at a
midtown Greek restaurant.

I know a fair amount of atheists, seeing as I live in a relatively godless town. But there's no way that you could drag any of my atheist ac-
quaintances to a meeting of New York City Atheists. Some of my
friends are atheists precisely because they want to avoid joining a group
that meets on a weekend and talks about plans for a cable-access TV
show.

An atheist club felt oxymoronic, like an apathy parade. But against
all odds, it exists. The gathering of the godless takes place in a back
room with a long table. A big blue atheism banner hangs from the ceiling—right next to the Christmas decorations of cardboard silver angels,
an irony several of the atheists point out.

I meet my neighbors. One is a compact woman with graying hair
and a Darwin cap. How was she converted to atheism? "I grew up with
a Methodist aunt who was basically a Victorian," she tells me. "I couldn't

say the word *leg*. I had to say *limb*. I once said the word *constipation* and got smacked. The hypocrisy was too much for me."

Then there is the big guy who looks like he's either a stevedore or hockey coach. "I'm a second-generation atheist," he says. "My dad spat when he walked by churches or synagogues."

There is a short-haired woman who seems quite eager to steer the conversation to her self-published book, which is about an atheist arena cleaner in ancient Rome. "The main character's job was to clean up the carnage after the gladiators."

They ask me, eyeing my unkempt beard, why I'm visiting the atheists club, and I tell them about my project. They seem relieved, at least, that I'm not an Orthodox Jew or militant Muslim. But further discussion will have to wait.

"Shhhh-shhh."

The shusher is Ken, the leader of New York City Atheists. Ken looks a bit like Jackie Mason, but a strapping, broad-shouldered Jackie Mason. He's at the front of the room, wearing a blue-and-white atheist baseball cap. My neighbor, the one with the Darwin hat, tells me that Ken worked at IBM for thirty-seven years, and instead of golf, atheism is his retirement hobby.

Ken starts with the week's announcements. They are looking for guests for the weekly atheist cable access TV show.

Also, the weekly movie night will be at five-thirty on Thursday, and they will be watching the Nazi war-crime film *Judgment at Nuremberg*.

"Judgment at Nuremberg?" says a bald guy in the back. He doesn't seem happy.

"Yes," says Ken.

"What does that have to do with atheism?"

"You'll see," says Ken.

"It doesn't seem like it has a lot to do with atheism."

"It has a lot to do with atheism. And a lot to do with skepticism."

The bald guy was, as you might have guessed, skeptical.

Then Ken goes into his sermon proper—the importance of confronting "believers."

"We have to stop being polite. We may not make as many friends. But we have to say, 'The Bible is literature, not history.'"

"Moussaka! Who has the moussaka!"

Ken pauses while the waiter delivers the moussaka. There's only one server, causing some "feed the multitudes" jokes.

"You know the saying there are no atheists in a foxhole?" says Ken. "You know what? I think they should stop praying and dig a deeper foxhole."

"Greek salad? Who ordered the Greek salad?"

Ken is a good speaker, even charismatic, as close as you can get to a godless preacher. He has a booming voice, he slaps the palm of his hand to punctuate a point, he all but says amen. Problem is, no one believes Ken's authority derives from God—which means it's much harder to command attention. There's lots of murmuring and cross talk during his sermon.

I leave the meeting early—child-care duties—but return a week later to chat with Ken. He says his road to atheism began when, as a kid, he figured out there could be no Santa Claus.

"It just was not feasible to deliver all those presents," he says. "This was before FedEx."

So Ken was tipped off to the Santa Claus falsehood because of faulty logistics. Very IBM of him, I think.

"I started to ask myself, what else are they telling me that's not true?" says Ken.

I ask him if it's hard to lead a group of atheists. Like herding cats, he says. Atheists aren't, by nature, joiners. "They're individualists," he says. Which perhaps explains why we had thirty separate checks for lunch.

Ken has, in fact, boosted the group's membership and started some programs. But go to an atheist meeting, and you'll see why the religious lobby doesn't have to worry about the atheist lobby quite yet. You'll see why there are no soaring atheist cathedrals and why hotel room nightstands don't come with a copy of *Why I Am Not a Christian* by Bertrand Russell in the top drawer. It's hard to be passionate about a lack of belief.

Recently, atheists have made a good effort, with authors like Sam Harris, Richard Dawkins, and Christopher Hitchens acting as the movement's antipopes. But if organized religion is Goliath, then organized atheism still qualifies as David.

Keep your tongue from evil . . .

—PSALMS 34:13

Day 70. A lot of my friends expect me to speak like a walking King James Bible. They want me—or at least my alter ego Jacob—to spout words like *thou* and *woe unto* and *whosoever shall*. I get a lot of emails that start "Give ear, O Jacobs." And phone calls that begin, "Verily, I ask thee, would you like to meet us for pizza?"

I try to play along as best I can ("Yea, I shall rejoice in a feast of pizza"). But it's not high on my list of priorities. Such language is more a reflection of seventeenth-century England than of ancient Israel.

No, speaking biblically requires a far more radical change than raising my diction a few notches. It requires a total switch in the content of my conversation: no lying, no complaining, no gossiping.

They're all hard, but let me just focus on the gossip for a bit, because that's turning out to be a killer. The Bible has at least twenty passages condemning gossip. In English editions, translators use words such as *slander* or *talebearing* or *unwholesome talk* or *evil tongue*.

This means I can't join in when my coworkers discuss a certain boozy actress who scribbled obscenities on a bathroom mirror, or the rumor that a news anchor is about to ditch his wife for a younger woman. That's a feat in itself, but I expected living biblically would require that.

The problem is, if you *really* want to be biblically safe, you should go much further. You should avoid almost all negative speech whatsoever. Here's how one of my Bible commentaries defines evil tongue: "This refers to any derogatory or damaging statement against an individual—even when the slanderous or defaming remarks are true—which if publicized to others would cause the subject physical or monetary damage, anguish, or fear."

In other words, about 70 percent of all conversations in New York.

In Hebrew, evil tongue is called *Lashon hara*, and the rabbis compare it to murder. As the Talmud says, "The gossiper stands in Syria and kills in Rome." Many Christians have a similar concept about negative speech. As Paul says in Ephesians 4:29: "Do not let any unwholesome talk come out of your mouths, but only what is helpful for building others up according to their needs, that it may benefit those who listen."

Parts of the Bible do allow some types of bad-mouthing—a gentle rebuke is OK, as is warning your friend that he's about to open a coffee shop with an embezzler. But for the most part, all sniping, snarkiness, disparaging, mocking, scoffing, and scorning is off-limits. Which is beyond difficult. I fail on a daily basis. An hourly basis.

Consider the scenario I faced last weekend. Julie and I went to a wedding on Long Island; the bride and groom, thoughtfully enough, had hired a van to schlep the guests back to New York. However, there would be no napping on this ride. Instead we would be forced to eavesdrop on a very loud, very drunk goateed guy.

For an hour, without pausing, he pontificates to this pretty blonde he's trying to pick up. She hears the following (as does everyone else):

"My one-man show *Why Try* is a dissertation on suicide," he announces. "It's very funny. I have a very funny mind. Death is funny. I haven't been to a funeral that I haven't laughed at."

She nods politely.

"My teacher said to me, 'You are a great actor.' And I said, 'I don't know what that means.' And I don't. All I know is the process."

Oh, man, I wanted so much to lean over to Julie and mock this bloviating putz with his greased-back hair and his pompous Buddy Holly glasses.

He continues:

"*Whhhhhy* do I admire George Clooney? I'll tell you. He wants to do something for society at large—and beyond."

I want to point out to Julie that he overpronounces his *t*'s and *wh*'s.

A couple of minutes later, apropos of nothing, he says:

"I've always wanted to write a comic strip called *Grizelda of Drunkopolis*."

When it becomes clear—even to him—that this woman is not going to climb into bed with him, he tries to engage the other passengers. Including me. A mutual acquaintance had mentioned that I write for a trivia magazine called *Mental Floss*. This is his way in. He shouts:

"Mental Floss Man over there! Mental Floss!! Tell us some trivia!"

His tone makes it clear that my job is not on the artistic level of his one-man show about suicide. I demur. After we get off the van, I hold back for three minutes. Julie and I just walk silently to our apartment. But there's something to the hydraulic metaphor in human behavior: the steam keeps building up and up in my brain. I have to let it out.

"Can you believe that idiot?" I say finally, as we wait at an intersection. "'Society at large—and beyond?' What is *beyond* society at large? Society at large *is* beyond."

Julie just nods her head. She knows.

Maybe taming my tongue will be good for me in the end. But it's pretty hard when you've got a world filled with idiots from Drunkopolis. It's like asking me not to breathe or blink. All I can say is, I'll keep trying.

> *And they fell on their faces . . .*
>
> —NUMBERS 16:45

Day 72. I've bought a lot of books this year, but this new Amazon delivery is a big one: the autobiography of my ex-uncle Gil. When I open the box, the first thing that strikes me is this: Gil is not opposed to graven images. The cover features no fewer than eleven photos of Gil. Gil in front of his hippie bus; Gil with his eyes shut, smelling flowers; Gil perched regally on a red armchair.

The book is called *Coming Back to Earth: The Central Park Guru Becomes an Old City Jew* and was published in 2004 by a small Jewish press. It was banned by some rabbis in Israel because, among other things, it contains four-letter words. I start to read, and it doesn't disappoint. His life is crazier than I anticipated, even if you make allowances for the occasional James Frey–like fabrication.

Gil grew up in a secular Jewish family in upstate New York. He became a financial consultant in Phoenix—and a successful one, by his account. But he felt something missing. So he dropped out and reinvented himself as a hippie.

Some of his adventures are typically hippie; the things you might see in an early Dennis Hopper film: He dropped acid and passed out for three days. He ate nothing but watermelon for two weeks straight in an attempt to cleanse himself. He got high in an opium den in Pakistan. He was arrested for skinny-dipping in Virginia. His wardrobe consisted of a tablecloth.

But other escapades are outlandish even by hippie standards. Gil trekked to an ashram in northern India where he lived in a squalid yard with five thousand other devotees. The ashram's guru—a man with a huge Afro and a crimson-colored robe—would emerge from his house every day but never deign to speak to Gil. Gil waited for weeks.

Finally, one day, the guru's pet elephant, Gita, went on a stampede in the ashram yard. Panic everywhere. Gil stood up, "threw my hand in the air toward the raging elephant and screamed, *'Stop!'* " The elephant stopped. From then on, Gil had a place in the guru's inner circle. This allowed him to meet John Lennon and Yoko Ono, who were disenchanted with their own guru—the Maharishi Mahesh Yogi—because, writes Gil, "he couldn't keep his hands off Mia Farrow's butt."

Gil came back to New York and opted to go into the guru business himself. He decided that God wanted him to start his sect on a bench on the corner of 86th Street and Central Park West. He sat there, gazing at the tip of his nose for eight months, amassing—by his account—dozens of followers who sat at his feet, soaking up his vibes: seekers, stockbrokers, poets, and movie stars (Sally Kirkland!).

Did I mention that he wasn't speaking at the time? Gil had given up vocal communication, remaining silent for three years. He dispensed wisdom (for example, "smoke the best bag first") to his followers through a sign language of his own invention.

Eventually Gil moved his "family" to Ithaca, New York. He lived in a yurt by a pond, meditating for—he says—twenty-three hours a day. All of his needs were attended to by his worshipful followers, who, by the way, had been given brilliantly sixtiesish names like Rainbow, Bliss, and Banana Tree. And I do mean worshipful. They literally fell on their faces in front of him.

Gil's Hindu phase came to an abrupt end when he read a pamphlet someone left in his bathhouse. It was about Christianity. Gil became a born-again Christian leader who, among other things, battled demons and healed a homeless man.

That phase, in turn, came to an equally abrupt end when Gil started to read the Hebrew Bible more closely. It was during this time that Gil followed the Bible literally: When he made tassels of yarn and attached them to every corner he could find on his clothes, and when he tied a wad of cash around his hand.

He eventually switched to more traditional Jewish practices. And nowadays, he spends his days in Jerusalem binding *tefillin* on tourists at the Western Wall and holding Shabbat dinner for young seekers. But I get the feeling that Gil is a very unorthodox Orthodox Jew. One of his theological precepts is that everything is God, sort of a Semitic pantheism. Other Hasidim say that God is everywhere—but Gil takes it to the extreme.

He writes that he was once sent to a psychiatrist who diagnosed him as a megalomaniac. Gil writes: "I had to look it up in a dictionary. It said, 'someone who believes they are God.' I had to agree with that. I not only thought I was God, I thought (and still think) *all* is God."

Gil's life inspired another obscure book that I figured I should read as well. Called *Yea God*, this 1980 biography painted a much darker picture of Guru Gil. If Gil's was the Disney version, this was the Grimm's.

Here we meet a Gil who was sexist (men in his cult got cushy yurts, women had to suffice with tepees) and controlling (he went so far as to instruct his followers how to go to the bathroom properly). Worse, according to this book, Gil sometimes smacked around members of the family. And here's the crazy part: They allegedly liked it. "Thank you for loving this one enough to beat him," it quotes one follower saying, in the odd third-person language of the family. (Gil says he was "out of his mind" during this part of his life, so he can't remember everything, but that the allegations about his violence are overblown.)

There's a scene about the father and mother of one of Gil's cult members. They feel like they no longer know their daughter—who has started to refer to them as her "body family." It's a heartbreaking story. And it makes me understand what my grandparents must have gone through when Kate became Gil's number-one follower.

It's exactly what I was always most afraid of with religion. To embrace religion, you have to surrender some control. But what if it's a slippery slope, and you lose all control, slide right past the Judeo-Christian mainstream, and end up in a yurt kneeling in front of a guy wearing a tablecloth who has renamed you Lotus Petal?

It's why I don't know what to do with Jasper. If I give him some religion, then he might become obsessed and go Guru Gil on me. Then again, if I give him no religion, he could descend into moral anarchy. They're both so risky. I feel like I can't win.

You shall not make for yourself a graven image, or any likeness of anything
that is in heaven above, or that is in the earth beneath,
or that is in the water under the earth.

—Exodus 20:4

Day 75. I've added another commandment to my Most Violated List: no making images. It was a surprise entry. Until I focused on it, I didn't realize the pervasiveness of images or how often I made them.

The loose interpretation of the Second Commandment—which starts out "You shall not make for yourself a graven image"—is that it prohibits idolatry. God is telling us not to bow down to golden calves or carved pillars.

But the more severe interpretation, which still echoes through Judeo-Christian tradition today, is that we should allow no images whatsoever. No drawing or sculpture or photography. No painting, unless you're Rothko or Mondrian. This is because the latter part of the commandment forbids us from making the "likeness of anything in the sky, or earth, or in the water." Which pretty much covers it.

The strictest adherents in America right now are probably the aforementioned Amish. Modern-day conservative Islam is also famous for its avoidance of images. It's the reason why the Taliban shut down all movie theaters and riots erupted after that Danish newspaper published cartoons of Muhammad.

Since I'm following the Bible literally, I figure I should take a rigorous approach, somewhere between the Amish and the Taliban. Which is enormously difficult.

I can't absentmindedly doodle. I can't use smiley face emoticons, which I never used anyway, but it was nice knowing I had the option. I can't turn on the TV (though I decide that it's OK to watch TV if it's already on, because that cannot be construed as "making an image").

I used to entertain Jasper by doing Google image searches of his favorite animals; no more. This is probably good, because typing in something like *kitty* inevitably turns up a woman in a skimpy cat outfit licking her hand.

I've tried to stop taking photos. Well, as much as possible, anyway. When I balked at snapping a picture of my wife and her mom at her mom's birthday, Julie said, "Can we have a sidebar conference, please?" The result of that tense negotiation: I'll take this photo, but after that, I'm done.

Granted, my starvation diet from images can be a headache. This morning Jasper dumped his Play-Doh on the table. And, as usual, he instructed me what to make. He's now moved beyond grunts to a vocabulary of twenty-odd words.

"Ball!"

"How about a circle?" I respond.

I figure Platonic shapes are OK. I make a circle.

"Car!"

"You want to see a square?" I make a square.

"Nemo," says Jasper. (*Nemo* is Jasper's word for any type of fish; as a good protoconsumer, he speaks in brand names.)

"Here you go," I say, making an oval. I'm starting to run out of shapes.

Jasper seems disappointed by my Play-Doh geometry. I feel ridiculous for refusing to make him a fish, but I also know that I have to do this experiment full bore, or else I'll risk missing out on key spiritual discoveries. No cutting corners.

At least I have plenty of historical precedents. The Second Commandment played a huge part in the Protestant Reformation. Several Protestant leaders—including John Calvin—urged the removal and/or smashing of paintings and statues from churches. Riots erupted in Switzerland and Scotland, among other places. Aside from provoking idolatry, images were thought to be a sign of human vanity. People were trying to compete with the God of creation.

Jews have also obeyed this commandment on and off. Orthodox Jews still won't make a sculpture of a human. Some Jews of fourteenth-century Germany wouldn't draw people, though they did find my favorite loophole: They illustrated their texts with bird-headed humans. You see, the commandment forbids the likeness of anything in heaven or earth—and, technically, bird-headed humans don't exist in heaven or earth. Ingenious, no?

My vacation from iconography has been surprising, even enlightening. Despite the inconvenience, I do like image avoidance.

First, it suits my job. Images are taking over, and writers are a dying breed. The Norman Mailers of today are reduced to writing pun-filled captions for paparazzi photos. Blogs—which were threatening enough to professional writers—are being replaced by video blogs. We writers need to embrace the Second Commandment as our rallying cry for the importance of words. In a literally biblical world, all publications would look like the front page of the *Wall Street Journal*. Or the way it used to look, anyway.

Second, I think there's something to the idea that the divine dwells more easily in text than in images. Text allows for more abstract thought, more of a separation between you and the physical world, more room for you and God to meet in the middle. I find it hard enough to conceive of an infinite being. Imagine if those original scrolls came in the form of a graphic novel with pictures of the Lord? I'd never come close to communing with the divine.

The Bible is right: A deluge of images does encourage idolatry. Look at the cults of personality in America today. Look at Hollywood. Look at Washington. I'd like to see the next presidential race be run according to Second Commandment principles. No commercials. A radio-only debate. We need an ugly president. I know we're missing out on some potential Abe Lincolns because they'd look gawky and gangly on TV.

Love not sleep, lest you come to poverty.

—Proverbs 20:13

Day 77. The other day, my grandfather asked me, "Do you sleep with the beard under the covers or over the covers?" Now that I'm aware of it, I can't stop thinking about it. I switch positions every few minutes.

It's just one of the reasons I'm having trouble sleeping. The problem is, I'm downloading so much spiritual information during the days that

I spend my nights awake in bed trying to process it. (Incidentally, the author of Proverbs would be fine with my lack of sleep; he considers sleep a sign of laziness that will lead to poverty.)

As I lie in bed tonight, I think about Answers in Genesis, which just sent me another colorful brochure. Maybe I let myself off the creationism hook too easily. As unlikely as the six-day scenario may be, shouldn't I at least give it the benefit of doubt?

So I do an experiment. I try to put myself into the mind of my biblical alter ego Jacob. I convince myself that the earth was formed a handful of generations ago. I can't 100 percent believe, but for a few minutes, I almost believe it.

And it is fascinating. The first thing I notice is that I feel more connected. If everyone on earth is descended from two identifiable people—Adam and Eve—then the "family of man" isn't just pabulum. It's true. The guy who sells me bananas at the deli on 81st Street—he's my cousin.

But even more powerful is this feeling: My life is more significant. If the earth is ten billion years old, I'm barely a drop of water in the ocean that is the universe. But if the earth is six thousand years old, then I've been alive for a decent portion of the world's existence. I'm no bit player. I've got a speaking part in the movie of life.

My thought experiment crystallized a key tension I've noticed in the Bible. On the one hand, the Bible teaches extreme humility. Humans are sinful, barely worthy of praying to God.

On the other hand, there's a certain—I don't know if arrogance is quite the right word. Maybe pride. Humans are the pinnacle of biblical creation, the ones God saved until last on the sixth day, beings that are vastly superior to the beasts and nature. We are made in God's image. (As the seventeenth-century philosopher Baruch Spinoza said, if triangles could think, their God would be eminently triangular.)

I believe that's a key motivation to creationism: the need to feel less inconsequential. I remember Mark Looy—the publicist for the Creation Museum—saying, "Evolution says that we are the product of random processes. That we evolved via pond scum. When we say that, we're not applying much value to humanity. If we say we're a product of accidents and random processes, how much purpose and hope does that give to our youth?"

Since I'll never convert to creationism, I have to find some dignity and self-esteem and sacredness even with our mucky origins.

> *Train up a child in the way he should go, and when he is old*
> *he will not depart from it.*
>
> —PROVERBS 22:6

Day 78. I've started to wear sunglasses more often. I can't find anything in the Bible prohibiting them, and they make my beard—which is now approaching my Adam's apple—look slightly hipper. More indie record producer, less Crown Heights. Today I've taken my shades on a trip to the playground with my wife and son. Julie's reading her *People* magazine on the bench, and I'm scampering around after Jasper.

He wants to go on the swing.

"OK, just give me a second," I say.

I take a bottle of Purell antibacterial lotion from the stroller bag. These playgrounds, they're like a germ free-for-all. I wipe the chain on the left side of the swing, then start in on the right side. Jasper is whining that he wants to get on already.

"Almost ready," I say.

Julie looks up from her magazine to see the battle in progress. "A. J.," she says. "Helmet."

Helmet is Julie's code word to me that I'm being a crazy overprotective father. We've had so many fights about this, she thought it'd be easier to just sum up her position with a single word: helmet. She chose helmet because, at one point, without irony, I checked out the prices of baby helmets on the internet.

It's just that these kids are so fragile, you know? They've only got that mushy little skull separating their brains from the sidewalk. They have only two years of an immune system built up.

Last week Julie and I got into an argument because I said I didn't want him going to something called the International Preschool. This is a preschool where a lot of UN workers send their kids.

I said I don't want him to become too interested in foreign countries because then he might live in one when he grows up.

"You're kidding, right?"

"No, I want him to live in the same town I do."

"That's why you don't want him to go there?"

"Yes."

"That's demented."

She told me that I have to back off. Otherwise I'll be cutting his hot dog into tiny pieces when he's nineteen and chaperoning him to the prom. That's when she came up with *helmet*.

Maybe she's right. Maybe I should treat Jasper more like God treats humans in the Bible. He gave us free will. He relinquished some control because He wanted us to be able to make our own mistakes and have our own victories.

Maybe I should. But I can't. I can't expose him to an unsanitary swing with its millions of microorganisms. So I give the right-hand chain another squirt of Purell. Julie shakes her head.

> *It is better to go to the house of mourning*
> *than to go to the house of feasting . . .*
>
> —ECCLESIASTES 7:2

Day 80. The extended family has gathered at my grandfather's apartment in midtown for a late lunch. It's to honor my grandmother, who died two years ago. It's our own secular ritual—we get together once a year to reminisce. My grandmother was a remarkable woman—smart, funny, elegant, organized beyond belief (each of her six children was assigned a different color, and got towels only in that color, left notes in that color, and so on).

And man, was she secular. For her, family was the alpha and omega, so she found the story of Abraham's near sacrifice of his son Isaac on a mountaintop particularly inexplicable.

"How could a father even think about killing his son?" she once told me when I was a kid. "What a horrible story."

After her daughter's switch to Orthodoxy, my grandmother—though she never stopped loving Kate—went from being secular to fiercely anti-religious. I remember walking down 57th Street with her. We passed a

Hasidic man draped in his black hat and black coat. I looked at my grandmother, who was staring at the man, almost scowling—and then she darted her tongue out. Quick as a snake, just poked it out.

"What was that?" I asked.

"I always stick my tongue out at people like that," she said.

"Do you think he saw?"

"He saw," she said. "He knows."

She was torn between her usual polite, elegant self and her real hatred for what she saw as religious fundamentalism. I often wonder what she would have thought of my experiment.

Everyone is at the lunch, including both Kate and my vegan-feminist aunt Marti from Berkeley. Marti gives me some stern pointers on politically incorrect, violence-laden religious words to avoid.

"You shouldn't use the word *sacred,* because it comes from the same root word as *sacrifice.* As in animal sacrifice."

"OK."

"And *bless* comes from the Old English word *bletsian,* which means 'consecrate with blood.' So don't use that."

"What about *Bible*?"

"I'm not sure about that one."

"It comes from *byblos,* the Greek word for *papyrus.* Made from the corpses of once-living plants."

"Yes, maybe avoid that too," she says.

Kate also gives me suggestions on language. Right before lunch, Jasper wants to show me a fascinating trick in which he jumps from the rug to the wooden floor, so he tugs on my pants and says, "A. J.! A. J.!"

"Yes, I'm watching."

"He calls you A. J.?" asks Kate.

"Yeah. We're on a first-name basis."

I've tried to convert Jasper to the more traditional "Dad" or "Daddy," but he insists on A. J. So I've gotten used to it.

"Children aren't supposed to use their parents' first names," says Kate. "It's disrespectful."

Kate's probably right; in biblical times, there was no such thing as an informal I'm-friends-with-my-kid father. Without me knowing it, Jasper was violating the "honor your parents" commandment.

A few minutes later, when we all sit down to lunch, my grandfather asks me, "What's the strangest rule you have to follow?"

I mentally scan my list of Five Most Perplexing Rules. I choose one at random. "Probably the one about how if you're in a fistfight, and the wife of your opponent grabs your private parts, you must cut off her hand."

"That," he says, "is very strange indeed."

And it is. But that's exactly what the Bible says in Deuteronomy 25:11–12:

> When men fight with one another, and the wife of the one draws near
> to rescue her husband from the hand of him who is beating him, and
> puts out her hand and seizes him by the private parts, then you shall
> cut off her hand; your eye shall have no pity.

So far (knock on wood) I've avoided getting in a brawl with a man whose wife looks like she has a firm grip. So I guess I'm obeying the commandment by default and can congratulate myself on that.

But, as with the mixed fibers, it baffles me. Why the specificity? Why does the Bible ban this particular below-the-belt maneuver and not, say, a kidney punch or a kick between the thighs? Julie suggests it's because the writer of Deuteronomy had this precise unpleasant scenario happen to him and so decided to forbid it for all eternity.

Unfortunately, Kate is within earshot when I tell my grandfather about the private parts rule. Damn. I thought she had been in the kitchen. I didn't want her hearing me talk about the crazy ones without balancing it with some good ones.

And sure enough, she looks stricken. Like she just discovered that her son smokes two packs a day. She had studied the Bible for years but had never learned about the husband-grabbing part. It's just not one that gets a lot of play at synagogue.

The next day, I get three voice mails. All from Kate. "Is part of your biblical life that you're not allowed to answer the phone?" she says.

I call her back.

"I talked to my rabbi," Kate says. "And, yes, it is in the Torah." But . . . it's supposed to represent something broader: Do not embarrass others. The wife here is embarrassing her husband by assuming he needs help. And the wife is embarrassing the husband's opponent by, well, grabbing his privates. Plus, adds Kate, you didn't actually chop off the wife's hand. That's metaphorical. The woman was required only to pay a fine.

OK. It does seem more rational if interpreted that way. But my question is: Why didn't the Bible just say that? Why not just say "Don't embarrass others"? Why the mysterious code?

I've asked all of the Jewish members of my spiritual board this question. The best answer I've gotten is this, from a rabbi named Noah Weinberg, a founder of Aish HaTorah, the outreach group: Life is a jigsaw puzzle, he told me. The joy and challenge of life—and the Bible—is figuring things out. "If a jigsaw puzzle came numbered, you'd return it to the store." Same with life.

It's a good answer, but only partly satisfying. I have to keep digging.

Cursed shall you be in the city, and cursed shall you be in the field.

—Deuteronomy 28:16

Day 82. Tonight I break the Eighth Commandment—no stealing—and I pay the price.

It happens when I try to research different types of biblical incense on the internet. Problem is our wireless connection is on the fritz. So I go in search of a signal. I take my laptop to the gray-walled emergency stairwell and descend to the fourth floor. I figure maybe I can glom onto a neighbor's network. I try one called Sonicboy. No dice. Password required. I go down another flight. Zildo y Zelda? Nope. Also requires a password. But down another flight, I find a network with the beautifully generic name Wireless. An excellent sign. If they can't be bothered to come up with a name, maybe they don't know about this newfangled thing called passwords. Yes, I get a signal. But it's not coming in strong enough, so I climb down another two stairs. At which point I trip and slam my knee into the railing and bash my laptop against the wall.

So I deserved it. The Bible says thou shalt not steal; I stole my neighbor's wireless signal. And I'm now limping around the house with a bum knee.

Was this God's punishment? I don't know. I don't honestly think so. Would my ancient Israelite ancestors have thought so (assuming I explained wireless internet etiquette to them)? Maybe. As with everything biblical, there's no simple answer about the consequences of sin. You can find several major themes.

The first is that God will punish you, and He will punish you in this life. This motif is best seen in Deuteronomy 28, which contains the three most terrifying pages in the history of publishing. Here you read every horrible disease and weather pattern that will befall you if you don't live by the Bible.

The Lord will "smite you with consumption, and with fever, inflammation, and fiery heat, and with drought, and with blasting and with mildew."

And that's just a little warm-up. It continues:

"And the heavens over your head shall be brass, and the earth under you shall be iron. And the Lord will make the rain of your land powder and dust."

It's actually oddly beautiful. Take away the fact that the words condemn you to a life of aching, thirsty, itchy torment, and it's poetic, breathtaking.

"You shall grope at noonday, as the blind grope in darkness . . ."

"You shall betroth a wife, and another man shall lie with her . . ."

It goes on to say that you shall be reduced to eating your own children and trying—unsuccessfully—to sell yourself as a slave. That's right. You aren't good enough for *slavery*. There is also a section on the good things that will happen if you follow the law. But it's only one-quarter the length of the curses. It's the curses that stay with you.

In some hyperreligious circles, this type of thinking persists. Jerry Falwell, for instance, argued that 9/11 was God's punishment for America's depravity.

I find myself slipping into the bad-people-get-what's-coming-to-them mind-set now and again. But only for a second. The world doesn't seem to work that way. Just look at the evil people in America. They don't have boils on their legs, and they're not eating their children. Many are living in penthouses, and some have their own reality shows.

Thankfully, the Bible is a big book, an infinitely complex book, and there are many alternatives. One recurring theme—found mostly in the New Testament—says that you will be rewarded in heaven. Another strain—found in books like Ecclesiastes and Job—takes a modern, almost agnostic, view.

Ecclesiastes is probably my favorite book of the Bible. I first read about it in the *Encyclopaedia Britannica,* and I have loved it ever since. Called *Qohelet* in Hebrew, the book is a collection of wisdom and reminiscences from a man who identifies himself as King Solomon. If you believe modern biblical scholars, the author was probably not Solomon but instead a now-anonymous poet from the third century BCE. Whoever he was, the writing is awe inspiring.

Every time I read it, I feel myself doing a little silent call-and-response with the text. "Yes." "That's right." I feel the thrill of recognizing thoughts that I have had myself, but that I've never been able to capture in such beautiful language. And I feel the oddity of finding myself on the same wavelength as a man who lived two thousand years ago. It's the closest I've come to proselytizing—telling friends they *have* to read Ecclesiastes.

In any case, the author of Ecclesiastes says: "The race is not to the swift, nor the battle to the strong, nor bread to the wise, nor riches to the intelligent, nor favor to the men of skill; but time and chance happen to them all."

Ecclesiastes says that life is uncertain. "Vapor of vapors . . . all is vapors." (This is a more accurate translation of the phrase usually rendered: "vanity of vanities . . . all is vanity.") We can never hope to plumb the mystery of God's mind. Bad things happen to good people. Idiots and geniuses, saints and sinners—we all die. The best we can do is try to appreciate the great things that God has given us—food, drink, the pleasure of honest work. We should follow the commandments, but we should do so with no guarantee that they will pay off in this life.

This is so wise. Be good for goodness' sake, as someone once said. It's a pragmatic worldview. The thing is, it's not a solid worldview. It's vapor, all vapor. If I knew for sure that I'd be punished for sinning, then I'd have an undeniable reason to follow God's word. But I doubt I'll ever believe that for certain. So what to do? Part of me wants something more tangible than the vapor. Can I find it by the end of the year? Or is that, as Ecclesiastes says, chasing the wind?

> *He who despises his neighbor is a sinner . . .*
>
> —PROVERBS 14:21

Day 84. I've been trying to love my neighbor, but in New York, this is particularly difficult. It's an aloof city. I don't even know my neighbor's names, much less love them. I know them only as woman-whose-cooking-smells-nasty and guy-who-gets-*Barron's*-delivered-each-week, and so forth.

Well, except for Nancy in 5I. We met because our son and her beagle are about the same age, have pretty much the same vocabulary, and share similar interests, such as running around the hall.

Nancy is a former hippie who was once friends with Jimi Hendrix and Janis Joplin. In fact, she looks like what Janis Joplin would have looked like if Janis Joplin had lived another thirty-five years. In the sixties, Nancy took a lot of drugs, had a couple of disastrous relationships with men, did some waitressing, wrote some poetry, and now lives alone with her dog and listens to Howard Stern every morning. She almost always wears sundresses and knit caps. She calls herself "the kooky lady with the dog."

She's painfully shy, almost skittish. She'll visit our apartment occasionally, but when I knock on hers, she always just cracks the door open and pokes her head out. "I'm painting one wall at a time," she once explained. "I don't want anyone to see it till it's done." She also once told me that I unnerved her because I maintained too much eye contact. (Which is, in fact, a problem for me. I often forget to glance away intermittently during conversations, and have to remind myself to do so; otherwise people will think I'm a psycho who keeps a cup of noses in my freezer.)

Nancy was married for a while after college, but she couldn't have kids. So she's become the unofficial godmother to our son. For the past few months she's been sketching a portrait of him. "I'll be finished soon," she promises. "By the time he takes his SATs."

And today she brings Jasper an early holiday present: a wooden Noah's ark with a menagerie of little painted animals. She thought it'd be good to get him a biblical present. I make Jasper say thank you, a phrase he pronounces without those tiresome consonants, so it sounds like *a-ew*.

"You know, it's interesting," I say to Nancy as we sit at the kitchen table watching Jasper march the giraffes onto his boat. "I was reading in one of my Bible commentaries about how the flood is such a tragic story—the drowning of millions of people and animals—and how strange it is that it's always made into cute kids' toys."

Nancy looks wounded.

"I didn't . . ." Ugh. What a putz. I had tried to show off my biblical knowledge, and I ended up insulting my only friendly neighbor. The Bible tells us not to be know-it-alls—"A prudent man conceals his knowledge . . ." (Proverbs 12:23).

"I love his ark," I say. "It's adorable . . ."

"Don't worry," she says, recovering. "At least I didn't get him the stuffed ten plagues."

Nancy is a good neighbor, probably the best I've had in my time as a New Yorker. I decide that this will be one of my missions for the year: Do something righteous—a good deed, a *mitzvah*—for my neighbor in 5I.

"Therefore he may lie with you tonight in return for your son's mandrakes."

—Genesis 30:15 (NAB)

Day 87. As of this week, Julie and I have officially been trying to be fruitful and multiply for a year. Still no luck. So we've decided to take radical measures. We're going to try in vitro fertilization.

This is more morally fraught than I had realized. Thanks to my religion-soaked life, I now know that several higher authorities condemn the procedure. The Catholic Church, for instance, denounces IVF for several reasons. Among them: it breaks what one Catholic magazine calls "the unity and integrity" of "conjugal fruitfulness." Which means that the conception takes place outside the woman's body, not where God intended it.

On the other hand, most rabbis don't have much of a problem with IVF—and some Jewish scholars even argue that "be fruitful and multiply" means that there's a moral imperative to get pregnant by any means necessary. Which is why New York fertility clinics are often crowded with black hats and voluminous beards.

The Bible, of course, never addresses the issue directly. There's nary a mention of IVF in Scripture, even by its long-forgotten name of "test-tube baby." There is, however, a biblical story about fertility drugs—or their ancient equivalent, anyway. You remember Jacob, who was married to two sisters: Leah (the baby machine) and Rachel (the one with the barren womb). At one point, Rachel got so desperate, she pleaded with her sister for some mandrake. Mandrake is the forked Mediterranean root that was thought to be an infertility cure. Rachel got her mandrake, but the scheme backfired. Because Rachel, to secure the mandrake, had traded to Leah a night with Jacob—and on that very night, Jacob was apparently at maximum virility. Leah got pregnant. Rachel got nothing, at least for the time being. So . . . you could argue that the Bible subtly disapproves of fertility treatments.

But, honestly, that seems like speculation. If I take the Bible literally—at its word—I can't find any guidance pro or con.

So we're going to try IVF. It helps that my new insurance plan covers it. And it helps, too, that we have a family connection to the procedure. My cousin David—now twenty-three—was the very first test-tube baby in New York State, and he got his little technologically assisted face on the cover of the *Daily News*. He seems to have turned out all right. He fits in fine with my family—with the exception of my ultraliberal aunt Marti, who squabbles with him every time they're in the same room. David, former president of his fraternity, likes manly things such as baseball and a big, juicy piece of meat. Marti does not. Whenever someone takes a family photo, she tells us all to say *"Soy cheese!"* which always prompts David to shout a gleefully malicious *"T-bone!"* (To be technical, Marti has since decided that soy causes health problems, so she now prefers us to say *"Vegan."*)

IVF is a startlingly complicated process. The buildup to the actual fertilization involves forty days of shots, pills, alcohol swabs, and a fearsome array of syringes. Granted, I get the better half of the deal. Julie actually has to be poked by a needle every day. But I do have to be her RN, mixing together white powders and sterile water in what seems the most stressful chemistry experiment of my life.

The first night, a Russian-accented nurse came to our apartment to show me how to inject my wife. She asked Julie to drop her pants and lean over. "It's just like throwing a dart," the nurse told me. Though with this dart, you miss, and the target starts bleeding.

"Each night, you alternate cheeks—first right, then left, right, left." And, she advised, you have to make sure the needle hits the sweet spot of the upper butt.

I don't like vagueness. So I opened a drawer, took out a green magic marker, and requested the nurse to draw me the exact location of these "sweet spots" on Julie's butt. Which she did. And which helps me enormously. But not Julie. She complains that whenever she wears white pants, everyone can see two green orbs on her butt.

"I hope this works," Julie told me yesterday. "Because I don't think I can go through this again."

. . . For God is with the generation of the righteous.

—PSALMS 14:5

Day 91, the end of month three of Project Bible. Thanks to the beard, my alter ego Jacob is looking more and more religious. Or, to be precise, more and more Jewish. I know this because I was stopped by some tourists on the street the other day and asked "Where in New York can we get a good knish?" More to the point, I was told by a guy at the soup kitchen where I volunteer, "You look really Jewish." Hard to misinterpret that one.

On the other hand, my ethical state leaves much to be desired. This occurs to me as I am sitting on the crosstown bus today reading Ecclesiastes.

I'm concentrating hard. Too hard. I feel a tap on my shoulder. I'm annoyed. I don't like strangers touching me. I look up. It is a fiftyish man.

"Excuse me, this lady is feeling sick. Could you give her your seat?"

He points to a tall brunette woman who was standing right in front of me. How did I miss this? The woman looks horrible: Her face is sallow, nearly the color of lima beans. She is doubled over. And she is weeping.

I get up in a hurry with mumbled apologies. To paraphrase Ecclesiastes, there's a time for reading and a time for getting off your butt.

I realize that I was what is known in Hebrew as a *Chasid Shote*. A righteous idiot. In the Talmud, there's a story about a devout man who won't save a drowning woman because he's afraid of breaking the no-touching-women ban. He's the ultimate pious fool.

The moral is the same as Jesus's parable about the Good Samaritan: Don't be so caught up in the regulations that you forget about the big things, like compassion and respect for life. The righteous idiot is what the Christian Bible calls a Pharisee—one of the sanctimonious legalistic scholars who criticize Christ's followers for picking grain on the Sabbath.

As I mentioned in the introduction, one of the reasons that I embarked on this experiment was to take legalism to its logical extreme and show that it leads to righteous idiocy. What better way to demonstrate the absurdity of Jewish and Christian fundamentalism? If you actually follow all the rules, you'll spend your days acting like a crazy person.

I still believe that. And I still plan on making a complete fool of myself to get this point across. But as with everything involving religion, my project has become much more complicated. The spiritual journey now takes up far more of my time.

My friend Roger was right. It's not like studying Sumo wrestling in Japan. It's more like wrestling itself. This opponent of mine is sometimes beautiful, sometimes cruel, sometimes ancient, sometimes crazily relevant. I can't get a handle on it.

Month Four: December

For everything there is a season . . .
—Ecclesiastes 3:1

Day 93. December has arrived, and everyone is gearing up for the big Judeo-Christian holidays. New York is packed. I tried to walk through Rockefeller Center the other day, and I got flashbacks to the mosh pit at the Hasidic rave.

I feel oddly out of sync. This is because the Bible itself has surprisingly little to say about the December holidays. The New Testament talks about the birth of Jesus, of course. But there's no description of how to celebrate that birth—no tree, no services, no carols, no eggnog, no Frank Capra films. Which means that some of the more literalist Christian denominations—including the Jehovah's Witnesses and the Worldwide Church of God—don't celebrate Christmas at all.

Hanukkah doesn't make it into the Bible either. The story of Hanukkah—the revolt of the Jewish rebels the Maccabees against their Greek oppressor Antiochus—appears (though only in a section of the Bible called the Apocrypha, which in Judaism is considered noncanonical). But there's nothing in the Scriptures about the lighting of eight candles or eating oil-soaked latkes.

I'll be sitting out this holiday season. Well, as much as I can. I still have to buy some gifts for Julie. I can't get away with skipping that, and the Bible is actually pro-gift-giving ("It is more blessed to give than to receive," Acts 20:35). Fortunately, buying gifts won't take too much time; Julie is so absurdly organized, she always hands me a stack of catalogs with the gifts she wants circled in red Magic Marker and marked with Post-it notes. It's a great thing. As is the conviction with which she says the inevitable "Oh my God! How did you know?"

Let your garments be always white.

—Ecclesiastes 9:8

Day 95. I looked in the mirror today and decided it's official: I've become someone I'd cross the street to avoid. To complement my beard and tassels, I've begun wearing all white, as prescribed by King Solomon in Ecclesiastes: "Let your garments be always white." White pants, white T-shirts, a white sweater, and a white zip-up jacket from the Gap, all without mixed fibers, naturally.

Which means that when I say good-bye to Julie in the morning, I get one of two responses. Either

1)   A *Saturday Night Fever* hand twirl and accompanying arm thrust
or
2)   A Fonzie-like "Aaaaayyyyyy!"

The John Travolta reference I understand, but the Fonzie one stumped me.

"In the first season, Fonzie wore white because black leather was considered too menacing," Julie explained. (This is a woman who still has her childhood collection of *TV Guides*.)

Personally, I prefer to think of myself in a more highbrow mold—a biblical version of Tom Wolfe. Or perhaps a modern Emily Dickinson, who became a recluse in the 1870s and refused to wear anything but white.

Regardless, it's a bizarre sensation walking around the Upper West Side in white garments—or "tusk" garments, as the Gap calls them. As with many New Yorkers, my regular wardrobe is made up mostly of bleak colors: blacks, browns, a daring splash of navy blue. It seems to suit the city's soot and cynicism. Dark clothes for a dark city.

I rarely see New Yorkers wearing all white unless they're behind a bakery counter. So I'm getting even more wary glances than ever on the subway. I like to play a game: I swivel my head around quickly and see how many gawkers I can catch. Usually at least two.

But the thing is, I'm enjoying it. My white wardrobe makes me feel lighter, more spiritual. Happier. It's further proof of a major theme of this year: The outer affects the inner. Behavior shapes your psyche as much as the other way around. Clothes make the man. As I walk down

Columbus Avenue on this brisk day, with the wind flattening my white pants and jacket against me, I think to myself, "Life can't be too terrible if I'm dressed like I'm about to play the semifinals at Wimbledon or attend P. Diddy's birthday party, right?"

The "white garment" line from Ecclesiastes is usually interpreted metaphorically—as a call to remain pure and joyous. But it's not beyond-a-doubt metaphorical. Maybe it means what it says: Dress in white. An ancient Israelite sect called the Essenes dressed in white, as do some kabbalists. I should have been wearing all white from day one, but it was one of those rules I felt I had to build up to. Now that I'm doing it, I don't want to stop.

> *Remember the sabbath day, to keep it holy.*
>
> —Exodus 20:8

Day 97. It's a Tuesday afternoon in December, but I feel like I've just experienced my first real Sabbath.

Let me explain: The doorknobs in our apartment fall off on an alarmingly regular basis. They're mercurial little suckers. We don't even need to be touching them—it's more of a natural-life-cycle type of situation, like icebergs calving or my hairline retreating. I'll be in bed, reading my Bible, and I'll hear a thud and know that another doorknob succumbed to gravity.

Usually, I screw the knob back on. Problem solved—for a week or two, anyway. No big deal. But this morning, it became a big deal. At 9:30 I stop typing my emails and shuffle over to the bathroom—and close the door behind me. I don't realize what I've done until I reach for the nonexistent inside doorknob. It had molted sometime during the night.

For the first ten minutes, I try to escape. I bang on the door, shout for help. No answer. Julie is away at a meeting, and Jasper is out with his babysitter. I've seen *Ocean's Eleven*, so I know to look for the grill in the ceiling that I can unscrew, climb into, slither through an air chute, drop into my neighbor's bedroom, make a clever comment like "just thought I'd drop in," and then return home. No grill. I'm trapped.

The next half hour I spend going through a checklist of worst-case scenarios. What if I slip, cut my forehead on the bathtub, bleed to death, and end up on the front page of the *New York Post*? What if there's a fire, and I'm forced to hang by my fingernails from the window ledge?

Even more stressful to me is that the outside world is speeding along without me. Emails are being answered. Venti lattes are being sipped. George Bush's childhood friends are being appointed to high-level positions.

At 10:30 the phone rings. I hear a muffled voice leaving a message. This almost qualifies as human interaction. At 10:35 I make a pledge to myself to put more reading material in the bathroom if I ever escape. A Bible would have been nice. I'm stuck with an old Levenger catalog and a candle with an Omar Khayyam poem on the side: "A jug of wine, a loaf of bread, and thou." Khayyam seems to be taunting me. I don't have a jug of wine, or a loaf of bread, or thou. I have a tube of Neutrogena shaving cream and some towels. That's not paradise enow.

By 11:00 I've become the world's greatest expert on this bathroom. I know the fake marble tiles with their spider-vein pattern and the power outlet that is tilted at a rakishly diagonal angle. I spend a half hour tidying the medicine cabinet. I notice that the ingredients in Chlor-Trimeton go all the way from A (acacia) to Z (zein), which, as a former encyclopedia reader, appeals to me.

By noon I'm sitting on the floor, my back against the shower door. I sit. And sit some more. And something odd happens. I know that, outside the bathroom, the world is speeding along. That blogs are being read. Wild salmon is being grilled. Reggaeton is being explained to middle-aged white marketing executives.

But I'm OK with it. It doesn't cause my shoulders to tighten. Nothing I can do about it. I've reached an unexpected level of acceptance. For once, I'm savoring the present. I'm admiring what I have, even if it's thirty-two square feet of fake marble and an angled electrical outlet. I start to pray. And, perhaps for the first time, I pray in true peace and silence—without glancing at the clock, without my brain hopscotching from topic to topic.

This is what the Sabbath should feel like. A pause. Not just a minor pause, but a major pause. Not just a lowering of the volume, but a muting. As the famous rabbi Abraham Joshua Heschel put it, the Sabbath is a sanctuary in time.

At about 1:30 I hear Julie come home. I call out and pound on the door.

"Where are you?"

"In here! In the bathroom!"

I hear her footsteps approaching.

"You can't get out?"

"No, I can't get out."

"How long have you been in there?"

"Four hours."

There was a pause. I knew she was weighing her options. A few months ago, when she had trouble opening our bedroom door, I had made her pretend she was in a prison movie and shout "Attica! Attica!"

Julie is more mature. After a few seconds, she just opened the door. I am free. I can return my emails, make my calls. It's kind of a shame.

All my sleep has fled because of the bitterness of my soul.

—Isaiah 38:15

Day 101. Another sleepless night. I lay in bed, adjusting and readjusting my pillow, unable to stop obsessing about this horrible news segment I caught on TV. It said that the recidivism rate for meth addicts is 80 percent. This freaks me out. If Jasper someday tries a little meth—"What's the harm?" he'll say to himself, "my parents were always in favor of experimentation"—he'll get addicted forever and end up hollow eyed and slack jawed in a county jail. Maybe it's true. This whole loosey-goosey parenting style is too dangerous.

A few months ago, right before my biblical year began, Julie and I went to Baltimore to attend the wedding of Sara, the daughter of my Orthodox aunt Kate, and I sat next to one of Kate's friends. She had a wide-brimmed white hat that wouldn't be out of place at Prince William's wedding, a peculiar counterpoint to the black-hatted Hasidim who were there.

She told me that her background was completely secular. But when she had kids, she and her husband made a deliberate decision to become religious.

"I didn't trust American culture."

"No?" I asked.

"Well, what does American culture teach?"

I wasn't sure what to say. "I think there are lots of different American cultures."

This was the wrong answer.

"If you turn on the TV, you see 'buy, buy, buy, sex and violence, buy, buy, buy.' We decided to live by a different code."

They explored several religions, including Hinduism, but ended up diving into Orthodox Judaism, since they were born Jewish.

They didn't become ultrareligious because of a charismatic leader or the truth of the Bible—they did it for the structure. And now their kids have grown up into responsible young adults. I met one of them. A nice computer geek.

It's something I should consider. More structure for Jasper. In my pop culture–tainted mind, I keep coming back to this conundrum:

Would I rather have Bart Simpson or one of the Flanders kids? A couple of years ago, I would have chosen the loveably spunky Bart. No question. But nowadays, now that I have my own three-dimensional son, I'm leaning toward the Flanders progeny. Yes, they may be a little creepy, they may sing loud songs about Noah's ark, but at least you know they won't spend their free time burning down the cafeteria or skateboarding off a canyon. I'd sacrifice some individuality for the knowledge that my son will outlive me.

> "Behold, I have taken upon myself to speak to the Lord,
> I who am but dust and ashes."
>
> —GENESIS 18:27

Day 103. I'm trying to pray for a half hour a day in three ten-minute intervals, usually in the corner of Julie's office, a couple of feet from the basket full of *Real Simple* magazines. A half hour's no record, I know. But at least I'm not glancing at the clock every minute as I did in the beginning.

And once in a while, I actually find myself looking forward to those ten-minute sessions, especially at night. It's a decompression. When I was a kid, I spent several minutes each night before bed picturing water-skiers slaloming over choppy waves. I don't know how I came up with the ritual. It's not like I was a big fan of water skiing—I had tried it at camp and ended up with a gut full of lake water. But I found visualizing it relaxing. Maybe prayer will serve the same purpose. I get to close the door, close my eyes, and sink into a meditative state, or as close to one as my brain will allow me.

Plus, I've discovered another category of prayer that I like: praying on behalf of others, for the sick, needy, depressed—anyone who's been kicked around by fate. Intercessory prayer, as it's called.

I've read a bunch of articles about intercessory prayer recently—mostly about how it's sprouted up all over the internet. You can place prayer requests on websites like ePrayer.com and CyberSaint. (Recent examples include "I am expecting my first child. Please pray for a speedy delivery," and "Please pray for me to complete my thesis work, it is delayed by eight months.")

Intercessory prayer can be found sprinkled throughout the Bible—with everyone from Moses to Paul pleading with God for the sake of others. Abraham is the first to try it, and he's far from successful. It's a curious scene. God announces to Abraham that he's considering laying waste to the wicked cities of Sodom and Gomorrah.

Abraham asks him: "Suppose there are fifty righteous within the city; wilt thou then destroy the place and not spare it for the fifty righteous who are in it?"

And the Lord said, "If I find at Sodom fifty righteous in the city, I will spare the whole place for their sake."

Abraham answered, "Behold, I have taken upon myself to speak to the Lord, I who am but dust and ashes. Suppose five of the fifty righteous are lacking? Wilt thou destroy the whole city for lack of five?"

And He said, "I will not destroy it if I find forty-five there."

It continues. Abraham is able to haggle the Lord down to ten people—if there are ten good people in Sodom, God agrees not to smite it.

In the end, though, as you know, Sodom didn't meet the quota.

At first I found the whole passage comical. I mean, here's Abraham sounding like a salesman at a bazaar trying to get rid of his last decorative vase. But on reflection, what's wrong with what he did? It's actually a noble, beautiful—if ultimately doomed—attempt to save the lives of his fellow humans.

I'm not finished with my year, so I'm withholding judgment, but my rational side says that intercessory prayer today is no more effective than Abraham's effort. I still can't wrap my brain around the notion that God would change His mind because we ask Him to.

And yet I still love these prayers. To me they're moral weight training. Every night I pray for others for ten minutes—a friend about to undergo a cornea operation, my great-aunt whose sweet husband just died in their swimming pool, the guy I met in a Bible study class whose head was dented in a subway accident. It's ten minutes where it's impossible to be self-centered. Ten minutes where I can't think about my career, or my Amazon.com ranking, or that a blog in San Francisco made snarky comments about my latest *Esquire* article.

The Bible says not to boast, so I'm not going to say that I've turned into Albert Schweitzer or Angelina Jolie. But I do feel myself becoming a slightly more compassionate person.

The odd thing, though, is that to be fully compassionate, I might not want to tell these people I'm praying for them. I recently read about a new study of 1,802 coronary artery bypass patients. The patients who knew they were being prayed for actually had *more* complications than those who didn't. Perhaps they thought, "Well, if I'm sick enough that I need people to pray for me, I must really be in bad shape." In case that's true, I'll pray secretly and hope they don't read this chapter.

. . . The treacherous are taken captive by their lust.

—Proverbs 11:6

Day 105. So, lust. This week, my job at *Esquire* has forced the issue.

Before I explain, let me confess that lust has been one of my biggest failings so far this year. Ever since that first day when I spotted that gym ad of two gorgeous sweaty people clutching each other after what was apparently a very vigorous workout, I've been trying to smother my libido.

I try not to think about sex. I try not to talk about sex. I try not to glance at women on the street. The problem is, my heart's not in it. Thanks to my thirty-eight years of staunchly secular life, I'm having a hard time adjusting to the worldview that sexuality is sinful. Well, some sexuality is sinful, as anyone with a DSL line can tell you. But I'm having trouble getting worked up over a moderate amount of sexuality in culture.

I'm guessing that this has a lot to do with my previous wrestling matches with sex. In high school and college, I experienced some startling dry spells. To justify my involuntary abstinence, I told myself that I was above such crass human motivations as sex. I had better things to do than think about women. And what is sex, anyway? Just some skin contact necessary for DNA mixing during procreation. I didn't need it. I tried to turn myself into a neo-Puritan. I was pure intellect, with my body just a shell to transport that brain from place to place.

It didn't work. My attempt to stifle my sex drive didn't make me a more righteous person—I just got more frustrated and unhappy and preoccupied with sex. So for years, I've thought that as long as I remain faithful to Julie and don't let my libido run rampant, what's the harm in a little sexuality in culture? A racy joke, an unacted-upon fantasy, a movie with partial nudity? It never bothered me much.

But now everyone expects me—or more precisely, Jacob, my biblical alter ego—to embrace extreme modesty and total restraint. No carnal thoughts, no carnal words. It's a reasonable expectation, I suppose. Modesty has been a huge part of the Judeo-Christian tradition for a long time. Orthodox Jews follow rigid modesty rules: women cover their hair and cannot wear a dress revealing their collarbone. Some conservative Christians also conceal flesh and shun R-rated movies.

So I've been trying. The difficulty is, the level of sexual imagery in modern life is astounding. I knew intuitively this was true, but when you tune into it, you just can't believe it. I click on the Yahoo! finance page, and there's this blond model in a low-cut dress looking at a computer screen and nibbling alluringly on the temple of her glasses, apparently very aroused by the latest S&P 500 report. Even the suburban-mom character on *Dora the Explorer* has clothes that are disturbingly form fitting. Or maybe that's just me.

A few weeks ago, I heard that the Rev. Billy Graham, before he arrives at a hotel, has his room swept for potentially tempting images. I decided to sweep my own apartment. I stashed away all magazines that we had lying around, like the one with Jessica Alba in a blue skintight suit.

Next I took out a roll of masking tape and got to work censoring the images around the apartment. Anything that has the potential to stir my libido got covered with a piece of tape.

- The woman in a geisha outfit on the box of Celestial Seasonings tea.
- The photo of a cute chef with the unlikely name of Crescent Dragonwagon on the spine of a cookbook.
- The bosom of Julie's friend Sharon in a photo from our wedding, since said bosom is both ample and prominently displayed.

My censorship raids were actually pleasantly nostalgic. When I was a kid in the 1970s, my dad subscribed to *Playboy*, which he got, as they say, for the articles. My mom did not approve. Whenever a new *Playboy* would arrive, my mom would give me a black Magic Marker, and, while Dad was at work, we'd go to town on the latest issue. We'd scribble thick black bikinis on all of the Playmates of the Month and Girls of the Big 10. I liked this a lot. Too much. Mom eventually caught on that I was spending several minutes inspecting each photo before I censored it. So the raids ended.

And these late-2005 censorship raids are about as effective. In other words, they are completely counterproductive. Every time I spot the masking tape, I'm reminded of what lies beneath. It makes me think about sex more, not less.

Anyway, back to my job and lust. *Esquire* is a tastefully lascivious men's magazine, but lascivious nonetheless. So avoiding sexual imagery there is even more difficult than in my home. And it got worse a few days ago. My bosses decided that it'd be funny to assign me an article about a hot young actress. You know, tempt the Bible guy.

The actress I'm interviewing is named Rosario Dawson. And to be a properly prepared journalist, I have to rent her movies, which is a quandary in itself. Because from the looks of it, there's a good deal of wantonness and harlotry and coveting.

So I joined a movie rental service called CleanFlicks. A Utah-based company started by a Mormon man, CleanFlicks is the Netflix for the highly religious. It sends you sanitized Hollywood movies with the violence and sex chopped out. Also, profanity, including "the B-words, H-word when not referring to the place, D-word, S-word, F-word, etc." (The S-word and F-word I know. But the B-word? The D-word? So many options. It's like working on a dirty *New York Times* crossword puzzle.)

A week later, I get a couple of DVDs of Rosario's movies in bright yellow envelopes: *25th Hour* and *Josie and the Pussycats*. I pop them into my player. It is a confusing couple of hours. The CleanFlicks films are full of non-sequitur jump cuts and intermittent sound, like what I imagine a Voice over Internet Protocol phone call from Tanzania is like. (When I was finished with Rosario's movies, I couldn't resist ordering *Kill Bill* on CleanFlicks, because I figured it'd be about five minutes long. It actually broke the hour mark, but made no sense whatsoever.)

A couple of Rosario's movies weren't available on CleanFlicks—but they can be found on one of its competitors, ClearPlay. This is an even more sophisticated bowdlerizing service. You download the censoring filter from the internet and then plug that into a specially equipped DVD player. The beauty of ClearPlay is that you can customize which offensive material to block and which to let through. (Incidentally, Clean-Flicks has since been forced to stop cleaning flicks; a Colorado court ruled that it was violating copyright laws by slapping fig leafs on the movies. But ClearPlay is still going strong.)

I download the filter for one of Rosario's movies—Oliver Stone's *Alexander*—and it looks like I hit the sin mother lode. Take a look at what it's got:

NonSensual/NonCrude Sex Talk
Thematic Sexual Situation(s)
Homosexual/Lesbian Characters

Implied Marital Sex
Implied Premarital Sex
Implied Extramarital Sex
Revealing Clothing
Some Suggestive Dancing
Some Suggestive Dialogue
Threatening Dialogue
Intense Action/Adventure
Intense Life/Death Situations
Scary Moments
Nongraphic Injury/Wound
Intense Battle Sequences
Alcohol Consumption
Rape Topic
Intense Thematic Elements
Suicide
Murder Topic
Dysfunctional Relationships

In other words, Thursday night at Tommy Lee's house. (My friend David pointed this out; I can't make such comments myself.)

I suppose CleanFlicks and ClearPlay mean well. But they weren't so helpful. I had the same problem as I did with my masking-tape endeavor. I was so focused on what they were cutting out, I probably conjured up far more sinful things in my mind than if I had just watched the suggestive dancing and thematic sexual situation(s) all the way through.

I have made a covenant with my eyes; How then could I look upon a virgin?

—Job 31:1

Day 107. I flew out to Los Angeles yesterday and drove to the hotel. I noticed that my sense of geography has changed. I paid attention to the locations of all the churches and synagogues in the same way that I used to pay attention to pop culture landmarks (Look, that's where they filmed the mall scene in *Fast Times at Ridgemont High*)!

Today is my interview with Rosario. I arrive at our meeting place: an aggressively Californian café with organic root beer and whole wheat bagels. Rosario comes a half hour late, as is required by a secret celebrity handbook.

Things start off better than I expected. Yes, she's beautiful, with skin out of a Clinique ad, but she's wearing a bulky beige sweater and jeans. Very discreet, not overly revealing. Second, she seems unfazed by my project. This is L.A., after all, home to calf implants and Crispin Glover, so the strangeness bar is set pretty high.

And, finally, she is one of about three people thus far who claimed my topiary looked good. "I've always loved big beards," she says, adding cryptically, "When I was a kid, I wanted a beard of my own. I thought it'd be nice to stroke it."

So I am feeling good.

And then we start the interview proper. It soon becomes clear that my bosses could not have picked a worse celebrity for me to interview. She is the single most raunchy actress in Hollywood. She has absolutely no ClearPlay-like filter in her brain. Over the course of two hours, I hear about her grandmother's sex life, her sex life, her conception with a broken condom, her breasts, her mom's R-rated piercings, her ex-boyfriend's bedroom noises, and on and on.

I feel like there are three people at this interview: Rosario Dawson, my regular old secular journalist self, and my biblical alter ego.

Every time she talks about the handcuffs you can buy at the Hustler store, my alter ego Jacob winces. Meanwhile, the secular journalist does a silent little cheer. Because I know that a racy quote from a beautiful woman is men's magazine gold.

I have two heads, two sets of eyes, two moral compasses. They're battling for supremacy. Maybe one will win—or maybe I can keep both. A friend of mine said that we shouldn't underestimate people's ability to hold totally contradictory opinions and be just fine with it. It's a uniquely human trait, like speech and blushing.

Sustain me with raisins, refresh me with apples; for I am sick with love.

—Song of Solomon 2:5

Day 109. Back in New York, I go out to lunch with Robbie Harris—the rock and roll professor from the Jewish Theological Seminary. I tell him about the racy conversation. And he makes a fascinating point: Maybe my secular self and Jacob were fighting each other for no reason.

I had always assumed that the entire Bible had an antilust, proto-Victorian point of view. And parts of it—especially passages in the New Testament's letters from the Apostle Paul—do say that celibacy is the ideal.

But much of the Hebrew Bible, if you read it carefully, isn't really antisex. Robbie directed me to the Song of Solomon, which is probably the bawdiest section of the Bible. It's a collection of love songs that contain, among other things, the B-word: "Your two breasts are like two fawns, twins of a gazelle, that feed among the lilies." And later again: "Oh, may your breasts be like clusters of the vine, and the scent of your breath like apples."

The Song of Solomon has sometimes been interpreted as an allegory about humans' love for God. And that may be one aspect of it. But, says Robbie, don't forget that it's also a paean to erotic love.

"But married love, right?" I ask. That's the traditional view, that the Bible sanctions husband-wife marital relations and nothing else.

"They don't sound married to me," says Robbie. "They sound to me like young lovers hightailing it to the woods."

When I get home, I look up Song of Solomon 2:10–13, one of the passages Robbie was referring to. It says:

> My beloved speaks and says to me:
> "Arise, my love, my fair one,
> and come away;
> for lo, the winter is past,
> the rain is over and gone.
> The flowers appear on the earth,
> the time of singing has come . . .
> . . . Arise, my love, my fair one,
> and come away."

He's right. It does sound like a couple of not-necessarily-married kids off for a tryst in the wilderness. This is liberating information.

You shall not commit adultery.

—Exodus 20:14

Day 110. The Bible isn't a free-love manual, though. Not all types of sex are permitted. The Bible forbids bestiality and incest. It famously calls homosexuality an "abomination," a troubling (to put it mildly) notion that I'll talk more about later.

And, of course, it bans adultery.

But I should clarify: Adultery in the Hebrew Bible is not what modern Americans think of as adultery. It's a much narrower concept. Adultery means sex with a married woman. Married women are not allowed to sleep around. They're off-limits. Married men, on the other hand . . . well, they have more leeway—as long as the woman who is the object of their lust doesn't already belong to another Israelite man.

And I use the word *belong* on purpose. The ancient Israelite culture was passionate about some forms of social justice, but gender equality was not high on the list. Women belonged to men. You can't sleep with a married woman because it's an affront both to God and to her husband's rights. And if you sleep with a virgin, you should make sure that her father is compensated properly.

The compensation could take the form of paying off the father. Or you could take the woman off his hands and marry her.

Now here's the interesting thing: You could marry the woman even if you already have another wife. Polygamy was, if not the norm, completely accepted. The Hebrew Bible is packed with examples of polygamy. Jacob had two wives (and two concubines). King David had eight. Solomon holds the record with seven hundred wives. (Solomon's proverbs warn against adultery, which I find curious, since I can't imagine he had any time or energy for other men's wives.)

Ashkenazi Judaism officially banned multiple wives in the eleventh century, when the great French rabbi Gershom ben Judah laid down the one-spouse-only law. But you can still find a handful of Jews who want a return to the old days. As one propolygamy Jewish web page says: "Polygamy is a Jewish institution. It is practiced, albeit underground, in Israel today. If the present trend to Orthodoxy among Jews continues, we can expect open polygamy to return soon."

Christianity hasn't had much polygamy in its history, with the famous exception of early Mormonism and a handful of outlying sects of fundamentalist Christianity that got a little bump in publicity when HBO's multiple-wives drama *Big Love* debuted a couple of years ago.

One such sect is called the Christian Polygamy Movement. It is headed by an Arizona-based man named Pastor Don Milton. Most of his justification seems to lie in the fact that the great men of the Hebrew Bible had many wives. The New Testament, contrary to popular opinion, does not overturn this, he says.

Yes, the Apostle Paul did say that "each man should have his own wife and each woman her own husband" (1 Corinthians 7:2). But here's the catch: Pastor Don says the Greek word for *own* in that sentence doesn't mean "one and only." The marriage is still a sacred covenant between one man and one woman. It's just that the man can have several simultaneous covenants—sort of like a psychologist and his clients.

I call up Pastor Don and ask him, "If I'm trying to follow the Bible, and I'm interested in having a second wife, how do I convince my current wife that this is a good idea?"

Pastor Don pauses, then says, "You don't want to bring it up unless you have a prospective second wife."

"Why is that?"

"What if you tell your first wife and then never meet anyone that you wanted to be your second wife? You'll end up causing a rift in your current marriage for nothing."

In fact, Pastor Don continues, I might want to consider the preemptive strike—a strategy he's seen employed successfully over the years.

"You find a prospective wife, have a ceremony, and consummate the marriage. Then go back and tell the first wife that you have a second. There is conceivably a better chance that your first marriage will survive."

Isn't that a bit . . . sneaky and unbiblical?

"It can end up being more cruel to put a wife through a year, five years, ten years of worrying that you're going to take a second wife."

Pastor Don's tone is friendly, informal. His website has a lot of fire and brimstone, warning detractors that "You are required by it [the Bible] to confront me in person if you accuse me of sin, then with witnesses to the alleged sin (Deuteronomy 19:16), and finally before a Christian assembly worthy of wielding its authority over us." But on the phone, Pastor Don's tone is that of a married man giving his bachelor buddy some girlfriend advice.

I ask Pastor Don if I should tell the prospective second wife about the first wife. Definitely, he says. You have to. And the good part is, it might even be a turn-on.

"Some women are drawn to men who are bold enough to say they have more than one wife. It's a bad-boy thing."

I ask him if he has any other tips about making the first wife see the light.

"First, pray like you've prayed only when you're in trouble. Then bring her into Bible study."

Show her that the Bible doesn't forbid polygamy. And, in fact, the Old Testament heroes were often polygamous. "You have to get her to see that the men of the Old Testament were great men. David—he wrote the Psalms! And Solomon—he wrote the Proverbs. These are great men. Get that point across. Polygamy is not only acceptable, but it's fabulous, and these women [the wives] are holy."

In fact, says Pastor Don, the father of the human race probably had several ceremonies.

"I think Adam was the first polygamist. Here was the healthiest man in history with the healthiest sex drive ever. And he had only one wife? Come on."

Pastor Don asks me if I have a prospective second wife.

"Well, I do like our nanny," I say. Des is, indisputably, adorable—she's twenty-six and text messages me things like "gud am," which take me five minutes to figure out (that's "good morning," for all you over-thirty people out there). Julie agrees she's ideal, and has given me permission to have an affair with her, à la *Curb Your Enthusiasm*. Of course, Julie gave me the offer only because she knew there was no chance Des would ever be interested. It's like giving me permission to become a linebacker with the Miami Dolphins. Completely moot.

"What religion is she?"

"She's Catholic."

Pastor Don exhales loudly. Catholics are tough to crack, he says. On the other hand, if I ever do marry Des, I have a good line of reasoning when I tell Julie.

"You can tell her that you can stop paying the nanny. Save on the price."

At one point, Pastor Don's voice rises, and I imagine on the other end of the line, his face is red and a vein has popped up on his forehead. He is talking about the persecution against polygamists. He is furious that they would put polygamists in jail—next to criminals and homosexuals.

Yes, homosexuality. Apparently, polygamists aren't so tolerant of other types of sexual behavior.

You shall not steal.

—Exodus 20:15

Day 111. When I'm jotting down tips on how to land a second wife, it's clear that the pendulum has swung too far into the Bible's crazy territory. I need to refocus. Get back to basics. The Ten Commandments. So I'm going to delve into the Eighth again: Thou shalt not steal.

Actually, many modern biblical scholars think that the word *steal* is a mistranslation. A closer word would be *kidnap*. You should not kidnap people and force them into slavery. This would be easier to follow. I could do that for a year. But it also feels like a cop-out.

So I'm going to stick with the traditional on this one, especially since there are plenty of other "do not steal" commands in the Bible (such as Leviticus 19:11).

I informed Julie that I can no longer raid the *Esquire* supply closet for manila folders for personal use. I've also stopped with the wireless piggybacking—we've seen what that can lead to.

And today I clamp down on some attempted theft at Starbucks. We are out for a walk: Julie, Jasper, and Julie's stepdad, who looks and acts exactly like George Burns. We stop for a coffee at Starbucks, and Jasper grabs a handful of straws from the counter. He's got a straw fetish. He loves to unwrap a dozen or so at a shot, perhaps thinking that the next one will have a special surprise, maybe a Willy Wonka–like invitation to tour the straw factory.

"No, Jasper. Just one."

Starbucks doesn't have a strict straw policy. But I think there's an implicit contract—you are supposed to take one straw for every beverage.

Does Starbucks need my money? Not so much. But the Bible's command is absolute. It doesn't say "Thou shalt not steal except for small things from multinational corporations with a faux Italian name for *medium*." It says, "Thou shalt not steal." There's no such thing as "petty theft."

"Just one," I repeat.

"Let him take 'em," says Julie's stepdad.

"No, we're supposed to take only one. Otherwise it's stealing."

"Let him take a few. It's not stealing."

"What if I took five thousand straws in a Starbucks every day?" I say. "Would that be stealing?"

"Well, there's got to be a relative—"

"Why? Why should it be relative?"

"Well, look," says Julie's stepdad. "One murder is OK. But fifty murders isn't OK."

I'm stopped short.

"Got you there, huh?" he says.

I'm not sure how to answer a man who has stolen my argument.

Jasper screams and grunts and points for about forty-five seconds. I stand my ground; I've got to ratchet up that justice-to-mercy ratio. Finally, I give him a napkin to rip up, which calms him down.

I could have rationalized the straws. That's one thing I've noticed this year. I can rationalize almost anything. For instance, I could take the utilitarian approach: The amount of pleasure it gives Jasper outweighs the couple of cents it'll cost Starbucks. Or I could argue to myself that, in the end, it helps out the struggling straw industry.

Same with when I stole the internet connection in my apartment building; I could have rationalized it by saying that I was using the internet to learn about God and make myself a better person.

I have a tendency toward ends-justify-the-means thinking. But this year isn't about that. It's about following the rules. Strictly. To the letter. And seeing what happens.

I know of only one other person who follows the "no stealing" commandment to the letter. My dad. Whenever we're on a road trip, he refuses to pull over at any old Holiday Inn or McDonald's to use the bathroom. Not unless we buy something. Otherwise, he says, we'd be stealing their soap and paper towels. So I feel like I'm honoring my father here as well.

> *She quickly let down her jar from her shoulder, and said,*
> *"Drink, and I will give your camels drink also."*
>
> —Genesis 24:46

Day 114. Mr. Berkowitz, the man who inspected my wardrobe for mixed fibers, is still calling. He wants to meet up and pray with me, but I've been busy with my own biblical duties and my own prayers, so I've been dodging his calls.

This morning, he leaves me a message at eight-thirty.

"Hello, Arnold," he says. (He calls me by my real name, Arnold; I must have told him about it once, and it somehow stuck.) "It's Bill Berkowitz. It's very important that you call me back."

I get nervous. Very important? That sounds bad. Maybe he's got a kidney stone and needs help getting to Mount Sinai Hospital. I phone him—it turns out he's going to be in my neighborhood and wants to pray with me at my apartment. Well, how can I refuse a house call?

Mr. Berkowitz arrives a couple of hours later, and he's as disheveled and kindly as ever. He comes bearing gifts: books and candles for the Sabbath.

"Can I get you anything?"

"A cup of water, please," he says. "Oh, and it has to be bottled water, please."

Oh, yes. I'd heard of this. A few rabbis in Brooklyn had made a controversial ruling declaring New York City tap water nonkosher. They said it contained tiny multicellular organisms that could qualify as forbidden crustaceans. Which is why, if you want to make a lot of money, you should open a Poland Spring concession in Crown Heights.

I look in the fridge. We have bottles of Dasani, but Julie refills them from the faucet. Tap water in Dasani clothing.

"Can I offer you anything else?" I ask. "Maybe juice? Soda?"

"No. Water."

Here I face a dilemma. The poor guy has schlepped several miles from Washington Heights in a thick black coat and black hat. No doubt he's parched. And the Bible tells me to ease my fellow man's suffering.

So I decide: What he doesn't know won't hurt him. And lots of rabbis say the tap water is fine to drink. Everyone will be happier.

I pour him a cup from the bottle.

"Thanks," says Mr. Berkowitz, as he lifts the cup to his lips, then puts it down to tell me something about the Sabbath. I'm not sure what he said. I'm too busy staring at that cup. He does it again, like the clueless husband in a forties *noir* film who keeps almost—but not quite— sipping the poisoned milk.

Finally, before he can actually drink, I lunge.

"You know what? I think this may be refilled with tap water."

Mr. Berkowitz is grateful. He puts the cup on the table gingerly, like it's filled with hydrochloric acid.

I just couldn't do it. What if, on the off-chance, Mr. Berkowitz is right? What if the water would have tainted his soul? I couldn't take the risk, even if his body will suffer.

> *So Abraham rose early in the morning, saddled his ass,*
> *and took two of his young men with him, and his son Isaac.*
>
> —Genesis 22:3

Mr. Berkowitz says it'd be good for me to get a minute-by-minute guide to the properly devout day. So he starts at the beginning: I should wake up early, just like Abraham woke up early on the day he was to sacrifice Isaac.

"Abraham didn't say, 'Hey, God, it's five o'clock in the morning. You sure you want me to get up so early?' Abraham got up early."

After that, there are many rituals to be done: You must wash impurities off your hands. Recite several prayers. Bind the commandments to your hand and forehead. Go to the synagogue to worship. Mr. Berkowitz tells me he loves going to synagogue; it's not an obligation, it's a gift. I'm jealous; I want that kind of hunger for spirituality.

He hates being late to prayer, so he lays out all of his religious gear the night before: his prayer shawl, his fringes, and so forth.

"It's like a fireman," he says. "The fireman has his hat, jacket, and boots on a peg, so when there's a fire, he doesn't have to think. Everything is set up."

He once again stresses the importance of being punctual to services.

"If it means I have to run with my shoelaces untied, then I will."

Mr. Berkowitz pauses, then decides he's gone too far.

"Well, I don't do that. That's an exaggeration. But I like to be on time. I don't want to run like a madman. I walk briskly."

Speaking of shoes, Mr. Berkowitz tells me that you don't just put them on any old way. There's a proper procedure. You put on your right shoe. Then your left shoe. Then you tie your left shoe. Then you go back and tie your right shoe.

Why that order? Mr. Berkowitz doesn't know.

"That's what the rabbis tell us to do. I don't have to think about it. It saves me a lot of thinking. It allows me to concentrate on more important things."

If this were on TiVo, I would have rewound it to make sure he said what I think he said. How much thinking could that possibly save? Do I really waste a lot of brainpower deciding the order in which I should slip on my Rockports? It seems like some serious religious micromanagement. I didn't want to say this to the sweet and no-doubt-thirsty Mr. Berkowitz, who was on to the next topic, but at the time, I thought: "crazy."

In retrospect, though, I'm starting to think that maybe it's not completely insane. My dad always talked about how his hero Albert Einstein owned seven identical suits, so that he wouldn't waste any neuronal activity on choosing what to wear. Similar idea.

In fact, it's part of a bigger theme I've been mulling over: freedom *from* choice. I'd always been taught to fetishize freedom of choice. It's the American way. It's why I went to Brown University, where they don't have any requirements, and you can go through all four years writing papers about the importance of Christian Slater's oeuvre.

But more and more I'm starting to see the beauty in a more rigid framework. The structure, the stable architecture of religion.

My brother-in-law Eric—now getting his doctorate in psychology—likes to lecture me about an experiment at a grocery store by researchers from Columbia and Stanford. They set up two tables offering free tastes; one table had six flavors of jam, the other had twenty-four flavors of jam. Oddly, more people bought jams from the table with six flavors. Nearly ten times more people, in fact. The conclusion was that the big table was just too overwhelming, too many options.

The Bible takes away a lot of those jam jars. What should I do on Friday night? Stay at home with the family. Should I waste my time reading about Cameron Diaz's love life? No. Should I give to the homeless guy on 77th? Yes. Should I be stricter with Jasper? Yes. There's something relieving and paradoxically liberating about surrendering yourself to a minimal-choice lifestyle, especially as our choices multiply like cable channels.

I recently heard a rabbi give a talk on Moses, and how, in a weird sense, he was a slave even after his release from bondage. He was a slave to goodness. He had no choice but to do the right thing.

There's a Jewish book that restricts choice even more—far more—than the Bible itself. It's a massive work from the sixteenth century called the *Set Table*—or *Shulchan Aruch* in Hebrew. It's an amazing book; it gives practical instruction on everything you can think of: eating, sleeping, praying, bathing, sex. Some Orthodox Jews follow a lot of the *Set Table*'s guidelines, but it'd be darn near impossible to follow every directive. There are thousands of them. One stipulates that when going to the bathroom outside, you should face north or south but not east or west.

Most of the *Set Table*'s rules are postbiblical. The Scriptures don't get into shoe-donning procedures per se. But the Bible still has plenty of laws to keep me busy—some that I like (the Sabbath) and some I don't (monthly wife avoidance). The key question seems to be: How do you choose which choice-restricting rules to follow in the first place? I don't know. It's like an M. C. Escher drawing. It hurts my brain.

Mr. Berkowitz, by the way, finished his lesson and the prayers, and left about an hour later. As he said goodbye, he reminded me to prepare for Sabbath by reciting a little ditty:

A Shabbos well spent
Brings a week of content.

I agree with the sentiment, if not the grammar.

I the Lord your God am a jealous God, visiting the iniquity of the fathers upon the children to the third and the fourth generation of those who hate me.

—Deuteronomy 5:9

Day 117. My son, Jasper, has finally improved his vocabulary, but not in the way I was hoping. And I'm the one to blame.

Perhaps I can explain what happened via a quick biblical story: In Genesis 12, Abraham traveled to Egypt with his beautiful wife, Sarah, to escape a famine. Sarah was so stunning, Abraham feared that the Egyptians would kill him and steal Sarah for themselves. So Abraham lied. He said that Sarah was his sister. Abraham took the deception so far that the Pharaoh, thinking Sarah was single, married her. And when the Pharaoh found out that he'd been deceived, he was—somewhat justifiably, I think—furious, and ejected Abraham from the land.

Abraham and Sarah eventually conceived a son named Isaac. When he's grown, Isaac and his wife Rebecca moved to the land of the Philistines to avoid a famine. And what does Isaac do? He pretends Rebecca is his sister. He doesn't want the Philistines to kill him and steal Rebecca.

This is a big recurring theme in the Bible: Children mimic their parents' behavior, even the flaws, perhaps especially the flaws. (One other example: Rebecca played favorites with her son Jacob; Jacob played favorites with his son Joseph.)

I've always known that parents influence their kids. It's not an obscure concept. But it didn't sink in on a gut level until I saw Jasper aping our words and deeds.

I first noticed it when he adopted one of Julie's more endearing habits. After Julie takes a sip of a drink, she'll often let out a satisfied "Ahhh," like she's secretly taping a Sprite commercial. Now Jasper is doing it. He'll polish off his watered-down apple juice, plunk the sippy cup on the table, and exhale noisily.

But with me, it's taken a darker turn. A few days ago, Jasper's Elmo plate slipped out of my grasp, scattering cubes of cantaloupe all over the kitchen. I shouted a four-letter word that is a synonym for the biblical verb "to know." (I'd type it here, but I think that'd be breaking the rules again.) Apparently Jasper was paying close attention. He has now decided this is a great word. It has replaced the perfectly acceptable "uh-oh" as the go-to exclamation.

When I've seen kids cursing on TV or in the movies, it's kind of adorable. When my two-year-old niece said the S-word? I chuckled. But when my own kid squeaks out swear words in his high-pitched voice, it's not funny at all. I immediately picture him fifteen years down the road with a syringe sticking out of his arm sprawled on the floor of some train station bathroom.

In Deuteronomy 5:9 the Bible says "I the Lord your God am a jealous God, visiting the iniquity of the fathers upon the children to the third and the fourth generation of those who hate me." I used to find this an appalling sentence. Why should God punish my grandson for my sins? It seemed outrageously un-American. What about everyone being entitled to a clean moral slate? And, yes, if you interpret this as a threat that God will smite your child with leprosy when you worship a carved idol, then absolutely, it's cruel.

But I've come to appreciate it. The trick is, you have to see the passage as a warning that your moral failings will affect your kids' ability to make the right choices. If you beat your son, he'll be more likely to beat his son. If you get angry at cantaloupe-related mishaps, your son will too. What better deterrent could there be to bad behavior?

It had even more resonance in biblical times. As Jack Miles points out in his excellent book *God: A Biography,* ancient Israelites didn't have the clearly formed concept of immortality of the soul, as we do now. You achieved immortality through your children and children's children, who were physical extensions of you. The basic building block of society was the family, not the individual.

With no afterlife, God dispensed justice to a family—a person's actions reverberate through his descendants' lives. The most extreme example: When Adam and Eve disobeyed God and ate the fruit of knowledge, the family of humanity has been paying ever since.

I can't say why for sure—maybe the Bible has seeped into my brain, maybe there's an inevitable mental shift that accompanies parenthood—but I've edged away from extreme individualism. My worldview is more interconnected, more tribal.

Ask now, and see, can a man bear a child?

—JEREMIAH 30:6

Day 120. On this brisk December morning, Julie and I trek to the fertility clinic on the East Side. They've been steeping two of Julie's eggs in a test tube for five days. The doctors are implanting both, in the hope that one will stick.

Man, does it feel unnatural. Surgical caps, antibacterial lotion, gurneys, charts. This is about as far from Adam and Eve as you can get.

They wheel Julie out a few minutes later. And it is done. She is, God willing, pregnant. For reasons I still don't understand, Julie has to lie in a hospital bed with a full bladder for about a half hour.

"Distract me, please!" says Julie. "Talk about anything."

I start in on a biblical story about Tamar.

"Anything but that."

OK. But it's a good story, a relevant story—and a profoundly strange story. Julie, feel free to skip this section, but here goes:

Tamar's tale is found in the Book of Genesis. Tamar was married to a man named Er, son of Judah. Er died before they could have kids. There was a custom in biblical times—as bizarre as it sounds now—that a widow who has no children stays within the family: She must marry the brother of her dead husband. It's called "levirate marriage." So Tamar married Er's younger brother, Onan. Onan, too, died. Tamar was understandably distraught. Two husbands, two deaths. But her father-in-law, Judah, told Tamar not to worry—she could marry his youngest son, Shelah. But Judah failed to follow through. Tamar was left without a husband.

Tamar was desperate to get pregnant. So she came up with a plan: She put on a veil, disguised herself as a prostitute, and intercepted her father-in-law, Judah, as he was on his way to shear his sheep. The unsuspecting Judah slept with Tamar, and then gave her his staff and personal seal as a IOU for payment. The plan worked. She got pregnant.

Judah, unaware he had been duped, found out that his widowed daughter-in-law was with child and accused her of loose morals. He wanted her burned to death. So Tamar showed him his staff and personal seal. Now he understood. *He* was the father of her child. He backed down and repented. Tamar had twin sons by Judah. They were named Zerah and Perez. And here's an interesting twist: Perez eventually became the ancestor of that remarkable leader of ancient Israel, King David.

When I first read this, it was too outlandish to have any meaning for me. A woman having sex with her father-in-law? In a prostitute disguise? But after rereading it four times, I've wrung a powerful moral out of it. And that is this: Even great things can be born from ethically murky origins. Even an illicit, deceit-filled union can lead to someone like King David.

So . . . perhaps in vitro fertilization is the same. It's ethically complicated, but maybe our child will be great. Or maybe I'm justifying like crazy here.

In the end, I do end up distracting Julie by finding some common ground. We play a name-a-movie-with-a-biblical-title game.

I will never forget thy precepts, for by them thou hast given me life.
—Psalms 119:93

Day 122. It's New Year's Eve, and Julie and I pull our rental car into the driveway of our friends' house in New Jersey. We'll be staying there for a three-day weekend.

After hellos and avoided hugs, I lug our suitcase upstairs to the guest room, heave it onto the bed, unzip it—and immediately realize my mistake. I forgot to bring my ram's horn. It's back in my closet in New York. Damn. I won't be able to blow a horn on January 1, the start of the new month.

I try to argue with myself that, well, January 1 isn't the Hebrew calendar, so maybe it's not really a new biblical month. Doesn't help. I feel surprisingly anxious and off-kilter, like I'm back in high school and forgot to study for a big physics exam. I take it out on Julie by picking a fight with her about the volume of Jasper's baby monitor.

The truth is, I've begun to get really rigorous with my rituals. I hate missing my daily routine—the praying, the binding, more praying, the tassels, the white clothes, the praying again. Why? Perhaps because these rituals dovetail beautifully with my obsessive-compulsive disorder.

Thanks to my OCD, I'm prone to weird little rituals, like touching the shower head four times after turning off the faucet. Or opening my jaw into a yawnlike position whenever I look in the mirror. Or making sure never to start a conversation with the word *you* because when I was eleven I saw an *Eight Is Enough* episode in which an estranged father's first words to his son were "You doing all right?" and the relationship went sour after that—probably not because the father started his sentence with "you," but you never know.

I've been doing my own rituals less and less frequently, as the Bible rituals take over more and more of my time. And why not? People have been doing these Bible rituals for thousands of years. They're time tested. Why should I try to invent my own ceremonies, when my heritage provides me with a book full of them? Mr. Berkowitz doesn't waste his days concocting his own rituals; he takes them off the rack.

At least in this way, I'm preprogrammed for biblical living. Religion—especially ritual-heavy religions like Judaism and High-Church Christianity—have three key OCD traits. First, the repetition (every day the same prayers, every week the same candle-lightings). Second, the fascination with taxonomy—everything in its proper category: good or evil, holy or profane. And third, especially in Judaism, the fixation on purity and impurity (the equivalent of my constant hand washing). I'm drawn to all three.

Of course, I'm not the first to make this connection. Sigmund Freud, a Jew who, as a child, regularly attended Catholic mass with his Czech nanny, believed that religion was the "universal obsessional neurosis of humanity."

If so, I think it can be a healthy neurosis. I'm more open to the *chu-*

kim nowadays: those inexplicable commandments such as keeping apart wool and linen. Without realizing it, I had been practicing my own self-generated chukim for years. How long had I wasted turning on and off the radio because I needed the final word to be a noun? Compared to my radio ritual, strapping commandments to my forehead looks positively rational. Instead of compulsively repeating the list of my freshman year classes—French, math, biology, and so on (don't ask)—I compulsively repeat certain passages from the Bible that I am mandated to remember. Like, that God gave us the commandments. And that God brought us out of Israel. And gave us the Sabbath. And that God instructed us to blow a horn at the start of every month.

Month Five: January

*Do not pay attention to every word people say, or you may hear
your servant cursing you—for you know in your heart that many
times you yourself have cursed others.*
—ECCLESIASTES 7:21–22 (NIV)

Day 124. January 2. We're back in New York. I'm not supposed to
make New Year's resolutions—probably a pagan ritual—but if I did,
here's what mine would be: I have to start thickening my skin. It's
right there in the Ecclesiastes: Don't pay attention to everything everyone says about you; you know you've talked trash about other people, too.

Today I was reading the Amazon.com reviews for my encyclopedia
book (I know, not biblical), and I ran across one that was very strange.
The reviewer said she looked at my author photo and discovered that
I'm not really that ugly. In fact, I'm kind of "normal looking." Which I
guess is sort of flattering. Normal looking.

But she didn't mean it as flattery. She said that I'm normal-looking
enough that I have no excuse to be socially awkward, neurotic, or beset
with an inferiority complex. So I should shut my normal-looking trap
and stop complaining. This is the most backhanded compliment I've
ever received. It sank me into a bad mood for three hours. The Bible is
right: I have to toughen up.

And I must, absolutely must, stop self-Googling. It's a horrible habit
that I still haven't kicked in my biblical year. I found one blogger in Sin-
gapore who got my book for a birthday present, though he seemed more
excited about another present, a T-shirt that read, "I'm Looking for
Treasure. Can I See Your Chest?" I've done image searches on myself,
and found an outtake from an appearance on C-Span's Book TV where

the website froze on a particularly unflattering moment that makes me resemble Sean Penn in *I Am Sam*.

This is all very unrighteous, very vain. I should think instead of the well-being of my family and my neighbors—and on God.

I should be more like Noah. It took Noah decades to build his ark. Can you imagine the mockery he must have received from doubting neighbors? If Noah were alive today, he wouldn't be wasting his time checking out what blogs said about him. He'd be down at Home Depot buying more lumber. Starting today, I'm going to be like Noah. Toughen up.

You shall teach them diligently to your children.

—Deuteronomy 6:7

Day 126. There's one upside to my son not talking a lot: I don't have to figure out what to tell him about God yet. Because I have no idea what to say.

The subject came up at dinner tonight with our friends Jessica and Peter, up from Washington, D.C., for a visit. Here's how Jessica answered the question when their daughter asked her about God.

"I told her God is in the wind, in the trees, He's in the rocks, He's everywhere."

Her husband Peter looks dismayed.

"Well, maybe not everywhere," says Peter.

"Yes, everywhere," says Jessica.

"God's in that cement mixer?"

"Yes," she says.

"In the forklift?"

"Yes, why not?" says Jessica.

Peter shakes his head. "You've got to draw the line somewhere."

But I know what Jessica is saying. In the past couple of weeks, I've taken not quite a leap of faith, but a cautious baby step of faith. I'm not sure why. I think it's that the three-times-a-day prayers are working their mojo.

The point is, I don't see the world as a collection of soulless quarks and neutrinos. At times—not all the time, but sometimes—the entire world takes on a glow of sacredness, like someone has flipped on a unfathomably huge halogen lamp and made the universe softer, fuller, less menacing.

I spend a lot of time marveling. I haven't stared at a forklift yet, but I'll marvel at the way rain serpentines down a car window. Or I'll marvel at the way my reflection is distorted in a bowl. I feel like I just took my first bong hit. I feel like Wes Bentley rhapsodizing about that dancing plastic bag in *American Beauty*.

I've noticed that I sometimes walk around with a lighter step, almost an ice-skating-like glide, because the ground feels hallowed. All of the ground, even the ground outside the pizzeria near my apartment building.

All well and good, right? The only thing is, this is not the God of the Israelites. This is not the God of the Hebrew Scriptures. That God is an interactive God. He rewards people and punishes them. He argues with them, negotiates with them, forgives them, occasionally smites them. The God of the Hebrew Scriptures has human emotions—love and anger.

My God doesn't. My God is impersonal. My God is the God of Spinoza. Or the God of Paul Tillich, the Protestant theologian who believed that God was "the ground of being." Or the God of the Jedi knights. It's a powerful but vague all-pervasive force; some slightly more sophisticated version of pantheism. I don't even know if my God can be said to have a grand plan, much less mood swings. Can I keep edging toward the true biblical God? I'm not sure.

And the Lord said to me, "Arise, go on your journey . . ."
—Deuteronomy 10:11

Day 127. Before I buy my tickets to Israel, I want to make sure my ex-uncle Gil will be there. I get his phone number from an Orthodox friend of mine in Israel, which was surprisingly easy. And I call.

My plan is to make it a stealth mission. I won't reveal that I'm his former nephew. That's not lying, right? That's just omission of information. If he doesn't know I'm an ex-relative, he can't think that I'm giving him tacit approval, the family's big fear.

I dial the fourteen digits. The phone rings.

My heart is thumping. I haven't been this nervous since I called Julie for our first date.

"Hello?"

I don't know what I expected—a booming voice speaking Aramaic?—but his pitch was a regular old midrange American.

"Is Gil there?"

"Speaking."

"Yes, well, I'm a writer, and I'm writing a book about trying to live by the Bible, and I'm coming to Israel, and—"

"What's your name?"

Part of me was hoping I could just be known as "the Writer." So what do I do now? Should I give him a fake name? That would be lying. Well, maybe he won't know my name. I've never met him, and I have a different last name from his ex-wife.

"My name is A. J. Jacobs"

"Oh! You're related to my daughters."

Well, there goes that theory. We set a date for me to come to his house for dinner. I'm tense enough about breaking the family taboo that it takes me three hours to go to sleep.

You shall write them on the doorposts of your house . . .

—Deuteronomy 6:9

Day 128. I've devoted a lot of time both to my physical appearance and my soul. But I feel I haven't sufficiently Bibli-fied my house. The only thing I've done is to strip our apartment of those images that verge on idolatry, even if it's of the celebrity kind: the poster of Ray Charles at the Monterey Jazz Festival, the half-dozen photos of Julie standing next to celebrities she accosted at events or on the street. (Julie with a reluctant Willem Dafoe, Julie with a skeptical Tupac Shakur, et cetera.)

So today, as instructed in Deuteronomy, I'm going to write a section of the Bible on our doorpost. I tell Julie, who has two stern commandments of her own.

1. Do not, under any circumstances, let Jasper see you write on the doorpost. We've been battling his tendency toward crayon abuse. This would not help.

2. Please, please do it in pencil. "I don't want to get a call from the co-op board about this. I don't want to have to pay for a painter."

I promise.

At the end of the Israelites' forty-year journey in the desert, Moses commanded them to write God's words on their doorposts and their gates. It's the origin of the mezuzah—the diagonally positioned box that we (and most other Jews) have nailed at the entrance to our homes.

The tradition has been to delegate the writing of the mezuzah to an officially sanctioned scribe. It all comes prepackaged. But the Bible's literal wording—and presumably what some Israelites did back in ancient times—says that we should write on our door frames ourselves.

But what to write? Moses says "these words which I command you." I briefly considered trying to squeeze in hundreds of commandments in tiny font but settled on the famous ten—they appear in the Bible right before the doorpost passage. (Incidentally, traditional mezuzahs instead have a scroll that contains famous prayer known as the *Shema:* "Hear, O Israel! The Lord is our God. The Lord is One!")

I get out my No. 2 Officemate pencil, make sure that Jasper is safely distracted by Legos, prop open the front door, and start slowly, very slowly, writing God's words on the avocado-colored door frame. It takes an hour. All the while I am inhaling the mysterious odor that always wafts from apartment 5R (I think they have an illegal albacore cannery in there), taking a break between every commandment to shake out my wrist and elbow, and being vigilant not to make a stray loop or spike.

At first I feel absurd, like a biblical version of Bart Simpson at the chalkboard. Absurd and nervous—am I committing an egregious sin by ignoring the centuries-old tradition? Orthodox Jews might say so. Probably would say so. There are an astounding 4,649 instructions that go into creating a certified mezuzah. You must write with a quill taken from a kosher bird, like a goose or a turkey. The scroll must have twenty-two lines. And on and on. By comparison, I am winging it.

But after a half hour, I sink into a quasitrance. I haven't done any monklike copying by hand in years—not since the invention of digital cut and paste, anyway. But there's something to it. You are forced to linger over every letter, every cadence. You absorb the text. It's the difference between walking to town and taking the bus—you can't help but notice the scenery.

I notice the minimalist beauty of commandments six, seven, and eight:

You shall not kill.
You shall not commit adultery.
You shall not steal.

And I notice the syncopated rhythm of the list of people banned from working on the Sabbath: "You, or your son, or your daughter, your manservant, or your maidservant, or your cattle, or the sojourner who is within your gates."

I think about how every word that I am writing has launched a thousand debates. Even something as straightforward as: You shall not kill.

This is widely regarded as a mistranslation. The Old Testament features plenty of God-sanctioned killing—from capital punishment of blasphemers to the annihilation of enemies. The actual commandment is more like: You shall not murder.

Nothing is free from dispute, even the number ten. Depending on how you parse the language, you could argue that it's actually the Thirteen Commandments. "You shall not make for yourself a graven image" is one commandment. "You shall not bow down to them" is another. But those two are generally lumped together.

They are deceptively simple, those Ten Commandments.

Do not go around as a gossiper among your people . . .
—Leviticus 19:16

Day 131. I keep thinking back to Amos, the harmonica-playing Amish man, and how he answered most questions with a monosyllable or a nod. And that's if you were lucky. Sometimes he just stared over your shoulder until the silence got so unbearable that you asked another question.

I'm no Amos, but I feel myself drifting in his direction. Guard your tongue, I tell myself. Ration those words. Just nod your head and smile and don't get provoked when they say "Hey, chatterbox, over there!" as my coworkers did at a recent *Esquire* dinner at an Italian restaurant.

I feel I have to clam up. It's the best way to battle the overwhelming urge to spew biblically banned negative language. The pastor out to pasture, Elton Richards, gave me a good metaphor on this topic: think of negative speech as verbal pollution. And that's what I've been doing: visualizing insults and gossip as a dark cloud, maybe one with some sulfur dioxide. Once you've belched it out, you can't take it back. As grandma said, if you don't have anything nice to say, don't say anything at all.

The interesting thing is, the less often I vocalize my negative thoughts, the fewer negative thoughts I cook up in the first place. My theory is, my thoughts are lazy. They say to themselves, "Well, we'll never make it out into the world, so why even bother?" It's more powerful than repression. The thoughts don't even form enough to require being repressed.

Yes, the sales guy at the biblical bookstore sold me a hardcover copy of *What Would Jesus Eat?* when, as I found out today, there's a paperback version that costs ten dollars less. But I refuse to complain about him to Julie. Maybe he didn't know, or maybe he thought I'd prefer a good durable cover for posterity. I refuse to let that toxic cloud gather in my brain. It's a purifying feeling, the verbal equivalent of wearing white clothes.

Tonight, over dinner with Julie, I was in fine no-negative-speech form. My wife's job is all about creating fun; she works for a company that organizes scavenger hunts—they do corporate events, public events, bar mitzvahs—but apparently her day had not been fun at all.

She had this client who insisted on doing an outdoor event. Julie told her that it would be much better to do the scavenger hunt indoors this time of year, but the client said no. And, of course, the day turned out to be ear-numbingly cold. And now the client is freaking out and demand-ing a refund.

"She is such a pain in the ass," says Julie.

I don't know this woman. Technically, I shouldn't say harmful speech about her.

"It's a difficult situation."

"I told her three times to do the hunt indoors, and she refused to lis-ten," says Julie.

"Maybe next time will be better."

"I hope to God there won't be a next time."

"Sounds like she has some pluses and minuses, just like everyone."

"What?"

"Everyone has their good and bad sides."

"What does that mean? 'Everyone has their good and bad sides.'"

"Well, it sounds like there was an unfortunate lack of communica-tion."

"There was no freakin' lack of communication. I told her to do it, and she ignored me."

Julie paused.

"Why aren't you supporting me?"

"I am. But I don't want to say anything negative. It's gossip. *Lashon hara.*"

"Well, you sound like a creepy child psychologist."

I'm jolted. But she's right. I do sound ridiculous. I faced one of the many cases in which two biblical commandments butted heads: The com-mandment to refrain from gossip and the commandment to treat my wife as I would have her treat me. I chose the wrong one. I should have broken the ban against negative speech. Even absolutism must have exceptions.

> *I will multiply your descendants as the stars of heaven and*
> *as the sand which is on the seashore.*
>
> —Genesis 22:17

Day 132. It's been twelve days since our visit to the clinic, and Julie and I just got the call from the nurse. She should have some news. Julie takes the call on the black cordless in our living room.

"Uh-huh. Uh-huh."

Julie smiles. Gives me the thumbs-up.

She's pregnant! Yes!

She gives another thumbs-up, this time with an overly clenched smile.

"OK. Yeah. Thanks."

Julie clicks off the phone. She's not just pregnant—she's *really* pregnant. Her hormone levels show that she's probably carrying twins. The doctor put in two fertilized eggs, and they both appear to have stuck.

Huh. Twins.

I knew there was a higher chance of twins with IVF, but still. That's hard to process. I always felt ambivalent about taking the "be fruitful and multiply" commandment too far. The world is in the midst of a scary Malthusian population boom—I had figured that two kids would be about right for me.

Julie and I sit on the couch together, stunned silent for a minute.

"Two-for-one deal," she says flatly. "Double the fun."

I guess compared to biblical families—Jacob had thirteen kids, David had at least fifteen—three isn't too bad. Be thankful, I remind myself. Be thankful.

Offer to God a sacrifice of thanksgiving, And pay your vows to the Most High.

—PSALMS 50:14

Day 133. Twins are, to use religious language, a mixed blessing. But they are a blessing nonetheless.

Two kids. It's no doubt the biggest news I've gotten all year, and I decide that I need to express my gratitude somehow. I need to do more than just clasp my hands and utter thanks with my lips. If I really want to be biblical, I should sacrifice something.

So today in Union Square, I put some olives and dates on a platform of stones and left them there as an offering to God. I said a prayer and walked away. I don't know what I was hoping for—a vision, a pillar of fire—but whatever it was, I didn't get it. Instead I felt like I'd just spent $15.46 at the grocery store contributing to New York's rat problem.

It was a letdown, especially after my previous experience with sacrifice. That one was profound, enlightening, and deeply disturbing.

Let me rewind a few months.

When I first read the Bible, it became clear that sacrifice isn't a weird footnote in the Hebrew Scriptures—it's central to it. The biblical rules for sacrifice go on for pages and are staggeringly complex. I've since read them dozens of times and still don't have a handle on them.

I have, however, figured out three things:

1. Animal sacrifice is preferable to other types of sacrifice, including fruit, grain, and incense sacrifices, which are seen as B-level offerings.

2. The ancient Israelites sacrificed an impressively wide range of species: oxen, she-goats, he-goats, turtledoves, rams, lambs, and so on.

3. They sacrificed often, very often. Sins, death, birth, holidays—all required sacrifices at the Temple. After reading the sacrifice section of the Bible, you start to wonder how there was any time left to reap or sow or beget or anything else ancient Israelites had to do.

Luckily for me—and more luckily for the animals—practically no Bible followers sacrifice animals anymore. Sacrifices were allowed only at the Temple in Jerusalem, and the Romans destroyed the Second Temple in 70 C.E. So maybe that's my loophole. Perfectly understandable.

And yet, animal sacrifice is such a huge part of the Bible, I feel I have to experience it somehow. Which won't be easy. Being a city boy, I've never killed anything larger than a water bug.

Over lunch one day, my adviser, the history teacher Eddy Portnoy, told me that there is still one ritual that borders on animal sacrifice. The ritual is called *kaparot,* and it's practiced by some ultra-Orthodox Jews once a year—on the night before Yom Kippur. The idea is that you buy a live chicken, hold it over your head, say a blessing, and have the bird slaughtered in front of you. The chicken is then donated to the poor.

Kaparot is not in the Bible. The earliest mentions of the ritual are in ninth-century literature from what is now Iraq. But it's the closest thing I'll find to legal sacrifice in the tristate area, so on a drizzly night back in October, I hop the subway to Crown Heights, Brooklyn.

I know I am getting close by the smell. As I walk from the subway station, the smell segues from the traditional New York City garbage-and-car-exhaust odor to a startling Arkansas-poultry-farm odor.

I arrive a few blocks later. I'll say this: There wasn't much of a chance I'd walk by without noticing. Hundreds of Orthodox Jews mill around in their black hats and long black coats and prayer books, all soggy from the light drizzle.

The black hats are outnumbered only by chickens. Chickens in cages, chickens on the street, chickens tucked under arms. It could be a Lithuanian town in 1805—minus the ever-present cell phones and digital cameras.

My guide is Rabbi Epstein, a round-faced Hasid originally from Tennessee. We meet on a predetermined corner.

We start by talking about our beards—common ground.

"Do you do any trimming?" I ask.

"No trimming allowed," Epstein says.

"But you can try to clean it up a bit," says his friend, another rabbi. With that, the other rabbi grabs his beard and does a quick roll-and-tuck-under-the-chin. Real sleight of hand, Ricky Jay stuff. But it makes his beard a half foot shorter.

The atmosphere is oddly festive, like a Jewish Mardi Gras. We have to talk loudly to be heard over the clucking and squawking and flapping. And just in case the scene needed to be more surreal, Rabbi Epstein has a noticeable Southern accent, so his Hebrew words are filtered through a Garth Brooks twang.

I ask about the sacrifice part of the ritual.

"Kaparot is definitely not a sacrifice," says Epstein kindly but firmly. "You can only sacrifice at the Temple, and the Temple does not exist anymore."

"How is it different?"

"The chicken does not die for our sins. It reminds us what could or should be happening to us because we are sinners."

"But isn't it in the same ballpark as the original scapegoat?" I ask.

I was referring to an ancient biblical ritual in which, on Yom Kippur, the Israelites transferred their sins to a goat and ran it over a cliff. It's the origin of the word *scapegoat*.

"Maybe," he says reluctantly. "But it's very different. The sins aren't in the chicken. It's to arouse within us the knowledge that 'there but for the grace of God go I.'"

I try to keep an open mind, but I am having trouble.

"I've gotta tell you," I say. "I feel bad for these chickens."

Epstein shakes his head. "No, it's kosher slaughter. These butchers use the sharpest knives. It's like a paper cut. You know how paper cuts don't hurt for a while after you get them? This doesn't hurt."

The crowd is thick. Kids with boxes ask for donations for charity. Friends snap photos of one another holding up fluttering chickens. We bump into Rabbi Shmuley Boteach—he's the third most famous Orthodox Jew, right after Joe Lieberman and reggae rocker Matisyahu. Boteach wrote the book *Kosher Sex* and, for a brief moment, was Michael Jackson's spiritual adviser. Boteach has a Treo clipped to his belt, a show in development on The Learning Channel (which has since aired), and is alarmingly media savvy.

"We've had documentary crews here before. And if you show this alone, out of context, it seems barbaric and irrational."

Rabbi Boteach is right. I know I'll be committing the same sin. Since I can't devote my entire book to explaining ultra-Orthodox rituals, kaparot will, by necessity, seem out of context.

"Is it any more irrational than a lot of things in our culture?" he asks. "Is it more irrational than Botox? Or more irrational than transubstantiation?"

Again, maybe he's got a point: In my admittedly brief encounters with the Hasidim, I've found them to be a lot more reasonable than I imagined. The ones I've met have been, for the most part, bright and friendly. And they have a fascinating self-awareness. Early on, Rabbi Epstein told me he took his kids to Colonial Williamsburg. One of his kids asked him, "Do people still live like this?"

And Rabbi Epstein told him, "No one lives like they did in the eighteenth century. Well, except for in Crown Heights."

So they aren't wackjobs. Well, let me qualify that. Most of them aren't wackjobs. There are exceptions.

Case in point: the short Hasidic Jew wandering among the chickens with a sandwich board over his black coat. The sandwich board has a huge photo of Rabbi Menachem Mendel Schneerson, the leader of the Lubavitchers, the huge Brooklyn-based Hasidic movement.

"The rebbe is coming soon!" he says with an Israeli accent.

"I thought Rabbi Schneerson died a few years ago."

"Well, we interpret it as dying, but he's not dead. He's going to come back, and there will be the Messianic Age."

This guy had drunk the kosher Kool-Aid.

"What does that mean? What will the Messianic Age look like?" I ask.

"Money will grow on trees. And clothing will also grow on trees. And the sand will be like candy. Everything will be provided for, so all we have to do is study Torah all day."

What an amazingly detailed vision. I expected some vague generalizations, not beaches of Skittles and orchards of chinos. As for the activities, I already study the Bible all day, so this wasn't too enticing.

"Have you ever studied anything but religion?" I ask.

"I had a little math and science when I was a kid, but not much. When I'm done with religion, I'll study other topics." He smiles.

"But you'll never be done with religion, right?"

"I'm not done yet."

Man, do I hate that insular thinking. It makes me think of my distant ancestor, the rabbi named Vilna Gaon. He railed against that mind-set, saying an understanding of the Bible required a broad education, including, as the *Britannica* describes it, "the study of math, astronomy, geography, botany, and zoology."

I find Rabbi Epstein again. Enough procrastinating. It's time for me to actually do this ritual. I pay ten dollars to a man behind a table and am directed to the open back of a huge truck. It's packed with chickens fluttering in coops.

"One male," says Epstein. Men get male chickens, he explains, women get females, and pregnant women get one of each to cover all contingencies.

The truck guy hands me my chicken—white feathered, red beaked, very much alive.

"Hold it under the wings," says Epstein. He takes the chicken and demonstrates for me a full-nelson grip.

"Really? But—"

"It's comfortable for them, totally comfortable," he assures me.

The chicken squawks. I stroke him to calm him down.

Now here's the thing: I know the rotisserie chicken I get at Boston Market did not die of natural causes. It did not drift off to eternal sleep in its old age surrounded by loved ones and grandchicks at a chicken hospice. It had its throat slit too. But modern society has done an excellent job of shielding me from this fact.

I look at my chicken again. Oh, man. I have an awful epiphany: The chicken kind of looks like Jasper—the same big eyes, same cocked head; it all but says "Da-da" (or actually, "A. J.").

You don't have to be Maimonides to see where this is going. I'm playing Abraham to the chicken's Isaac. And I don't have even a speck of Abraham's faith. I feel nauseated and loosen my grip. The chicken flaps out of my hands and starts scampering down the street. Epstein scampers after it, scoops it up, and brings it back to me. I stroke the chicken's head again.

"Now wave it in a circle over your head."

This is one of the strangest parts of the kaparot ritual—you are supposed to gently twirl the bird three times in the air.

Epstein is holding the prayer book for me to read: "This is my exchange," I say. "This is my substitute, this is my expiation. This chicken shall go to its death, and I shall proceed to a good, long life and peace." I was hoping I'd feel my sins flow out of me, but I don't. I'm too focused on holding the flapping chicken.

Next stop is the kosher slaughterers. There are three of them standing behind a counter on a raised platform, bringing to mind very violent pharmacists. They're wearing black garbage bags over their bodies to protect themselves from splattered blood. And, my goodness, is there blood—it coats the ground, it spots the faces, it soaks the gloves. The smell of chicken blood is so strong, a girl in line is dry heaving. In the era of avian flu, can this be a good idea?

I give my chicken to the slaughterer. He takes it, flips it over, bends back the neck, and makes three quick strokes with the knife. The chicken is dead, just like that.

The butcher tosses my chicken in an upside-down red Con Ed traffic cone, which is where it will stay as the blood drains out of its body. My chicken will then be plucked and packaged and trucked to a needy family somewhere in Brooklyn.

I'm elbowed out of the way. I'm still in my city-boy stupor: My chicken was alive; now, three knife strokes later, it's dead. Epstein is saying something, but I can't really focus. I'm too dazed.

As I said, I've started to look at life differently. When you're thanking God for every little joy—every meal, every time you wake up, every time you take a sip of water—you can't help but be more thankful for life itself, for the unlikely and miraculous fact that you exist at all.

What I mean is that I do admire the sentiment behind kaparot. I think it's good to be reminded that I could be scampering around the street one minute, and the next minute find myself gone from this world—that life is so absurdly precious and fleeting. And yet I don't admire the method. Perhaps if I grew up as a Hasid, it'd make more sense to me. But as Rabbi Boteach says, out of context, it just seems barbaric. If I ever do kaparot again, I'm going to do it like my Aunt Kate. Some Orthodox Jews, Kate included, practice a tamer—but still approved—version of kaparot: Instead of poultry, they wave money over their heads.

As I walk to the subway and the smell of chickens fades, I thank God that He discontinued the daily need for ritual slaughter. I had enough trouble with a chicken. I'd hate to try a goat or an ox.

And you shall not strip your vineyard bare, neither shall you gather
the fallen grapes . . . you shall leave them for the poor

—Leviticus 19:10

Day 135. Our living room table is covered with four large terra-cotta pots containing cucumber plants. Or at least scraggly, struggling versions of cucumber plants.

I've been trying to engage in some agriculture, seeing as so many biblical laws involve farming. I bought cucumber seeds online (cucumber was eaten by the Hebrews when they were slaves in Egypt, along

with melons, leeks, and garlic) and planted them in soil. For good measure, I added a couple of dozen cinnamon-colored plant-food pellets that
called to mind that discussion of rabbit digestion at the Creation
Museum.

The cucumbers do grow—they each get to be the size of a Good &
Plenty candy. And then they promptly die. I don't understand why. To
date I've grown and killed about a hundred dozen tiny, prickly, inedible
cucumbers.

My hope had been to leave cucumber "gleanings." The idea of gleanings is one of my favorites in the Bible. It goes like this: When you harvest your field, don't reap the entire field. Leave the corners unharvested
so that the leftovers—the gleanings—can be gathered by the poor.

It's a beautiful and compassionate rule. Plus, the commandment rewards people for doing a half-assed job, which I think is a nice notion.
Part of the idea is that, ultimately, the land belongs to God, so you respect that and be sure to provide for God's children. It's been called the
first welfare system.

And it can lead to unexpected blessings. Consider this great, roman-
tic story in the Old Testament's Book of Ruth: Ruth was an impover-
ished foreigner who had followed her mother-in-law Naomi to Israel.
To survive, Ruth gathered gleanings of barley. One day the rich owner
of the land—a man named Boaz—spotted Ruth gleaning and was smit-
ten. When she found out about his crush, she bathed herself, anointed
herself, put on her finest clothes, and sneaked into Boaz's room to "lie
at his feet." (Some say the phrase is a euphemism for lying elsewhere.)
Boaz was startled but pleased. They were soon married—and it all
started because of the command to leave gleanings.

In any case, how to apply this amazing notion of gleaning to my life,
since the cucumber experiment is flopping? I suppose that gleaning could
be generalized to mean "give to the poor." But I'm already doing that,
thanks to tithing and other commands. Gleaning is a slightly different
creature.

I decide to try to figure out how to update it. Which is hard. If I do a
lax job on an *Esquire* article, it doesn't help the poor. It just means a
copy editor has to fill in Scarlett Johansson's age and unsplit my infini-
tives.

But then I have this idea: What's the closest thing to harvesting in my life? Going to an ATM. What if I leave twenty dollars in the machine whenever I take out two hundred? I do this twice, and it isn't bad. Though I get the queasy feeling that Ron Perelman is coming in after me, and that he's using my twenty-dollar bill as Kleenex.

So I came up with a new plan: if I accidentally drop anything valuable on the street, I'll leave it there. It would be God's will. I would not gather it up.

Perhaps I psyched myself out: For several days, I don't drop a thing, not even so much as a nickel or a clump of lint. But then, yesterday, I am pulling out my wallet on the corner of 81st and Columbus, and a crumpled five-dollar bill falls out. I glance at it for a second and keep walking.

"Excuse me, sir!"

I turn around. A woman is holding up my bill.

"You dropped this!"

"Uh, that's OK," I say.

"It's yours. I saw it drop out of your pocket," she says.

I pause.

"No, it wasn't mine," I say, and keep walking. This lying has to stop.

Praise the Lord with the lyre; make melody to him with the harp of ten strings!

—PSALMS 33:2

Day 138. My white garments have gotten a shade darker, thanks to food stains and general urban pollution. But I still love wearing them. They make me feel buoyant, like I'm floating a couple of feet above the sidewalk. They're such a success, I decide that I should have an even more biblical appearance, which is how I settle on following Psalms 33:2. This instructs us to praise the Lord on a harp of ten strings.

"Do ten-string harps even exist anymore?" I wondered. Or would I have to make my own? Maybe I'll gain worldwide acclaim as the only living ten-string harpist.

One Google search later, I discovered that I would not be the only ten-string harpist. Far from it. When will it sink into my skull that there is no such thing as an obscure Bible verse?

Turns out there's a thriving underground world devoted to the biblical instrument. You can buy ten-string harps on eBay. You can send a Christmas e-card featuring ten-string harp music (the harp is plucked by a computer-generated angel who looks like a winged, demure Victoria's Secret model). You can read about how the Messianic age will usher in ten-string harps that will miraculously expand the octave from eight notes to ten notes.

The Tiffany of ten-string harps is an Indiana-based shop called Jubilee Harps. (Motto: "Home is where your harp is!") The website features audio samples of harp music, a photo gallery, accessories such as amplifiers and charcoal gray harp cases, and promises of spiritual rewards: "Although not fully understood, people today are experiencing the healing powers of the harp. Just hold this harp close to your heart, rest your face on the side of its arm, and feel peace and serenity surround you."

I call to find out more. The co-owner, Mary Woods, gets on the phone; she tells me that she and her husband, Rick, have sold more than one thousand of their handmade wooden King David–inspired harps to clients in sixteen countries.

They set up shop soon after Rick was downsized from his job as a scientist at Bristol-Myers Squibb. He made his first harp for a celebration at their church.

"It was late one night," Mary recalls, "and Rick got me to come out to his workshop, and I looked at the harp, and I couldn't quit crying. He thought I was mad because he spent three months in the workshop, and all he had was this harp. But I went over and hugged it, and I couldn't quit crying."

At this point, two things happen: Mary starts choking up on the other end of the phone. And I start feeling like more of a voyeuristic schmuck than I have since this year began. Much has touched me in these months—the humility of the Amish, the joy of Hasidic dancing, the power of prayer—but I can't relate to Mary's passion for a biblical harp. It's totally foreign to me. I thank her and hang up.

In the end, I did buy a ten-string harp online—a $40 one from a secondhand store, not the $800 version offered by Jubilee. Mine is made of coffee-colored wood and is about the size of a cafeteria tray. I play it twice a day, as instructed by the Psalms. I don't really know what I'm doing, but the good news is, it's hard to screw up too badly on a harp. A pluck here, a glissando there, and it sounds soothing.

I sometimes take it out for walks, which mostly inspires the cautious sideways glances I've become so accustomed to. I have had a couple of notable reactions, though. When I strummed my harp during a recent stroll on Columbus Avenue, a woman walking her dog offered me a dollar. Also, a white-haired man near Rockefeller Center started yelling at me. "A ten-string harp? The Bible actually says an *eight*-string harp, not a ten-string harp!" He could have been playing with my mind, or he could have been your garden-variety crazy, hard to tell.

In the end, though, the harp isn't transporting me. I'm going to have to find another PIN code to spiritual transcendence.

> *These are the living things which you may eat among*
> *all the beasts that are on the earth.*
>
> —LEVITICUS 11:2

Day 140. The Bible is filled with so many Thou Shalt Nots that I've started to take advantage of anything the Bible *does* allow. Even if said allowed activity isn't so alluring. Which is how, today, I ended up eating a bug.

To start at the beginning: Before this project, I'd had just a little exposure to the Bible's food laws. When I was in college, I used to order kosher meals on airplanes because someone told me that they were better—the reasoning was that the airlines have to give the kosher meals special attention and can't throw them in the vat with everyone else's slop. Frankly, I found the meals no tastier than the airline's secular lasagna. So I stopped doing that. Which is probably good, since feigning piety to upgrade your lunch is ethically dubious.

My airline adventure wasn't a total waste, though. I did pick up the very basics of the Bible's dietary restrictions. Namely these rules, found in Leviticus:

- You shall eat no pork or bacon or any other pig meat (land creatures must have cloven hoofs and chew their cud to be edible).
- No shellfish (sea creatures must have both fins and scales to be edible; shrimp, clams, and their cousins have neither).
- No blood.
- No rabbits.
- Certain birds—most of them birds of prey, such as eagles, vultures, and falcons—are off-limits.

Why the food taboos? The Bible itself doesn't give a reason. I'd always thought they developed as a primitive way to avoid trichinosis and other nasty diseases. But apparently I was wrong. Most anthropologists now dismiss that idea. The more popular theory nowadays is that the food bans were all about creating holiness and separation. The Israelites wanted to keep themselves apart from other tribes such as the pork-loving Philistines. They were marking their territory with menus.

Observant Jews follow the Bible's laws today. In fact, they follow a far more elaborate version of the laws, a system recorded by the rabbis over the centuries. The strictest kosher eater abides by hundreds of other rules, including regulations about separating milk and meat that could take years to learn.

A handful of Christians keep the basic rules, including the evangelical author of a book I own called *The Maker's Diet,* who writes: "In an odd twist of logic, many religious Americans dismiss the Jewish dietary laws as outdated legalism, invalid for the modern era. Yet they embrace the fundamental truths of the Ten Commandments as universal and timeless." This guy's in the minority. Most Christians believe that Jesus's sacrifice freed Christians from the food laws.

Over the last few months, I've been trying to abide by the rules explicitly listed in the Bible (as opposed to the full rabbinical kosher laws). It's been an enormous challenge.

Granted, in some sense, I've gotten lucky. The laws align with my own preferences. I've never liked shellfish. Lobsters, for instance, remind me too much of something you'd kill with Raid. So it wasn't a hardship to give up the ocean's bottom-feeders. I don't eat much bacon, either; my cholesterol already hovers around the score of a professional bowler, and I don't need it to break 300.

The problem is, forbidden foods are hiding everywhere. Bacon lurks in salad dressings. Gelatin is sometimes derived from pig bones, so an argument can be made—and often is—that it's forbidden. And pig fat. That terrifies me. Typical is this recent exchange I had with a waitress at a midtown restaurant:

"Do you know if the piecrust is made with lard?"

"I don't think so, but I'll check."

"Thanks. I can't eat lard."

"Allergies?"

"No, Leviticus."

It's a conversation stopper, that one. It's hard to trot out the Bible at a New York restaurant without sounding self-righteous or messianic. But the Proverbs say I must tell the truth, so I told the truth.

It's often pointed out that following religious food laws sharpens your discipline. The famous twelfth-century philosopher Maimonides says this is precisely their purpose: "[They] train us to master our appetites; to accustom us to restrain our desires; and to avoid considering the pleasure of eating and drinking as the goal of man's existence."

The thing is, I've been mastering my appetites since my cholesterol first bubbled up in my early twenties. For years, I've been eating Styrofoam-like fat-free cheese and scouring ingredient labels for the evil hydrogenated oil. It seems most people nowadays have some sort of food restriction, whether it's avoiding carbs, sugar, or nonorganic vegetables. My friend's sister refuses to eat nightshades, whatever they are.

So if self-regulation of our urges is the purpose, perhaps the Bible laws are no longer necessary. As a society, we've outgrown them. I told this idea to my Orthodox adviser Yossi. He shook his head. "You can't know the mind of God," he said. "There may be benefits beyond what we know now or can imagine."

So I sucked it up and stuck with the laws, still hoping to trip over one of those elusive benefits. And maybe I did. It happened about three weeks ago. I was following one of the most obscure food taboos in the Bible. This one concerns forbidden fruit. According to Leviticus 19:23–25, you cannot eat fruit unless the tree that bears said fruit is at least five years old. If a tree is four years old or younger, its fruit is not for human consumption. (Some Orthodox Jews follow this but say it applies only to fruit grown in Israel or fruit grown with your own hands.)

I tried to find out the ages of all the fruits I ate by emailing and calling grocery stores and companies. This was not a success. I got a lot of terse responses like this one, from the corporate headquarters of Polaner All-Fruit spreads:

> Mr. Jacobs,
> Unfortunately there would not be any way for us to guarantee the age
> of the plants from which our suppliers pick the blackberries.

I was reduced to researching which kinds of fruits came from slow-bearing trees and which from fast-bearing. I learned that peach trees can bear fruit in two years. Too dangerous. Pear trees in four. Again, too risky. But cherry trees, those are slowpokes. They take at least five to seven from planting to produce.

Cherries are safe. Not my favorite fruit, but they will be my fruit for the year. I went to Fairway supermarket, bought a half pound and began eating them out of the plastic bag on the walk home, spitting the seeds into garbage cans on the street corners.

Each cherry took about three seconds to eat. Three seconds to eat, but at least five years in the making. It seemed unfair to the hard-working cherry tree. The least I could do was to devote my attention to the cherry in those three seconds, really appreciate the tartness of the skin and the faint crunching sound when I bite down. I guess it's called mindfulness. Or being in the moment, or making the mundane sacred. Whatever it is, I'm doing it more. Like the ridiculously extended thank-you list for my hummus, the fruit taboo made me more aware of the whole cherry process, the seed, the soil, the five years of watering and waiting. That's the paradox: I thought religion would make me live with my head in the clouds, but as often as not, it grounds me in this world.

Of them you may eat: the locust according to its kind . . .

—LEVITICUS 11:22

But anyway, back to the bugs. To really connect with my forefathers through my stomach, I decided the food taboos were only half the story. I'd have to do more. I'd have to eat the same foods Moses and Jesus did.

To help me with this, I bought the aforementioned *The Maker's Diet,* a 320-page book by an evangelical nutritionist named Jordan Rubin. It's a helpful guide. The basic idea is a modified Mediterranean diet, which means our refrigerator is now packed with even more hummus, tahini, and pita bread. At the suggestion of *The Maker's Diet,* I've also cut out all cow's milk. Cows in biblical times were mainly used for dragging farm implements. The beverage of choice for Israelites was goat's or sheep's milk.

I called around, and, sure enough, I found a health food store in midtown that stocks fresh goat's milk from upstate New York. They stash a few half-gallon cartons in the fridge behind the massive display of vitamin B and echinacea.

Every morning I splash a little goat's milk on my oatmeal. It's not bad, really. It's like regular milk but thicker, the consistency of those overpriced blackberry Odwalla smoothies.

Also, I'm eating a lot of honey. Honey is one of the few certain pleasures in the Bible. It's the very description of the Promised Land—a place God says is "flowing with milk and honey"—so my oatmeal gets a healthy dollop of honey.

(My aunt Marti, the vegan and animal rights activist, found out about my honey eating and sent me a rebuking email. The subject header was "The bitter truth about honey." She listed all the ways the commercial honey industry mistreats bees. I won't reprint it here, but her description of artificial bee insemination was disturbingly graphic. She signed the note, "Your eccentric aunt Marti.")

The Mediterranean cuisine is working out well. Maybe it's buried deep somewhere in my DNA, this love of chickpeas and flat bread. It's my kind of Semitic food. Incidentally, I can't stand that other Jewish food: the Eastern European variety. I don't know why—a shrink would probably say it's because I have conflicted feelings about Judaism in general—but I can't eat it. The single most nauseating meal I've ever had was at a Lower East Side Jewish restaurant called Sammy's Roumanian Steak House. This is a place where, instead of salt and pepper, the condiment of choice is liquefied chicken fat. They put a big bottle of thick yellow chicken fat—*schmaltz* is the official term—smack in the middle of the table, just in case your potato pancakes aren't quite sopping wet enough with grease already. I ate at Sammy's with a guy who, after a couple of vodkas, mistook the chicken fat for a complimentary bottle of orange juice, and downed several gulps before turning white and excusing himself for the bathroom.

Where was I? Oh yes, the bugs. Now, this doesn't get much play in *The Maker's Diet,* but there was one other source of protein in biblical times: insects. Leviticus forbade the ancients from indiscriminate bug eating, condemning most insects as "abominations" (anything that creeps, swarms, or has four legs and wings is off limits). So, no beetles, no mosquitoes, no bees, and so on.

But there are exceptions: "Of [insects] you may eat: the locust according to its kind, the bald locust according to its kind, the cricket according to its kind, and the grasshopper according to its kind." (Leviticus 11:22) In other words, locusts, crickets, and grasshoppers are fine.

It's not clear from the Bible how often our forefathers actually ate them. Were they a popular meal? Or just in case of famine? The Bible's only other reference to bug consumption comes in the story of John the Baptist, who was reported to have survived on locusts and wild honey (though even this is controversial; some say the word *locust* here is a mistranslation, and he really ate carob pods).

Regardless, since the Bible diet contains so many restrictions, I figured I'd try to take advantage of this loophole. Maybe it'll make me feel manly and adventurous. It'll be *Fear Factor,* Old Testament style.

It isn't hard to find the bugs. The internet is teeming with edible insects, or "microlivestock," as they are called. There are chocolate wafers with ants sprinkled in. And beetle toffee bars. And larva cheddar cheese snacks. And plenty of crickets, which are apparently called "the other green meat" (high in protein, low in fat). The most promising supplier is named Fluker's Farms, which describes its crickets as "oven roasted to perfection and then covered with the finest chocolate available to create one truly unforgettable exotic snack." Plus, you get an "exclusive" I Ate a Bug Club button.

A few days later, I get a purple box with two dozen individually wrapped chocolate crickets. I'm going to need a fellow traveler on this one. I ask Julie, but she gives me another in a long line of overly enthusiastic "Thanks for asking! But I'm going to take a pass this time!"

So I take a couple of crickets along to dinner with my friend John. For my last book, John went to singles bars and tried to pick up women using facts from the encyclopedia about penguin mating rituals, so I figure he might be willing. He wasn't so sure.

"If I feel sick in the next couple of days, I'm going to blame you."

"Fair enough," I said.

"I'll think about it."

After we finish dinner at a downtown diner, I eat my cricket. Or at least I swallow it. I pop the cricket in my mouth, bite down twice, then chug water, ingesting it like a chestnut-sized pill. I tasted nothing.

I offer the other one to John.

"Come on. Just one."

"Fine," he says.

John unwraps his cricket and takes a bite, chewing slowly while looking at the ceiling, brow furrowed in thought.

"You like it?"

"A little crunchy," he says. "Hard to actually taste the cricket."

"I read it's supposed to be tangy. Is it tangy?"

"The chocolate is overpowering. But you do get a nice crispness."

He takes in the other half.

"It tastes like that candy bar Krackel. Same consistency."

A couple of days later, I am at my grandfather's house boasting about my insect eating. My cousin Rick, who is a high-school sophomore, isn't impressed.

"You eat insects all the time," he says. "There are insect parts in everything."

Rick has embraced entomology with a passion that most kids reserve for baseball and illegally downloaded music. If E. O. Wilson had a poster, Rick would have it on his wall. So presumably he knew what he was talking about.

And he did. I found a tremendously disturbing Food and Drug Administration website that lists the "natural and unavoidable" amounts of insects for every kind of food.

One hundred grams of pizza sauce can have up to thirty insect eggs.

One hundred grams of drained mushrooms may contain twenty or more maggots.

And if you want oregano on your mushroom pizza, you'll be enjoying 1,250 or more insect fragments per 10 grams.

So I was violating the Bible rules even without intending to. Or maybe not. Depends on the interpretation. Orthodox Jews usually reason that since they didn't have microscopes in biblical times, then a bug must be visible with bare eyes to be forbidden.

Why would God weigh in on any insects at all, visible or not? Once again, my secular mind wanted to know the reason for the Lord's decrees. What's the logic? The Bible doesn't say—it's one of the unexplained laws.

But one book I read—*The Unauthorized Version* by Robin Lane Fox—had a theory. It said that in biblical times, swarming locusts would often devour the crops and cause famines. The only way for the poor to survive was by eating the locusts themselves. So if the Bible didn't approve of locust eating, the poorest Israelites would have died of starvation. This I like. More and more, I feel it's important to look at the Bible with an open heart. If you roll up your sleeves, even the oddest passages—and the one about edible bugs qualifies—can be seen as a sign of God's mercy and compassion.

You shall rise up before the grayheaded and honor the aged . . .
                                        —LEVITICUS 19:32 (NASB)

Day 142. I'm currently in Florida. Julie and I have made a trip to Boca Raton for the wedding of Julie's college friend. We got through airport security without a second glance, which made me both happy and slightly concerned about the screeners' vigilance.

It's the day before the ceremony, and we're at a strip mall restaurant. It's 5:00 p.m., Jasper's mealtime. Florida, 5:00 p.m. dinner. As you can imagine, the average age approached that of a Genesis patriarch—maybe not Methuselah's 969 years, but perhaps Mahalalel, who saw 895 years.

The Bible has a lot to say about your elders. In fact, there's this one law that I keep meaning to abide by, but so far it has gotten lost in the avalanche of other rules. It is Leviticus 19:32: We should not only respect our elders, but stand in their presence. If there's a time to laser in on this rule, it is now. So as we wait for our pasta, I start standing up and sitting down. I pop up every time a gray-haired person enters the restaurant. Which is pretty much every forty-five seconds. It looks like I'm playing a solitaire version of musical chairs.

"What are you doing?" asks Julie.

I tell her about Leviticus 19.

"It's very distracting."

I stand up and sit down.

"I thought you had a wedgie," Julie says.

I stand up and sit down.

"Are you going to do this for the rest of the year?"

"I'm going to try," I say. I know I'll fail—there's just too much to remember to follow in biblical living—but I don't want to admit that yet.

There's a reason the Bible commands us to respect the elderly. According to scholars, many of the ancient Israelites lived a subsistence-level nomadic life, and the elderly—who couldn't do much heavy lifting—were seen as a liability.

The command seems disturbingly relevant today. After the ancient times, the elderly did have a few good centuries there. Victorian society especially seemed to respect those with white hair and jowls. But now, we've reverted back to the elderly-as-liability model of biblical times. This has become increasingly troublesome to me as I speed toward old age myself. I'm thirty-eight, which means I'm a few years from my first angioplasty, but—at least in the media business—I'm considered a doddering old man. I just hope the twenty-six-year-old editors out there have mercy on me.

And I have pledged to have mercy on those even older than I. A week ago, when I volunteered at the soup kitchen, I sat next to this fellow volunteer; she must have been in her seventies. And she complained . . . for a half hour straight. She was like the Fidel Castro of complainers—she spouted a never-ending stream of faultfinding. She spent five minutes alone on how the tree roots in her neighborhood make the sidewalk uneven. But instead of trying to stuff my ears, I attempted to empathize. Yes, that must be hard. Uneven sidewalks. I never noticed it, but, yes, someone could trip.

As Julie and I finish our dinner, we watch an old man get up from his table and shuffle off to the bathroom. He emerges a few minutes later and sits down at an empty table. It is a table two tables away from the table with his wife and kids. He sits there alone for several minutes, his head cocked, staring into the middle distance. What's going on? Is he mad at his family? I didn't see them fighting. Why his banishment?

Suddenly the daughter notices her father sitting two tables away.

"Dad!" she calls. "We're over here. Over here!" He looks over, suddenly remembering. He returns to the table, still somewhat dazed.

I turn to Julie. She looks like she's about to cry.

"The standing stuff I could do without. But I think it's good that you're honoring your elders. That's a good thing."

Let your eyes look directly forward, and your gaze be straight before you.

—Proverbs 4:25

Day 143. My glasses broke today. Jasper grabbed the wire-rimmed frames and stretched out the temples, so the glasses keep slipping off my nose. I'm reduced to keeping my head tilted up at a forty-five-degree angle as we walk around Boca Raton. My neck is killing me.

Plus, I look arrogant; my nose stuck in the air all day. I wonder if I'm breaking a biblical rule. I'm not sure. Maybe. In the Talmud, there's a ban against walking more than four cubits in what one translator calls "a jaunty, insolent, upright position." This is one reason you see some old Jewish men and women walk with such a pronounced stoop, their hands folded behind their backs. In America, land of Trump and self-esteem, humility isn't much of a virtue. But my ancestors wouldn't even stand up straight for fear of looking boastful.

I keep my chin in the air while watching the wedding the next day. It's a lovely, quiet outdoor ceremony in a Japanese-style garden. You can barely hear the bride and groom, but it doesn't matter.

I try not to think about the propolygamy parts of the Bible. That would be disrespectful to the event at hand. I try to focus instead on those parts of the Bible that say one wife per husband is a good ratio. In Genesis 2:24—a passage quoted by Jesus—we read about how man and woman are not complete until they cleave to each other. They are two halves. Only together can they create a full being.

So you shall do with any lost thing of your brother's,
which he loses and you find.

—Deuteronomy 22:3

Day 148. On the flight back from Florida, I found the checkbook of a Fort Lauderdale woman in the seat pocket in front of me. The Bible says that if your neighbor loses an ox or a sheep—or anything, for that matter—you are to return it to him or her.

So I sent back the checkbook. I felt good, honorable. I'm not a hardhearted New Yorker: I'm acting with random kindness. And the beauty part is, it actually worked out to my benefit. The Fort Lauderdale woman sent me a thank-you note (the stationary had a cartoon of a fat guy wearing an "I'm Too Sexy for My T-shirt" T-shirt), and enclosed a Starbucks gift card.

The checkbook triumph gives me such a moral high, I use the card to pay for the latte of the guy behind me at Starbucks. I got the idea from a religious website devoted to kindness. Just tell the cashier that three bucks of the next guy's bill is on you.

I'm opening the door to leave, when I hear him call.

"'Scuse me," he says. He is about forty, squat, wearing biking shorts despite the chilly weather.

I turn around.

"Did you pay for my coffee?"

"Yes, I did."

"I really don't feel comfortable with that."

I pause. Huh. I don't know what to do here. Does he think there must be a catch? Does he think I was hitting on him?

"Uh . . ." I say. Then I walk out the door very quickly and don't look back till I am a block away.

Ye shall not round the corners of your heads.

—LEVITICUS 19:27 (KJV)

Day 153. A physical update on my/Jacob's appearance: The beard has gone wild. You can see only about 40 percent of my face nowadays. It's got its disadvantages, of course—my wife now will kiss me only after covering her face with her hands so that just her lips are exposed. But I try to look on the bright side. It's keeping me warm from the wintry New York winds, like a sweater for my cheeks. Plus, it's providing me a level of anonymity. Not that I've ever been mobbed on a subway platform by adoring fans. But if I happen to see my former boss on the street, it's nice to know I could stroll by unrecognized.

I've even started to get the occasional positive comment about my looks. The Italian woman who works at the corner deli said she feels more sacred in my presence and is afraid to curse or gossip. And my coworker Tom, whom I hadn't seen in months, said he was all ready to greet me with a one-liner about Mel Gibson's facial hair, then decided he couldn't make a joke because he felt almost reverential. *Reverential,* that's the word he used. I was on a high for two days afterward.

The beard is the most noticeable, but I'm making other changes to my appearance too. I'm pleased to report that I got a new set of tassels. For the first few months, I tried the homemade approach: I attached four tassels from Tassels without Hassles to my shirt with safety pins. But here was a case where I decided I didn't need to reinvent the wheel: Why not use the prefab tassels, or fringes, known as *tzitzit* and worn by Orthodox Jews? For about twenty dollars, you can get a towel-sized rectangular cloth with four clusters of meticulously knotted white strings tied on each corner. The cloth has a hole in the middle, and you simply slip the entire thing over your head and wear it under your shirt.

If you're really hardcore, like I'm trying to be, you need to go further. The Bible says you must attach a blue thread to your fringes (Numbers 15:38). For centuries, almost all Jews skipped the blue thread because no one could figure out the exact shade of blue used in biblical times. No more. Archaeologists in the last two decades have discovered a type of snail that the ancient Israelites used for blue dye. The snail is still around and still capable of making blue. So for the first time in hundreds of years, a handful of ultra-Orthodox Jews are, once again, wearing four blue threads tied to their fringes. As am I.

And then there's my hairdo, which is starting to take on a personality of its own. The Bible has a lot to say about hair. In general—despite claims to the contrary that I read on a website for pious heavy-metal rockers—the Bible comes down on the side of short hair for men.

Consider Absalom, the vain and nefarious prince whose flowing locks got tangled up in an oak tree during battle. They cost him his life. And in the New Testament, the Apostle Paul is even more to the point. He asks: "Does not nature itself teach you that for a man to wear long hair is degrading to him?" (1 Corinthians 11:14).

But what of Samson? Granted, he did lose his superhuman strength after Delilah gave him a haircut—but his was a special case. Samson was part of a holy sect called the Nazirites whose members took a vow to drink no wine, touch no dead bodies, and cut no hair. He broke the vow. He suffered the consequences.

I'm no Nazirite, which is why I've been getting monthly haircuts at the local barbershop. Of course, as with everything in my biblical year, a haircut is not a simple matter. You want your hair mostly short, but a typical number 4 buzz cut is out of the question. Leviticus says you are forbidden to chop off the sides. This has led to some extreme micromanagement at the barbershop. First I requested for a male haircutter—purity issues. Then, after giving him elaborate pretrim instructions, I periodically piped up:

"You won't cut the temples, right?"

"I won't cut the temples."

Two minutes later:

"You know not to cut the temples, right?"

"Yes, I know. No cutting the temples."

By the end, I think he was ready to slay me with the jawbone of an ass.

He did tell me that he needed to clean up the hair on my neck.

"So you look religious, not dirty," he said. "No offense."

Most biblical scholars believe the purpose of the uncut side locks was, as with the food laws, to distinguish the Israelites from the pagans.

Apparently the pagans cut and shaved the sides of their hair short, perhaps, says one commentator, to give it the shape of a "celestial globe," perhaps as some sort of mourning ritual.

But in Jewish tradition, the hairstyle has taken on moral significance as well. One scholar told me that if you pass by a harlot on the road, God will blow your side locks into your eyes to shield you. Another rabbi has said that one day he will grab hold of the side locks to pull his students out of hell.

The ultra-Orthodox twirl their side locks while praying or studying—resulting in those amazing curlicue stalactites, frequently as long and thick as rolling pins. The Bible doesn't require this. So I've left my side locks untamed, leading to these odd hair formations that grow upward and outward, bringing to mind an ethnic Pippi Longstocking.

> *But to this day the Lord has not given you a mind to understand,*
> *or eyes to see, or ears to hear.*
>
> —Deuteronomy 29:4

Day 154. The more I research these side locks, the more confused I am about whether I've been properly following this commandment. The word *payot* in Hebrew is often translated as "corners." Do not cut the corners of your head.

What are the corners of the head? Not being a robot or cartoon sponge, my skull is reasonably ovoid. And if it is corners, shouldn't it be four corners? So maybe I should grow sideburns, a rattail, and a unicorn-type forelock. Could be interesting. But there's only so much I can subject my wife to. Payot is sometimes translated as "edge." But this doesn't clarify much.

The Hasidic-style payot have been around for centuries, but what did they do in biblical times? Can we ever know? I'm growing more and more skeptical that I'll ever hit biblical bedrock and discover the original intent. The Bible's meaning is so frustratingly slippery.

Yossi told me that the Bible has seventy faces. The ancient rabbis themselves don't even claim to have struck the bedrock. The Talmud—the huge Jewish book with commentaries on biblical law—is far from black and white. As writer Judith Shulevitz puts it in *Slate* magazine: "You cannot compare the Talmud to, say, the United States civil code, a series of prescriptions issued from Congress, or to Catholic doctrine, which comes directly from the pope. The Talmud is more like the minutes of religious study sessions, except that the hundreds of scholars involved in these sessions were enrolled in a seminar that went on for more than a millennium and touched on every conceivable aspect of life and ritual."

Even more exasperating: If I do get to the bedrock, it may be such strange bedrock that I won't be able to process it. In Karen Armstrong's terrific book *A History of God,* she says that the ancient Israelites weren't really monotheists. They believed in the existence of many gods: Baal, El, and so on. It's just that Yahweh is the boss of all Gods. Hence the command "You shall have no other Gods before me." It doesn't say "You shall have no other Gods at all."

Could I ever hope to get into the skull of an ancient Israelite who believed in several gods? Do I want to?

Month Six: February

*If you chance to come upon a bird's nest . . . you shall
not take the mother with the young.*

—DEUTERONOMY 22:6

Day 155. As a New Yorker, I've generally avoided interacting with pigeons, much like I avoid dark alleys or the Jekyll and Hyde theme restaurant. But living biblically makes you do some strange things.

Tonight I got a voice mail from Mr. Berkowitz, the man who inspected my wardrobe for mixed fibers a while back.

"Good evening, Mr. Arnold Jacobs. It's Bill Berkowitz of Washington Heights. There's a pigeon with an egg under her tonight, if you want to come over."

You bet I do.

You see, Mr. Berkowitz, in addition to *shatnez,* also specializes in another commandment. This one is likewise among the least known in the Bible. You won't find it on stone tablets in front of any federal courthouses.

The commandment says that if you discover a mother bird sitting on her egg in a nest, you cannot take both mother and egg. You are permitted only to pocket the egg; you must send the mother away.

The Bible doesn't say why. Most commentators think it has to do with compassion—you don't want the mother to have to watch her offspring snatched up for the breakfast table, so you nudge her away. In fact, many rabbis have expanded the meaning of this commandment to forbid cruelty to all animals, not just expectant birds, which is a great thing. I'm glad mainstream Judaism stresses kindness to animals, despite the sacrificial past.

But the actual wording of Deuteronomy 22:6 is solely about birds and nests, and it is this formulation that Mr. Berkowitz—along with others in his community—has taken to the literal limit. He has set up two pigeon nests on his third-floor windowsill in his northern Manhattan apartment. Whenever there's a newly laid egg, he allows a faithful seeker to come over, pay one hundred dollars to charity, shoo the mother pigeon away, pick up the egg, hold it aloft, say a prayer, place it back in the nest (or, in some cases, eat it), and thereby check off this commandment as officially "fulfilled."

This I needed to do. In fact, I'd been waiting for several months for my egg, tempted by a half dozen false alarms and missed opportunities. Tonight is the real thing.

I get to Mr. Berkowitz's apartment at seven-thirty, and he is all business. He has an appointment in a half hour, so we are on a tight schedule. He gives me a quick orientation on how this commandment works.

"It must be a kosher bird," says Mr. Berkowitz.

Pigeons, interestingly, are kosher—they're related to the doves mentioned in the Bible.

"It has to be a wild bird, not domesticated. It has to be female, it has to be sitting on the eggs, not next to the eggs."

We're at his dining room table, which is covered with half-open books and plastic cups. Mr. Berkowitz occasionally pauses in his speech to flip through his books. There's a colorful tome on kosher birds and a tablet-sized book on Jewish law. There's also a Hebrew manuscript devoted exclusively to the study of this single commandment, complete with diagrams of men climbing ladders, and photos of backlit eggs.

I express my concern that maybe the pigeons don't love the experience. Mr. Berkowitz shakes his head.

"Don't feel bad, because, first, God gave us this mitzvah. And, second, you ever eat an egg before?"

"Yeah."

"You feel badly about that? Your wife makes a scrambled egg, do you feel bad?" Mr. Berkowitz takes on a mock-petrified voice: "Oh no, don't do that! Not a scrambled egg!"

Speaking of which, most of Mr. Berkowitz's clients put the pigeon egg back in the nest—the option I've chosen. But some take their egg home for a hard-boiled snack.

"Have you tried it?" I ask.

"I once tasted it. I ate it raw."

"Raw? How'd it taste?"

"Tasted like a regular egg."

He shrugs his shoulders. No big deal.

The time for egg gathering is at hand. He leads me into a dark room off the entrance hall and flips on his gray flashlight. It's a huge and powerful flashlight—the kind used for spelunking or locating fugitives in the woods—and more than bright enough to help me see the nests.

The nests are actually two white plastic boxes—originally olive boxes from the grocery—each with a pigeon and some shredded newspaper inside. Mine is on the right.

"You have to do something to send her away," says Mr. Berkowitz. "You can't just scream at her, 'Fly away, birdie!' That won't work. It has to be a physical action."

I stamp my feet, wave my arms. Nothing. The pigeon—a big one, about the size of a football—clucks contentedly, enjoying the show.

"Open the window and reach in."

"Won't she fly into the room?"

"Don't worry about it."

I open the window and reach in. I'm wearing thick blue insulated ski gloves, official pigeon-shooing equipment provided by Mr. Berkowitz. Overcoming a lifelong revulsion to pigeons, I nudge the bird with my index finger.

She flutters up and away.

I take off the glove and pick up the egg. It's cream colored and warm, about the size of a walnut. I hold it up for Mrs. Berkowitz to snap a photo.

Mr. Berkowitz tells me now is the time to ask God for anything. "To have more children, make a million dollars a year, become a big scholar. Whatever you want."

In the outlying edges of Judaism (and I should stress that most Jews have never heard of this commandment, much less fulfilled it), the bird's nest ritual has taken on mystical meaning, seen as good luck, especially for infertile couples.

I make my wish for a safe delivery for our twins and soon after am shooed gently away from Mr. Berkowitz's apartment.

On the subway home, I'm euphoric. I just followed a rule that maybe a few dozen people in America have followed. I'm one of the faithful elite. But that feeling soon fades to worry. If there is a God, did I just please Him? Or did I maybe get Him angry? If His nest egg rule is meant to teach compassion, wouldn't it have been compassionate not to pester the pigeons with a high-wattage flashlight and a crazy dance?

> *"O my son Absalom, my son, my son Absalom!"*
>
> —2 Samuel 18:33

Day 161. Jasper has been suffering from what Julie calls, in honor of my project, a series of minor plagues. Rashes, colds, coughs. And today he got hit with a bad one. He suffered a major fracture in his left leg.

I was at a meeting when it all went down, but apparently he stepped on his toy truck the wrong way and snapped his thigh bone. He paused that terrible calm-before-the-storm pause and then just let out a category five wail.

The doctor told us that Jasper must be a invalid for at least the next six weeks. No playground, no sports, no playdates, no dancing, no walking. Just sitting. A baby Buddhist.

I can't tell you how depressed this makes me. So far we've been lucky to avoid much time in the hospital with Jasper. And this will, God willing, eventually heal. But Jasper's stunned. He looks beaten for the first time in his life. He looks like Jack Nicholson after getting electroshock therapy in *One Flew over the Cuckoo's Nest*.

I got a taste—just a little taste—of what King David meant when his rebellious son, Absalom, was killed:

> And the king was deeply moved, and went up to the chamber over the gate, and wept; and as he went, he said, "O my son Absalom, my son,

my son Absalom! Would I had died instead of you, O Absalom, my son, my son!" (2 Samuel 18:33).

As I sit here with Jasper on my lap watching Dora's singing backpack on the TV—it's two in the morning, and he won't sleep—I waste a lot of time retroactively bargaining with God about Jasper's leg. It's a habit of mine, this fake bargaining. I say, "God, let me break my leg instead of him. I would break *both* legs. I'd break both legs and both arms. Would I amputate my legs? I don't think so. But I'd amputate one toe. OK, two toes." It's a macabre game, and a waste of God's time.

> *Tell the people of Israel to bring you a red heifer without defect, in which there is no blemish . . .*
>
> —Numbers 19:2

Day 168. I finally got a call back from a Mississippi minister I've been trying to reach for weeks.

I want to talk to him about red heifers. The Bible's rule on red heifers makes my list of the Top Five Most Perplexing Commandments. It is found in Numbers 19, and it tells us to purify ourselves by finding a red cow. And not just any red cow—it must be a perfect red cow, an unblemished one, and one that has never plowed a field. Once I do this, I have to sacrifice the cow, burn it with cedar wood, mix the ashes with water, and have the resulting blend sprinkled on me by someone holding some hyssop. Only then will I be spiritually clean.

So how do I find an unblemished red cow in Manhattan? Well, I don't. They don't exist here. They don't exist anywhere yet. But maybe soon. On and off for the past twenty years, at a handful of ranches across America, people have been trying to breed just such an animal. The quest has created a bizarre alliance between ultrafundamentalist Christians and a group of ultra-Orthodox Jews, both of whom see it as a key to the end times.

The Jews need it because it will make them ritually pure from contact with dead people. Without that, they can't build the Third Temple in Jerusalem. Without the Third Temple, the Jewish Messiah will never come.

The ultrafundamentalist Christians need it for the same reason. Sort of. To them, the Jewish Messiah will be the false Messiah, the Anti-christ. The true Christ will have an apocalyptic battle with the Antichrist, which will bring on the thousand-year reign of peace on earth. The Jews will convert to Christianity or be destroyed.

Cattle ranchers in Israel, Texas, Nebraska, and Mississippi have all tried or are currently trying to breed the ultimate rust-colored cow. It's a lot tougher than it sounds. According to tradition, the cow must be at least three years old and cannot have a single nonred hair. One promising Israeli calf got believers excited a couple of years ago. But in the end, she sprouted white hairs.

The Mississippi minister who called me today is a man named Dean Hubbard, a Kia car salesman who has been working on the red heifer project for years. He caught me on my cell phone as I was walking out of my building. But I was so eager to talk to him, I didn't want to call him back. I plopped down on a lobby chair and grilled him for an hour, nodding at my neighbors as they passed by.

Dean is hard not to like. He's got a big voice and a big laugh. Dean became a minister in 1974 after he was zapped by 4,600 volts of electricity during a mishap at a radio station. He says God meant for him and me to talk. God has blessed him so far in life. Even when his wife died a few years ago, he says God provided him with another.

"I prayed to God for a new wife. I prayed I don't want a big one. I want a small one—about five foot three. I want her between fifty and sixty years old. I want her cute. And I said, I don't want to go far to find her. I want her to show up in my driveway. I gave God all these criteria. I prayed at two in the afternoon, because it says in the Bible that a man needs a female. And at seven that evening I walked to the end of my driveway to my mailbox, and there she was in a tennis skirt carrying a bunch of gardenias."

They are still happily married. And she's still small.

Hubbard works on the red heifer project with a born-again cattle rancher and preacher named Clyde Lott, also of Mississippi. About three years ago, Lott bred a cow they thought could be unblemished. But there was a problem.

"The thing about Mississippi is we have something called hoof-and-mouth disease," says Hubbard. "The thing about Israel is there's a coming war. We don't want the cows over there now." So for safety, they shipped the cow off to Nebraska. Hubbard and Lott believe that the true world-changing red heifer must be born in Israel, so they are waiting till the political situation calms down before exporting this—or any other— potential red mothers.

Their contact in Israel is a Massachusetts-raised rabbi named Chaim Richman. Richman runs the Temple Institute, which is a remarkable place staffed by people who make my ex-uncle Gil look moderate. Richman and his colleagues are awaiting the establishment of the Third Temple and the restoration of animal sacrifices. They aren't just waiting, though. They're preparing. They have a museum in Jerusalem with dozens of vessels and vestments preapproved for Temple use. If you want, you can browse the photos online. There's a three-pronged fork for turning over the roasting goats. There's a golden flask, a menorah cleaner, and the sacred jewel-bedecked breastplate of the high priest. And so on.

I like Dean, but I'm no fan of his and Chaim Richman's project. It's not just that it's zany—I'm certainly not opposed to occasional zaniness—it's that it's potentially dangerous. If the red heifer arrives, it'll be seen by some as divine permission to build a Third Temple. Where would it go? On the Temple Mount, which is currently under the administration of Muslims—home to their sacred Dome of the Rock and Al-Aqsa Mosque. Then it really might be the end of the world.

Frankly, the apocalypse sections in the Bible leave me cold. It's one of the few topics in my biblical year that I can't even begin to wrap my brain around. Not that I don't believe we could be living in the end times. I do. I think about it way too much. I worry about which lithium-deprived manic-depressive misfit will finally decide to use the nuclear bomb.

But I don't believe the Bible predicts how the world will be destroyed. The main apocalyptic text in the Bible is the Book of Revelation (not Revelations, as I always thought). The writing is poetic, vivid, and terrifying. Killer horses with heads like lions and tails like serpents stampede across the earth. People are thrown into lakes of fire. The sky opens up like a scroll being unfurled. If it weren't in the public domain, I could see Jerry Bruckheimer optioning it.

How to interpret this notoriously complex text?

A few fundamentalists go with the ultraliteral. In the very near future, just like Revelation says, seven angels will sound seven trumpets. The sun will go black, and locusts will cover the earth. A red dragon with seven heads will try to attack the Messiah as a child, but God will save him.

A step down the literalism ladder are those who say that the main points of Revelation are true—the world will end in a battle between Christ and the Antichrist—but some passages use symbolic language.

For instance: I was watching Pat Robertson's *The 700 Club*—the fundamentalist version of the *Today* show—and there was a news story about how the Israeli army is using nanotechnology with the hopes of creating "killer bionic hornets." Robertson—actually, it was Robertson's son Gordon, sitting in for Pat—said this was fulfillment of Revelation prophecy. Specifically, this passage about deadly insects:

> And the noise of their wings was like the noise of many chariots with horses rushing into battle. They have tails like unto scorpions, and stings, and their power of hurting men for five months lies in their tails.

So that's one side. At the other end of the spectrum are the religious moderates who say that no part of the Book of Revelation should be taken literally. And, just as important, no part of the Book of Revelation should be taken as a Nostradamus-like prediction of events in centuries to come. Instead the Book of Revelation referred to the political situation *at the time it was written.*

In this view, the book is an extended allegory about the persecution of the Christians by the Roman Empire. The seven-headed beast, for instance, is the city of Rome, a reference to the seven hills it was founded on. The elaborate symbolism was partly to avoid censorship, partly because it's a hallmark of a then-flourishing genre called apocalyptic literature.

"To take Revelation literally is entirely missing the point," says Elton Richards, my pastor out to pasture. "It'd be like taking Aesop's fables as literally true."

Their hearts are far from me . . .

—Isaiah 29:13

Day 169. I've taken a step backward again, spiritually speaking. My faith is fragile. Little things jolt me back to pure agnosticism. All that talk of red heifers and pigeons—that did it. As will a story about a suicide bomber, which reminds me of religion's dark side. Or even a quote like the one from the philosopher interviewed in the *New York Times,* in which he said that ethical monotheism is the single worst idea that humans have come up with.

If my spirituality could be charted like the NASDAQ, the general trend so far is a gradual rise, but there are many valleys, and I'm in a deep one now. It's making me lazy. I forget to put on my fringes, and I tell myself, well, what's the big deal? I'll put them on tomorrow.

I'm still praying several times a day, but when I do, I'm saying the words with as much feeling as I give to a Taco Bell drive-through order. I often think of this verse in Isaiah where he lashes out against the Israelite hypocrites:

> Because this people draw near with their mouth
> and honor me with their lips,
> while their hearts are far from me,
> and their fear of me is a commandment of men learned by rote.

That describes me right now.

I even find myself being skeptical of those times when my heart *was* near to God in the last few months. Perhaps it was an illusion. If I prayed to Apollo every day, would I start to feel a connection to Apollo? And what if I'm drawn to spirituality simply because I'm bored of the dry, dusty, rational mind-set that I've had these many years? I get bored easily. I can't sit through a sequel to a movie because I'm already tired of the characters. Maybe spirituality attracts me for its novelty factor.

> *Do not say to your neighbor, "Go, and come again,*
> *tomorrow I will give it . . ."*
>
> —Proverbs 3:28

Day 177. I may have found a way to help my neighbor Nancy, the self-described "kooky dog lady" who lives in apartment 5I. She knocked on my door today.

"Can I ask you a favor?" she says.

"Sure."

I could tell she hated this conversation already. I think she considers it an imposition to ask a waiter for the check, so asking me for a favor kills her.

"But I don't want you to do it because the Bible tells you to. I want you to do it because you want to."

"OK," I say. "Sometimes I can't tell the difference anymore, but OK."

"I have a book idea."

"Yup."

I guess I should have said something else, because Nancy gets skittish.

"I don't know." She turns to go away.

I finally squeeze it out of her: Nancy wants to write a book about her life in the sixties. About hanging with the classic rockers: Janis Joplin, Frank Zappa, and especially Jimi Hendrix. She was good friends with Jimi. She sketched him for the cover of one of his albums and collaborated with him on still-unpublished poems.

"What were the poems about?"

"Hippie stuff. Clouds. Sky. Love. I'll give them to you when I'm done with the book."

"How much have you written?"

"Only fifteen hundred pages. I've got a ways to go."

She smiles. She says she'd always been resistant to writing about her rocker days, but, well, it's been a long time. And, frankly, she needs the money.

I tell her I'd be happy to give whatever advice and/or referrals I can. I do want to help. Aside from a few blissful moments in the sixties, Nancy's life has been an unhappy one—an abusive mother, a rough marriage, inability to have kids, a fizzled career. She deserves something good. And if I help her, I will be "making a deposit of righteousness in God's bank," as I heard one preacher say.

But her question also nags me: Am I doing this just because of the Bible project? Or would I be this eager to help her no matter what?

"In the end, people appreciate frankness more than flattery."
—Proverbs 28:23 (TLB)

Day 179. I'm still wrestling with the no-lying commandment. It's brutal. But the Bible says to tell the truth, no matter what. People appreciate frankness. I need to follow the lead of those biblical heroes who take enormous risks to tell the truth.

Consider the prophet Nathan, who confronted King David. It's one of the Bible's most dramatic tales. The background is that David had wronged his loyal soldier Uriah by sleeping with Uriah's wife, Bathsheba, while Uriah was away at war. David got Bathsheba pregnant. To try to cover up his act, he arranged for Uriah's death.

So Nathan, one of the wisest people in the kingdom, told David a parable: There's a rich man and a poor man. The rich man has a vast herd of sheep. The poor man owns but one lamb. One day the rich man gets a visitor. What should he feed him for dinner? The rich man decides to slaughter the poor man's only lamb and serve that for dinner.

When he heard the parable, King David had the reaction most people have: The rich man is a horrible person. He's greedy and pitiless.

At which point Nathan reveals to King David: *You* are the rich man. Nathan's point was, King David had everything—including multiple wives and concubines—and still chose to steal Uriah's wife.

Nathan was taking a huge risk—criticizing the king to his face could have backfired. But in this case, the truth worked. King David realized the prophet was right. He had acted evilly.

As you might imagine, I'm not the prophet Nathan. So far, my truth telling hasn't laid bare the hypocrisies of great men. But I have managed to slash my total production of white lies by one-third.

Sometimes this works well, other times not so much. Tonight, Julie, Jasper, and I go for a five o'clock dinner at Homer's, a greasy spoon tastefully decorated with a flat-screen TV playing nonstop Nickelodeon.

I'm busy cutting Jasper's hot dog while simultaneously making sure not to touch the skin myself, as it's impure. At the next table, as at pretty much every other table, is a family. A dad in typical Upper West Side khakis, a mom with a ponytail, a three-year-old girl busy with some Crayolas.

"Julie Schoenberg?" says the ponytailed woman.

It's an acquaintance Julie hasn't seen since college. Hugs are exchanged, compliments toward babies are extended, spouses introduced, mutual friends discussed.

At the end of the meal, we get our check, and Julie's friend says: "We should all get together and have a playdate sometime."

"Absolutely," says Julie.

"Uh, I don't know," I say.

Julie's friend laughs nervously, not sure what to make of that.

Julie glares at me.

"You guys seem nice," I say. "But I don't really want new friends right now. So I think I'll take a pass."

A few weeks ago, I read a book called *Radical Honesty,* which was about telling the truth in all situations. It talks about the scary thrill of total candor, the Six Flags–worthy adrenaline rush. I felt that. I heard myself saying the words, but they seemed unreal, like I was in an off-Broadway production.

Julie is not glaring at me anymore. She's too angry to look in my direction.

"It's just that I don't have enough time to see our old friends, so I don't want to overcommit," I say, shrugging. Hoping to take the edge off, I add: "Just being honest."

"Well, I'd love to see you," says Julie. "A. J. can stay home."

Julie's friend pushes her stroller out of Homer's, shooting a glance over her shoulder as she leaves.

> *And it shall be to you as a sign on your hand and as*
> *a memorial between your eyes . . .*
>
> —Exodus 13:9

Day 180. Today marks the twenty-sixth time I've been asked whether I'm going to sacrifice Jasper during my biblical year. No, I say politely, only Abraham was commanded to do that.

"No binding your son on top of a mountain?" asked David, a friend of Julie's who has drifted slowly toward Orthodox Judaism over the years.

"No binding him."

David clearly knows his stuff: "The binding" is what some Jewish scholars call Abraham's near sacrifice of Isaac. Binding, I've noticed, is a huge theme in the Bible. Isaac's is the most famous, but there are plenty of other less violent examples. And those I am trying to do.

Last week I scratched Deuteronomy 14:25 off my list: "You shall bind money to your hand." This is one of the verses that my ex-uncle Gil took literally, and though most take it metaphorically (as advice to be careful with your money), I wanted to follow Gil, at least for a day.

When I woke up, I found a rubber band in Julie's desk and used it to strap a five-dollar bill on top of my left knuckles. I went about my day—I visited the grocery and Starbucks. But it felt like I was tempting fate. New York still has a sizable crime rate, so this seemed about as clever as walking around Yellowstone National Park with a salmon strapped to my hand. Luckily, despite lingering stares, no one tried to grab my exposed cash.

There's another type of binding I've been doing every day. This one comes from Deuteronomy 6:8. It tells you to bind the commandments to your hand and between your eyes.

Since I began my year, I've been using this homespun method: I take two xeroxed copies of the Ten Commandments and fold each to the size of a Polaroid photo. Every morning I tie one around my wrist with a white string, the other around my head.

It's been startlingly effective. Just try forgetting about the word of God when it's right in front of your eyeballs, obscuring a chunk of your view. Sometimes I imagine the commandments sinking through my skin and going straight to my brain like some sort of holy nicotine patch. If you look really closely, "Thou shalt not steal" is branded somewhere on my frontal lobe.

Even after I take off the string for the day (usually at about noon), I still have red indentations on my hand and head for hours afterward.

So in that sense, my binding feels good, righteous. But lately, my daily binding has also become tinged with guilt. I feel a tug from my ancestors or conscience or God that maybe now is the time to try the traditional Jewish method of binding the commandments to my arm and forehead: I should try to wrap tefillin.

I had a passing familiarity with the Jewish prayer straps (they're usually called tefillin, but sometimes they're known as phylacteries). When I was fourteen, on an El Al flight to Israel, I saw the ritual for the first time: A group of Orthodox Jews stood in the airplane aisle with leather boxes on their heads that looked like jewelers' loupes. They wrapped straps, they bounced their heads back and forth, they chanted. It was mystifying and a bit frightening.

My only other brush with tefillin was a book I was sent a few years ago at *Esquire*. It was by Leonard Nimoy—*Star Trek*'s Spock himself—who, as it turns out, is also a photographer and a quasireligious Jew. His book contained racy black-and-white photography of half-nude women wrapped in tefillin, a sort of Mapplethorpe-meets-Talmud motif. (Brief but relevant side note: You know Spock's famous split-fingered "Live long and prosper" salute? It's actually a sacred hand position used by the Jewish priestly class, the *kohanim*.)

Tefillin have been around a very long time—archaeologists found a pair near the Dead Sea in Israel dating to right around the time of Christ. And some claim that Jesus himself put on tefillin every day, though he did criticize the bulky versions worn by the Pharisees.

But what about the origins of tefillin? What did they do in the beginning? In the time of Moses? No one's sure. Biblical scholar Oded Borowski—author of *Daily Life in Biblical Times*—told me it might have been much more primitive, perhaps a string with a scroll. Others say that perhaps nothing was worn at all: The passage was originally meant metaphorically.

However it started, tefillin have evolved into an enormously intricate ritual. There are dozens of rules, right on down to a ban on passing gas while wearing them.

I would be needing some help. I ask Yossi, one of my Orthodox advisers, to be my tefillin-wrapping tutor. He invites me to his house on the Upper West Side. It's late in the afternoon—ideally, tefillin should be wrapped early in the morning, but it's still acceptable to do it now.

Yossi welcomes me with a handshake, goes to his closet, and takes out a small blue velvet pouch. Inside are two black leather boxes, each with tiny scrolls of scripture inside and leather straps attached.

"Are you right-handed or left-handed?" asks Yossi.

"Right."

"OK, then give me your left arm."

I stick out my arm, palm up, and Yossi places the black box on my left biceps. As prescribed by custom, I wrap the band around my arm seven times, starting below the elbow and ending at the wrist. Well, actually, I do it five times and then run out of arm. So I start over with Yossi's help, which isn't easy for him, as it requires him to do reverse wrapping.

"It's like tying a tie on someone else," he says.

He finally wraps it the proper seven times. Yossi puts the other black box on my forehead, and points to a part in the prayer book. I read, "Blessed be the Name of His glorious kingdom for ever and ever."

The tefillin is tight, creating six little lumps of forearm. The experience isn't frightening or odd, as I'd imagined. It is more . . . comforting. The wrapped arm reminds me of getting my blood pressure taken, so my unconscious logic probably went like this:

Getting my blood pressure taken is good for me.

This feels like I'm getting my blood pressure taken.

Therefore it must be good for me.

Or maybe it's that it reminds me of getting swaddled. I used to envy Jasper whenever I rolled him into a human burrito in his swaddling blanket. Perhaps this was God swaddling me.

Or maybe it's something about connecting with my father's father. My aunt had recently told me that my grandfather used to wrap tefillin. Which startled me. I knew that he was more religious than most of my secular family. But wrapping tefillin? That's seriously religious. And if he did it, you know *his* dad did it. And so on back for hundreds of years.

As Yossi helps me unwind the straps from my arm and head, I feel relief. Not just that I hadn't totally messed up the ritual. But relief that, after trying to do DIY religion for months, I'd finally done it the approved way. The Vilna Gaon would be happy.

It didn't send me into the mystical trance that I seek, but it was far more moving than I thought it'd be. As strange as the ritual is, it also has beauty. As I walk home, I feel my red heifer–inspired skepticism ebb away.

Finally, Moses finished writing all the words of these teachings in a book.

—DEUTERONOMY 31:24 (GWT)

Day 181. My *Esquire* boss just sent me a final version of the article I wrote about the Wikipedia, the online collaborative encyclopedia. I admire the Wikipedia, though I do so with much guilt, since it's the enemy of my beloved *Britannica*.

In any case, I've decided—and my aunt Kate would kill me if she heard this—that the Wikipedia and the Bible have a lot in common. Hardcore believers say that the Bible emerged from God's oven like a fully baked cake. Or, to be precise, several fully baked pieces. Moses transcribed the first five books. King David wrote Psalms. The Gospel of St. Luke was written solely by St. Luke. Every book of the Bible was written by a single author who transcribed God's words.

The alternative is called the documentary hypothesis. This says that the Bible has many, many authors and editors. The first five books of Moses didn't come from Moses alone. They are a patchwork from four anonymous sources who have been named J, E, P, and D. Each writer has his own linguistic quirks and theological passions. P, for instance, short for "Priestly," was fascinated by the laws. The sections on food and sex prohibitions in Leviticus, for instance, come from the Priestly source.

The passages have been chopped and pieced together by various editors. In short, the hypothesis says that the Bible has evolved, like humans themselves. Like a Wikipedia entry.

I believe the documentary hypothesis. And, as with creationism versus evolution, I just can't see myself ever embracing the alternative. I'm too in awe of archaeology and secular historical scholarship to reject it. I'm too attached to the idea that everything has untidy origins.

The challenge is finding meaning, guidance, and sacredness in the

Bible even if I don't believe that God sat behind His big oak desk in heaven and dictated the words verbatim to a bunch of flawless secretaries. Or maybe the fundamentalists are right, and this is impossible.

> *For the company of the godless is barren . . .*
>
> —Job 15:34

Day 181, afternoon. I was on the subway today, sitting a few seats down from a Buddhist monk. He looked at me, with my white raiment and bushy beard, I looked at him, with his orange robes, and we exchanged a knowing nod and smile.

It was a great moment. I felt like I'd been let through the velvet rope at a holy nightclub.

Here, at the halfway mark of my journey, I've had an unexpected mental shift. I feel closer to the ultrareligious New Yorkers than I do the secular. The guy with the fish on his bumper sticker. The black man with the kufi. The Hasidim with their swinging fringes. These are my compatriots. They think about God and faith and prayer all the time, just like I do.

Yes, there's still a difference between me and my alter ego Jacob—but Jacob is gaining strength. In fact, he's often the dominant one, quizzically observing my secular self. Jacob looks at the world and says, "Secular people are the freaks, not religious people. How can you *not* think about the Big Questions all the time? How can you put so much energy into caring about earthly matters, like basketball games or *Esquire*'s sell-through rates or the divorce proceedings of TV actresses?"

I'm still aware of the Bible's crazy parts. I haven't forgotten about the red heifer. But I find myself compelled to look for the Bible's good parts—or at least put the insane parts in context. Yes, it's crazy that I have to grow a huge beard. But if you think about it, it's actually a humane hairstyle. You're not supposed to shave the corners—the payot—the same word used when God tells us to leave the corners of the field unharvested. As with the side locks and edible crickets, maybe the beard teaches us to remember the less fortunate.

Last week, as part of my equal-time policy, I read Mark Twain's

Letters from the Earth. It's both very funny and wildly sacrilegious. At one point Twain says he doesn't understand why the Bible so despises those who piss against a wall. He's referring to this verse in the King James version of the Bible:

> And it came to pass, when he began to reign, as soon as he sat on his throne, that he slew all the house of Baasha: he left him not one that pisseth against a wall, neither of his kinsfolks, nor of his friends (1 Kings 16:11).

Twain writes: "A person could piss against a tree, he could piss on his mother, he could piss on his own breeches and get off, but he must not piss against the wall—that would be going quite too far."

Yet I knew from my research that those who "piss against the wall" was an idiom for adult men, since men would go behind a wall to get a modicum of privacy. Not quite as nonsensical. I want to stick up for the Bible, maybe insert a footnote in Twain's book.

Today a friend of mine who knows of my biblical quest sent me a funny email. It's the third time I've gotten this email since I started. Depending on the version, it's either an open letter to conservative Jewish radio host Dr. Laura Schlessinger or one to a strict evangelical minister. It first started circulating a few years ago and inspired a scene on *The West Wing* in which President Josiah Bartlet dresses down a barely disguised fictional version of Dr. Laura.

The email thanks Dr. Laura/the minister for reminding us that the Bible condemns homosexuality (Leviticus 18:22). But the writer has some questions.

Should he stone his mother for working on Saturday?

If he sells his daughter into slavery, as sanctioned in Exodus, what would be a good price for her?

He wants to burn a bull in sacrifice, but what should he do about his pesky, complaining neighbors?

The Bible says we can't touch the skin of a dead pig, so he should avoid directly touching a football. But can he play football if he wears gloves?

The first time I read this email, I thought: Excellent. What a great critique of those who follow the Bible literally, but haphazardly. It imagines a world of biblical literalism free from picking and choosing—the world I'm trying to create.

And now, here it was again, for the third time. As always, I was amused, and agreed with the gay-rights thesis. But here's the odd thing: I also got a little defensive. I wanted to send the author a note. Yes, the mixing fibers sounds berserk, but maybe the emailer should talk to Mr. Berkowitz about the glory of following things we can't explain.

Also, I know from my encyclopedia-reading days that a football is not made of pigskin anymore. NFL footballs are made of regular old cowhide. And my son's football is some sort of plastic. The email commits the same fallacy that it satirizes: It overliteralizes the word *pigskin*.

The email did make me think twice about touching pig carcasses. I don't have any pigskin clothes, so that's good. But to be really safe, I'm avoiding contact with playing cards, because they're often made of gelatin, which can be made of pigs. So even if poker didn't lead to greed and coveting, it would be off-limits for me.

Month Seven: March

He who winks his eyes plans perverse things . . .
—PROVERBS 16:30

Day 184. Julie's dad is visiting from Florida. We're out to dinner at a Chinese restaurant. It's proving to be a trying experience, mostly because her dad—a former software salesman—is indulging his weakness for particularly excruciating puns.

I can't even remember how it came up, but over entrees he punned on the word *olive* and the first letter of the Hebrew alphabet, *aleph*.

Then he looked at me and winked.

"You know, the Bible is antiwinking," I say.

"Really? What's the origin of that?"

"Not sure."

"Well, when you get down to it, the Bible is all about the *prophet motive.*"

I purse my lips and nod. A little part of me dies.

"Proph-*et*," he says. "Like the Prophet Elijah."

"I got it."

The Bible's antiwinking bias (there are at least four warnings against winkers) is one of the least-studied scriptural motifs around. I found negligible literature on the topic. But it does seem wise and ahead of its time, the wink being perhaps the world's creepiest gesture, with the winker coercing the winkee into being a part of his little cabal. If the Bible condemned people who call me "Captain" . . . well, a man can dream.

The Lord has made everything for its purpose.
—PROVERBS 16:4

Day 187. I blew my shofar on the first of the month, and frankly, I'm feeling much better about my skills. Mr. Berkowitz gave me a few pointers—including holding my shofar between my fingers like a giant cigarette—so it's begun to sound respectable. I'm no Miles Davis, but I can hit a couple of clear notes.

Today, Julie and I have an appointment at Mount Sinai to get a sonogram. Julie is dreading it. It's not so much a fear of hospitals. It's a fear that we'll find out the twins' genders—and that they'll both be boys. She's wanted a daughter from day one.

"We'll be fine," I say. "There's a seventy-five percent chance we'll have at least one girl. My guess is two."

An hour later, the Italian-accented nurse is sliding the microphone-like sonogram gadget over Julie's stomach. She stops on the right side.

"OK, Baby A is a boy. That's very clear. Baby A is a boy."

Julie starts laughing nervously. She's muttering, "Please be a girl, Baby B, please be a girl."

The nurse is digging the gadget into the left side.

"And I'm sorry," the nurse says.

At which point, my stomach drops, my pulse triples. What? What's wrong?

"I'm sorry to say that you have two boys. Baby B is a boy."

I'm relieved. For a moment, I thought that there was something seriously wrong with Baby B. But the only thing wrong is that he has a Y chromosome.

Julie isn't relieved. Her face crinkles. She starts crying, then sobbing. My relief fades to mild depression.

"I know it's stupid," says Julie. She's caught her breath now. "I'm mad at myself for being so upset. But it's just the finality of it. I'll never have a girl. That's it."

It's true. I love Jasper—but three boys? That's far too much testosterone for a two-bedroom New York apartment. That's a future filled with hundreds of lacrosse games and countless hours discussing vehicle parts like backhoes and racks and pinions.

The doctor, a stout fiftyish man, comes in. He sees Julie's wet cheeks.

"I used to do a lot of sex change operations," he says, chuckling. "I could do one for you guys."

Julie and I don't even so much as smile. This doesn't deter him.

"You know, Daniel is a nice name. A strong name. Dan. Daniel and the lion's den." The doctor's name is Daniel, you see.

Daniel puts some petroleum jelly on Julie's stomach for the sonogram. "Yesterday I used grape. This is raspberry." The guy is relentless.

After the sonogram, Julie and I go out to lunch. We barely talk.

I've got to focus on being thankful. Perhaps this is God's will.

"Maybe it's not so bad. Think about *My Three Sons*," I say. "They seemed happy."

"That doesn't help me," says Julie. "The mother was dead."

We sit silently for another couple of minutes.

"You know what my spiritual adviser Yossi would say?"

"What?"

"What seems terrible at first may turn out to be a great thing. You can't predict."

Yossi had been talking to me about this the other day. We were discussing the biblical story of Esther. This is the tale of a pagan king who went on a kingdomwide search to find a new queen for himself. He set it up as a beauty pageant, and a surprisingly carnal one. Each contestant would be primped for an entire year—six months with oil of myrrh, six months with perfumes and spices—then be sent in to spend the night with the king. The winner—the one the king loved "above all the women"—was a Jewish exile named Esther. The king crowned her his queen. This mixed marriage would have been viewed with horror by the Jews of the day. But here's the twist: It turned out to be the best thing that could have happened. Because Esther ended up convincing the king to spare the Jews, against the wishes of his evil adviser Haman. Bad can lead to good. We don't know the greater plan.

"I agree with that intellectually," Julie says. "But right now, it's a little hard to swallow."

Yeah. It's not helping me much either.

My mouth is filled with thy praise and with thy glory all the day.

—PSALMS 71:8

Day 191. Speaking of Yossi, he gave me a stern talking-to today. I was over at his house on the Upper West Side. We are sitting on a couch in his living room, a room dominated by books. There's a huge set of shelves stuffed with hardcovers, paperbacks, and pamphlets on whatever biblical topic you can think of, even the obscure ones like polygamy and gleanings.

"I love saying prayers of thanksgiving," I say, "because it makes me more grateful for life. But I still have trouble with the prayers where you're glorifying God . . ."

"You're on thin ice there," he says.

He told me: Stop looking at the Bible as a self-help book. That is the way I view it a lot of the time. I ask myself, "How can religion make me more joyous? How can it give my life more meaning? How can it help me raise my son so he won't end up an embezzler or a racketeer?"

But religion is more than that. It's about serving God. Yossi tells me this story:

Two men do their daily prayers while at work. One spends twenty minutes in his office behind a closed door and afterward feels refreshed and uplifted, like he just had a therapy session. The other is so busy, he can squeeze in only a five-minute prayer session between phone calls. He recites his prayers superfast in a supply closet.

Who has done the better thing?

"The first," I say.

"No," says Yossi. "The second."

The second guy was doing it only for God. He was sacrificing his time. There was no benefit to himself.

I think: That's interesting. Prayers are a good way to teach me the concept of sacrificing my time for the higher good. I'll become a more selfless person. A better person.

And then I realize: I'm back to self-help again. I can't escape it.

"I will ask you a question; hide nothing from me."

—Jeremiah 38:14

Day 196. Wednesday morning, March 15, I wake up early to make my pilgrimage to the Holy Land. That is, if I can get through El Al airline security at Newark.

The security officer—a feisty, olive-skinned Israeli woman—grills me but good. I don't fit into any of her categories—a beard, but not the traditional black hat or coat? Thus commences a half hour of questions.

"What was your mother's maiden name?"

"Kheel."

"Why do you have such a big beard?"

"I'm writing a book about the Bible, and [here a one-minute summary of my premise]."

"Hmm. Did you celebrate Purim?'

"Technically, it's not mandated by the Bible proper, so no."

"What does the 'J-R' at the end of your name stand for?"

"Junior."

"Why are you a Junior if you're Jewish?"

"My parents weren't so observant."

"Did you have a bar mitzvah?"

"Uh, no."

By the end, my mouth is dry, my palms are damp, and I feel like I have just been on worst first date in history—but for some reason, she lets me board.

Go up to a land flowing with milk and honey . . .

—Exodus 33:3

Day 197. The plane touches down in Tel Aviv, and I hop on the one-hour shuttle bus to Jerusalem with a couple of Scandinavian tourists.

I'm a mess. I'm jet-lagged and energized at the same time. And above all, I'm jittery. I'm jittery about meeting Gil. I'm jittery about trying to wrap my brain around this unfathomably historic place in a mere week-long stay. I'm jittery about Jerusalem syndrome: the bonafide psychological disorder in which tourists become delusional during their time in Israel and end up wandering the streets in a white gown and spouting moralizing sermons. Among the symptoms: "the need to scream, shout, or sing out loud psalms, verses from the Bible, religious hymns, or spirituals." I doubt I'll fall prey to it—I'm too self-controlled—but you never know. Also, as I have been since 9/11, I'm jittery about terrorism.

After I check in at the hotel, I meet a friend of a friend—a curly haired twenty-six-year-old TV producer named Neta—who has agreed to show me around. We go to a café of her choosing, a laid-back place with couches and patterned pillows. I eat pastries and pick her brain about what I should see.

As we leave, she takes me around to the side window of the café.

"I didn't want to show you this before we ate, but do you see this plaque?"

I nod. It's a stone plaque engraved with a flame and a half dozen names.

"This is to memorialize the people who died in a terrorist attack here a couple of years ago."

My shoulders tense up. She anticipates my question before I ask it.

"It's not out of the ordinary," she says. "Pretty much all the cafés in this neighborhood have been bombed at one point or another."

She wasn't blasé, but she wasn't overly dramatic either. It's a fact of Jerusalem life; she talked about it with the same tone you'd hear from a Los Angeleno talking about earthquakes or an Alaskan talking about the blizzards. If you love Israel as she does, she tells me, you live with it.

The Lord is my shepherd . . .

—Psalms 23:1

Day 198. The next morning I head off to the Negev Desert. That's where I want to go first.

Chronologically, it appears earlier in the Bible than Jerusalem does—it's the arid land where Abraham and Isaac once pitched their tents. I'm also hoping it'll get me into the biblical mind-set. I'd been reading about these patriarchs for months. Now I want to walk the ground they walked.

I rent a small car from Hertz, get hooked up with a translator by Neta, and we set off at ten o'clock with two cups of strong Israeli coffee. The landscape gets sparser and sparser. The wind picks up. The street names become more biblical: Jacob Street and Abraham Street. And then, a couple of hours later, we arrive.

The Negev is an extraordinary place. Step out of your car and look around, and you can visualize what it was like to live in biblical times. Well, you could if you removed the yellow-and-black camel-crossing signs. And the cigarette boxes littering the roadside. And the omnipresent electrical wires with weird orange balls on them to keep planes from flying into them.

Over the last three millennia, the desert has become a bit cluttered. But it's still as biblical a landscape as we have on this earth: dunes that stretch to the horizon, fine sand that coats your mouth whenever there's a gust of wind.

Unfortunately, aside from the view, the trip is turning out to be a bit of a letdown. The best we can muster is a visit to a Bedouin museum, which had a faux Bedouin tent that felt too sterile and orderly, like a room at an ancient Ramada Inn.

We are actually heading back to Jerusalem when we spot the thing that will save us. On the right side of a twisty, empty road: a flock of sheep. And a shepherd.

As even the most casual Bible reader knows, sheep and shepherding imagery pervades the Scriptures. The Twenty-third Psalm talks about the Lord as shepherd. Exodus compares the Israelites to a flock of sheep. Jesus is the lamb of God. Plus, most of the patriarchs were shepherds at one time: Jacob, Moses, King David.

So lambs have been very much on my mind. (My strangest lamb sighting before this: At a Judaica store on Manhattan's West Side, there was a kids' video of a Passover dinner with Dom DeLuise, Shari Lewis, and the sock puppet Lamb Chop, which must have been disturbing for Lamb Chop, seeing as seders traditionally include a roasted shank bone to represent a sacrificed lamb.) But here, finally, was the real thing.

The shepherd is a Bedouin man in his twenties wearing a red sweater and an orange jacket. He is shy and quiet, but in keeping with Middle Eastern hospitality, he invites me to tend with him.

We stand side by side, watching the sheep graze. I expected shepherding to be a silent occupation, but it's not. The sound of two hundred sheep chomping grass is surprisingly noisy. And that's not to mention the constant *b-a-a-a*-ing. And lambs do say just that: "*B-a-a-a-a-a.*" It reminds me of how Julie sneezes; she lets out an "*Ah-choo!*" as if she's reading from a script.

The shepherd does not have a flute or harp or staff (the hook-shaped instrument). But he does have a rod. He carries a black rubber tube that looks like it might have once been part of a tractor.

I ask through the translator, "What do you do with the rod?"

"It's just for appearance," he admits.

I love that. Even shepherds are concerned with superficial things.

I ask him a few other questions.

"How long have you been doing this?"

"Two years."

"Is the black sheep really rebellious?"

"No, it acts the same way as the white sheep."

"Do you like being a shepherd?"

"Yes, very much."

And then the conversation dies. Which is a relief to him, and OK by me. We just stroll along silently, listening to the chomping and *b-a-a-a*-ing.

My mind is clear, settled, still. At least for a few minutes, the separation between me and my biblical alter ego Jacob dissolves. Theoretically, if God is everywhere, then He should be just as present in a New York forklift as he is in an Israeli sheep pasture. But what can I say? Maybe I lack vision, but the idea of God is just easier to sense out here, away from the beeping of trucks backing up and the sight of gym ads.

Occasionally one of the lambs strays too far away. The shepherd teaches me to chuck a rock near it to get it to return to the flock. It's the method that's been in use since the days of King David, which is how David was so adept at embedding a rock in Goliath's forehead.

Perhaps the biggest revelation from my afternoon of shepherding is this: It's astoundingly good for your confidence. I have minimal management skills, but even I could handle a couple of hundred sheep. Because in addition to "*ba-a-a*-ing," sheep fulfill another stereotype: They are sheepish. A loud "Hey!" or a tossed stone, and the sheep fall right into place. Everyone can be a Jack Welch in the pasture. You can see why shepherding was the ideal first job for patriarchs. There's a reason Moses led sheep before leading the Israelites out of bondage.

"It is not good that the man should be alone . . ."

—Genesis 2:18

Day 198, late afternoon. If the desert is relatively empty (not counting the accumulating twenty-first-century detritus), then Jerusalem is the most packed place I've ever been. Every square inch seems drenched with people, history, and religion.

This afternoon, as I am walking along some twisty cobblestone streets of the Old City, I turn a corner and witness what has to be the highest density of spiritual devoutness on planet earth. The scene is this:

Dozens of brown-robed, Franciscan Friars are slowly, solemnly walking the stations of the cross, their hands clasped in front of them. They are singing "Ave Maria," accompanied by a single-speaker boom box strapped over the right shoulder of one friar. Another friar is swinging a miniature umbrella in the exact same way that altar boys swing incense lamps.

Then, slicing through the crowd of friars comes a family of Orthodox Jews. The father—his head topped by a brown fur hat the size of a manhole cover—leads the way, with eight Hasidic children trailing behind in single file. And, at that same moment, mingling with the "Ave Maria," comes the Muslim call to prayer over a tinny loudspeaker. A man with a fez edges past the Hasidic Jew. All three Abrahamic faiths intersecting on the same street.

It's an astounding sight. And it makes me feel more alone than I've felt since Project Bible began.

Here I am, a stranger in a strange land, away from my wife and child, in a city where everyone belongs to his or her own gated spiritual community. It drives home a disturbing point: My quest is a paradoxical one. I'm trying to fly solo on a route that was specifically designed for a crowd. As one of my spiritual advisers, David Bossman, a religion professor at Seton Hall University, told me: "The people of the Bible were 'groupies.' You did what the group did, you observed the customs of your group. Only the crazy Europeans came up with the idea of individualism. So what you're doing is a modern phenomenon."

I've loved that crazy European individualism all my life. To use author Robert Putnam's phrase, I bowl alone, and I've always preferred it that way. It gives me more control, or at least the illusion of it. It's made me resistant to joining anything. No frats, no Rotary clubs, not even the Kiss Army when I was a kid.

This year I've tried to worship alone and find meaning alone. The solitary approach has its advantages—I like trying to figure it out myself. I like reading the holy words unfiltered by layers of interpretation. But going it alone also has limits, and big ones. I miss out on the feeling of belonging, which is a key part of religion. I experienced this most keenly once before, during the biblical holidays of Yom Kippur and Rosh Hashanah back in October. I tried to do them alone. I fasted. I ate sweets. I sent portions to the poor. But I was doing it cluelessly and by myself, and it felt empty. I couldn't even bring myself to write a chapter about the holidays, because I failed to wring anything approaching the proper level of meaning from them. And many of my more profound experiences have come when I've joined a group, even momentarily, whether that group be huge (the Hasidic dance party) or small (Amos, Julie, and I singing "Amazing Grace").

Maybe I have to dial back my fetishizing of individualism. It'd be a good thing to do; the age of radical individualism is on the wane anyway. My guess is, the world is going the way of the Wikipedia. Everything will be collaborative. My next book will have 258 coauthors.

You shall surely tithe all the produce . . .

—Deuteronomy 14:22 (NASB)

Day 201. Before I left for Israel, my adviser Yossi had given me a list of commandments that—according to traditional Judaism—can be fulfilled only in the homeland. Many involved sacrificing animals. But one was relatively bloodless: tithing fruit.

Today I buy an orange at an Israeli farmers' market for a couple of shekels. Outside, I meet a man named David. He is a portly guy in a Gilligan-style hat who is reading a passage aloud from the Bible. I can't remember the exact passage, but I know it involved the word *harlotry*. His audience consists of me and a tall guy in ripped jeans.

David seems like a good candidate.

"I want to give you ten percent of my fruit," I say. "I need to give it to my fellow man on the street."

"Oh, you're tithing?" David knew all about this and thought this was a good idea. "Problem is," he says. "I don't eat oranges. Give it to Lev here." He motions at the tall guy.

Lev is unsure.

"Come on!" says David. "He can't eat the orange unless you take a tenth of it."

"Fine," says Lev.

So I peel the orange and, with my index finger, dig out two sections.

"Here you go!"

Lev recoils. Understandable, actually. I wouldn't take a manhandled orange slice from a stranger.

"Take it!" urges David.

Lev thinks about it.

"How about I take the ninety percent and you take the ten percent?"

He's not kidding. I agree and keep the small chunk for myself. It's true, what they say. Everything's a negotiation in the Middle East.

> *But a Samaritan, as he journeyed, came to where he was;*
> *and when he saw him, he had compassion . . .*
>
> —LUKE 10:33

Day 202. The next day I climb into a small Israeli cab to go visit a Samaritan. Before my project, I figured I'd have to climb into a time machine to visit a Samaritan. I assumed they had gone the way of the Hittites and Canaanites and other long-lost biblical tribes. But, no, the Samaritans are still around twenty-one centuries later.

The Samaritans get a couple of brief mentions in the Hebrew Scriptures, but they are far more famous for their role in Jesus's parable. When Jesus is asked by a lawyer, "Who is my neighbor?" he answers:

> A man was going down from Jerusalem to Jericho, and he fell among robbers, who stripped him and beat him, and departed, leaving him half dead.

Now by chance a priest was going down that road; and when he saw him he passed by on the other side.

So likewise a Levite, when he came to the place and saw him, passed by on the other side. But a Samaritan, as he journeyed, came to where he was; and when he saw him, he had compassion, and went to him and bound up his wounds, pouring on oil and wine; then he set him on his own beast and brought him to an inn, and took care of him. (Luke 10:30–34)

It's a powerful story—all the more powerful when you understand the historical context. The Judeans and the Samaritans hated each other, so the idea of a Samaritan helping this man was deliberately shocking, like a modern-day Hezbollah fighter tending to an Israeli soldier.

The Samaritans are particularly relevant to my quest because they lean toward biblical literalism. They disregard the interpretations of the rabbis in mainstream Judaism and place great—though not exclusive—emphasis on the Bible itself.

So I called Benyamim Tsedaka, the community's unofficial spokesman—he edits the Samaritan newspaper—and he invited me to his home outside Tel Aviv. He's waiting in his front yard when the cab pulls up.

"Tell me your name again?" asks Benyamim.

"It's A. J."

"Ah. Like C. J. on *Baywatch*."

This takes me aback. I knew that, at one time, *Baywatch* was beamed to all of earth's seven continents, but it is still a bit startling. Here is a member of the Samaritans, the most ancient surviving biblical tribe, and the first words out of his mouth are about TV's top-heavy harlot Pamela Anderson?

"I think that is a good icebreaker," says Benyamim. He laughs.

"Yes, a good icebreaker," I agree.

Benyamim, sixty-two, has gray hair combed straight back, a neatly trimmed white moustache, and a thick accent. He's wearing a gray skirt down to his ankles, the traditional Samaritan dress for the Sabbath, which he has kept on in my honor. His apartment feels clean, modern; it somehow reminds me of a Middle Eastern version of my late grandmother's condo in Century Village. As with everyone I've visited so far, Benyamim offers food and drink moments after I enter his door. He brings out a pot of tea and a plate of Samaritan cookies that look like madeleines but taste more spicy than sweet.

We wander around his apartment, looking at the gallery of Samaritan photos on his wall. I stop at a picture of a group of Samaritans gathered on top of a mountain, the men in white suits and white fezzes.

"That's the entire Samaritan community in 1914," says Benyamim, "One hundred forty-six people."

The current population has grown to all of seven hundred Samaritans, he says. Which is still an astounding statistic. Seven hundred people. His whole ethnic group could be comfortably seated in a high-school auditorium.

Think of it this way: Benyamim tells me about how a Samaritan mother recently gave birth to severely premature twins. They survived— but if they had died, Benyamim says, it would have been the equivalent of "wiping out your Kansas City."

The seven hundred remaining Samaritans either live near Benyamim—in a city called Holon—or in the West Bank. Neither Israeli nor Palestinian, they feel slightly out of place in modern-day Israel, trying to remain friendly with both sides. As Benyamim puts it, "We dodge the political raindrops."

They weren't always such a minority. The Samaritans—who trace their descent to ancient Samaria, which was in northern Israel—reached a peak in the fourth century BC with more than a million followers. They were wiped out in the centuries that followed by Romans, Ottomans, and the plague. Benyamim and his fellow Samaritans believe that they are one of the lost tribes of Israel, upholding the true biblical tradition.

"Should we take a walk?" asks Benyamim.

We step outside and into the Samaritan enclave—a quiet little maze of backstreets. We see no one except for a half dozen teenagers playing soccer and a neighbor out for a late-night errand. Benyamim points out that each house's exterior has a stone tablet with a biblical passage carved into it, their way of writing on doorposts.

About three blocks from Benyamim's house, we arrive at the Samaritan temple—a squat white-walled structure—which is closed for night. But inside, says Benyamim, is the Samaritan Bible.

It's a fascinating thing, the Samaritan Bible. Because it's almost exactly like the Hebrew Bible—with one key difference. The Ten Commandments aren't the ten that we know. Instead, one of the commandments tells followers to build an altar on Mount Gerizim, which is located on the West Bank. To the Samaritans, Mount Gerizim is the most sacred place in the world, the mountain where Noah beached his ark, where Abraham nearly sacrificed his son.

To this day, it is the site of their annual lamb sacrifice. Yes, unlike the Jews, the Samaritans still practice animal sacrifice. Every year on their Passover, the head of each Samaritan household slits the throat of a sheep. Then all the sheep—about forty of them—are skinned, put on stakes, and roasted over pits for eating.

"It's a beautiful ceremony," says Benyamim. "The smell is delicious. It's next week—you should come."

I had enough trouble with the chickens.

"I'll be back in New York, I'm afraid."

When we get back to the house, Benyamim introduces me to his wife, a short-haired woman who, frankly, doesn't seem in the mood to chat with me. She nods her head, and that's about it. Benyamim's wife is a convert from Judaism. Apparently there are a sprinkling of Jewish women who make the switch, but not too many. As one commentator points out, the Samaritans' superstrict menstruation laws are a hard sell.

"In the Torah, a woman in her period has to be departed," says Benyamim. This is why, he explains, Samaritan houses have a special room for women in their cycle. "My wife has her own TV and small refrigerator. It's like a hotel room."

Can she come out?

"Yes, and we can talk, but not face to face, because of the saliva. And we do talk. Mostly about my cooking."

Benyamim must cook the meals, since his wife cannot touch the food. Benyamim tries to put an upbeat gloss on it: It's a vacation from household chores for the women.

"Fifty years ago, there was a special tent for the women. And I believe it was the happiest tent in the camp."

I don't know. I still have trouble accepting the menstrual laws, whether Jewish or Samaritan.

Before I leave, I ask the obvious question: What do the Samaritans think about the parable of Good Samaritan? Well, not surprisingly, they don't object. They like it. There is even a Samaritan-owned Good Samaritan Coffee Shop in the West Bank.

Benyamim tells me he has given Jesus's parable a lot of thought and has his own take on it: It was autobiographical. Benyamim believes that the wounded man is meant to represent Jesus himself. And Jesus chose to have a Samaritan rescue him because he'd had a good experience in Samaria. When Jesus fled the Pharisees and passed through Samaria, the locals treated him kindly and believed he was the savior (John 4).

On the cab ride back to the hotel, my mind keeps coming back to the Samaritan Bible. So similar, but so different, too. What if history had taken a left turn? What if the Samaritan Torah had become the standard, and millions of Semitic faithful flooded to Mount Gerizim every year to sacrifice lambs, except for a few hundred people called the Jews, who worshipped at an obscure site known as the Western Wall?

> *I give thanks to thee, O Lord my God, with my whole heart,*
> *and I will glorify thy name for ever.*
>
> —PSALMS 86:12

Day 204. I can't stop thinking about the two praying guys in Yossi's story: the one who emerges refreshed and the one who emerges more harried than before. Sometimes I'm the first guy, sometimes the second.

Today I'm taking a rest from a walk on a set of stairs near the Jaffa Gate. Or maybe near the Lion's Gate. I'm not sure. Frankly, I'm lost. But I'm resting here on the stone steps, which are cool and shaded and have a bumpy surface that makes them look like a Rice Krispies treat.

I have my head bowed and my eyes closed. I'm trying to pray, but my mind is wandering. I can't settle it down. It wanders over to an *Esquire* article I just wrote. It wasn't half bad, I think to myself. I liked that turn of phrase in the first paragraph.

And then I am hit with a realization. And *hit* is the right word—it felt like a punch to my stomach. Here I am being prideful about creating an article in a midsize American magazine. But God—if He exists—He created the world. He created flamingos and supernovas and geysers and beetles and the stones for these steps I'm sitting on.

"Praise the Lord," I say out loud.

I'd always found the praising-God parts of the Bible and my prayer books awkward. The sentences about the all-powerful, almighty, all-knowing, the host of hosts, He who has greatness beyond our comprehension. I'm not used to talking like that. It's so over the top. I'm used to understatement and hedging and irony. And why would God need to be praised in the first place? God shouldn't be insecure. He's the ultimate being.

Now I can sort of see why. It's not for him. It's for us. It takes you out of yourself and your prideful little brain.

Therefore the people of Israel shall keep the sabbath . . .

—Exodus 31:16

Day 205. As I wander over to a café near the hotel for a bagel, I realize something: Walking around Jerusalem in my biblical persona is at once freeing and vaguely disappointing. In New York—even though it's home to the Naked Cowboy and Gene Shalit—I'm still unusual enough to stand out. But in Israel I'm just one of the messianic crowd. A guy with strange outfits and eccentric facial hair? Big deal. Seen three dozen today. Jerusalem is like the Galápagos Islands of religion—you can't open your eyes without spotting an exotic creature.

Speaking of which, it's Friday. The day I'm finally going to meet him, the most exotic creature of my family, the official black sheep, the man who gave me the germ of the idea for this book: Guru Gil.

When I called up Guru Gil a couple of weeks ago, he said he wanted to meet me at the Western Wall, the holiest site for Jews in Jerusalem. He's there every day. I arrive on a drizzly, chilly Friday afternoon. It's an amazing place: dozens of mostly Orthodox Jews chanting and swaying, their fringes swinging, some so deep in ecstatic prayer that they are clenching their fists and shuddering. It's impossible not to be moved by the combined kilowatts of faith.

Gil is nowhere to be found. When I ask his whereabouts, I discover that my family isn't the only one with mixed feelings about Gil. An Orthodox man from the Netherlands tells me that he and Gil no longer speak. What's the feud about? He won't say. But whatever Gil did, he did "these things *again* and *again* and *again!*"

Finally I spot Gil. I recognize him from the many, many photos on the cover of his book. He's walking down the steps, his long beard forked in half by a headwind, a big white tuft blowing over each shoulder.

"Gil? It's A. J. Jacobs."

"You're A. J? You look so religious," he says, eyeing my beard. "I was expecting something else."

"Well, it's not as long as yours."

"You'll get there," says Gil.

He's smaller than I thought. Somehow, in my mind, thanks to years of family legends, he had grown into a Paul Bunyanesque super-Jew. But in real life, he's far south of six feet. And with the beard, he looks his sixty years.

I tell him I'm in the middle of reading his book.

"In the middle of it? Well, you're the first person to ever put it down."

I can't tell if he's joking or if he's actually offended.

He grabs a chair and a prayer book, and we sit down to worship next to the sixty-foot wall. It turns out that this is Gil's second trip to the wall today. Every day he wakes up at 1:45 a.m., takes a ritual bath, then arrives at the wall at 3:00 a.m. He stays there for a few hours, wrapping tefillin—the leather prayer straps—on willing tourists, then goes home for study, only to return in the afternoon. If you think, as I did, that 1:45 a.m. is an ungodly hour, you'd be wrong. At least according to Gil, the most spiritual time of day is midnight to eight.

After an hour or so of prayers, we head back to Gil's apartment for Shabbat dinner. His guests arrive a few minutes later.

"Come in and sit down," he says sternly. "You're late."

Gil's dinner is quasifamous, a minor tourist attraction for students and seekers. Tonight we've got a couple of Russian yeshiva students, a pair of rabbi's daughters from Jersey, an Orthodox shrink and his wife, and this spaced-out Berkeley dude in a rainbow-colored yarmulke. Gil warned the Berkeley dude not to hit on the rabbi's daughters, or "I'll break both your legs."

"Hello?" shouts Gil, after we're seated. "Shut up! Earth to people! Earth to people!"

We stop chattering. Time for the ground rules.

"Whoever asks the most questions gets the biggest dessert. But they have to be good questions. They can't be 'What's for dessert?'"

Gil runs the dinner like he's still head of his yurt cult in upstate New York. Though nowadays he talks. And during two minutes of the introductory prayers, no one else does—or else you have to go wash your hands, as required by Orthodox custom.

He looks at the Berkeley dude.

"Are you going to talk?"

"Uh . . . no."

"You just did. Go wash your hands."

The Berkeley dude is already walking on eggshells. He was the first guest to arrive and made the mistake of touching his cutlery prematurely, prompting Gil to snap, "Stop with the plates, stop with the spoon, knock it off!"

Not wanting to make eye contact, I glance at the surroundings. The dining room table takes up most of the floor space. The walls are filled with photos of white-bearded rabbis. In the corner, I spot a snapshot of Gil playing a . . . ten-string harp. Yes, one alarmingly like mine. Gil tells me later that he designed the harp himself. "I based the notes on the sounds of a Hawaiian waterfall," he says.

One of Gil's big themes is that everything has a reason. Julie has the same point of view, but Gil takes it to the extreme: Absolutely nothing is an accident. A few years ago, he tells us, he got bird droppings on his tefillin. He was devastated. "I thought, 'God hates me! He hates my prayers. All these years I've been trying to please him, this is how he feels about me.' He took the tefillin to an expert, and it turned out that one of the parchments was upside down. God didn't hate him—He was just letting him know.

Each of the Bible's laws has a reason, too. A perfectly rational explanation.

"I thought some of them we don't know the reason for," I say.

"Whoever told you that wasn't a deep person," says Gil.

And remember, the little rules are just as important as the big ones.

"If you were in medical school to study brain surgery, would you want to follow all the rules? Or just the 'main ones'?" asks Gil.

One of the rabbi's daughters has a question:

"Why is it important for a guy to have a beard?"

"Because Abraham had a beard."

"He also had two wives," replies the rabbi's daughter.

"I beg your pardon. One was a concubine."

"Solomon had seven hundred wives," I pipe up.

"Shut up," says Gil. "In those days you could. But since it was going to be forbidden later, Jacob was buried with Rachel, not his other wives."

The rabbi's daughter isn't satisfied. Gil tries again:

"If you see a guy with a long beard, you know he's not a warrior. There's no way. You can't fight with one of these things. The first they'd do is grab your beard. It's a handle on your head."

That is one I hadn't heard. Gil takes a big swig of his red wine, about half of which dribbles into his beard. He gets up to clear the first course, a vegetable soup. The chatter at the table devolves to whom we know in common. Gil comes back. He is not well pleased.

"Only holy topics!"

"But what is holy?" says one of the twentysomething Russians. "Every topic can be holy."

This guy had given Gil some lip earlier in the night—he kept asking to sing a Russian song—and now Gil has had enough.

"You have no idea how hot things can get around here," Gil thunders. "One time, I had a guy from a yeshiva sitting right over there, and he was giving me a hard time. And I said, 'Look, I have two black belts in judo.'

"And you know what the guy says?

"'Oh, yeah? I know martial arts too.'

"So I jump up and grab him in a choke hold, and he turns blue in the face and goes '*Ahhhggghghh!*' And I let go, and from then on, he was the sweetest guest I ever had.

"*Don't . . . push . . . the . . . buttons,* kid. OK?"

The Russian says nothing.

I decide that Gil's shtick is part bully, part vaudevillian, part charismatic leader. He's an ultrareligious Donald Trump, and this is his boardroom. Maybe because I'm ex-family, I never get fully shellacked. He doesn't call me "klutz" or "idiot," as he does the others. The most I got is a "bozo!" when I wash my hands incorrectly.

I can see how he was a cult leader. You can't take your eyes off him. When he's telling a story, he'll jump out of his wicker chair to preach an important point. He'll laugh for no apparent reason—during prayers, he just started giggling, his face reddening, apparently filled with the joy of God. He also weeps. He was talking about a rabbi he knew, stopped midsentence, looked away, and cried for a good minute, as the rest of us silently contemplated our wineglasses.

He talks about his days as a cult leader only occasionally. At one point he grouses about the burden of having forty servants. "You know what I said every day? 'God, get them out of here!' What a pain in the *tuchus* to have to tell forty people what to do."

When he finds out that one of the girls speaks American Sign Language, he boasts of the sign language he invented as a cult leader—and how it swept New York in the 1970s.

"I found that a lot of my signs were the same as deaf sign language. Like the word *understand*."

Gil puts two of his fingers on his palm.

"You just did the sign for *toast*," says the girl.

Gil shrugs.

"Well, it wasn't the most important thing that I invented in my life."

At about nine o'clock, Gil says it's nearing his bedtime, so we say the final prayers and pass around a cup of water for hand washing. At least the men do. When the shrink's wife tries to, Gil explodes.

"*Ahhhhhhh! Ahhhh!!* No woman will wash hands at my table!!!"

Gil is not a feminist. He calms down, tries to soften it.

"No foxy woman, anyway. A short, fat woman, yes."

I look at the shrink's wife, a sixtyish woman who would fit in well at a Palm Beach bingo game. She isn't in the traditional sense foxy.

"Why not women?" she asks.

"Because you'll give this guy bad dreams!" says Gil.

He points at me. I smile weakly.

After the hand-washing incident, I get ready to go. Gil grabs my hand, looks me in the eyes, and says, "I love you." Oh man, my family would have a heart attack if they heard that one. How to respond?

"Uh . . . thanks for dinner!" I say.

As I walked down the cobblestone streets of the Old City, I remembered that Gil, when he first met my aunt Kate at a party, said those same words: "I love you." I can understand my grandfather's alarm. I sure wouldn't want my daughter marrying the Guru Gil of the twenty-first century.

Granted, he didn't end up strangling that Russian. In fact, he seems to me more of a religious clown than a felon. And I even agreed with a couple of his teachings. This one seemed kind of wise: "Whenever you're sad, things aren't working out for you, look around, see if there's someone else in trouble, go and help them. And I promise you, I promise you, I promise you, your problems will be solved."

But, overall, what I found offensive and subtly dangerous about Gil was that he claimed to have all the answers. As he reminded me several times. "I'm glad you found me," he said. "Because I have all the answers." And later: "If you have any questions, call Gil. Others will lead you astray."

He's a spokesman for the arrogant side of religion. My favorite parts of the Bible are the ones that take the complete opposite tack, that admit that we don't know everything, that stress the mystery of God and the universe. Like Ecclesiastes 6:12 says:

For who knows what is good for man while he lives the few days of his vain life, which he passes like a shadow? For who can tell man what will be after him under the sun?

Month Eight: April

Let my people go.

Day 215. I've been home for a week. Julie's still recovering from her stint as a solo mom, and I'm still trying to decompress from Israel.

Israel was so intense, I need a week of as little activity as possible. I've been spending a lot of time slack jawed on the couch watching Scripture-themed movies. Julie ordered me Charlton Heston's *The Ten Commandments* on Netflix. Man, I hadn't remembered it being quite so gloriously cheesy as it is. God sounds like Darth Vader. The seductive bare-midriffed Egyptian dancers look like they strayed off the set of Elvis's *Clambake*. And director Cecil B. DeMille is the most unhumble man in the world. Just in case there was any question of who is responsible for this masterpiece, he fills the screen with DIRECTED BY CECIL B. DEMILLE in 8,000-point font. He gets higher billing than God.

It's a nice break from ruminating about Israel. Because Israel has got me tied up in knots. On the good side, it can humble you. Even physically it humbles you. The vastness of the desert humbles you. The height of the Western Wall humbles you. The echoing interior of the Church of the Holy Sepulchre humbles you. And the history. All those millions of seekers who have walked the exact same cobblestone streets asking the exact same questions—it's hard not to feel like you're part of something much larger than yourself.

But Israel can also be dangerous. It can bring out the fundamentalist in all of us. It can bring out everyone's inner Guru Gil. It can nurture your self-righteous side. I saw this even as I took the cab back from Newark Airport. I looked at the pedestrians yammering away on their cell phones, no doubt speaking evil tongue and coveting. Ugh. "I'm not like that," I tell myself. "I'm so much more biblical than these people. These secular losers." Which, I know, is a completely unbiblical way to think.

> *You shall not harden your heart or shut your hand*
> *against your poor brother . . .*
>
> —Deuteronomy 15:7

Day 219. One unavoidable side effect of biblical living: You think a lot about your forefathers. In my case, I find myself fascinated by my father's father.

My grandfather, who died when I was in high school, wore a gray fedora and lived by the Hudson River in an apartment with a plastic-covered couch. I remember him being perhaps the gentlest man I've ever met, a man who spoke so quietly that you'd have to lean forward to hear.

And I remember him giving away money. Whenever we'd go for a walk—which usually meant that we were either traveling to or returning from moo shoo chicken at Szechuan Palace—we'd inevitably pass a homeless person, and my grandfather would inevitably fish a couple of quarters out of his pocket. No doubt it was a reaction to his past. He grew up in a tenement on the Lower East Side. He'd never tell you, but his stepmother—a woman straight out of Grimms'—kept a lock on the icebox so that my grandfather wouldn't try to sneak an extra slice of bread.

Today, I'm waiting on the subway platform for the downtown B train, trying not to get annoyed that express trains keep whooshing by while the local is MIA. About twenty feet away, I spot a woman in an Adidas T-shirt and blue jeans. She is working the platform, going from commuter to commuter asking for change.

She is making absolutely no headway. These people have perfected the art of ignoring the homeless. Their body language is very clear: "I am unable to look up for even a second because I am so deeply involved in observing this discarded Tropicana pineapple juice carton on the track." It's heartbreaking.

The homeless woman does her best; she stares at them, open palmed for a good half minute, then moves on. She comes to me. I am biblically obligated to give, so I get out my wallet and hand her a dollar. She takes the money and smiles. I feel good.

And then she throws open her arms for a hug. I wasn't expecting that. As a germaphobe, I've never been a hugger. More of a polite nodder. And with my biblical living, I've become even more leery of hugs, seeing as the Hebrew Scriptures caution against touching women. But what am I going to do? Be a callous schmuck? I hug her.

At which point she goes for a kiss. I swivel my head in time so that she misses my lips and gets my cheek.

She steps back and looks at me.

"Did you just take advantage of me?"

I laugh nervously. "No."

"I think you took advantage of me. I think you made a pass at me."

More nervous laughter from me.

"I'm going to report you!" she says, her voice rising. She isn't smiling. She just glowers at me as I sputter denials and apologies for any misunderstanding. By this time, most of the commuters have stopped reading their papers to check out this grabby, hirsute, fringe-wearing pervert who has tried to fondle the panhandler.

"I'm going to report you," she repeats.

The C train comes. It's not the train I need, but close enough for me. "Sorry, I have to go."

As I sit down, I look out the window to see if the Adidas woman is following me. She isn't. She is, instead, cracking up—having a good stomach-clutching laugh. She'd been playing me. She'd homed in on a lanky guy with a beard and decided to spice up her day. Can't blame her for that. Maybe it was an even better gift than the dollar.

A false balance is an abomination to the Lord, but a just weight is his delight.

—Proverbs 11:1

Day 222. Julie is feeling slightly better about the impending three-sons situation. Part of her problem had been that the male-female ratio in our house will be 4:1. She'll be outnumbered. She'll be the One Who Doesn't Belong.

As self-prescribed therapy, she's made a big list of sons who treat their mothers well. And, conversely, another big list of sons who have terrible relationships with their dads. She consults this list often. It doesn't seem quite biblical. But I'm not about to stop her. In fact, I decide to throw in a couple of dysfunctional father-son Bible stories to help her cause.

"Absalom led a rebellion against his father, King David," I tell her.

"OK," she says.

"And you know Reuben?"

"The firstborn son of Jacob," she says. (Julie's favorite musical is *Joseph and the Amazing Technicolor Dreamcoat*.)

"Well, he slept with his father's concubine. And his father was so angry, he took away Reuben's birthright."

By the way, I can't tell you the number of people who try to console us by telling us that, with our three boys, we can start our own team. They never say what *kind* of team. Three-man bobsled? Arena polo? The options seem somewhat limited.

Julie's also feeling better because she's been able to avoid getting too huge, at least so far. Her legs, arms, and face look remarkably unbloated. Her stomach, though, is hard to ignore. It looks like she ate a wrecking ball for breakfast.

She's off to the ob-gyn's office for a checkup this morning. "I hate the scale there," she says. "It's always two pounds heavier than the one at the gym. Plus, the nurse rushes me. I never have time to take off my sneakers before getting weighed."

I nod. I decide not to tell Julie, since I know I'd be met with an eye roll, but she's hit on an important biblical theme: inaccurate scales. I'm guessing that the scales in question measured barley and spelt, not wives in their second trimester, but, regardless, the issue gets a lot of play.

How much? The law of fair weights and measures appears an impressive six times in the Bible. By way of comparison, the passages often cited to condemn homosexuality: also six.

The laws about weights and measures are generally given a wide interpretation; the Bible here is demanding fair business practices. Which does seem like a good idea. But if frequency of mentions counts for anything, I should probably be focusing my wrath on improperly calibrated truck weigh stations.

Wine is a mocker, strong drink a brawler; and whoever is led astray by it is not wise.

—Proverbs 20:1

Thou dost cause . . . wine to gladden the heart of man

—Psalms 104:14–15

Day 223. I'm in the kitchen drinking a glass of red wine as Julie microwaves some pizza. Julie tells me that she wants me to give up alcohol for the rest of her pregnancy.

"It'll be a sign of solidarity," she says. "Paul did it when Lisa was pregnant."

I make a note to have a discussion with our friend Paul.

"And isn't there something in the Bible about not drinking?" she asks.

I tell her it's complicated. After a couple of minutes of back-and-forth, Julie reveals her true motivation: She thinks a few weeks of abstemiousness would help shrink my gut.

"Look at that stomach," she says. "How many months are you? Four? Five? You having twins too?"

OK, OK, very good. And, yet, there must be a better way to shed pounds. I'm no wine enthusiast—despite the bizarre and inexplicable fact that I edited the wine page at *Esquire* for a few months (it mostly involved spell-checking words like *Gewürztraminer*)—but I do like an occasional glass.

Before I started living biblically, I had feared that I'd be forced into a year of sobriety. After all, I knew some Puritans banned booze. And certain fundamentalist Christians think of alcohol as up there with adultery, idol worship, and *South Park*. A few even argue that the "wine" drunk in the Bible is not wine at all but actually grape juice. This was the thinking of a temperance advocate named Thomas Welch, who tried to sell "unfermented wine" in the late nineteenth century for communion services. He failed. At least until his family changed the name to grape juice and marketed it to the secular.

The truth is, biblical wine is wine. But is it a good thing or a bad thing? In some passages, wine seems like a gift from God. In other passages, it's portrayed as a wicked toxin: "[Wine] bites like a serpent, and stings like an adder. Your eyes will see strange things, and your mind utter perverse things. You will be like one who lies down in the midst of the sea, like one who lies on the top of a mast" (Proverbs 23:32–34).

To clear things up, I found the expert of all experts, a conservative Christian oenophile named Daniel Whitfield. Whitfield has made an astoundingly exhaustive study of every alcohol reference in Scripture—all 247 of them. I quote his findings here:

> On the negative side, there are 17 warnings against abusing alcohol, 19 examples of people abusing alcohol, 3 references to selecting leaders, and one verse advocating abstinence if drinking will cause a brother to stumble. Total negative references: 40, or 16 percent.
>
> On the positive side, there are 59 references to the commonly accepted practice of drinking wine (and strong drink) with meals, 27 references to the abundance of wine as an example of God's blessing, 20 references to the loss of wine and strong drink as an example of God's curse, 25 references to the use of wine in offerings and sacrifices, 9 references to wine being used as a gift, and 5 metaphorical references to wine as a basis for a favorable comparison. Total positive references: 145, or 59 percent.

Neutral references make up the remaining 25 percent.

If I could add one observation to Whitfield's study: There is also one reference to medicinal alcohol: "No longer drink only water, but use a little wine for the sake of your stomach and your frequent ailments" (1 Timothy 5:23).

It comes down to the battle between the Bible's gusto for life, and the Bible's wariness of excess. Between its Epicureanism and Puritanism. You can find both themes in the Scriptures. The Epicurean side is best seen in Ecclesiastes:

"There is nothing better for a man than that he should eat and drink, and find enjoyment in his toil. This also, I saw, is from the hand of God" (Ecclesiastes 2:24).

The key seems to be to enjoy wine as one of the many great things that God has provided us. But don't enjoy it too much. Use what Anheuser-Busch public service announcements call "responsible drinking."

Otherwise, bad things happen. For instance, there's the remarkable story of what happened when Lot—the one who fled Sodom—drank too much. Lot had escaped to a cave with his two daughters (his wife, as you know, had been turned into a pillar of salt). The daughters, thinking all other men in the world had died, got their father very, very drunk—and slept with him. Both got pregnant. Their incestuous offspring founded two nations, Moab and Ammon, which became enemies of Israel.

Too much wine is an abomination. But a glass or two? That seems fine. I show Julie the results of Whitfield's wine study. I tell her I'd be willing to water down the wine a bit, since most scholars think that biblical wine had a lower alcohol content.

Incidentally, I just did an internet search for marijuana and the Bible. As I suspected, someone has figured out a way to make the Bible seem in favor of pot smoking. Not only does the website Equal Rights 4 All! quote Genesis 1:29 ("Behold, I have given you every herb bearing seed which is upon the face of all the earth . . . To you it will be for meat"), but it claims that Moses's holy anointing oil contained a high concentration of THC. This, as my high-school hero Jeff Spicoli used to say, seems totally bogus.

> *"You shall eat nothing leavened; in all your dwellings you shall eat unleavened bread."*
>
> —Exodus 12:20

Day 229. It's April 12, perhaps the most famous biblical holiday of them all: Passover. If you're even remotely Jewish, you know it as the religiously themed, springtime version of Thanksgiving. And if you're Christian, you probably know it, at the very least, as the meal that Jesus was eating at the Last Supper.

Secular as my family was, even I have attended a handful of Passover dinners, mostly at my dad's cousin's house in Long Island. We'd tell an abbreviated story of the Jews' flight from Egypt, eat our matzoh, and then talk about movies. They were lovely meals, but biblically literal? Not so much. To give you an idea: We recited the *Nine* Plagues. The tenth one—the killing of Egypt's firstborn—was left out for being too harsh. Which seems like leaving that unpleasant throwing-herself-in-front-of-the-train business out of *Anna Karenina*.

This year I wanted an uncensored Passover. I wanted to tell the whole story of the Exodus. More, though, I wanted to try to re-create that very first Passover as much as I could. Today's seders—even the strict ones—bear little resemblance to that original meal. Which I discovered may be a good thing.

I hold my attempted biblical seder at our apartment. My parents and parents-in-law show up around five o'clock. I greet them in my biblically mandated outfit. Exodus says to eat with your "loins girded"—I wear a belt around a white robe. "Your sandals on your feet"—Tevas. "And your staff in your hand"—the maple-wood "Walden Walking Stick" I bought on the internet.

We sit down, and I pass around a plate of unleavened bread. I had made this myself; no store-bought matzoh for me. That very first unleavened bread, the Bible says, was cooked by the Israelites as they wandered out of Egypt. They didn't have time to put the bread on stones, so they put it on their backs and let the sun harden it.

I decided to do the same. That morning, I had taken some kosher flour, added water, made a hubcap-sized pancake, slipped it into a plastic Ziploc bag, and slapped the whole mixture on my back. I walked, hunched over, a few blocks to the hardware store, bought some C batteries for Julie, and came back. Maybe the dough was too well-camouflaged by my white shirt, because the guy at the hardware store didn't bat an eye.

The plate returns to me untouched. No one has taken a piece.

"I had it in a plastic bag," I say. "It's not like I sweated on it."

They shake their heads. Not surprising, I guess. "More for me." It isn't bad; kind of chewy, what I imagine pizza dough tastes like after thirty seconds in the toaster oven.

As I am eating the matzoh, I lose control of the table. I am supposed to be the leader, the one telling the great story of the Exodus, but already the topic of conversation has lapsed into a discussion of the prices at local parking lots. I think back to my ex-uncle Gil, and how he screamed, "*Only holy topics!*" I wish I had his maniacal charisma.

Instead I go to fetch the lamb from the kitchen. The ancient Israelites ate the sacrificed lamb—all of it, from head to feet. (Today many Jews don't eat lamb on Passover, as it can't be sacrificed properly without the Temple.) The closest I could get to this original meal was a fifteen-pound hunk of kosher lamb I bought at an Upper West Side butcher, and which I somehow conned my mother-in-law into roasting.

The lamb at that first Passover was key, because it provided the blood that saved a nation. God ordered the Israelites to paint the lamb's blood on the doorposts—the secret sign so that the Angel of Death would know to skip over their houses and not slay their firstborn.

That's another thing: lamb's blood; I needed to do something about that. After several phone calls, I had determined that selling lamb's blood in the U.S. is illegal. Which was a relief. I didn't really want a bucket of blood in the fridge—too Dahmer-esque. Instead I improvised by using the lamb juice from the saucepan, which I figure contains at least a hint of blood. And as for painting it on my doorpost? The paintbrush, says the Bible, should be made of hyssop, a minty herb. I discovered an online store called Blessed Herbs—cofounded by Martha Volchok, "herbalist and mother of four home-schooled children"—and ordered a bag that looked alarmingly like something I would buy in senior year of high school from a guy named Boo on 68th Street.

"If anyone wants to watch me paint the doorposts, come with me now," I announce.

Most everyone stays at the table, but Julie comes along to supervise, and my nieces follow out of curiosity. I go into the building hallway and carefully dab lamb juice on the sides and top of our door frame, leaving brownish stains and a couple of stray hyssop leaves. Julie isn't happy about the stains but is more worried about our neighbor Nancy's dog.

"He's going to go berserk when he smells the blood."

Back at the table, I take out my ex-girlfriend's Bible and read a section from Exodus. I figure this is better than trying to summarize the story myself. I read for about three minutes, starting with this passage:

"Afterward Moses and Aaron went to Pharaoh and said, 'Thus says the Lord, the God of Israel, "Let my people go, that they may hold a feast to me in the wilderness."'"

I close my Bible and let the story sink in. "Does anyone else have anything they want to say?" I ask.

My dad does. He has brought a packet of photocopied handwritten pages. They are a collection of childhood memories that his mother—my grandmother—had written before she died. My dad reads the section about her memories of family seders in the 1920s.

Before the seders, my mother would buy a very large live carp and bring it home (how, I don't know). She put it into the bathtub to swim until it was time to prepare the gefilte fish we all relished so much. We kids loved watching it swim, but it was so big it could barely (and sometimes not at all) negotiate a turn at the end of the tub. We all took our showers downstairs until after the fish was removed.

She wrote about how the kids would file up and down the stairs carrying the kosher-for-Passover dishes, "all of us like ants, trip after trip, one after the other." And about how Uncle Oscar once ate a dozen hardboiled eggs on a dare. About how, when the seder dragged on, the prayers went "express, no local stops."

Her writing is vivid, fresh. The references to the customs are no longer confusing or foreign. The whole thing felt familiar. My Biblical rituals—the door painting and sandal wearing—were interesting on an intellectual level, but, frankly, I wasn't as moved as I hoped I might be. I didn't feel like I had been swept back to the time of the Pharaohs.

But this writing from my grandmother—that did sweep me back. Perhaps to make a ritual resonate, I can't skip directly from my stain-resistant dinner table in New York to a desert three thousand years ago. I need some links in between. I need my grandmother and her memories of the leviathan-sized carp of Hinsdale Street in Brooklyn.

Do not boast about tomorrow . . .

—Proverbs 27:1

Day 230. Here's a sample from a phone conversation I just had with my wife. I was at the *Esquire* office for a meeting.

"What time are you coming home?" Julie asks.

"Six o'clock, God willing."

"Also, John Munzer left a message on the answering machine."

"Thanks. I'll call him back, God willing."

"See you soon."

"God willing."

It's not an atypical snippet. For the last month, I've been saying "God willing" at least eighty times a day.

Both the Old Testament and the New Testament say this is a good idea. Proverbs advises us, "Do not boast about tomorrow, for you do not know what a day may bring forth." In the New Testament, James 4:13–15 cautions against saying: "Today or tomorrow we will go to such and such a city," but "Instead you ought to say, 'If the Lord wills, we will live and also do this or that'" (NAS).

It has become a reflex. Every time I use the future tense, I try to tag on those two words: "God willing." My mother hates it. She told me I sound like someone who sends in videos to Al Jazeera. And I know my verbal tic comes off as weird in secular settings. But I find it a profound reminder of the murky instability of the future. Yes, I hope to return home at six, but God or fate might have other plans. This, in turn, makes me value the present even more. As James 4:14 says, "For what is your life? It is even a vapor that appears for a little time and then vanishes away" (NKJ).

I've got to try to squeeze all I can out of that vapor.

When her time of delivery came, there were twins in her womb.

—Genesis 38:27

Day 232. Julie and I spend the morning at the doctor's office to get another sonogram. Julie lifts her shirt, and the boys pop up on the little monitor. They're starting to look human now. They both have the oversized skull of a bobblehead doll or talk show host, perched on a tiny body with reptilian limbs. You can see them move—they wiggle and jostle and . . . um . . . smack each other.

"Did you see that?" Julie asks.

"I saw it."

The boy fetus on the right had given the boy fetus on the left a jab to the head. Actually, more of an uppercut. He just took his olive-pit-sized fist and thrust it directly into the ovarian wall, stretching it till it cuffed his brother in the face.

"You think it was intentional?" asks Julie.

"I don't know. Could have been a spasm. Though it did kind of look intentional."

"Oh, man. These next few years are going to be hard."

Of course, being Bible-obsessed as I am, my mind goes straight to the Scripture's most famous twins: Jacob and Esau, who also waged war in utero. A far more serious war.

> The children struggled together within [Rebecca].
> And she said, "If it is thus, why do I live?"
> So she went to inquire of the Lord.
> And the Lord said to her,
> "Two nations are in your womb,
> and two peoples, born of you, shall be divided" (Genesis 25:22–23).

I've been thinking a lot about Jacob and Esau lately (the real Jacob, not my biblical alter ego). The brothers are relevant—almost eerily relevant—not just to my family life, but also to my quest for biblical truth.

The story of Jacob and Esau provides a classic example of the gap between, on the one hand, what the Bible literally says, and, on the other, the centuries-old layers of interpretation that have built up around those words.

If you read the Bible cold, as if you'd been raised on one of Jupiter's moons, you would, I'd wager, have this reaction: Jacob is a conniving scoundrel. And Esau, though maybe not a Mensa member, got a raw deal.

But the tradition—at least the more conservative tradition—says just the opposite: Jacob is a righteous man. And Esau, if not totally evil, is certainly depraved and impetuous and untrustworthy.

How does this work?

Consider the story of the swapped birthright. Esau, the older brother, owned the birthright, a privilege that Jacob coveted. The Bible says:

> Once when Jacob was boiling pottage, Esau came in from the field, and he was famished.
> And Esau said to Jacob, "Let me eat some of that red pottage, for I am famished!" . . .
> Jacob said, "First sell me your birthright."
> Esau said, "I am about to die; of what use is a birthright to me?"
> Jacob said, "Swear to me first." So he swore to him, and sold his birthright to Jacob (Genesis 25:29–33).

My first thought on reading this was: What kind of demented brother is Jacob? Why wouldn't he just ladle out a bowl of red pottage for his starving sibling instead of blackmailing the poor guy?

But the tradition has a different read: Esau wasn't really about to die; he was just hungry. He's a slave to his urges, pure id, and an exaggerator to boot. He'd do anything for a snack, including selling the sacred birthright; he showed no respect for what God had given him.

Just a few pages later, Jacob dupes his brother again. This time, their father, Isaac, who is blind and on his deathbed, wants to give a blessing to his eldest son. He sends for Esau. But Jacob—at his mother's urging—disguises himself as Esau, putting a goatskin over his hands and neck to mimic his brother's hairiness. Jacob announces himself as Esau. Isaac checks by feeling the faux hairy hands and proceeds to give Jacob the blessing. Again, a first-time Bible reader might think Jacob a rascal for fooling his dying dad. But the tradition says that Esau deserved it.

You have to remember that Jacob is a patriarch, one of the original fathers of God's people, so biblical interpreters had all the reason in the world to put a positive spin on his exploits. Esau wasn't a patriarch. Well, not of righteous people, anyway: In the rabbinic tradition, Esau spawns an evil race—either the Romans or the Edomites, depending on the source (both were frequent enemies of the Israelites).

Even when Esau seems to act with nobility and forgiveness, the tradition doesn't buy it. Take Jacob's and Esau's reconciliation. The two brothers, estranged for twenty years, finally meet up in the desert.

The Bible says: "Esau ran to meet [Jacob], and embraced him, and fell on his neck and kissed him, and they wept" (Genesis 33:4).

Sounds innocent enough. But my friend Nathaniel Deutsch, who teaches religion at Swarthmore College, told me about a fascinating *midrash*—a Jewish legend—about what really happened. The midrash says that Esau's "kiss" was not a kiss at all, but actually an attempt to bite Jacob on the neck. And not a love bite, mind you, a malevolent bite. Jacob, being a man of God, was saved when his neck miraculously turned to marble.

I'm not immune to the interpretative tradition. Now that I read the Bible again with the rabbinically tinted lenses, I agree that Esau sold his birthright too quickly. He needed to engage in more long-range thinking. And Jacob is surely the smarter of the two—and a homebody like me—so maybe it's a good thing that he tricked the doltish Esau to become the patriarch.

Still, I don't want to whitewash Jacob. I love the complexity of the patriarchs, that their flaws are as numerous as the stars in the sky and, in some cases, come close to eclipsing their righteousness. And I am awed by the profound and extraordinary fact that the entire Judeo-Christian heritage hinged on a bowl of soup.

"You shall not join hands with a wicked man . . ."

—Exodus 23:1

Day 233. I hate the nonsensical, bacteria-ridden custom of the handshake. And the Bible project—with its many purity laws—has given me an excellent excuse for avoiding shaking hands with women. Now I have figured out something beautiful: I can expand my prohibition to the rest of the population too.

The Bible says not to join hands with a wicked man. And what are the chances of a man being wicked? Remarkably high, especially with the strict standards I'm employing nowadays. So I find it's best to keep my hands in the pockets of my white pants and just nod politely.

To be fair, the "not join hands" command occurs in relation to conspiring to give false evidence. So maybe it doesn't apply all the time. Which is why I've come up with a backup excuse.

The Bible's female impurity laws are more famous, but there are, in fact, corresponding laws of male impurity. Men don't get off scot-free. Leviticus says that a man shall be unclean for the day after his "emission of seed," as the Bible phrases it, and must take a bath to purify himself. In the twenty-first century, the male impurity laws are rarely observed, even by the strictest of the strict. The reason given is that such laws applied only in the era of now-destroyed Jerusalem temples. But if I'm trying to re-create biblical life, I should probably pay heed to the male laws.

My male friends usually assume that I'm evading the handshake because of germs. Since I'm biblically required to tell the truth, I say, "No, not germs." And then I explain. Which somehow turns out to be even more awkward than discussing the monthly cycles with women. Men just don't like talking about their emissions.

"Well, I haven't in a week," said John. "Not that it's any of your business."

I've learned that men of my vintage aren't having a whole lot of sex. I think I'm hanging out with too many new fathers.

I like the male purity laws, and not just because they allow me to stay in my antiseptic bubble. I like them because they make the female impurity laws seem much more palatable. It's not only women who experience a miniature loss of life and must be avoided. Men do, too. The Bible has its moments of egalitarianism.

"Honor your father and your mother . . ."
—Exodus 20:12

Day 234. I feel like I've dishonored my father and mother by even embarking on this quest in the first place. They wanted me to write a book about something safer, like taking a year of salsa lessons. Worse, I still haven't told them about my visit to Gil.

Tonight Julie and I are going over to my parents' house, and I plan to make a conscious effort to be more honorable. Honoring your parents is not one of the inexplicable *chukim*. It's eminently rational, perhaps even more so in biblical times.

If you were a nomad—as many ancient Israelites were—the aging parents would be cumbersome. They couldn't help with the heavy lifting or nailing down tent pegs. The temptation to leave them behind must have been great. But you couldn't. Because God commanded us to honor them.

I've read objections to this commandment. The problem is the absolute nature of it. What if your parents don't deserve honor? Should Stalin's daughter honor him? It's a hard question, and I don't have an answer. But in my case, my parents do deserve honor. Despite the embarrassingly early curfew they gave me in high school, despite the daily guilt trips about not seeing them enough, despite the quibbles, they've been, on balance, very good parents. Just last week I figured out something about my dad. I realized that he checks my Amazon.com page every day, and if there's a bad review up there, he clicks on the "Not helpful" box. It makes me want to hug him—if we weren't both so repressed.

I don't treat them nearly well enough. I honor them only in a lip-service way. I call them every weekend, but I spend the twenty minutes of the phone call playing hearts on my PowerBook or cleaning the closet while tossing out the occasional "mm-hmmm." I delete without reading my mom's emailed jokes about vacuous blondes or wacky etymology. And when I do reply to her emails, I often do the I'm-so-important-I-don't-have-time-to-capitalize-or-punctuate thing.

So in this biblical year, I've been on a mission to reform. I've been trying to capitalize my emails to my mom. And to actually listen to what my parents say during our weekly calls. Listening is a key theme in the Scriptures. Or, in Hebrew, *Shema*. In fact, the Shema—a passage from Deuteronomy that begins "Hear, O Israel"—is considered the most important prayer in Judaism.

Tonight it's dinner and a DVD. They chose *Gods and Generals*, a civil-war movie that opened to wide apathy a few years ago. The title smacks of polytheism to me, but I don't object, and we settle into our respective chairs to watch it.

About forty-five minutes in, during another musket loading scene, I look over and notice my mom asleep in her chair. And not just light dozing. We're talking mouth-agape, head-slumped-on-the-chest deep slumber.

I nudge Julie. At this point, I am planning to whisper something clever along the lines of "Looks like my mom is really enjoying the movie." Or perhaps I would have gone with a sight gag—an impression of my mom with her jaw slack. But I stop myself. This isn't good-natured jesting. It has a tinge of mockery to it. And the Fifth Commandment kicked in. So I just smile vacantly at Julie, who then goes back to watching Jeff Daniels.

I realize I nearly committed a major biblical sin. Or at least a G-rated version of one.

Consider this story from Genesis: After the floodwaters had receded, Noah planted a vineyard, grew some grapes, and made wine. One day he drank too much and passed out in his tent, naked. Noah's bare body was spotted by his son Ham, who then told his brothers about it—we assume in a disrespectfully jovial manner. For this, Ham would pay. Or more precisely, Ham's son Canaan would pay. Noah thundered, "Cursed be Canaan; a slave of slaves shall he be to his brothers."

What exactly was Ham's sin? Perhaps seeing his father's nakedness. Or maybe Ham did more than just look: Some believe that Ham perpetrated something X-rated on his dad, though this isn't stated in the text itself. To me, perhaps the biggest offense was that Noah was asleep. We're never more defenseless and vulnerable than when we're asleep. If you mock a napping person, you might as well be putting a stumbling block before the blind (to use another biblical phrase).

So as difficult as it is to restrain myself from teasing my mother, it's best that I did. When I get home, I check in on Jasper, who is sleeping as soundly as a drunken Noah. He is in my favorite sleeping position: on his knees, kowtowing before some invisible Chinese magistrate. I watch him for a good three minutes and smile like an idiot the whole time.

"When you make your neighbor a loan of any sort, you shall not go into his house to fetch his pledge."

—DEUTERONOMY 24:10

Day 236. The writing on our doorpost is starting to attract more attention. The building manager—a tall Russian guy with a goatee—knocks on our door today. He tells me I have to paint over it. Someone has complained. I ask him if I can wait a few months, till my year ends.

"Why so long?" he says.

"Well, I'm—"

"What is the writing, anyway?"

"It's the Ten Commandments. From the Bible."

"The Bible? Oh, religious?"

He puts his hands in the air and backs away. He looks flustered, like he just stepped on my cat's tail or got caught feeling up my wife.

"Leave it there, leave it there."

It certainly wasn't our neighbor Nancy who was doing the complaining. I run into her in the hall while she is walking her dog.

"I love the writing," she says. "I was thinking of doing it to my door."

Excellent! My first disciple.

"Anytime," I say. "I'll write it for you myself."

"OK, I may take you up on that."

She pauses.

"You know what? Wait here."

Nancy vanishes into her apartment and emerges with a blue paperback.

"I'm not very religious," she says, "but I like this book. It's *Pirkei Avot: Ethics of the Fathers.*"

She flips to a page with a passage highlighted in yellow.

She reads: "'In a place of no humanity, strive to be human.' That's my motto for living in New York."

That's good wisdom. It may not be from the Bible itself, but it's good.

"Here, take it." Nancy says. Before I can say no, she's shoved the book into my hands and is on her way into the apartment.

"How's your Hendrix proposal?" I ask before she shuts the door.

"Just a few thousand more pages, and I'll be done."

> *You shall remember that you were a slave in Egypt . . .*
> —Deuteronomy 16:12

Day 237. I got an unexpected email today. It arrived in my in-box at 1:07 p.m. from a guy named Kevin Roose. "Allow me to introduce myself. I'm an eighteen-year-old native Ohioan in the middle of my first year at Brown."

Kevin went on to explain that he's going to be working at a café in New York this summer, but he wants to be a writer, and he noticed I went to Brown as well, and . . . would I be willing to take him on as a part-time personal intern?

This was an unusual request in several respects. First, there's the fact that he wants to be a writer in this day and age, since it seems about as pragmatic as getting into Betamax sales. Second, that he took the initiative to email me. I don't inspire many groupies. I still have a special place in my heart for my one and only rabid fan—the guy who took off his sweatshirt at a Texas signing to reveal passages of my book scrawled on his T-shirt in Magic Marker. Other than that, I'm not in the market for bodyguards.

alive nothing that breathes." Pretty shocking stuff. But when talking about this in the *midrash,* the rabbis completely ignore the bloodletting. Instead, they focus on the part in which the Israelites offer peace. They say, *See! The passage is all about compassion* (I'm paraphrasing). "It's clear the rabbis have moral objections to this passage," professor Galambush says. "So they pretend it says something they do believe in—peace—rather than something they object to. You can't underestimate the radicalness of the rabbis."

My slave Kevin seems like a nice guy, so I'll probably take option number 4 on those passages that allow me to give him a biblical beat-down.

> *Give ear, O Lord, to my prayer . . .*
>
> —PSALMS 86:6

Day 237, afternoon. Jasper got out of his cast a couple of weeks ago. But the medical traumas never end. Today he trips and falls while dancing a bit too enthusiastically to The Wiggles masterpiece "Fruit Salad." I watch him as he tumbles face forward and smacks his forehead hard against the door frame. It makes a horrible sound, a crack like a line drive off the wall at Shea Stadium.

I pick him up. He is crying by now. I inspect his forehead—a small bump.

"Should we get you some ice?"

He just keeps wailing, openmouthed.

I look at the bump again. It is bigger. Scarily bigger. It has become a bump you'd see on Fred Flintstone's head after he got hit by a rock at the quarry. It looks like a golf ball had been sewn into Jasper's skin.

I run into our bedroom to show Julie, who is still sleeping. We call the doctor, who tells us that if he starts vomiting, bring him to the ER. Otherwise, just ice it down and expect him to have a black eye tomorrow. Toddler's foreheads apparently distort like that.

It's a horrible moment—and also a milestone of sorts. My first reaction, as I was running to show Julie, was to pray to God for Jasper to be OK. It was like reflex praying. Unplanned, unforced.

Can . . . the leopard change his spots?

—JEREMIAH 13:23

Day 238. A spiritual update: I'm all over the place. My belief in God changes by the hour. I have three phases, about evenly split throughout the day. As I type this, I'm in phase two. But that could change by the time I finish the next paragraph.

First, there's the comfortable old position: agnosticism. I haven't erased that totally, and it especially pops up whenever I read about religious extremism.

The second phase is all about a newfound reverence for life. Life isn't just a series of molecular reactions. There's a divine spark in there. The official term is "vitalism." I'd always thought of vitalism as a nineteenth-century relic—in the same category as leeches and phrenology. But now I'm a believer, at least sometimes.

The third phase, the highest level, is when I believe in something more specific, a God who cares, who pays attention to my life, who loves. Why wouldn't there be a God? It makes just as much sense as having no God. Otherwise, existence itself is just too random.

Phase three is an amazing and uplifting state. For instance, my Hollywood dreams are in meltdown mode. My previous book—the one about the encyclopedia—was optioned for a movie. But now the director won't email me back. And when I call his assistant, she always tells me to hold, then returns to report—surprise!—he's not there right now but I am welcome to leave a message. Hmmm. I wonder: Could he be breaking the commandment not to lie?

It's annoying, but things happen for a reason, right? It wasn't meant to be. Perhaps something better will come out of it. Maybe Scorsese will call me out of the blue and tell me that encyclopedias have replaced bloodshed as his new obsession.

Julie always told me that things happen for a reason. To which I would reply, Sure, things happen for a reason. Certain chemical reactions take place in people's brains, and they cause those people to move their mouths and arms. That's the reason. But, I thought, there's no greater purpose. Now I sometimes think Julie's right. There *is* a reason. There has to be. Otherwise, it's all too absurd. The world can't be that Dadaist.

It's certainly a healthier way to look at life. I feel better when I see the world this way. I ask Elton Richards, the pastor out to pasture, about this. Maybe I should commit myself to believing in God for the simple reason that it will make my life better.

"You could," he says. "But it feels a little too calculated for me."

It smacks of Pascal's wager. This was devised by Blaise Pascal, the seventeenth-century French mathematician. He said we should believe in God because the cost is minimal, but the potential benefit of heaven is huge. Believe in God just to avoid hell. Pretty cynical, really. Or to use a more recent metaphor, maybe it's the *Matrix* wager. Am I taking a blue pill just because it's a happier worldview?

"I think you should believe for a more organic reason," says Elton. "If you're going to believe at all."

He who pursues righteousness and kindness will find life and honor.

—Proverbs 21:21

Day 239. I've been trying to be as compassionate as possible. Often this requires energy and planning—going to the soup kitchen, for instance.

But today God or fate gave me a big, juicy softball: An old lady asked me to help her across the street. Never in my thirty-eight years has an old lady asked me to help her across the street. I didn't think those things happened anymore. I thought it was just an expression, like kittens getting stuck in trees.

But after lunch, outside the Jewish Theological Seminary, where I was meeting a friend, this kindly old octogenarian woman tells me that she is worried about making it across Broadway's six lanes alone, and could I maybe help.

I'd be glad to. Though actually *ecstatic* is a better word. She locks her arm in mine—I figure she's safely past the age when I can't touch her—and we walk across, me holding my right hand out in a stern stop-traffic position, which was totally unnecessary, since the cars were safely motionless at the red light.

I am so happy about the situation, I stay with her for another several blocks, which, oddly enough, doesn't creep her out.

Be glad in the Lord, and rejoice, O righteous, and shout for joy,
all you upright in heart!

—PSALMS 32:11

Day 240. Mr. Berkowitz is over to pray again today. I can only say no to him so many times. He's giving me another kind but stern lecture.

"You have to say a prayer in the morning," says Mr. Berkowitz.

"Right," I say.

"You have to say a prayer over bread."

"Right."

"Did you say the prayer over bread today, Arnold?"

"Right."

"Arnold, I asked you a question. Are you paying attention?"

I am busted. I had tuned out. Mr. Berkowitz is frustrated; not angry, but frustrated.

"Yes, yes, I said the prayer over bread."

"OK," he says.

Then it's on to learning the Hebrew alphabet.

"*Aleph, beth, daleth.*"

"No, aleph, beth, *gimel.*"

"Aleph, beth, gimel, daleth."

It's a time-consuming visit—a ninety-minute chunk out of my day. But in the end, I'm glad he came over, because Mr. Berkowitz said two things that struck me as astoundingly wise.

The first was about how much he loves doing the commandments. "To me, going to pray is like going to do a hundred-thousand-dollar deal," he said.

This is a mind-set I'm trying to adopt. I shouldn't look at the Bible as a collection of pesky tasks on my to-do list. I have to look forward to the commandments. I have to love them.

And in a few cases—just a handful, really—I'm starting to. Like, with the Sabbath. I used to orient my week around Monday, the start of the secular workweek. Now it's the Sabbath. Everything leads up to the Sabbath. On Friday morning I start prepping for it like I'm going on a big date. I make a huge pot of coffee so that I don't have to do anything resembling cooking on the Sabbath. I pile my research books in a corner.

And when the sun sets, I flip off my computer and get to work not working. Because resting is, paradoxically, difficult. The writer Judith Shulevitz talks about how avoiding business requires much effort. She's right. You can't talk about work, you can't even think about work. A notion about *Esquire* will creep into my brain—I have to write that article on weddings for Thursday—and I'll squash it down. Another will pop up. It's like mental Whac-a-Mole. By the end of Saturday, as the sun finally sets, I feel as if I've done something strenuous but healthy, like I've taken a run through Central Park. I feel good, like I deserved the endorphin rush the Sabbath gave me. And then I start to look forward to next week's Sabbath.

The second thing Mr. Berkowitz says is this: "It's a different way of looking at the world. Your life isn't about rights. It's about responsibilities." It's the biblical version of that famous quote from our first Catholic president: "Ask not what your country can do for you, ask what you can do for your country." It's a good way to think. It's not my natural mind-set, far from it, but I'm giving it a shot.

Consider speech. As a journalist—even though I spent most of my career as a frivolous entertainment journalist—I've been obsessed with my right to free speech. If I was an absolutist in any sense, then it was as a zealot for the First Amendment. Journalists should be allowed to say whatever they want. It's our right. The American way. Take no prisoners. But now I'm trying to balance that mind-set with my responsibility not to engage in evil tongue or the written equivalent. In my article on tuxedos, do I really need to make a cheap joke at David Arquette's expense? Does it make the world a better place? As much as it pains me, I leave my article free from Arquette abuse.

Month Nine: May

In the beginning was the Word . . .
—JOHN 1:1

Day 243. Today is the first day of my New Testament life. I'm as nervous as I've been since the start of this experiment, more nervous than even the very first day, more nervous than when I called up Guru Gil.

On the one hand, I can't wait to dive in. It should be a massive education. Before this year, I knew only the very basics of the New Testament and Christianity. Well, the basics plus the random facts that I still remember from the encyclopedia (for example, some early Christians believed that the creation of the world was equivalent to conception, and it occurred on March 25, lending symbolic weight to Jesus's birth nine months later on December 25). But I want more in-depth knowledge. So this will be good for me.

Plus, it feels timely. It's hard to argue with the fact that the New Testament holds more sway in America today than the Old. Or, to be more precise, the Christian literal interpretation of the Bible holds more sway than the Jewish method of exegesis. I don't buy that we're on the verge of a theocracy, but certainly evangelical Christianity—both in its conservative and progressive forms—has a massive impact on our lives.

On the other hand, I'm freaked out. I've already been overwhelmed by the complexity of my own tradition, and now I'm going to venture into even more foreign territory. I told Julie I had a stress headache.

"You don't have to do it, you know," said Julie.

"If I don't, I'll only be telling half the story," I said.

"But it's a big half."

True. But like Nachshon, the Israelite who marched into the Red

Sea, I'm going to wade into the water and see what happens. Before I do, though, I have to wrestle with a bunch of Big Issues.

The first Big Issue is this: If I'm going to switch my focus to the New Testament, should I continue following all the rules of the Hebrew Bible? In other words, should I keep my beard and fringes? Or should I break out the Gillette Mach3 and order shrimp fajitas?

After asking this question to pretty much every Christian expert I meet, I've come to this definitive conclusion: I don't know.

You can find a small group—a very small group—of Christians who say that every single Old Testament rule should still be followed by everyone. The ultralegalist camp. They quote these words from Jesus found in Matthew 5:17–18:

> Think not that I have come to abolish the law and the prophets; I have
> come not to abolish them but to fulfill them. For truly, I say to you, till
> heaven and earth pass away, not an iota, not a dot, will pass from the
> law until all is accomplished.

Jesus is God, but he affirms that the laws of the ancient Israelites still stand.

On the other end of the spectrum are those Christians who say that Jesus overrode all rules in the Old Testament. He created a new covenant. His death was the ultimate sacrifice, so there's no need for animal sacrifice—or, for that matter, any other Old Testament laws. Even the famous Ten Commandments are rendered unnecessary by Jesus.

Consider Matthew 22:37–39, in which Jesus is asked by a lawyer what is the great commandment of the law.

Jesus responds:

> You shall love the Lord your God with all your heart, and with all
> your soul, and with all your mind.
> This is the great and first commandment.
> And a second is like it, You shall love your neighbor as yourself.

Some Christians say all of the other eight commandments flow from those two. You love your neighbor, so you don't lie to him. You love your neighbor, so you don't steal from him. The Old Testament is important historically, but as a moral guidebook, it has been superseded.

And then there's the vast middle ground. Most Christians I met draw a distinction between (a) moral laws and (b) ritual laws. The moral laws are the ones such as those found in the Ten Commandments: no killing, no coveting, and so forth. Those we still need to follow. Ritual laws are the ones about avoiding bacon and not wearing clothes of mixed fibers. Jesus made those laws obsolete.

What does obsolete mean? Is it a sin to keep a beard and avoid shellfish? Or is it just unnecessary, like wearing sunscreen indoors? Ask ten people, and, once again, you'll get ten different answers. But most seem to say, go ahead, wear that sunscreen. It won't hurt. You need to accept Jesus, but you don't need to shave the beard.

Which is a relief. I want to keep the beard. I'm not ready to give up my rituals. That would feel like I ran seventeen miles of a marathon. So unless there's a contradiction in the laws—for instance, the literal interpretation of eye for an eye contradicts the literal interpretation of turn the other cheek—I'll follow both Old and New.

My second Big Issue is this: As a Jewish person, how do I treat the issue of the divinity of Christ?

For the bona fide literal New Testament experience, I should accept Jesus as Lord. But I just can't do it. I've read the New Testament several times, and though I think of Jesus as a great man, I don't come away from the experience accepting him as savior. I've had no road-to-Damascus moment yet.

The closest I've come to such a moment was probably during college when I grew strangely envious of my best friend's Catholicism. He went to mass several times a week and did the sign of the cross before every meal. We ate together at least once a day, and I always felt awkward while I waited for him to finish his prayer. Awkward and superficial. Here he was, funny and smart, but he had something deeper going on than I did. I'd pretend not to look, but I was fixated by the sign of the cross. It's such a simple and beautiful ritual. What if I started doing it with him at dinner? Just to see what it's like? To see if I felt anything? Would my friend be weirded out? Probably. So I never tried it.

Same goes for now. I could adopt the cognitive-dissonance strategy: If I act like Jesus is God, eventually maybe I will start to believe that Jesus is God. That's been my tactic with the God of the Hebrew Bible, and it's actually started to work. But there's a difference. When I do it with the Hebrew God, I feel like I'm trying on my forefathers' robes and sandals. There's a family connection. Doing it with Jesus would feel uncomfortable. I've come to value my heritage enough that it'd feel disloyal to convert.

Which naturally leads to this quandary: If I don't accept Christ, can I get anything out of the New Testament at all? What if I follow the moral teachings of Jesus but don't worship him as God? Or is that just a fool's errand? Again, depends whom you ask.

The more humanist mainline Christian denominations say, yes, it's OK to follow Jesus's ethics without converting to Christianity. Ask a Unitarian or more liberal Lutherans, and they'll tell you there is much to be learned from Christ the moral teacher. This is Christianity with a strong dash of Enlightenment.

The most extreme example of this comes from Enlightenment's archbishop himself, Thomas Jefferson. His version of Christianity is so one-sided it almost seems a parody of this position. In the early 1800s Jefferson created an edition of the Bible called the Jefferson Bible. He stripped away all the supernatural references. Gone was the Resurrection. Gone was the miracle of the loaves and fishes. Gone was the virgin birth. Jefferson's idea was that Christ was a great moral philosopher. So Jefferson kept only Christ's moral teachings: forgiveness, loving thy neighbor, and striving for peace. He called them "the most sublime and benevolent code of morals which has ever been offered to man."

The Da Vinci Code tilts the way of Jefferson. Dan Brown doesn't come right out and say that Christ was totally human, but a Christ who marries and has kids sure makes him seem more like us mortal men.

So that's one side. On the other side, most evangelical Christians would say that simply paying attention to Jesus's moral teachings is missing the point. The central message of the Gospels is that Jesus is God, He died for our sins, and He rose again on the third day. You need to accept Him.

The emphasis on faith is a key difference between modern Judaism and current evangelical Christianity. Judaism has a slogan: deed over creed. There's an emphasis on behavior; follow the rules of the Torah, and eventually you'll come to believe. But evangelical Christianity says you must first believe in Jesus, then the good works will naturally follow. Charity and kindness alone cannot save you. You must, as the saying goes, be "justified by faith."

Here's an email I got from a conservative evangelical Christian I contacted. He runs a website that tries to reconcile science with biblical literalism. He wrote:

> It is through being in Christ and following Him that we become transformed. Unless one takes this step, one cannot be truly transformed. So, after your year is over, you will go back to being a man who finds purpose in weird projects and writing assignments. Becoming a follower of Jesus Christ is much more rewarding.

In short, I got schooled.

And yet . . . I still want to explore Christian biblical literalism. It's not a minor thing. It's hugely relevant to my quest. So here's my revised plan: I'm going to visit some Christian communities that interpret the Bible literally. I will try to learn about them. And, when inspired, and when possible, I've decided that I should try to experience some of their teachings firsthand. Overall, it will be much less Do It Yourself than my trip through the Hebrew Scriptures. It'll be more like a guided tour.

Which brings me to my final Big Issue. Where to go on my tour? Christian biblical literalism comes in dozens of flavors. No way I could cover them all. I'll do my best. But I'll spend much of my time looking at the two poles that shape our moral debate:

1. The Pat Robertson–Jerry Falwell–style conservative fundamentalists, who place a lot of emphasis on the issues of homosexuality, abortion, the Apocalypse, and George W. Bush's foreign policy.

2. The Red-letter Christians, a growing evangelical group that focuses on social justice, poverty, and the environment.

Both accept the Bible as the word of God, both accept Jesus as their savior, but they come out with radically different agendas.

A disclaimer: I'm going to try to be fair, but I'm probably going to fail. It's the same problem I had when I went to the Creation Museum. There are limits to how far my mind can leap. I've been a moderate New York liberal all my life. Will I really be able to get inside the mind of a conservative evangelical from Virginia?

> *"Judge not, that you be not judged."*
>
> —Matthew 7:1

Day 247. This evening I spend an hour on the phone talking to Pastor Elton Richards. He wants to give me a theological inoculation.

I tell him I'm about to make a road trip to Jerry Falwell's church, and he wants to make sure I know that, in his opinion, Falwell's version of Christianity bears practically no relation to Jesus's message.

"Take what they say, and in most cases, it's the exact opposite of Jesus's message. Jesus's message was one of inclusion. Theirs is of exclusion."

"OK," I say.

"And they're so focused on the other world and the end times. Jesus cared for the downtrodden and outcasts in this world."

"Got it," I say.

"It's this god-awful certainty that they have."

I promise him and promise him again that I'll spend as much time looking at other, more progressive interpretations of Christianity.

Falwell—who died several months after my visit—embodied a certain ultraliteral brand of Christianity. For decades he was the go-to guy when the mainstream media wanted a quote from the Christian right about homosexuality or abortion. He was the liberal's nightmare, the man who launched a thousand Aaron Sorkin plotlines.

Here's my chance to see Falwell unfiltered. I take a flight to Richmond, Virginia, and drive a rental car to Thomas Road Baptist Church in Lynchburg. It's a big week in the Falwell universe. For its fiftieth year, the church has moved from its three-thousand-seat house of worship to a splashy new six-thousand-seat one.

At nine-thirty in the morning, I park my car along with hundreds of others, pull open the glass, mall-like front doors, and step inside Falwell's enclave. Like all megachurches, it's not just a church. It's a complex.

There's a massive, brightly lit walkway called "Main Street." There's a playground with a Noah's ark theme featuring pairs of wooden zebras and tigers, along with a huge whale's mouth that kids can climb into à la Jonah. There's a Starbucks-ish coffee shop called The Lion and the Lamb Café, where I get a pretty good iced coffee. Nearby a player piano tinkles Mrs. Falwell's favorite hymns.

Services don't start for a while, but at ten, many of the parishioners attend one of the Bible studies in the classrooms off Main Street. You have an astounding range to choose from—thirty-eight in all, from a tutorial on the Apocalypse to a meeting targeted at Christian biker dudes.

With the imminent increase in my household, I opt for a class called Growing Families, in room 255. There are about thirty churchgoers already assembled, mostly white, mostly crisply dressed, engaging in a prestudy mingle.

"Hello, I'm glad you could come," says a fortysomething woman. She eyes my beard. "We welcome people from all, uh, walks of life."

"Thanks."

"Do you have a growing family?" she asks.

"Yes, I have a son—and two more on the way."

"Wow! And you live here in Lynchburg?"

"No." I pause. "New York."

"Great! What are you doing here?"

"Um, just traveling around the South a bit."

Oh, man. Biblically, I should have been honest and told her about my book, but I only have a day here at Falwell's headquarters, and I didn't want to waste any time.

"You're here with your wife?"

"Uh, yeah. She's back at the hotel."

Another lie. I didn't want to seem like a lout who abandoned his pregnant spouse, which is what I did.

"She didn't want to come?"

"She was going to, but, uh, she had morning sickness."

And on it grows, the tangled web. She keeps asking questions, I keep spitting out lies.

Mercifully, the meeting starts. The pastor, a man who looks like a thinner, younger, brown-haired Falwell, has some announcements. An upcoming luau, a couple's twentieth wedding anniversary—and a welcome to me, soon-to-be-father of twins. The parishioners applaud. I wave a sheepish thank-you.

Man, these people are friendly. That's the overwhelming first impression: They're disorientingly friendly. When I walked into the church, an official greeter named Tip said "Good morning!" with such enthusiasm, I'd have to append a half dozen exclamation points to get across his tone. Nobody is aloof. Everybody keeps eye contact. Everyone smiles. In my four hours there, I got more pats on the back, arms on the shoulders, and double-handed clasps than I've gotten in ten years in New York.

I know that this friendliness has limits—and disturbing ones. I know that Falwell has said "AIDS is the wrath of a just God against homosexuals." I know that after 9/11 he said "the pagans, and the abortionists, and the feminists, and the gays, and the lesbians . . . the ACLU . . . I point the finger in their face and say 'You helped this happen.'" I know that he recently said that we shouldn't worry about so-called global warming because, in Psalms 119:90, it says God has "established the earth and it abideth." I know that his magazine crowbarred poor purse-carrying Teletubby Tinky Winky out of the closet.

Presumably, Tip and others share these views. But that intolerance coexists with a stunning bonhomie. The place is a study in sweet and sour.

After about fifteen minutes of announcements with no end in sight, I decide I need to get out of there. This was no different than a thousand other churches or temples in America. I need something more spicy.

"Be right back," I lie to the guy next to me, as I slip out. "I have to go to the bathroom."

I wander down a flight of stairs to the singles seminar. That could be good.

The woman at the singles welcoming table asks how old I am.

"Thirty-seven," I say.

"You're right in there," she points. "It's for singles thirty-five to fifty."

That hurts. I am in the oldsters' group. By the way, another fib. I am thirty-eight. Vanity.

The leader of the singles group is a burly ex-military guy with a bald head, a gray goatee, wire-rimmed glasses balanced on his forehead, and a huge amount of energy. He seems more into tough love than the folks at the Growing Families class.

He paces back and forth, telling us that we should give up the idea that we're perfect.

"Anyone ever say bad things about other people?"

We nod.

"Anyone ever think bad sexual thoughts?"

Yes.

"Anyone ever have envy?"

Yes.

"Anyone ever lie?"

It's a sermon directed at me.

"Did I ever tell you the story of when I was working as Dr. Falwell's bodyguard?" says our leader. "I handed him the mail one Tuesday, and he says to me, 'Did you vote today?' And I said, 'Um . . . um . . . um . . . yeah.' But I hadn't. I lied. I lied to Dr. Falwell. I had forgotten that it was Election Day. But I know that I have voted in every election since."

I can't figure out how this applies to dating, but there's no time for questions. The class ends at eleven o'clock, and the featured show begins right after: Falwell's sermon.

The sermon takes place in an enormous room with comfy, Loews Cineplex–style seats; three swiveling TV cameras; and two huge screens that display the hymn lyrics karaoke-style over photos of seagulls and purple orchids.

On the side are two "Cry Rooms." When I saw the words *Cry Room* on the church map, I thought it was for parishioners who became too wildly emotional. Actually, it's a soundproof space for screaming babies.

Falwell himself walks onto the stage. There he is: He's got that familiar silver hair with the tidy part. He's packing a few more pounds than he used to. As the three-hundred-person choir sings a hymn, Falwell leans way back on his heels, his hands clasped together in front of him, smiling beatifically.

Falwell starts with some announcements of his own—that the café is open from eight in the morning to eleven at night, that Rick Stanley, the stepbrother of Elvis Presley, is visiting today. And then Falwell puts his hands on the pulpit and begins his sermon proper. And here's the thing about the sermon. It is kind of . . . bland. There was no fire, no brimstone, no homophobic remarks, no warnings of the imminent Apocalypse.

I've read dozens of Falwell's sermons online since that visit. And this wasn't a total aberration. More than half of the content is run-of-the-mill stuff: the importance of passing the baton to today's youth. The suggestion to keep a prayer journal. A moral lesson about being optimistic, another about having patience—both of which I find hard to argue with.

I noticed the same thing from watching hours of Pat Robertson's *700 Club*. Sometimes you'll get a crazy "Let's assassinate Hugo Chavez"–type comment. But a lot of it is indistinguishable from standard morning TV: an interview with a gospel singer, or a health segment on the club's weekly "Skinny Wednesday" feature (the wackiest thing I learned there was that Robertson has a side business in "age-defying protein pancakes").

That's the big secret: The radical wing of the Christian right is a lot more boring than its liberal detractors would have you believe.

Falwell's sermon today ties his church's fiftieth anniversary to the concept of the Jubilee in the Bible, which occurs once every fifty years. He encouraged us to be "soul winners" and win over the two hundred thousand souls in the Lynchburg area.

It's not a particularly offensive sermon, but I will say that it has absolutely nothing to do with the Jubilee the Bible talks about. The Bible's Jubilee year is about forgiving debts and returning all property to the original owner, about social justice, about evening the balance between rich and poor. Falwell's was about expanding his church.

After the service, the curious seeker can get one-on-one counsel with one of Falwell's pastors. I am assigned to Tom, who looks to be in his twenties, and has a spiky boy-band hairdo to offset his suit and tie.

Tom works at Liberty University, Falwell's nearby college. It's an amazing place, Liberty, the total opposite of my permissive, grades-optional alma mater. The Liberty rulebook contains such items as: "Six reprimands and $25 fine for attendance at a dance, possession and/or use of tobacco" and "twelve reprimands and $50 fine for attendance at, possession or viewing of an 'R,' 'X,' or 'NC-17' rated movie, or entering the residence hallway of the opposite sex."

I decide I have to redeem myself. I have to stop lying, so I tell Tom that I'm Jewish and writing a book about my spiritual quest. He's interested. I ask if I could gain anything from following the moral teachings of Jesus without being born again.

"It's OK to follow his teachings. It can make you a better person," he says. "But it's not enough. You need to accept Him, to be born again."

"I got saved when I was a freshman in high school," Tom continues. "I was a good Christian already. I went to church. I acted as morally as I could. I had accepted Jesus here." Tom points to his head. "But not here." He points to his heart. "I was off by twelve inches."

He talks so passionately, so intensely, with such freedom from irony, I feel myself becoming unanchored. Perhaps to counter this, as a defensive measure, I bring up the gay issue.

"I have a lot of trouble with the Bible's stance on homosexuality," I say. Adding somewhat lamely: "I have a lot of gay friends."

"So do I," Tom says.

This takes me aback. A Falwell pastor hanging with Lynchburg's gay community? It turns out, Tom meant formerly gay people trying to overcome their gayness, which made more sense.

"Yes, homosexuality is an abomination," says Tom. "But I'm a sinner too. We're all sinners. You just have to love them."

This is a pretty mild stance—the hate-the-sin, not-the-sinner idea. I'm guessing he toned the rhetoric down for his Northeastern Jewish audience of one. But, still, I find this stance intolerant in its own way. It's like saying that we should love Jesse Jackson, except for the fact that he's black.

After about a half hour, my questions slow, and Tom asks if we could pray together. We close our eyes, bow our heads, put our elbows on our knees, and he begins addressing the Lord. "Thank you, Lord, for giving A. J. and me the time to talk today. And may you give him more guidance in his spiritual journey, Lord."

More guidance—that I need for sure. We can agree on that.

. . . The men likewise gave up natural relations with women and were consumed with passion for one another, men committing shameless acts with men and receiving in their own persons the due penalty for their error.

—ROMANS 1:27

Day 256. Back in New York, I'm continuing my tutorial in evangelical Christianity. It's Friday night, and I'm sitting in on a Bible study group. The group has been around for thirty years and meets every week on the Upper East Side of New York. Tonight we'll be delving into the Epistle to the Hebrews, chapter three. We'll be led by a man named Dr. Ralph Blair, who is a hardcore Christian evangelical.

Oh, I should mention one other thing: Ralph Blair is gay. And out-of-the-closet gay. Not, mind you, the I-once-was-gay-but-now-am-cured type of gay. Ralph—and all the other men in his Bible group—embrace their homosexuality with the same zeal that ultraconservative evangelicals condemn it. They're the anti-Robertsons.

"Come in," says Ralph. "You're the first one here."

Ralph has a calming, velvety voice. Which is appropriate—his day job is as a psychotherapist. The Bible study meets in his office, which is everything you'd want in a shrink's office: black leather chairs, indirect lighting, dark wood everywhere. The *Diagnostic and Statistical Manual of Mental Disorders* weighs down one shelf, *The Sex Atlas* another. And Ralph himself looks pleasingly shrinkish: bald except for a fringe of gray hair, dressed in a dark green corduroy jacket, a blue sweater, a red tie, and chinos.

"I'm glad you found us," he says. "It's not what your average gay man in New York is doing on a Friday night."

I chuckle.

"The *New York Times* wrote us up in the eighties, and that's how they started the article," he says.

Ralph has arranged a dozen seats on the edges of the room, each with a thick blue Bible on top. It's more than we'll need. Most of the regulars are out of town, so only three diehards show up: a stout songwriter who grew up in Florida; a square-jawed architect; and a dance teacher at a New Jersey college who takes copious notes.

They are all members of Evangelicals Concerned, an organization that Ralph founded in 1975 for gay and gay-friendly evangelicals. It's not a massive movement: Ralph has two thousand people on his mailing list. But its existence alone was a surprise.

We begin. Ralph appoints the dance teacher to read some verses from Hebrews 3 out loud. Ralph stops him to discuss. "Faith is not merely intellectual assent," Ralph says, taking off his wire-rimmed glasses to punctuate the point. "You have to be willing to act on your faith. In other words, talk is cheap. Except in therapy."

Ralph returns his glasses to the end of his nose. He's not overbearing, but he's definitely in charge. He's the analyzer, the parser, the one who knows the original Greek words.

"Go on," says Ralph.

The dance instructor reads a verse that likens Moses to a house and Jesus to the builder of a house.

This is an important verse. It's at the heart of Ralph's theology: Jesus isn't just a great prophet. He isn't, as Ralph says, "the fairest flower in the family of humanity." He is God, and the Resurrection was literal. Ralph quotes C. S. Lewis here: "A man who was merely a man and said the sort of things Jesus said would not be a great moral teacher. He would either be a lunatic—on the level with the man who says he is a poached egg—or else he would be the Devil of Hell. You must make your choice."

In short, Ralph is theologically conservative. That's what makes him an evangelical. The Scriptures' social and humanist message is important, but Blair puts the emphasis on the divinity of Christ itself.

The ninety-minute session glides by without a single mention of homosexuality. If an evangelist from Thomas Road Baptist Church happened to drop in, he might not even notice anything different. Well, let me revise that. Ralph and his group do, at least, fulfill one gay stereotype: They know a lot about clothes.

At one point, the conversation drifts to buttons, and the dance instructor starts throwing around terms like *placket*—which apparently means the part of a man's shirt that covers the buttons.

The architect tosses in a factoid about Eisenhower-style jackets, which were truncated to save fabric in World War II. They had no skirt.

"The skirt," he explains to me, "is the part of a man's blazer worn below the waist." He looks at Ralph: "You wear a skirt almost every day."

Ralph smiles.

After Bible Study, we go out for chicken kebabs at a Turkish restaurant and I get a crash course in Ralph's life. He grew up in a moderately religious Presbyterian home in Ohio. He knew he was gay early on, certainly by high school. He also knew he loved religion.

In his high school library, he found a catalog for Bob Jones University, the fundamentalist college. He was drawn to it, he says with a laugh, because it was bright yellow. "All the other catalogs were dull colors, black and white."

He liked Bob Jones U's emphasis on Christ, and enrolled in 1964. It didn't go smoothly. For starters, Ralph got chewed out by an apoplectic, finger-wagging Bob Jones Sr. for defending Reverend Billy Graham, who was considered too liberal. "I thought he was going to have a heart attack," he says.

Ralph didn't come out of the closet at Bob Jones U. He went public slowly, steadily, as he crisscrossed the country attending other seminaries and grad schools. He started Evangelicals Concerned in 1975 after the president of an evangelical college took him out to dinner in New York and confessed that he was a tormented, closeted gay man.

Of course, Ralph's organization is controversial. And at first blush, it makes about as much sense as an Association of Vegan Burger King Owners. It's at once inspiring and depressing. Inspiring that they have found one another, and depressing because they are part of a movement in which the majority thinks of their sexuality as sinful.

But Ralph says that you have to distinguish between evangelical Christianity and the religious right. The religious right's obsession with homosexuality comes "out of their culture, not out of Scripture."

"But there do seem to be antigay passages in the Bible," I say.

"Yes, the so-called clobber passages," he says. "But I call them the clobbered passages."

Ralph's argument is this: The Bible does not talk about loving same-sex relationships as they exist today. Jesus would have no problem with two men committed to each other. One of Ralph's pamphlets has this headline on the front: "What Jesus Said about Homosexuality." You open up the pamphlet, and there's a blank page.

Ralph says that if you look at the Bible's allegedly antigay passages in historical context, they aren't antigay at all. They are actually antiabuse, or antipaganism. Consider the famous Leviticus passage: "You shall not lie with a male as with a woman, it is an abomination."

"In biblical times, there was no parity between men and women. Women and children were just a little bit above slaves. To lie with a man like a woman was to disgrace him. It's what soldiers did to their conquered enemies, they raped them."

That famous Leviticus passage is actually merely saying: Do not treat your fellow man disgracefully.

Or take another commonly cited passage in the New Testament, Romans 1:26–27. Here the Apostle Paul rails against those who gave in to "dishonorable passions."

". . . Their women exchanged natural relations for unnatural, and the men likewise gave up natural relations with women and were consumed with passion for one another, men committing shameless acts with men and receiving in their own persons the due penalty for their error."

Ralph says that Paul is preaching here against pagan cultic practices—the loveless sex that went on in the idolatrous temples of the day.

I hope Ralph's right. I hope the Bible doesn't endorse gay bashing. But even if it does, there's another tack religious people can take. This one I learned from Ralph's acquaintance in the Jewish world, a man named Steven Greenberg. Greenberg is the first out-of-the-closet Orthodox rabbi in America. Like Ralph, he's an extreme minority. Most Orthodox Jews still believe that Leviticus bans same-sex relationships of any kind. Your average far-right Orthodox Jew is just as antigay as your average far-right evangelical; in 2006 the ultra-Orthodox Jews held violent demonstrations in protest of a planned gay pride march in Jerusalem, an event that was eventually canceled.

I call Greenberg. He has plenty to say about the Bible and homosexuality. But the point I find most fascinating is this: God and humans are partners in a quest to reveal new meanings of the Bible. The letters of the Bible are eternal, but not its interpretation.

"The whole Bible is the working out of the relationship between God and man," says Greenberg. "God is not a dictator barking out orders and demanding silent obedience. Were it so, there would be no relationship at all. No real relationship goes just one way. There are always two active parties. We must have reverence and awe for God, and honor for the chain of tradition. But that doesn't mean we can't use new information to help us read the holy texts in new ways. We don't have to sit back and passively accept that Leviticus bans sex between men at all times and in all ways if other convincing ways of reading can be found."

Or put it this way: Greenberg says that God is like an artist who is constantly revising his masterpiece. Sometimes He nearly erases his whole work, as with the Great Flood. Other times, He listens to what humans say. Moses, for instance, argues with God and convinces him to spare the lives of the complaining Israelites. "It sounds strange to say it," the rabbi says, "but in the Bible, God is on a learning curve."

Greenberg tells me, "Never blame a text from the Bible for your behavior. It's irresponsible. Anybody who says X, Y, and Z is in the Bible—it's as if one says, 'I have no role in evaluating this.'"

The idea that we can work with God to evolve the Bible's meaning—it's a thrilling idea. It makes me think back to Mr. Berkowitz and his shoes and the whole issue of religion providing freedom from choice. Greenberg is at the other end of the spectrum from Mr. Berkowitz. He says that just because you're religious doesn't mean you give up your responsibility to choose. You have to grapple with the Bible.

Give thanks in all circumstances . . .

—1 Thessalonians 5:18

Day 263. I feel myself becoming an extremist—at least in some areas. Like with my obsession with gratefulness. I can't stop.

Just now, I press the elevator button and am thankful that it arrives quickly.

I get onto the elevator and am thankful that the elevator cable didn't snap and plummet me to the basement.

I go to the fifth floor and am thankful that I didn't have to stop on the second or third or fourth floor.

I get out and am thankful that Julie left the door unlocked so I don't have to rummage for my King Kong key ring.

I walk in, and am thankful that Jasper is home and healthy and stuffing his face with pineapple wedges.

And on and on. I'm actually muttering to myself, "Thank you . . . thank you . . . thank you."

It's an odd way to live. But also kind of great and powerful. I've never before been so aware of the thousands of little good things, the thousands of things that go right every day.

Sometimes my thank-yous are directed at no one in particular. It's more of an appreciation than a thanks. A reminder to myself: "Pay attention, pal. Savor this moment." But other times, when I'm in a believing phase, my thanks have an addressee. I'm thanking God, or the universal laws of nature—I'm not sure which—but it gives the act of thanking more weight.

And he lifted up his eyes on his disciples, and said: "Blessed are you poor, for yours is the kingdom of God."

—LUKE 6:20

Day 264. In terms of stereotype busting, it's hard to beat Ralph Blair and his group of gay evangelical Christians. What could possibly top that? Evangelical Christians who don't believe in Jesus? Evangelical Christians who worship Poseidon? I don't know.

But I do want to spend some time with another group of evangelicals who, in their own way, have camped out far from the tent of Pat Robertson and Thomas Road Baptist Church. They're called the Red-letter Christians.

I'd never heard of the Red-letter Christians before my biblical year. They're still much smaller than the conservative evangelical lobby. They don't have TV shows with millions of viewers and 1-800 operators standing by. They don't have their own universities with facilities like the LeHaye Ice Hockey Arena. And, yet, even since the start of my year, I've watched them gain more and more national prominence.

The Red-letter Christians are a loose-knit, like-minded group of preachers, the most prominent of whom are a Philadelphia-based pastor named Tony Campolo, and Jim Wallis, the founder of *Sojourners* magazine and author of *God's Politics*. Bono is an honorary member.

Wallis writes in *Sojourners* about how he came up with the name. He was doing an interview at a Nashville radio station, and the DJ said:

"I'm a secular Jewish country music songwriter and disc jockey. But I love your stuff and have been following your book tour." He told me he loved my "riffs" and would like to spend an evening together just to get some lines for new music. "You're a songwriter's dream." Then he told me he believed we were starting a new movement, but noticed we hadn't come up with a name for it yet. "I've got an idea for you," he said. "I think you should call yourselves the Red-letter Christians, for the red parts of the Bible that highlight the words of Jesus. I love the red letter stuff."

In their own way, the Red-letter Christians are literalists. They probably would avoid that label, since the word has such negative connotations. And, true, they accept more figurative language in the Bible than, say, the Robertson camp. But they are literal in the sense that their goal is to return to the plain, primary, simple sense of Jesus's words, what *Merriam-Webster's'* entry for *literalism* calls "the ordinary meaning of a term or expression."

When Jesus said that you should invite the poor, the maimed, the lame, and the blind to your banquets, then you should. When Jesus talked about nonviolence, we should take him at his word. The problem with a lot of religion, says Campolo, is that people have "interpreted the Gospel so much, we've started to believe the interpretations instead of what Jesus said."

Campolo looks a bit like New York Yankees manager Joe Torre, but balder and with clunky glasses. He was, along with Rev. Jesse Jackson, one of Bill Clinton's spiritual advisers during Lewinskygate.

I call up Dr. Campolo, and I immediately like him because he addresses me as "Brother."

"Many of us in the evangelical community believe that evangelical Christianity has become captured and enslaved by the religious right," Campolo says right off the bat. "Its loyalty seems to be more to the platform of the Republican Party than to the radical teachings of Jesus."

Campolo and the Red-letter Christians claim not to be liberal or conservative, Democrat or Republican. Which may be true, but their social policies definitely are more MoveOn.org than Fox News. They're antiwar, anticonsumerism—and above all, antipoverty.

They point out that there are more passages in the Bible about the poor than any other topic save idolatry—several *thousand*, in fact. "The Christian call is to share," says Campolo. "There's nothing wrong with making a million dollars. There *is* something wrong with keeping it."

Some megachurch pastors subscribe to a doctrine called the Prosperity Gospel. The idea is this: Stay faithful, go to church, pay your tithes, and God will bless you by making you rich. God wants you to be successful. God has nothing against a Gulfstream jet and a private tennis court. The Red-letter Christians call this heresy. "Christianity is not a watered-down version of middle-class morality," says Campolo.

As for homosexuality, Campolo is no Ralph Blair. He doesn't endorse gay marriage. But . . . at the same time, he believes it's not a major Christian issue. It wasn't what Jesus preached about. It's not something on which we should waste spiritual capital. Jesus was concerned with breaking down barriers and embracing society's outcasts.

At the end of our conversation, Dr. Campolo calls me Brother again, which I love. If I were in the punditry business, I'd guess that Campolo and his movement will keep gaining steam. They may never fill Madison Square Garden with their sermons, but they'll become a powerful force. They've already gotten enough press to inspire a backlash from those who've been called Black-letter Christians. These are Christians who say the Red-letter Christians ignore troublesome passages that don't fit their agenda. Jesus may have a message of mercy, but he also has a message of justice. They cite his words in Matthew 10:34: "Do not think that I have come to bring peace on the earth. I have not come to bring peace, but a sword."

Regardless, the Red-letter Christians are just one of the cracks in the Republican-evangelical love affair. Some evangelicals don't necessarily go as far as to embrace progressive politics but say instead that churches should stay out of politics. The *New York Times* ran an article in 2006 about Rev. Gregory A. Boyd, a pastor of a Minnesota megachurch. As the article says, Boyd "first became alarmed while visiting another megachurch's worship service on a Fourth of July years ago. The service finished with the chorus singing 'God Bless America' and a video of fighter jets flying over a hill silhouetted with crosses. 'I thought to myself, "What just happened? Fighter jets mixed up with the cross?"'"

He gave a series of sermons saying that Christians should not seek political power but instead seek to have "'power under' others—winning people's hearts by sacrificing for those in need, as Jesus did." A thousand members of Boyd's flock were offended enough to leave the congregation. But another four thousand stayed on.

Jesus said to him, "If you would be perfect, go, sell what you possess and give to the poor, and you will have treasure in heaven; and come, follow me."

—Matthew 19:21

Day 268. I bought *The Purpose-Driven Life* today. This is the guide to a Christian life by Hawaiian-shirt-wearing megachurch minister Rick Warren that has been on the *New York Times* best-seller list for about a half decade now.

When I get it home and start to read it, the first thing I notice is that Warren has copyrighted the phrase "Purpose-driven." It has a little ® after it. This makes me angry. Did Jesus copyright "Turn the Other Cheek"®? Did Moses trademark "Let My People Go?"™

But then I see that, in fine print, it says that Warren gives away 90 percent of the Purpose-driven profits. Ninety percent. He reverse tithes. Now I just feel small. It reminds me that I have to finish my own tithing for the year. I go online and donate the final chunk of my 10 percent to a place called Warm Blankets Orphan Care International, which builds orphanages in Asia. The Bible commands us to take care of the fatherless, plus this charity got the maximum four-star rating on Charity Navigator's website.

As with that first tithing back in September, I feel a mixture of God's pleasure and my own pain. But I think, or hope, I felt less pain than before. It comes back to the idea of surrendering. I still haven't been able to fully surrender my spirit or emotions, but I have at least surrendered some of my bank account. I have to embrace the surrender.

But I won't say another word about it. I've already violated Jesus's teaching: "When you give alms, sound no trumpet before you, as the hypocrites do in synagogues and in the streets, that they may be praised by men."

Love . . . keeps no record of wrongs.

—1 Corinthians 13:4–5 (NIV)

Day 270. There's a passage in the New Testament that I keep coming back to. I think about it every day. It's not nearly as famous as the Sermon on the Mount or the Good Samaritan parable. It's mostly known for being read at weddings.

In the passage, the Apostle Paul is writing to the Corinthians and tells them, "Love is patient, love is kind. It does not envy, it does not boast, it is not proud. It is not rude, it is not self-seeking, it is not easily angered, it keeps no record of wrongs."

I think this passage speaks to me because I violate this one so literally, especially that last part.

I keep a record of wrongs.

It's in my Palm Treo in a file I've labeled "Stuff." I figured the name "Stuff" was vague and dull enough that if someone found my Treo on the subway, he or she wouldn't bother to look at the file. Because I know it's not something I should be proud of.

The problem is, Julie is always insisting that I have a terrible memory. She says I'm constantly getting things wrong. I respond that my memory is about as good as her memory—decent but not great. And that she gets things wrong a lot, too. Then she demands an example, and I can never think of one. So I've started to keep a list.

I'm aware of the irony that I have to consult a list to prove that I have a decent memory.

Here's a sample from my list:

- Vichyssoise is a potato soup like I said, not a fish soup like Julie said.
- The animated android Max Headroom did commercials for Coke like I said, not Pepsi like Julie said.
- We saw an Irish movie called *Waking Ned Devine* on our second date like I said, not another charmingly quirky movie called *Saving Grace*.

You get the idea. I've actually put my list into action only one time. This is because it's kind of difficult to look at the list in public without exposing the secret of the list's existence. During an unpleasant argument about who left the microwave door open, I sneaked into the bathroom, clicked on my Treo, then reemerged with an example of the time she left the keys in a rental car, and we had to call Avis.

In short, the exact kind of thing Paul was preaching against. I decide that not only should I erase my "Stuff" file, but I should confess to Julie about its existence. So that's what I'm doing.

When I show Julie my list, she looks at it for a good ten seconds without talking.

Then she laughs.

"You're not angry?"

"How could I be angry?" she says. "It's just so heartbreaking that you need this."

"Well, I have trouble remembering things in the moment."

I take the Treo back from her, highlight the "Stuff" list, then press delete. I feel good. I've cleaned the slate on my Treo, and I've cleaned the slate with Julie. I know it may seem like a small thing, but the "Stuff" incident made me realize my worldview is too much about quantification. It consists of thousands of little ledgers. Everything—people included—comes with a list of assets and liabilities. When I forgive, I file away the other person's wrongs for possible future use. It's forgiveness with an asterisk.

The Hebrew Scriptures encourage forgiveness—Leviticus tells us not to "bear any grudge"—but it's fair to say that it's a bigger theme in the New Testament. Start over. Be born again. Become a new creature in Christ.

Consider Jesus' parable of the prodigal son. Here's how the *New Catholic Dictionary* describes it:

> The story of the son who took his portion of his father's goods and squandered it by riotous living. When reduced to the depth of misery and obliged to eat the husks thrown to the swine, he bethought himself of his father and resolved to return to him penitent. The father was watching for him, greeted him affectionately, and killed the fatted calf to make merry over his return. The elder son resented the father's rejoicing. The father silenced him by the reminder that: "thou art

always with me, and all I have is thine, but . . . thy brother was dead and is come to life, was lost and is found.

When I first read the parable of the prodigal son, I was perplexed. I felt terrible for the older brother. The poor man put in all these years of loyal service, and his brother skips town, has a wild good time, then returns, and gets a huge feast? It seems outrageously unfair.

But that's if you're thinking quantitatively. If you're looking at life as a balance sheet. There's a beauty to forgiveness, especially forgiveness that goes beyond rationality. Unconditional love is an illogical notion, but such a great and powerful one.

> *The eyes of the Lord are in every place, keeping watch*
> *on the evil and the good.*
>
> —PROVERBS 15:3

Day 271. A spiritual update: Back when I was in seventh grade, I had this delusion. I thought that the girls on whom I had crushes might be watching me. Not at school, mind you. They ignored me there. But in my room, when I was alone, they were watching. I wasn't sure how the logistics of this worked (psychic powers? Hidden cameras like *The Truman Show*?), but it put a lot of pressure on me.

I had to make sure to act cool in case Kim Glickman was observing. I'd put on a David Bowie LP not because I wanted to hear Bowie but because I wanted Kim to *think* I wanted to hear Bowie. I'd brush my teeth in a rakishly nonchalant manner, just so she knew I was cool even when doing dental hygiene. Maybe she likes the tortured artists, I thought. So sometimes I'd channel Sid Vicious and do something crazy, like throw my three-ring school binder across my room and watch the pages splatter on the floor. (I'd then spend fifteen minutes cleaning up and putting the pages back into the rings.)

Sad, I know. Luckily, I got over that in ninth grade. But now I'm starting to have a similar feeling. Kim can't see me. But maybe something can. Something is keeping track of my life, of all of our lives. My existence is not a meaningless collection of actions, so I should take seriously every decision. I don't know what the payoff will be, if anything. But someone is writing this all down in the Book of Life.

> *When they had rowed about three or four miles, they saw Jesus walking on the sea and drawing near to the boat.*
>
> —JOHN 6:19

Day 272. My brother-in-law Eric does not embody the biblical virtue of humility. He's a prideful man.

He's Harvard educated, as he'll remind you not infrequently, and he's distressingly smart, as he also makes clear. He'll lecture you on everything from SALT II treaties to the symbolism in Zola's novels. I'm sure if Eric were around in biblical times, he'd have been chief architect of the Tower of Babel.

These days, Eric is getting his PhD in social psychology at Columbia, which means he says things like this: "Humans are a fascinating species." As if our struggles are all for his intellectual amusement.

When I went on *Who Wants to Be a Millionaire?*, Eric was my phone-a-friend. It seemed the most obvious choice. But when I called him at the $32,000 level, he choked. It was one of the most bittersweet moments of my life—bitter because I lost $32,000, but sweet because I thought he'd get taught a lesson: Pride goeth before the fall.

That lesson didn't quite pan out. The *Millionaire* fiasco didn't seem to dent his ego one bit. He still enjoys tormenting me with his superior knowledge. And the unfortunate thing is, the man reads everything.

Today, he's over at our apartment and gleefully telling me about the latest religion-themed article he read:

"So, did you hear about that study about Jesus walking on water?"

"No."

"This scientist says it's because the conditions in the Mediterranean at the time caused ice floes on the Sea of Galilee."

"I see."

Eric chuckles. He actually doesn't think that scientific explanations of miracles are worthy of serious discussion. They are, he says, more like crackpot science that tries to explain the physics of Road Runner cartoons.

But for me, such studies do present a problem.

The rivers of Egypt turning bloodred? It could have been red algae or volcanic ash. The darkness sweeping over the land? It might have been the khamsin, a hot wind of the Sahara, churning up the sand. When Moses sweetened the bitter desert water at Marah with a tree? He could have been using an ion exchange resin. Not that I know what that means. But it sounds convincing.

I don't need to hear scientific explanations of miracles. It plays too perfectly into my innate skepticism, which still runs deep.

I know plenty of religious people who see miracles as myths, not literal truth. They say that we don't need to believe that Joshua actually stopped the sun in the sky so he could finish a battle; the story can still have beauty and resonance even if Joshua didn't get a divine extension. And I imagine that, if I go religious at the end of this year, that's the camp I'll belong to.

But if I'm going to be literal, I must at least try to believe they happened and that God overturned the natural order. It's a heck of a mental hurdle and, as with creationism, one I'm not sure I can clear.

I take some measure of consolation from a book I just read. It's called *The Battle for God* by former-nun-turned-religion-scholar Karen Armstrong.

Armstrong makes the intriguing argument that people in biblical times did not believe the miracles happened. Or not in the same way that fundamentalists today do, anyway. Armstrong says that the ancients viewed the world simultaneously in two different ways. One was *logos*, the other *mythos*. Logos was the ancients' rational and practical side, the factual knowledge they used in farming or building houses. Mythos was the stories that gave their lives meaning. For instance, the story of the Exodus was not to be taken as factual but as a tale filled with significance about freedom from oppression. The ancients didn't necessarily believe that it happened exactly as told—with six hundred thousand people trudging through the desert for forty years. But it was true in the larger sense, in the sense that it gave context to their lives.

Fundamentalism, Armstrong says, is a modern phenomenon. It's the attempt to apply logos to mythos, to turn legend into scientific truth. I don't wholly buy Armstrong's thesis. It smacks of wishful thinking to me. I don't think the distinctions in the biblical minds were that black and white. But given the choice between her theory and fundamental-ism, I'll take hers.

"Whoever strikes his father or his mother shall be put to death."

—Exodus 21:15

Day 273. When Jasper wakes up from his nap, I go to retrieve him. He is standing at the edge of his crib, his hair sticking up in back, Alfalfa-style. In his hand he is clutching a plastic bowling pin, which is his version of a security blanket.

I lift him out. Jasper grins. It is a grin meant to convey that he is about to do something spectacularly witty—and then he hits me in the face with a bowling pin.

"Don't do that," I say. I have on my stern James Earl Jones voice.

He takes that to mean "Do it again, but harder." So he winds up and delivers another blow to my face. And another. These ones were power-ful leave-a-red-mark-on-my-forehead hits.

"Jasper!" I say. "Say you're sorry."

Jasper just grins.

"You do not hit people in the face with bowling pins. It's very dan-gerous. That's a no-no."

He looks at me bewildered, then angry. How could I not see the hu-mor in a flawlessly executed bowling-pin-to-the-face maneuver?

"Apologize to me, please."

"No."

"Apologize."

"No."

This is going to be ugly.

The Hebrew Bible says that hitting your parents can be punishable by death. Instead I turn the other cheek. I ignore my son.

Ignoring a rebellious son is, coincidentally, a strategy recommended by a secular parenting book I read months ago. So I put him on the ground, turn my back to him, and cross my arms. I look like a model posing for the label on the Mr. Clean bottle.

He starts to whimper.

"Say you're sorry, and we can go play," I say.

"No."

"No hitting people," I say. I say it with decisiveness, confident that I have thousands of years of tradition behind me.

I keep my back to him. He grabs my leg.

"A. J.!" he says. "A. J.! A. J.!"

There's something ineffably heartbreaking about a two-year-old calling to his father, and the father not answering. And I am that father. It's killing me. But Jasper is still too stubborn to say he's sorry.

The Bible talks about the importance of punishing your kids if you love them. And I think there's something to that paradoxical advice. The best punishment should be a sacrifice—you sacrifice a pleasant afternoon, you sacrifice some in-the-moment affection, to give them a better future.

Jasper stomps, he sulks, he mutters to himself. It's the longest fight we've had. Finally, four hours later, he tracks me down in the living room and gives me a sad little downcast-eyes "Sorry."

"Great!" I say. "I'm so proud of you for apologizing. What should we play?"

But Jasper would not be playing with me tonight. He would play alone. He goes to bed all mopey and martyrlike. It probably sounds like a minor skirmish, but for me the War of the Bowling Pin was an epic one. The next morning at about seven-fifteen, I hear Jasper screaming into the monitor: "A. J.! A. J.!" I open his door, stick my head in. I pick him up, he gives me a grudge-free hug around the neck. Yes, our relationship survived my dispensation of justice. It's a good lesson for me. I still spare the rod, but I'm trying not to spoil the child.

Month Ten: June

Nor should there be obscenity, foolish talk or coarse joking,
which are out of place . . .
—Ephesians 5:4 (NIV)

Day 277. "How was the birthday party?" I ask Julie.

She and Jasper had just returned from a party at a preschool on the East Side.

"OK. But they had this rabbit for the kids to pet, and there was rabbit shit everywhere."

"Huh."

I am shocked at her language. And then I am shocked that I am shocked. When I first met Julie, she rarely cursed, whereas I had no filter whatsoever. I chose a particularly adolescent curse word as my default computer password. I enjoyed watching TV with the closed captioning, because the captioners sometimes type in the dirty words that are bleeped out for the apparently more delicate hearing-unimpaired community.

But for the last two months, inspired by Orthodox Jews and evangelical Christians, I haven't used a single naughty word. And it startles me when others do.

What is a biblically naughty word? Well, there are two genres: blasphemy and profanity. Blasphemy is the subject of the Third Commandment, which orders us not to take the Lord's name in vain. What does it mean to take the Lord's name in vain? Is it when you say the word *God* in any secular context? Or is it only when you invoke God's name while lying under oath? Or is it uttering the word *Yahweh*, which might come close to the pronunciation of God's holy name? All three theories have their supporters.

If you want to be supremely safe, as I do, you should use the word *God* only when praying or talking about the Bible.

As for profanity—the S-word and the F-word and regular old bodily-function-themed cussing—things are even less clear. In fact, as science writer Natalie Angier points out, the Bible itself uses some adult language. In 2 Kings 18:27 the men "eat their own dung and drink their own piss."(KJV) In Ezekiel 23:20, you can read some very salty language about the size of Egyptian men's private parts.

Still, there are sections, especially in the New Testament, that indicate such language should be avoided. Consider the passage from Ephesians I put at the top of this chapter: "Nor should there be any obscenity, foolish talk or coarse joking, which are out of place." Or this one from Ephesians 4:29 (NIV): "Do not let any unwholesome talk come out of your mouths."

So to be totally protected, I've scrubbed up my vocabulary. My current curse words are: *fudge, sugar,* and *shoot.* When I say one of my new curse words, Julie usually responds with something like, "Hey, Opie! You going fishin' this morning?" Or just whistling *The Andy Griffith Show* theme.

She can mock me, but the weird thing is, I think my G-rated language is making me a less angry person. Because here's the way it works:

I'll get to the subway platform just as the downtown train is pulling away, and I'll start to say the F-word. I'll remember to censor myself. So I'll turn it into "fudge" at the last second. When I hear myself say "fudge" out loud, it sounds so folksy, so Jimmy Stewart-ish and amusingly dorky, that I can't help but smile. My anger recedes. Once again, behavior shapes emotions.

"Fudge" seems clearly within bounds, but what about words like "heck"? Those are more morally ambiguous, but probably should be avoided as well. In the 1600s "criminy" was considered a curse word for being too close to "Christ." Same with "gosh" and "golly" in the 1700s, which were meant to evoke God and God's body, respectively. Later, "Jiminy Cricket" and "Gee Willikers" were wicked code words for Jesus. "Tarnation" began as an offensive combination of "eternal" and "damnation." And "heck" was an only slightly better alternative to "hell."

A minister's daughter recently told me that when she was growing up, they used "Cheese and rice" instead of the name of her savior, which I imagine would also have been banned in the eighteenth century. Land mines lurk everywhere in the English language.

> *Jesus said to them, "Render to Caesar the things that are Caesar's, and to God the things that are God's."*
>
> —MARK 12:17

Day 279. I've been dropping in on another evangelical Bible study class—a straight one. They meet on Tuesday nights in the back room of the American Bible Society near Columbus Circle.

The dozen or so other members have been very welcoming of me, though a little perplexed at the same time, since I look more Jewish than your average diamond dealer on 47th Street. I'm glad they let me listen as we drill deep on a different passage from the Gospel of Mark each week. It's always humbling. I can keep up with them on the Old Testament—I can quote from Deuteronomy and Proverbs—but I'm still a third-string minor leaguer when it comes to the New Testament.

Anyway, I bring this up because last week at Bible study, the co-leader—a tall, precise, white-haired man named Kevin—was talking about how he tries to be a good and law-abiding person.

He told us that he was recently driving from New York to Ohio for business, and he had a battle with himself. He'd keep gunning his car up to sixty-five, then he'd feel guilty for breaking the law and slow back down to fifty-five.

"I said to myself, 'Do I really need to speed?'" he said. "'What's it going to save me? An hour? Is it worth it in the long run to break the law?'"

There is scriptural justification for strict observance of civil law, speed limits, and otherwise. You can see it in one of Peter's letters to his followers in the New Testament, where he tells them to obey the emperor: "Be subject for the Lord's sake to every human institution, whether it be to the emperor as supreme, or to governors as sent by him" (1 Peter 2:13–14).

When I ask the pastor out to pasture Elton Richards about whether

to obey every human institution, he cautions me: You can find the op-
posing idea in the New Testament as well. There's a story about Peter
and the apostles preaching God's word, and they are told by the authorities to shut up. They do not. They say, in effect, "We answer to a higher
authority."

Marcus Borg, author of *Reading the Bible Again for the First Time,*
says the two themes run throughout the Bible. Call them the status-quo
motif and liberation motif. Status-quo sections tell us to support our
earthly leaders. God appointed our leaders, so we shouldn't question
them—or even speak ill of them ("You shall not . . . curse a ruler of your
people," Exodus 22:28). The liberation parts encourage God's people to
throw off the yoke of oppression and flee the Pharaoh or his modern-day
equivalents. They say that God is with the people, not the rulers.

So which to choose? Well, in the case of traffic laws, Bible study
leader Kevin has got a point. I'm not doing any noble Gandhi-like civil
disobedience by going seventy in a school zone. I'm just trying to get
home faster to take a nap. This month I have pledged to try to really follow New York's street laws. To the letter. This has changed my life in a
more dramatic way than I could have imagined. Just try not to jaywalk
in Manhattan. It's almost impossible. I wait on the corner, usually alone,
or, if I'm lucky, with a German tourist couple and a class of first-graders
on a field trip to the aquarium. The rest of New York pedestrians see the
traffic lights as helpful suggestions and nothing more.

I won't pretend it's fun. It's a pain in the butt. It takes me about 30
percent longer to walk anywhere. And it's another source of stupid—but
increasingly frequent—arguments with my wife. Yesterday we got out
of a cab in the middle of the block, and I refused to cross the street there.
I walked to the end of the block, waited for the light to change, marched
over the zebra crossing, then walked back up the other side. Conveniently, it was raining. Julie was waiting for me under an awning.

"Hope you had a nice walk," she said, her voice more tired than
angry.

Driving is just as bad. Until I started to pay attention, I didn't even
know speed limits existed in New York. I figured the rule was: Gun your
car to get to the next light as fast as possible, then jerk to a stop. Then repeat. Or, more likely, sit in traffic and go 5 mph. But if you look hard

enough, you can find them. Actual speed limit signs—30 mph on most avenues. So whenever we rent a car to visit Julie's brother in New Jersey, I've made sure to cruise at a nice, smooth 25 mph down Columbus Avenue.

When we get to the highway, things get more complicated. Often, I'm the only one putt-putting along at fifty-five, certainly the only one without a "World's Best Grandpa" bumper sticker. I should probably have my hazards on. Cars whiz by me. They honk. They swerve. The drivers look at me like I'm the lone Red Sox fan at a Yankees game. The first time I drove on the highway, I couldn't stop laughing—I'm not sure out of nervousness or out of the absurdity of it or both.

So, in general, the whole experience has been a pain. But there are two upsides.

1. I've come to see obeying traffic laws as an urban version of the Sabbath. It's an enforced pause. When I stand alone on the corner, I try to spend the time appreciating the little things New York has to offer. Look at that: The street signs have changed from yellow and black to a much more pleasant green and white. When did that happen? Or else I watch the FedEx truck drive by and notice the secret white arrow embedded in its logo (it's between the *F* and the *E*).

2. I have freedom from worry. No one I know has ever been arrested for jaywalking. But whenever I violated the Don't Walk sign, there was always a tiny, faint pang from knowing that I was doing something wrong. I no longer have that. I feel in control. It's that same feeling of cleanliness, of relief, that I get when I actually fold all the sweaters in my closet or clean out all the emails in my in-box.

. . . Not in the passion of lust like heathen who do not know God.

—1 Thessalonians 4:5

Day 286. Julie is seven months pregnant with the twins, and wildly uncomfortable. She can hardly move. She gets out of breath opening the refrigerator door. When I asked her a couple of weeks ago if she wanted to be intimate, she said the following: "I can't think of anything I'd rather do less."

No sugarcoating there.

Speaking of sex, I think I dismissed the whole lust issue too glibly. I found a way to rationalize it. I told myself, well, the Hebrew Bible has prosex parts, so I don't have to bother with all that modesty business.

I took the easy way out. The truth is, there are plenty of sections of the Bible that do encourage restraint of the sex drive, sometimes even abstinence. Jesus says not to even think about other women aside from your wife: "You have heard that it was said, 'You shall not commit adultery.' But I say to you that every one who looks at a woman lustfully has already committed adultery with her in his heart" (Matthew 5:27–8).

And the Apostle Paul implies that celibacy is the ideal; marriage is a second-best solution, a concession to our urges. As he says in Galatians 5:24: "And those who belong to Christ Jesus have crucified the flesh with its passions and desires." So I decide that I should try to be ascetic for my final few weeks, and, as Paul says, put to death my earthly nature.

My previous strategy of censorship didn't work. We saw that with the CleanFlicks fiasco. It was too passive. I have to attack lust head-on. I have to change my way of thinking about sex. So after much reading, I've developed four strategies.

Last night I had the chance to road test all four. I went to a fashion show that Yossi had invited me to. He said the designer is an Orthodox Jew who grew up in Brooklyn, and I figured, Orthodox fashion? Sounds pretty tame. Lots of bulky, shapeless, earth-toned dresses. Perhaps a scandalous glimpse of exposed ankle. I could handle that.

I know I am going to be tempted from the moment I arrive. The event is held in Chelsea at the *Frying Pan,* a rusty boat docked off 23rd Street. The crowd is thick, packing both sides of the catwalk. Yes, there is a sprinkling of Orthodox Jews, but mostly it is gorgeous twentysomething fashion types with back tattoos and bare shoulders/midriffs/thighs. (There is also a man in a pink suit, pink shoes, and pink bowler hat, and on said bowler hat, a tiny billboard—about the size of a license plate—with a functioning electronic text scrawl. This did not make me lustful, but I thought you should know.)

I start out with strategy number one. Here you think of the woman in question as out of your league. You remember this advice from the medieval rabbi way back in the first month? You have to think of your-self as a peasant and her as a princess. She's so beyond your grasp, you can admire her aesthetically but not lustfully.

I try this out within the first five minutes. When Yossi and I take our place, we notice a woman with a small leopard-skin skirt, small bustier, and very large cleavage.

"You don't see that too much in Crown Heights," says Yossi.

Interestingly, this strategy has gotten much easier for me with my current appearance. A year ago I might have deluded myself that I had a shot at Leopard-skin Bustier Woman. Nowadays, not so much.

Strategy two: Think of the woman as if she were your mother.

This is another tip from the medieval rabbi. So I do it. I think of Leopard-skin Bustier Woman as my mom, and I feel revulsed. I feel like Malcolm McDowell in *A Clockwork Orange* undergoing the Ludovico technique. This is more effective than strategy number one, and also more disturbing.

Strategy three: Recite Bible passages to yourself.

After a few minutes, the fashion show itself starts, and the tempta-tions get worse. The models aren't hidden behind modest muumuus. They stomp down the runway with their exaggerated hip swivel, wear-ing alarmingly skimpy outfits that look like kimonos during a fabric shortage. One dark-haired model has no shirt or blouse whatsoever. The only thing around her chest is what appears to be an extralarge rubber band.

Here I try strategy number three. This one I picked up from a book called *When Good Men Are Tempted,* a guide to controlling your lust, by an evangelical Christian named Bill Perkins. He suggests you recite Bible passages: "I've found that memorizing large sections of the Bible gives me a safe mental focus when I'm tempted. By the time I recite a paragraph or two to myself, my spirit is strengthened, and my mind is cleared."

So I do that. I mouth to myself one of the verses he suggested. It worked, in a way. My brain was so busy with its recital project, it didn't have time to focus on the rubber band. The meaning of the passage is al-most beside the point. I could have probably recited the lyrics to *The Mikado* and gotten a similar benefit. It's all about keeping your mind distracted.

The show ends, and I tell Yossi I should probably go. He says, "You sure you don't want to just hang around for a few minutes?"

"Well, just a few minutes."

We bump into a friend of Yossi's. She is blond, Israeli, cute, and very drunk.

"She has a weird fetish," Yossi whispers to me. "She likes to fondle *payot*."

As in the side locks? Yossi nods.

Oh, man. Yossi introduces me to her.

"I'm very drunk," she says.

I smile noncommittally.

Was she checking out my side locks? I think so.

Here, I try out strategy number four: Do not objectify. This one I got from downloading an excellent sermon about lust by a Unitarian minister. The minister suggested that you can battle your urge to objectify women by focusing on them as a complete person. So I look at Fetish Girl and think about everything but her body: her Israeli childhood, what might be her favorite novel, how many cousins she has, whether she owns a PC or a Mac.

But she won't stop looking at my payot. This isn't working. In a panic, I switch to the less evolved but more efficient method: *Think of her as your mom*. I feel nauseated. Victory.

I've also noticed a strange phenomenon. I figured it'd get more and more difficult to suppress my sexuality. I figured it'd be like water building up behind a dam. But quite the opposite: it's more like my sex drive has evaporated. I'm sure it'll come roaring back like a dragon—to use the metaphor in my book *When Good Men Are Tempted*. But for now, it's pleasantly tranquilized.

And it makes me feel spiritually spotless. It makes me realize I have a hidden Puritan streak. On some level, I do consider sex dirty, or else why would I feel so buoyant when I've stamped it out? There's something lovely about putting your libido in storage.

And there's another advantage: The thousands of watts of energy devoted to sex are suddenly free for other pursuits. Sublimation is real. I've never been so productive as I have been in these past weeks. I can crank out two thousand *Esquire* words a day on this no-sex diet.

"Lord, how often shall my brother sin against me, and I forgive him?"

—MATTHEW 18:21

Day 287. Tonight, at nine-fifteen, Julie leaves our bedroom door open. I have repeatedly asked her not to do this. I can't sleep unless the room is Reykjavik-level cold, so I always shut the door at seven and flip the air conditioner on high. Julie, who could sleep anywhere and anytime, always forgets, leaves the door open, and lets my precious cool air slip out.

I snap at her. "Please shut the door!"

Huh. That came out a little too sharply. To soften things, I throw in a biblical literalism joke. "I forgive you this time. But if you do it another four hundred eighty-nine times, I won't forgive you."

Julie shuts the door without asking me to explain my wryly cryptic statement. So let me do it here.

I was referring to a passage in Matthew 18: "Then Peter came up and said to him, 'Lord, how often shall my brother sin against me, and I forgive him? As many as seven times?' Jesus said to him, 'I do not say to you seven times, but seventy times seven.'"

In other words 490 times.

When I first made my list of biblical rules, this was actually part of my plan. I'd take everything literally, even those sentences that were clearly metaphorical. I would forgive someone 490 times, despite the fact that Jesus almost surely meant you should forgive an infinite number of times.

I revised that plan for a couple of reasons. First, it would involve chopping off various parts of my body (see below), which I was reluctant to do. Second, it soon became clear that I could make my point—that biblical literalism is necessarily a selective enterprise—without intentionally warping the meaning of the Bible.

But here is a sample of the even more bizarre life I could have led:

- I could have plucked out my eye, since Jesus says, "And if your eye causes you to sin, pluck it out; it is better for you to enter the kingdom of God with one eye than with two eyes to be thrown into hell" (Mark 9:47). This is generally interpreted by Christian leaders to mean that you should get rid of those things in your life that cause you to sin. "If you are addicted to internet pornography, you should consider getting rid of your computer," says Dr. Campolo. Though as with most passages, there have been people who have taken it at its word. A psychologist of religion named Wayne Oates writes of mental patients who attempted to pluck out their eyes in literal compliance with Jesus's words.

- I could hate my parents, since Jesus says, "If any one comes to me and does not hate his own father and mother and wife and children and brothers and sisters, yes, and even his own life, he cannot be my disciple" (Luke 14:26). Here the idea is that given the difficult choice between God and your family, you should choose God—not that Jesus condoned parent hating.

- I could avoid uttering the word *good* for the rest of my year, in literal adherence to this passage from Luke 18:18–19: "And a ruler asked him, 'Good Teacher, what must I do to inherit eternal life?' And Jesus said to him, 'Why do you call me good? No one is good but God alone.'"

This approach reminds me of one of my dad's wacky practical jokes: He'll start pouring a glass of water for one of my friends and tell the unsuspecting chump "just say when." The chump will say "Stop," and my dad will keep pouring. The chump will say "That's enough!" and my dad will keep pouring. My dad will keep pouring till the water spills over the edge of the glass and splashes on to the table. Then my dad will look at him in faux bewilderment and say: "You never said 'when.'" A classic.

And here's the amazing thing: Those who overliteralize the words of God get mocked in the Bible itself. I learned this while reading a book called *Rescuing the Bible from Fundamentalism* by retired Episcopal bishop John Shelby Spong, who refers to the following passage in the Gospel of John:

In reply Jesus declared, "I tell you the truth, no one can see the kingdom of God unless he is born again."

"How can a man be born when he is old?" Nicodemus [a Pharisee] asked. "Surely he cannot enter a second time into his mother's womb to be born!" (John 3:3–4, NIV).

Nicodemus is like a sitcom dunderhead here. Born again? How is that possible? How can an adult squeeze back into his mother's uterus? He can't see that Jesus's words were figurative and poetic, and he becomes the butt of a joke.

"The truth will make you free."

—John 8:32

Day 290. Ever since my lying spree on the Falwell trip, I've recommitted myself to extreme honesty. In response, Julie has come up with a way to make my honesty more palatable. She's started to ask me a singularly terrifying question: What are you thinking about? We'll be walking to the playground, and she'll spring it on me:

"Hey. What are you thinking about?"

I can't just respond "nothing much." I have to tell the truth, the unvarnished truth.

"I'm thinking about that rude guy at the Judaica store on Broadway, and how I should have told him, 'You just became a villain in my book.'"

"Sounds like vengeance. Isn't that biblically forbidden?"

Julie loves her new trick. It's as if she's found a peephole into my soul and can discover who she's really married to, no deceptions. Or, as she puts it, "I feel like I've picked up a chance card in Monopoly."

We'll be unpacking groceries, and suddenly I'll hear: "What are you thinking about?"

"Oh, business stuff."

She's not falling for that. "What business stuff?"

"That I wish I could time travel back to 1991 and buy up hundreds of internet names like flowers.com and beer.com and cabbage.com, then I could sell them for millions of dollars to the flower and beer and cabbage industries, and then I'd never have to work again." (This is an alarmingly common fantasy of mine.)

"That's the saddest daydream I've ever heard. Plus, that's greed."

She's right. I'm wasting my time with greedy and angry thoughts. Not always, mind you. Sometimes, when Julie pops the question, I'll be thinking about something noble, like the environment or our son's future. In fact, compared to my prebiblical life, the percentage of brain space allotted to gratitude and compassion has inched up. But I still have way too many thoughts like this:

"What are you thinking about?"

"The Bible, actually."

"What about the Bible?"

"The story of Esther."

"What about the story of Esther?"

"Well . . . what it would be like to be the king in the Esther story and get to spend the night with each of the most beautiful women in the kingdom, like a test-drive or something, and then get to choose your favorite."

"You've really evolved."

In the last couple of days, I've been focusing on cleaning up my brain. It's possible that God is monitoring my thoughts, but it's certain that Julie is. So I've commanded myself to think positive thoughts. And today, it paid off.

"What are you thinking about?"

"How lucky I am to have a healthy wife and a healthy son and two so-far-healthy babies."

Julie pretends to gag. But it was true, that's what I was thinking.

> *Of making many books there is no end . . .*
>
> —Ecclesiastes 12:12 (NIV)

Day 292. I've got a decent biblical library going now. Perhaps a hundred books or so. And I've divided them into sections: Moderate Jewish. Fundamentalist Jewish. Moderate Christian. Fundamentalist Christian. Atheist. Agnostic. Religious cookbooks.

I've tried to keep the conservative books on the right side and the liberal ones on the left. When I started my year, I thought that nothing would go to the right of my Falwell collection. But of course, I was wrong. I just got in a book called *A Handbook of Bible Law* by a man named Charles Weisman.

I'd try to summarize it, but the subtitle does a pretty good job, so I'll just type that in: *An Indexed Guide to over 1500 Biblical Laws, Commandments, Statutes, Principles, Admonishments, Exhortations & Guidelines under 22 Different Subject Headings.*

When I found *The Handbook of Bible Law: An Indexed Guide to over 1500* (etcetera, etcetera), it seemed the perfect Fodor's guide to my spiritual trek. All the laws in one place! It was so well organized, I figured it might be worth talking to the author. So today I Googled Charles Weisman, and I found out that he probably does not want to hear from me. And vice versa.

Weisman runs a small publishing company in Burnsville, Minnesota, that distributes such gems as *The International Jew,* a collection of anti-Semitic rants originally published by Henry Ford. You can also buy a tome called *America: Free, White & Christian,* and books about how the "white Adamic race have [sic] been the innovators and builders of all advanced civilizations throughout history." You get the idea.

And when Weisman publishes *The Handbook of Bible Law,* it's not out of academic interest. He wants a theocracy in America now.

Weisman's got company. There are thousands of beyond-the-pale fundamentalists who want to set up a biblical government based on both Testaments. As in a society that executes homosexuals, adulterers, and blasphemers. As in one that shuts down every synagogue, mosque, and moderate church. They are the American Taliban. Not all are racist like Weisman—in fact, most claim not to be—but all scare me. Unlike mainstream Christians, they don't believe that Christ's death voided much of the law. And unlike mainstream Jews, they don't mute the harsher Hebrew Bible passages, the executions for adultery and blasphemy and the like.

So they are on the fringe, yes. But perhaps not as much as I'd hoped. The movement is called reconstructionism or dominionism (the differences are subtle, but as far as I can tell, dominionism is for the slightly less-extremist extremist). And writers such as Garry Wills and *Salon*'s Michelle Goldberg argue that dominionism has undue influence on some more respectable members of the Christian right. It's an influence they say far outweighs their numbers: Dominionists were a driving force behind the home-schooling movement and have helped shape Pat Robertson's worldview.

They're doing what I'm doing, but they aren't doing it as part of a spiritual quest/book project. They make me appreciate the comparative graciousness of the Falwell folks even more.

They will pick up serpents . . .

—MARK 16:18

Day 297. If you want to slam Christian biblical literalism, I've noticed, the go-to epithet is "snake handler." As in "The religious right is filled with knuckle-dragging snake handlers."

In fact, most evangelical Christians I met disapprove of snake handling. But it's easy to see why this small sect has become shorthand for religious extremism in America. You watch the Appalachian snake handlers on the Discovery Channel, and they look as weird as the guy on Coney Island who hammers six-inch nails into his nostrils, or Nick Nolte after a couple of vodka tonics.

I knew the basic idea behind serpent handling. I'd once assigned an *Esquire* article on the topic to Dennis Covington, a writer who penned a wonderful serpent-handling memoir called *Salvation on Sand Mountain*. As Dennis explains, the serpent handlers take their inspiration from a passage spoken by Jesus in Mark 16:17–18, which reads: "And these signs will accompany those who believe: in my name they will cast out demons; they will speak in new tongues; they will pick up serpents, and if they drink any deadly thing, it will not hurt them . . ."

Most Christians read the phrase "they will pick up serpents" to be a metaphor: Faith will help you overcome life's "serpents," its challenges and bad people and temptations. The serpent handlers don't see it as figurative. They show their devotion to Jesus by picking up snakes— venomous snakes—during their services.

You may criticize them for a loopy interpretation, but one thing is for sure: These are not the type of biblical literalists who had a pre-conceived political agenda and then dug up a few Scriptural passages to back up that agenda. They simply read a passage in the Bible and did what it said. They are the ultimate literalists. I needed to visit them.

I called up a man named Jimmy Morrow, whose phone number I

got from a professor of religion at the University of Tennessee. Jimmy was happy to hear from me and told me to come on down anytime.

"Will I have to handle snakes?" I asked.

"Absolutely not," said Jimmy. "You can come to the church for one thousand years and not handle a single snake."

After church, "if all goes OK," Jimmy says he's having a picnic, and I'm invited. *If all goes OK*. That's a scary concept. These snakes are real. Though it's uncommon, people do get bitten and die—more than sixty of them in the last century.

So, on a Saturday night, I fly to Knoxville, Tennessee, wake up in the morning, and drive ninety minutes to Del Rio, one exit past the Wal-Mart. I pull into the driveway of the Church of God with Signs Following. It's a small, wooden one-room structure. Outside a white-painted sign quotes Mark 16:17–18.

Jimmy arrives minutes later. He hugs me and invites me inside. He's a tall, gray-haired fifty-one-year-old with a big, jutting Clintonian chin. And he has the thickest accent I've ever heard. It takes me a while to adjust my ears—for the first half hour, I have to strain the same way I do when Shakespearean actors first start spouting their Elizabethan English.

Jimmy is the humblest fundamentalist you'll ever meet. Even his slightly stooped posture radiates humility. "I'm just a mountain man," he tells me. He peppers his speech with a lot of "Well, I think" and "It's my interpretation."

"I just tell the word of God, and people can take it or reject it," says Jimmy. "I've had Mormons here—I treat 'em good. I've had people from Finland here—I treat 'em good. I don't say anything against 'em. Just tell 'em the word of God."

Jimmy was saved when he was thirteen. He saw a snake in the road, and the snake tried to bite him, but "God locked the snake's jaws. So that's when I knew it was true." Since then, he's amassed what he believes is the largest archive of serpent handling material in the world. He unlocks a large church closet to show me. It's crammed with yellowed newspaper clippings, black-and-white photos, and videotapes of National Geographic documentaries. Here you can read about how serpent handling started—in 1908, when a Tennessee preacher and ex-bootlegger named George Hensley heard the word of God. You can read about how, since then, it's spread to nine states and Canada, with about two thousand followers.

Jimmy gets out his Bible. It's the King James Version, and nearly every passage has been highlighted in one color or another: pink, yellow, blue. He shows me Mark 16:17 and reads it so fast that it sounds like it's one long word.

I ask Jimmy what else serpent handlers believe. Some practitioners also drink strychnine because the passage says, "if they drink any deadly thing, it will not hurt them." They also avoid jewelry in accordance with 1 Timothy 2:9—". . . Women should adorn themselves in modest apparel, with shamefacedness and sobriety; not with braided hair, or gold, or pearls, or costly array." Some greet each other with a "holy kiss"—a kiss on the cheek or mouth—as instructed by Romans 16:16.

Jimmy's handled thousands of poisonous serpents. Most of them he picks up in the mountains right outside his house. He's taken up copperheads, cottonmouths, rattlers, an eight-foot king cobra, and a "two-step Vietnamese viper." Which is? "If you get bit, you fall in two steps. But God gave me victory over him."

He has been nailed, though. Twice. First in 1988. "It was just like a blow torch. I couldn't sleep for five nights. It throbbed like a toothache." The second time, in 2003, a northern copperhead got him in the chest. But he didn't feel a thing.

Jimmy built this church himself. It's a simple church: There's a linoleum floor, an electric organ, some wooden benches, and a dozen or so tambourines, some with crosses on them, one with a Fisher-Price turtle. Since I told him I'm Jewish, he points out a Bible passage on his wall written in Hebrew. "We believe the Jews are the chosen people," he says.

The Church of God with Signs Following doesn't quite fit into my oversimplified liberal versus conservative evangelical schema. Politically, Jimmy's a fan of LBJ-style Democrats. Theologically, he's more in line with Robertson, with an emphasis on end times.

The parishioners are trickling in. And I do mean trickle. Only about a half dozen show up, which makes me kind of sad. Jimmy doesn't seem to mind. "One time nobody showed up. I still got up on the pulpit and preached. And this guy walking by, he stuck his head in and said, 'What are you doing? No one's here. No one can hear you.' And I said, 'Well, you heard me, didn't you?'"

A couple of minutes past eleven, Jimmy asks his friend Matthew to do a warm-up sermon. Matthew steps up. He's young—twenty-eight—and looks a bit like the actor Steve Buscemi. He walks back and forth, his key chain jangling from his belt. He starts to preach.

"People say to me, 'I keep the Ten Commandments.' That's good. But there are many other commandments besides those ten. We should keep everything the Lord says."

Matthew's voice fills the church. He preaches hard, hunched over, his back almost parallel with the ground, as if he were doing a Groucho Marx impersonation.

"I've heard people say the Bible means this or the Bible means that. But, my friends, the Bible means exactly what it says. If God wanted it changed, He would have had the prophets change it."

"C'mon!" says Jimmy, who is sitting on a chair behind the altar. He lifts his hands in the air. "Amen!"

Matthew's carrying a blue handkerchief. Every minute or so, he wipes his brow or the saliva from the corner of his mouth. He's working on three hours of sleep—he preached late last night at another church.

Matthew was supposed to talk for only a few minutes, but it's been twenty minutes, and he's going strong. He jumps from topic to topic, wherever God takes him: healing, the chastening hand of God, his son's injured leg, Jesus' mercy, the war in Iraq ("We shouldn't be in Iraq, and God will punish President Bush").

The Catholic and Lutheran services I've been to have been like well-orchestrated Bach concertos. This is like Ornette Coleman free jazz. All spontaneous.

"I was trying not to get started again," says Matthew, "but I believe in obeying the Holy Spirit . . . *huh.*"

Matthew punctuates every sentence with a pronounced exhale. *Huh.* In the beginning, it was distracting, but now it seems sort of natural.

"Today is the day for salvation, *huh.* Right here in this church, *huh.*"

It's been an hour now. Jimmy is stamping his feet. Jimmy's wife, who is sitting behind me, is weeping and saying "Praise Jesus." Another woman a few pews back is speaking in tongues. "Shamamamamama," she says. Then her body jerks. "Shamamamam."

I feel myself getting hypnotized by those repetitive *huh*s. I feel like the top of my head is being swept upward. For a minute, everything fades to white except for Matthew and his shirtsleeves and his blue handkerchief and his godly riffs.

I snap myself out of it. It was too much. How could I come back to New York and tell Julie I was saved at a serpent-handling church in Tennessee? I force myself back down. I'm not ready to surrender yet.

Matthew preaches for an hour and a half before the Spirit moves him to stop. The warm-up act has gone on so long, there is no need for Jimmy's main event. Jimmy wraps up the service by anointing his parishioners with olive oil. Jimmy feels badly that I had come all the way down and missed the big show. Not a single snake had been handled, no strychnine drunk.

"Let me see if the Holy Spirit moves me," he says. From under the altar, Jimmy slips out a wooden box with a clear plastic top. Inside, a copperhead, about three feet long, slithers over itself, flicking its tongue.

Jimmy tells me he takes good care of the snakes. "I clean 'em, care for 'em, water 'em, and feed 'em mice." And afterward, he lets them go back to the mountains. (Regardless, my animal rights activist aunt Marti was furious at me for coming down here at all.)

Jimmy sits on a bench and closes his eyes. "*Ha-ta-ta-ta-ta-ta*," he says. He's speaking in tongues, a descending scale. "*Ha-ta-ta-ta-ta-ta.* Oh, thank you Jesus *Ha-ta-ta-ta*."

Jimmy opens his eyes and reaches down for the copperhead. He picks it up with one hand near the head, one near the tail, moving his hands in slow little circles. "*Ha-ta-ta-ta*." The snake just flicks its tongue. He does this for a minute, holding the serpent at eyes level. Then slowly, carefully returns the snake to its box. Jimmy is out of his trance. The weird thing is that his appearance has completely changed. He looks happier, fuller, transformed from two minutes ago. Maybe that's how Moses glowed when he came down from the mountain.

"How did the snake feel?" I ask.

"Not cold and slimy. More like velvet."

"And what did you feel?"

"It's joyful," says Jimmy. "Like a bucket of warm water pouring over your head."

I don't handle the copperhead myself. I had promised Julie I wouldn't. If I really needed to fulfill that literal part of the Bible, she pointed out I could always handle a garter snake, since the Scriptures never specify *venomous* snakes.

Afterward, Jimmy takes me to a picnic at his friend's house. We eat cake and chicken and look at his friend's brightly colored Chinese bird. We talk about family and black bears and the Apocalyptic times we live in. And then Jimmy hugs me and tells me I have to come down and stay with him for longer.

As I drive back to the airport listening to a country song about Moses's showdown with the pharaoh on AM radio, two things strike me: First, when you're there, when you're in that one-room church, serpent handling doesn't seem as bizarre as I had expected. It's like a great quote I once read: Religion makes the "strange familiar and the familiar strange." Here the strange had been made familiar.

My second thought is: I wish Jimmy would stop handling snakes. My college anthropology professors would be appalled. So would Ralph Hood, the religion teacher who hooked me up with Jimmy in the first place. He wrote a culturally relativist essay about how serpent handling is a valid mode of worship, how it lets the handler embrace life by conquering death. Judge not, lest ye be judged.

But I still have my risk-reward mind-set, and here the risk to Jimmy's life cannot outweigh the reward of transcendence. He's one of my favorite people from this year, and almost every Sunday, he's tempting death. And why? Because of a literalist interpretation of Mark 16:18—a passage that some New Testament scholars argue was not in the original Scriptures. I want Jimmy to find transcendence through dancing or hymn singing or Sufi spinning. Anything.

Well, there's an old mountain saying that Ralph Hood quotes: "If you don't believe in serpent handlers, pray for them." That I can do.

Month Eleven: July

"If any one thirst, let him come to me and drink."
—John 7:37

Day 306. I spend the morning at the Holy Apostles Soup Kitchen again. I've been studying who gets which job and why. I've noticed something: The beverage station—which is the very first stop in the main room, right next to the front door—is almost always given to . . . a hot female volunteer. Is this a coincidence? Or are they trying to give the place a little sex appeal?

My hunch is the latter. Which could be unbiblical. Aren't we supposed to be concerned with the spirit, not the flesh? I am stationed right next to today's official pretty lady. I pour the pink lemonade, she hands it out. She's a short, blond woman in a yellow T-shirt, the leader of a church youth group from Abilene, Texas. She hands out lemonades with a "Have a great day" and a smile out of a cruise line commercial. She seems to be doing well, but the soup kitchen elders can be tough. "Don't step forward when dispensing the lemonade," snaps a veteran volunteer. "It slows up the line. Just hand it to them."

The blonde nods, chastened.

There's almost always a church youth group at the soup kitchen. I have yet to see an atheists' youth group. Yeah, I know, religious people don't have a monopoly on doing good. I'm sure that there are many agnostics and atheists out there slinging mashed potatoes at other soup kitchens. I know the world is full of selfless secular groups like Doctors without Borders.

But I've got to say: It's a lot easier to do good if you put your faith in a book that requires you to do good. Back in high school, my principal—a strict guy who wore disconcertingly festive pink glasses—started something called "mandatory volunteering." Every week students had to spend two hours doing good if they wanted to graduate.

We students were outraged. Mandatory volunteering is oxymoronic! You can't legislate morality! It must be cultivated naturally. Plus, the policy came from the administration, so it had to be wrong.

But I wanted to graduate, so I went to a soup kitchen and cleaned trays. And it wasn't so bad. Looking back, I realize that mandated morality isn't such a terrible idea. Without structure, I would have been at home playing *Star Raiders* on Atari 800 or scouring at my dad's censored *Playboys*. Maybe Congress should take a page from my high school—or Mormon missionaries or the Israeli army—and require good citizenship from Americans. You graduate high school, and you get shipped off to AmeriCorps for a year—it's the law.

> *Make an incense blended as by the perfumer . . .*
>
> —Exodus 30:35

Day 309. Only two months left to go, which freaks me out. I have way too much to do. There are dozens of commandments I have yet to follow. And despite my shepherding and locust eating, I still haven't submerged myself enough in a primitive lifestyle. This month I vow to do just that. So I take out my thin, brown hardcover copy of *Daily Life in Biblical Times*, and get to work:

- Incense. I've started burning myrrh every morning. As you probably know, myrrh is one of the three gifts the wise men brought to Jesus. It's also mentioned several times in the Old Testament—God told Moses to make a sacred anointing oil using myrrh, along with cinnamon, aromatic cane, cassia, and olive oil (the recipe is so holy, you were exiled if you used it for nonsanctioned purposes).

  I bought my myrrh at a shop on Broadway, a cramped place filled with oriental rugs and brass jewelry and a surly guy behind the counter who was angry that I was wasting his time by having the gall to purchase items from his store when he had important sudoku to attend to. The myrrh comes in several congealed cones the size of a chocolate truffle, and I light one on the kitchen table when I wake up.

Julie scrunches her face and says, "It smells like a cathedral in here."

Yes. That's exactly what it smells like: the nave of Notre Dame or St. Paul's. It's not a frivolous smell. It smells old and serious and holy.

• Hospitality. They knew how to treat a visitor back in biblical times. If you're looking for the best host in history, Abraham has to make the short list. When three visitors appeared at Abraham's tent door, he ran and got them veal, cakes, and milk. He sat them under the shade of a tree. He stood nearby while they ate, just in case the veal was undercooked or they ran out of cakes.

This turned out to be a clever move. The strangers revealed themselves to be divine, so Abraham's hosting was not for nothing.

The zeal for hospitality continues in the present-day Middle East. When I was in Israel, it got to be oppressive, quite honestly. I peeked into a shop in the Old City section of Jerusalem, and the shop owner insisted that I come in, sit down, and have tea with him.

"I'd love to, but I actually have to run."

He looked at me like I had just taken a golf club to his car's windshield.

"Sit down and have tea."

It was not a request. I sat down and had tea.

Food and drink aside, the proper biblical host offered something else: water for the guest's feet. Everyone wore sandals, it was desert conditions—it's a nice thing to do. For the last two weeks, I've been trying this out.

"Come in!" I said to Julie's friend Margie. "Can I offer you food? Drink? Care to wash your feet in a bowl of water?"

In modern times, this always comes off creepy, no matter

which gender I'm offering it to. I've realized that foot washing is a surprisingly intimate and private thing, like gargling. In other words, no one's taken me up on foot washing. Margie went the furthest: She agreed to have a bowl of water brought out, but it just sat there forlornly on the table.

- Olive oil lamp. An olive oil lamp isn't just biblical, you'll be happy to know. It's also environmentally friendly. As it says in the appropriately named web magazine *TreeHugger,* "Olive oil lamps are a pleasing way to light your home. Olive oil is a renewable, nonpetroleum fuel which burns without fumes or odor. You can also burn any vegetable oil, or liquid fat, or grease in these lamps."

  I ordered a replica of an ancient "Samaria" lamp from Israel; it's terra-cotta, about the size of a grapefruit, comes with a thick white wick, and looks like a genie might puff out of it at any minute.

  I use it at night. I'm typing right now by olive oil lamp. The flame is solid and steady and casts a healthy glow over the table, but it's also disturbingly high. I can't figure out how to properly adjust the wick, so I've got this thing that could be carried in the opening ceremonies of the Olympic Games. I burn through a lamp full of olive oil in a half hour. Perhaps it's not so economical after all.

- The robe. I've been wearing white for a few months now—or off-white, by now—but I started to feel that wasn't enough. Before the end of the year, I wanted to sample some real biblical attire. I ordered a white robe off eBay, but when I tried it on, I looked like I was about to sing in a gospel choir. It wasn't working at all.

  The only genuine-ish biblical robe that didn't cost several hundred dollars was at a Halloween costume store. There it was, next to the Roman emperor togas: a shepherd's robe. It is white, with a V-neck, a belt rope. It's surprisingly comfortable. A man rarely gets to walk around in public with his legs unencumbered by pants. It's a nice change.

When I took it for a spin this week, I learned that a robe is a polarizing garment. At times I was treated as if I were a D-list celebrity—two Austrian teenagers asked to have their photo taken with me. At other times, I engendered not just the usual suspicion but flat-out hostility. As I was passing this man on the street, he looked at me, snarled, and gave me the finger. What was going through his mind? Does he hate shepherds? Or religion? Did he just read Richard Dawkins's book?

I've felt absurd many times throughout in the last ten months, but wearing a white man-skirt was a particularly embarrassing part of the experiment. My beard has drawn attention, but it is also—paradoxically—protective, since it shields my face. A robe is not. A robe makes me vulnerable.

My friend Nathaniel told me about a rabbi in nineteenth-century Lithuania who required his students do ridiculous things. He'd make them go into a bakery and ask for a box of nails. Or go into a tailor and ask for a loaf of bread. The idea was that he was trying to break down their ego, which he saw as a hurdle to true spirituality. That's what I try to think of when I walk around with my shepherd's robe, which sometimes billows up like Marilyn Monroe's white dress: I am breaking down the ego.

- The slave/intern. My slave-slash-intern started a couple of weeks ago. And it could be among the top ten best things that ever happened to me.

  I've had assistants before, but this is a whole other league. Kevin is a nice boy from Ohio. He's well-scrubbed, has dark blond hair, and looks like he stepped out of a commercial for herpes medication (I mean that as a compliment, by the way; they always cast the most vigorous American types, you know?). He's also part of an a cappella group that sings Jay-Z tunes. I heard them on his iPod, and they're really good.

  And, man, has he thrown himself into this role of biblical slave. Yes, he does a lot of regular intern stuff, like researching, making phone calls, and data entry (he set up an eBay account for me so I could sell some of my possessions—mostly DVDs and flannel shirts—and donate the proceeds to charity). But he also sends emails like this:

"Need any shopping done? Any baby clothes or things like that?"

Or:

"I'm willing to work eight hours a week or eighty."

I felt a bit guilty at first, but that faded soon enough. It's hard to complain when a guy zips off to the hardware store whenever a lightbulb blows out.

He also sent me this email yesterday: "If I can use your kitchen—mine's too small for these purposes—I'd love to bake you a loaf or two of Ezekiel bread tomorrow morning or afternoon, so that you can enjoy them over the weekend and on the Sabbath. Is this OK?"

Today I come home from a meeting, and Kevin is in my kitchen, his hands covered in flour, mashing a mixture of grains with a mortar and pestle. Ezekiel bread is one of the few recipes in the Bible. God told the prophet Ezekiel to bake a bread made with wheat, barley, beans, lentil, millet, and spelt. Kevin's Ezekiel bread was quite good. It reminded me of a less-crunchy graham cracker. Kevin later confessed that he tweaked the biblical recipe and added honey, but I felt it would be petty to rebuke him.

"Maybe we should give some to your neighbors," Kevin says. "That would be the biblical thing to do."

We knock on some doors, but no one's home. Well, actually, my neighbor Nancy is home, but she calls out from inside: "I'd love some, but I have a cracked rib, so I'm not getting up." I remind myself: I've got to get to work on that Hendrix proposal when she's better.

Kevin says he'd like to take a portion of bread to give away on his walk home. He reminds me of the good servant in Jesus's parable. The parable says that a master left for a trip, and gave five bags of money to his good servant and five to his bad servant. The good servant invested the money and doubled it to ten bags. By contrast, the bad servant buried his bag of money, which meant no increase at all. A good servant is proactive. Kevin would have doubled the money, maybe tripled it.

If a man begets a hundred children . . .

—ECCLESIASTES 6:3

Day 314. We go out to a Chinese restaurant with Julie's dad and step-mom. Julie is big enough now that the top of her stomach juts out at a ninety-degree angle, pretty much parallel with the table. She slides into the booth with impressive grace.

The waiter takes our orders. I get the steamed vegetables—bland but biblically safe. A few weeks ago I decided to make my Berkeley-based aunt Marti proud and go vegetarian. It wasn't so much an ethical decision as a pragmatic one. It's just so much easier to keep the Bible's food laws if you steer clear of the animals. Plus, according to the Bible, the human race started out as vegetarian—Adam, Eve, Cain, Abel, right on up until Noah, who was the first to eat flesh. So avoiding meat has scriptural backing.

I've also tried to cut out eggs. This is because of something I learned while interviewing a Karaite, a member of that sect of Judaism that follows the Bible as strictly as possible. "Let me drop an atom bomb on you," said this Karaite; his name is Nehemiah Gordon, and he runs the Karaite website, the Karaite Korner. "You can't follow all of the Bible literally because we can't know what some of the words mean."

In Leviticus 11, there's a list of birds that are abominations: the eagle, the vulture, the osprey, the pelican, and so on. Problem is, those birds are just our best guesses. The true identity of the birds have been lost in the haze of time. So to be safe, some Karaites don't eat eggs or poultry at all. It's a profound insight—and it has made my diet even more extreme.

Anyway, that was my dinner: vegetables that had been steamed into tastelessness. The conversation consisted mostly of Julie's stepmom trying to console Julie about the overload of Y chromosomes in our household.

"If you have another baby, I bet it's going to be a girl," she said.

When we get home, I ask Julie about the helpful tip.

"You think we should?"

"No. Absolutely not," she says. "These ovaries of mine are done."

"My thoughts exactly."

"Though we do have a frozen embryo at the clinic, right?"

I don't know. Do we have another frozen embryo? I can't believe I don't know. I should have been on top of that. The next day, I call the clinic and get a nurse on the phone. No, we have no embryos left. Nothing survived besides the two in Julie's swollen belly. Which is a relief. I don't have to figure out what to do with an extra embryo. One fewer moral decision to make.

The ethics of embryos—stem cells and abortion—are, of course, incredibly complex. Reasonable people disagree. And, frankly, the debate is beyond the scope of this book. So I won't try to argue for one side or the other. You can probably guess my position—it's typically liberal. But I will say this: When I read the Bible, it didn't seem to support either side. Religious tradition, church doctrine, rabbinical interpretation—those all weigh in on stem cells and abortion, and weigh in mightily. But the literal words of the Bible are, I believe, neither pro-life nor pro-choice.

Some pro-life advocates disagree. They point to several passages to prove that life begins at conception. Among them:

> For thou didst form my inward parts; thou didst knit me together in
> my mother's womb. (Psalms 139:13). (This passage is cited to prove
> that God is working on the fetus even as it is in the womb, thus mak-
> ing the unborn child sacred.)

> The Lord called me from the womb, from the body of my mother he
> named my name (Isaiah 49:1). (Here the prophet Isaiah says that God
> made him sacred him before he was even born. Again, God is at work
> in the womb.)

> And when Elizabeth heard the greeting of Mary, the babe leaped in
> her womb, and Elizabeth was filled with the Holy Spirit (Luke 1:41).
> (Here John the Baptist's pregnant mother meets the Virgin Mary, also

pregnant. John the Baptist jumps for joy—which is cited to show that unborn children have emotions.)

To base a major ethical decision on passages like these seems overreaching. They're too vague. They can be interpreted any number of ways—and, naturally, pro-choice Christians and pro-choice Jews do just that. But pro-choicers go further, which I wasn't expecting. They cite passages of their own. I read an article called "The Bible Is Pro-Choice" from a journal called *Humanist Perspectives*. The article talks about this quote from Ecclesiastes 6:3.

> If a man begets a hundred children, and lives many years, so that the
> days of his years are many, but he does not enjoy life's good things, and
> also has no burial, I say that an untimely birth is better off than he.

Here an untimely birth is interpreted as a phrase for miscarriage. This is meant to show that sometimes it is better that a life not be lived at all.

And there's also a controversial line in Exodus 21:22. This one says that if a man hurts a woman while she's pregnant and she loses her offspring, the man is liable. His punishment: He shall be fined some money. This, it's argued, shows that the unborn child is not considered a person. If it were a person, the man's punishment would be more severe. He'd be put to death.

Naturally, the pro-lifers have rebuttals to this. And their opponents have rebuttals to the rebuttals. (If you want to see a more in-depth look at the back-and-forth arguments, I recommend a website called ReligiousTolerance.org.) The abortion and stem cell debates always remind me of a William Blake quote. I wish I could say I read the quote while perusing Blake. Heck, I wish I could say I read the quote while reading a book by a Yale Divinity School professor. The sad truth is, I read it in a book called *Don't Know Much about the Bible*. But it's still a great quote:

> Both read the Bible day and night,
> But thou read'st black where I read white

> *He who is glad at calamity will not go unpunished.*
>
> —Proverbs 17:5

Day 324. I don't know what's happening to me. My friend Paul emailed me a YouTube video. I clicked it open. It showed a female newscaster reading some stock market news, when suddenly a huge stage light falls, smacking her on the head. She crumples off her chair and out of sight.

All the viewer comments said "LOL" or "laughing my ass off." But I didn't get it. It just seemed upsetting. I spent twenty minutes on Google trying to find the name of the poor newscaster so I could email her a get-well-soon or hope-you-win-your-lawsuit note. I couldn't track her down.

What's going on? What kind of an overly virtuous sap am I turning into? Next I'll be renting *Pay It Forward*.

> *By day the heat consumed me . . .*
>
> —Genesis 31:40

Day 332. It's a hot, hot New York summer weekend. I'm sweating heavily in my beard and *tzitzit*. Jasper's face is lobster red. So when our friends—who have a plastic blow-up kiddie pool in their courtyard—invite us over, it sounds like a good idea.

Jasper's right now splashing around in the pool with their daughter Lily, and he's having the time of his two-year-old life. He's laughing like Ray Liotta in *Goodfellas*. He's showing us how he can jump from one side of the pool to the other. I, on the other hand, am not having the time of my life. It's not good, this jumping. He's going to break his kneecap, crack his skull—something. I want to dial 9-1 and keep my finger poised over the other 1 in preparation for the inevitable disaster.

After three minutes of watching, I can take it no longer. I slip off my shoes, roll my white pants up to my calves, get up from the table, and step into the kiddie pool.

"What are you doing?" Julie calls out.

"I'm spotting our son," I say as I wade toward Jasper.

"Helmet," says Julie.

"Really?"

"Yes, helmet."

Fudge. Maybe she's right. Remember the example set by God, I tell myself. Remember that he gave humans free will. Which was a crazy generous thing to do. But God knew that humans are part-divine, so He wanted to give us the divine ability to make decisions. And just as importantly, to make mistakes.

So I should do the same with Jasper. Slowly, reluctantly, I step out of the kiddie pool. I sit down on a sticky white plastic chair and watch Jasper. Who eventually smacks his butt on the pool bottom, appears dazed for about ten seconds before returning to jumping like a maniacal monkey.

Month Twelve: August
(and Some of September)

Honor widows who are real widows.
—1 Timothy 5:3

Day 336. Today, I met my great-aunt Joelle for lunch. Joelle's the only other religious member of our family besides my Orthodox aunt Kate. She's a practicing Catholic who happily thanks God, even when surrounded by agnostics like my family. She's a former actress and singer (when our family sings "Happy Birthday to You," her vibrato gives it a professional sheen), and the single most talkative person I've ever met. Her husband—a sweet navy veteran—died a few months ago at their house in Miami.

The Bible says to comfort widows, which was one of the reasons I invited her to lunch. But as is often the case, I think she was more helpful to me than I was to her. She talked about God's love, His unconditional love. "Sometimes I can't believe how much God loves me. I think, 'How can He love me that much? I don't love myself nearly as much as He loves me.'" Even if life turns sour, or Joelle botches something, she can count on the unconditional love of God.

When I left the lunch, I felt at peace for the first time in a week. Last week, you see, I had a bit of a mental breakdown about my Bible project. In the final stretch, I've been frantically trying to read every single book on religion, trying to interview every religious leader, trying to figure out how to obey every rule. What if I miss an insight? What if I overlook a potential translation? I haven't paid God five shekels to redeem my firstborn son. I haven't talked to a Seventh-day Adventist yet. What if they have the secret? I've barely made a dent in the Bible.

But maybe God will forgive me for my lack of omniscience. If Joelle is right, He'll still love me. I'll never know everything. I can't compete with Him. And if you want to see what happens when you try, just look at the overachievers behind the Tower of Babel.

Again she conceived and bore a son . . .

—Genesis 29:34

Day 359. Today is the birth of our twins. The date is our choice. We scheduled to have them emerge onto God's Green Earth today, August 24, at nine in the morning. It's right there in Julie's computer calendar, like a routine eye exam with an ophthalmologist.

It seems highly unbiblical. I can't imagine that Rachel scheduled the birth of Joseph for the third day after the barley harvest. But our kids are positioned butt first in the womb, so the doctor says there's no choice but a Caesarian section.

It's all very civilized, this birth. Nothing like Jasper's. This time Julie has no contractions and lets out not a single lupine howl. She is wheeled on a gurney into the operating room with a little shower cap on her head. The anesthesiologist numbs her from the waist down, and that is it, she is ready to give birth.

I strap a surgical mask over my nose and mouth and join Julie in the OR.

"Uh-uh," says the nurse. "You need one for your beard."

She escorts me out and gets me a second mask for the bottom of my face. I return.

"We're going to take off your wife's gown now," the nurse says. "So if you want to leave, now is the time . . ."

"No thanks," I say.

An odd offer, I think. Oh, wait. She believes I'm an Orthodox Jew and might not want to see my wife's nakedness.

The atmosphere in the OR is an odd mix. It is, on the one hand, frighteningly gory. I'm stationed by Julie's head, and the doctor has hung a little curtain across the stomach so as to block the really messy stuff, though I still see enough to nearly make me pass out. On the other hand, the atmosphere is almost relaxed. The doctors are chatting about week-end plans as if they are having a chicken salad in the cafeteria.

"Hold my hand," says Julie.

"Well, you're impure for a week after the birth, so I can only hold it before the birth."

"Please don't—"

At 9:50 a.m. our doctor reaches in and scoops out one little man. At 9:52 she reaches in and scoops out another. I officially have a whole bunch of sons.

I look at my boys as they squirm around under a huge heat lamp. The boys themselves are another strange mixture. On the one hand, they're such little animals—tiny, naked, slimy little animals. They even sound like animals. Their crying isn't human, it's more like ducks quack-ing. On the other hand, I can already see something transcendent in them. When they pry their eyes open—blue eyes on both of them? where did that come from?—I spot what a nun I know calls "God's DNA." Those eyes are alive.

When the doctor plucks out our sons one after the other, I flash back to perhaps the most unforgettable delivery in the Bible. Yes, even in the OR, the Bible still colors my thinking. This was the birth of the twins Perez and Zerah. It goes like this: There was a struggle between the sons to see which one could be born first. One son—Zerah—stuck his hand out of his mother's womb, and the midwife tied a scarlet thread around his wrist. Then he pulled his hand back inside. The second son, Perez, then maneuvered around him and got out first. The Bible doesn't say who was considered oldest in this unusual scenario. I like to think it was Zerah, since he breached the womb with his hand, much as an NFL player scores a touchdown if he gets the ball over the line.

I'm glad I flashed to this story. Not because of the red ribbon twist. But because, if you remember, their conception is a good metaphor for my boys. Those ancient twins were conceived in complicated circumstances—the offspring of Judah and his daughter-in-law Tamar, who disguised herself as a prostitute. Mine, too, have a complicated ori-gin. But that doesn't, I hope, doom them.

And now that I type this up, I'm wondering if the Perez-Zerah story could be a Big Metaphor for my year. Maybe it applies to the Bible itself.

The Bible may have not been dictated by God, it may have had a messy and complicated birth, one filled with political agendas and outdated ideas—but that doesn't mean the Bible can't be beautiful and sacred.

Little children, you are of God . . .

—1 JOHN 4:4

Day 361. They released Julie and the twins from the hospital at eleven o'clock on the third day. It would have been sooner, but we lost about forty-five minutes to the hospital guards who double-checked and triple-checked our wrist bracelet IDs and social security numbers to make sure we hadn't swiped the wrong babies.

We've been home for two days now, and I've been spending the majority of that time snapping these little body suits on them. Man, these things have a lot of snaps. What the fudge happened to good old zippers?

Jasper has been dealing with his brothers with an interesting strategy: complete denial. He refuses to acknowledge them. Won't even look at them. They can be howling right in front of his face, but he'll use his X-ray vision to stare right through their skulls.

As for me, I know this will surprise you: I'm deliriously tired. Yesterday Julie was making a sandwich in the kitchen and I playfully patted her on the butt when I walked by. The only thing was, it wasn't Julie. It was my mom. My mom was visiting the twins. And in my bleary-eyed state, I had confused Julie for my mom. This is definitely forbidden by Leviticus.

I've barely been able to do anything biblical since the birth. I'm losing valuable time. I decided to extend my project another month, but Julie bargained me down to two weeks.

It doesn't help matters that the boys—Zane and Lucas—are on completely different schedules and refuse to cooperate. Their rivalry is, yes, biblical. The younger one is tiny—barely five pounds—and the older is a big lug, almost seven, and they're constantly battling each other to get access to Julie's milk supply. The younger one is sneaky. I think he can sense when the older one is stirring, and he'll start wailing to make sure he gets first crack. He's the Jacob to his brother's Esau—the mischievous underdog. Is it bad that I root for him? I've rooted for underdogs all my life, so I almost can't help it. I'm sure it's temporary. It better be. I've seen what favoritism can do—Jacob favored Joseph, and it got Joseph tossed in a pit by his jealous brothers.

> *Forgive, and you will be forgiven.*
>
> —Luke 6:37

Day 363. I finally told my parents that I had met my ex-uncle and was including him in the book. I emailed them the sections with Gil so they could be prepared.

They weren't happy. They told me I didn't expose Gil's dark side enough. They asked if I had to make him such a prominent part of the book. They wanted me to be clear he was an ex-uncle. They disputed the part where I said Gil was the most exotic creature in the family. But in the end, they were forgiving. They didn't make me change a thing. "We'll live with it," Mom wrote. "We love you." Their son did the equivalent of eating the husks thrown to the swine, and they welcomed me home with a hug.

> *He that is eight days old among you shall be circumcised.*
>
> —Genesis 17:12

Day 366. My twin sons have been in this world for eight days, which means today is the day to follow one of the first biblical commands: Circumcision.

I actually knew quite a bit about circumcision even before my biblical adventure. Perhaps too much. For a year or so in my early career as a journalist, I wrote a surprising number of magazine articles about circumcision. It was my first real beat. I was living in San Francisco at the time, and my eccentric aunt Marti introduced me to some anticircumcision activists who saw the snipping of the foreskin as cruel and unnecessary. As Marti put it: "It's the only men's issue I care about."

The hardest of the hard core didn't just want to outlaw circumcision, they wanted to reverse their own circumcisions. I remember attending a support group meeting that was bizarre even by the standards of San Francisco support groups. They called themselves RECAP, short for Recover A Penis (a rival group was called BUFF—Brothers United for Future Foreskins).

The meeting was held in the basement of a church—either an extremely liberal church or a church that didn't know to whom it was renting space. A dozen men sat in folding chairs arranged in a circle. Some were ponytailed hippies, some resembled the Leather Dude in the Village People, a few were just plain vanilla guys who looked like they could have worked in the loan department at Citibank.

"I don't feel whole," said one. "I want to feel whole again."

Another asked: "Can you imagine what it's like to have sex with a foreskin? It must be like watching color TV." (I never was able to confirm this, but the claim is that circumcision blunts the sensation.)

Most of the time was spent discussing homespun methods that would allow the men to regrow their foreskins. I'll spare you the details. I'm sure the internet has plenty more information for those who are interested.

Sexual sensitivity aside, the medical aspect of circumsicion remains a matter of debate. The American Academy of Pediatrics makes no recommendation either way. Circumcision may reduce penile cancer, and there's now compelling evidence it lowers men's susceptibility to AIDS. (After my biblical year ended, the World Heath Organization recommended medical circumcision be practiced in high-risk locales.)

So when our first son, Jasper, was born, I had mixed feelings about circumcising him. I didn't think he'd end up in a San Francisco basement venting his anger, but why put him through the pain? There's no rational reason for it. At least there wasn't before this latest round of AIDS studies. And even if it makes good medical sense, should we really turn the procedure into a party with sesame bagels and veggie cream cheese?

My aunts fueled my confusion. I was subjected to dueling campaigns. On the one hand, my Orthodox aunt Kate left voice mails encouraging us to go ahead with it. On the other, Marti sent pamphlets with stomach-churning stories of circumcisions gone bad.

In the end, Julie put her foot down. Jasper would have a circumcision, and it would be at our apartment, and it would be done by a family friend, Lew Sank, a New Jersey pediatrician who also has *mohel* credentials.

When the day came, and the family gathered, I did my best to ignore what was actually happening. I deluded myself into thinking of it as a brunch, with a short detour into some minor medical procedure.

I distanced myself with jokes. Of which Lew—like all mohels—had plenty.

"Did you hear the one about the guy who converted to Judaism as an adult? He has to get a circumcision, but he's nervous about it. So he asks his Jewish friend Abe, does it hurt? And Abe says, 'Oy. When I had mine done, I couldn't walk or talk for a year.'"

The only terrifying moment was when I spotted a knife on the table the size of a small machete. It turned out to be for the cutting of the ceremonial bread. So that, too, turned into something of a joke.

During Jasper's circumcision, Julie and I refused to watch the actual cutting. We both went into our bedroom and shut the door, and held hands, and talked very loudly about whether the dolphin-themed mobile took AA batteries or C batteries so as to drown out the crying. Two and a half years later, circumcisions two and three are upon me. And despite the existence of bagels and the mohel Lew, these feel different: This time I plan to watch. If I'm choosing to do this to my sons—this, the fifth and final law on my list of Most Perplexing Rules in the Bible—I can at least face up to my choice.

Circumcision is a huge part of the Bible; it merits eighty-seven mentions. It was seen as the way to seal the covenant between God and humans. A signature in blood. Abraham was the pioneer. God appeared to him and instructed him to circumcise all males in his house, and all newborns after eight days. Abraham had no newborns at the time, so the first inductees were his elder son, Ishmael (who was thirteen years old), and Abraham himself, who was all of ninety-nine years old.

In the New Testament, circumcision becomes optional, at best. The Apostle Paul—whose mission was to expand the Christian faith beyond the Jewish people—said that circumcision wasn't necessary. You didn't need the physical proof as long as you changed your heart. The phrase he used was circumcised "in the heart." Some passages do indicate that

Paul is fine with circumcision for those who are direct descendants of the Israelites.

"So are you going to do the circumcision yourself?" asks Julie's brother Eric.

"I hear there are some nice flint rocks in Central Park," adds her other brother, Doug.

"Very good," I say.

I'm not in the mood for jokes; I'm too anxious. My forehead is damp.

I mutter something about how the Bible doesn't mandate that the father perform the ceremony.

Actually, we're about as far from a flint rock as possible. Lew has come with a case full of gleaming metal equipment, which he's laid out on our dining room table. He snaps on his white surgical gloves, ties on a yellow apron, and pulls out a box of alcohol wipes.

"Who's first?" asks Lew.

"Zane?" I say.

"OK, bring him over."

He looks so tiny on the table, as small as a soup bowl at a dinner setting.

I glance around the room. My sister-in-law is staring out the window. My mom is flipping through a Thomas the Tank Engine brochure. Julie has her back to the table. No one is looking at Zane.

I gaze back at my son, who has started to cry. A bus rumbles by in the background. My teeth are clenched. I'm squinting, some sort of compromise between open and closed eyes.

Lew attaches some clamps. More crying. He takes out a brown leather strap. And scalpels. Drops of blood stain the towel. Zane is now wailing, openmouthed.

In a sense, it's all very hygienic, medical, sanitized. And yet . . . nothing can disguise the fact that what is happening on that table is deeply primitive. It's the most primitive thing I've seen in my entire biblical year.

There, on a patch of white gauze, is a piece of my son. He has sacrificed a part of his body to join an ancient community. Lew reads a prayer from a xeroxed sheet of paper. "May He who blessed our fathers, Abraham, Isaac, and Jacob, Moses and Aaron, David and Solomon, bless this tender infant . . ."

These are no longer just meaningless names. These are the men I'd spent my year with. Abraham, Isaac, Jacob. This was a chain that—if Lew continued spouting names for several hours—would presumably reach Charles Jacobowitz and Arnold Jacobs and A. J. Jacobs. Who am I to break thousands of years of tradition? Circumcision is a crazy, irrational ritual. But here's the thing: It's my heritage's crazy, irrational ritual. So maybe I shouldn't dismiss it.

So whatever you wish that men would do to you, do so to them.

—MATTHEW 7:12

Day 372. A few days ago, right before Labor Day weekend, the hallway outside our apartment began to smell.

"It's like rotten turnips," Julie said. "You smell it, don't you?"

I did, but told Julie it was probably nothing. Our mysterious neighbor in 5R—a woman I've never met—loves to cook exotic dishes made from animals unknown. This was probably just a recipe gone awry. But the smell didn't fade by morning. Julie called the building staff; they "checked it out" and found nothing. Over Labor Day, our neighbors all left Manhattan. The building was empty except for me, Julie, our kids, and that smell. Which got worse. And worse. You couldn't tell where it was coming from—it seemed to soak the hall.

When Julie and I would go out for a walk, we'd dart from our apartment to the elevator, our mouths and noses covered with our shirt collars. Julie called the maintenance staff again. They promised to look into it.

On Tuesday morning, I woke up to banging in the hallway. I opened our door a crack and peeked out. The building handyman, Victor, was outside apartment 5I—the one owned by our sweet hippie neighbor Nancy—trying to pry open her front door with a hammer. I could hear Nancy's dog barking. Four medics lingered nearby, occasionally clicking their walkie-talkies and speaking in low voices.

I knew before one of the medics asked me that question: "Have you seen your neighbor in the last few days?"

It took Victor a half hour of pounding before he broke down the door. He went in, reemerging a few minutes later.

"Alive?" I asked.

He shook his head.

They wheeled Nancy's body out on a stretcher covered with a sheet. They snapped a padlock on the door, along with yellow police tape ribbon and a Day-Glo sticker warning people not to even consider trying to come inside. They brought an industrial strength fan at the end of the hall to clear the smell.

I told Julie when she woke up. She sat down on the couch and put her face in her hands and didn't talk for what seemed like two full minutes. Finally she looked up, her eyes red.

"I saw her a week ago and she was all worried about me and how *I* was holding up."

I just shook my head.

"What'd she die of?"

"They don't know yet."

"I told them there was a smell," said Julie. "I told them. This is what I was afraid of."

Whenever something happens, I always try to think of a biblical precedent, a story that will help me put it into perspective. But with Nancy's death, there is none, really. The Bible doesn't talk much about living and dying in solitude. Adam starts out alone, but God doesn't let that last long: "It is not good for a man to be alone." In biblical times, the smallest unit of society wasn't the individual. It was the family. Nancy had no family, no husband, no children, just a handful of friends, few of whom she saw very often.

That night, Julie and I lie in bed, too spent to do much reading.

"Maybe we could . . . say a prayer."

Julie looks at me like I had just proposed a threeway with the waitress at Columbus Bakery.

"You serious?"

"A prayer of thanksgiving. I find them helpful. We don't have to call it a prayer. We just give thanks."

Julie paused. "OK."

"Maybe we'll start out simply."

"I'm thankful for our health and our kids," Julie says.

"I'm thankful we got to know Nancy," I say.

"I'm thankful you're ending your project soon."

The memorial service is held a couple of days later. It's in the apartment of a woman who knew Nancy just a little bit—they were both members of the building's informal dog owners' clique. Since Nancy had no family, Julie did most of the organizing, tracking down her few friends, posting a notice in the lobby.

About ten people show up. Her high-school friend Dan reads letters she'd written over the years, painfully honest notes about her loneliness and how she still has "the bends" after emerging from the sixties. We pass around the album cover she designed for Jimi Hendrix. Several people say something along the lines of: "She had a troubled life, but at least she found some peace at the end with her dog Memphis."

And we talk about the crushing irony, a twist that sounded like it was out of a Chekhov play but was true: She died of heart failure and asthma. The asthma was brought on by her dog.

If you try to literally follow Leviticus 19:18—"You shall love your neighbor as yourself"—well, you can't. That would mean putting your neighbor's dreams, career, children, pets, and finances on par with your own. This is why it's usually reinterpreted in the less extreme—but infinitely wise—version known as the Golden Rule: "Do unto others as you would have others do unto you."

While she was alive, I didn't do so well with the Golden Rule and Nancy. Here she was, my literal neighbor. Two doors down. And I had made a half-assed effort. I never invited her to dinner. I never rolled up my sleeves and helped her get her Jimi Hendrix book published. I never bought her a gift to repay her for the ones she bought Jasper. I never fulfilled my mission to do a mitzvah for her.

I got my chance to partially redeem myself. Nancy's beagle Memphis still wasn't adopted. He had a temporary home at another neighbor's apartment, but that family couldn't keep him long. So the next day I began a frantic quest: Find Memphis a home, and in so doing, make myself feel less powerless.

I clicked on to craigslist to put up a dog-adoption notice. But while there, I read a notice from the ASPCA. It warned of psychos who adopt dogs and then, for amusement, shoot them or toss them in the river. This didn't help my mood. Instead, I sent an email blast to everyone I could think of. I included a photo of Memphis. I had snapped the photo earlier in the day—the dog was born with a droopy face, but now it was positively dragging on the ground. Will anyone adopt such a forlorn-looking mutt?

A friend of a friend responded. He wanted to meet the forlorn dog. He came over, dressed in a suit and tie, his wife and children in tow.

"Let's think about it," said his wife, as the kids scratched Memphis's head.

She may have had a prudent idea. But the kids weren't about to wait, so just like that, Memphis was off to a suburban house with a yard and a porch.

The next day I felt like I'd at least done something Nancy would have liked. But I also flashed back to a question Nancy asked me months ago:

Did I help because the Bible told me to, or because I really wanted to?

Did I find the dog a new home as a pat and tidy way to quantify some moral progress for my book? Quite possibly.

I consulted one of my spiritual advisers about this—Greg Fryer, a Lutheran minister who lives in my parents' building. He told me the following:

"C. S. Lewis said the distinction between pretending you are better than you are and beginning to be better in reality is finer than moral sleuthhounds conceive." In short, pretending to be better than you are is better than nothing. Not only was this a great quote, but it also included dog imagery, so I thought it must be fated. I thanked Rev. Fryer and C. S. Lewis for letting my conscience off the hook.

A few days later three men in white Hazmat suits came to clear out Nancy's apartment. They had stuffed everything—her clothes, her frying pans, her papers—into black plastic garbage bags, about a dozen of which lined the hall. And they were just getting started.

I tied a red bandana to my face, put on some yellow dishwashing gloves, and stepped past them into the apartment.

"Just looking for something real quick," I said before they could ask for identification or permits.

I wove my way through the mess on the floor, and there, on a table in the corner, I found a stack of papers. I flipped through it. It was a very rough draft of her memoir. I took it.

"Thanks!" I said as I walked out.

When I got back to my apartment, I sat on my couch and read the handwritten pages. It's a tough but lovely book. It's also highly unfinished, sometimes with but a sentence fragment scribbled on top of a page. I don't know if it'll ever get published. I hope so. But in case it doesn't, here's a sentence on page forty-one that stopped me short. It is about her sketch of Jimi Hendrix, the one that became the cover to one of his albums.

"Eventually, I sold the original to the Hard Rock Cafe, not only because I needed a little money, but because I was afraid that, if I would die, it would be put on the street, like all stuff is put on the street when people die, in a black plastic bag. Now it was safe."

> *. . . It was in my mouth as sweet as honey.*
>
> —Ezekiel 3:3

Day 374. My niece Natalia is having her bat mitzvah in New Jersey today. As you probably know, the most important part of a modern bar or bat mitzvah isn't the Torah portion or lighting the candles, it's the theme. You've got to have a theme: sports, Camelot, whatever. I recently went to a bar mitzvah called Zach Wars: Revenge of the Torah, which seemed at odds with Leviticus's ban on vengeance. Natalia's theme is *Willy Wonka's Chocolate Factory*.

She and her mom have gone all out. The invitations were wrapped around a chocolate bar. Her mom spent weeks making twenty-two papier-mâché Oompa Loompas. Bowls of Skittles and M&M's cover the tables.

Jasper is getting fidgety, so I carry him onto the dance floor, where we joined all the thirteen-year-old classmates and sixty-eight-year-old cousins twice removed. We are dancing to some Beyoncé song, and I feel something happen. I feel something envelop me and then envelop Jasper. And then I feel it keep going. I feel it spread out like a drop of cranberry juice in a glass of water, sweeping through the room, swallowing my nieces and nephew and Julie and my parents. Here I am, at this gloriously silly ritual, surrounded by giant Twizzlers and Milk Duds, my defenses down, and this feeling has seeped out of my brain through my skull and filled the room. And kept going. For all I know, it has swept out the doors and windows and into the parking lot and through the driveway.

I'd had some close calls this year. There was that hypnotic trance while watching the serpent-handling preacher. But I've never fully let myself go, always hovering a few feet above ground like a hot-air balloon still stuck to its tether.

So at this suburban Jersey country club, my son's hands locked around my neck, his head pressed against my shoulder, I chose to accept this feeling and ride it to the end. To surrender. If I had to label it, I'd say the feeling is part love, part gratefulness, part connectedness, part joy. And that joy was like joy concentrate, far more intense and warmer than what I felt that night of dancing with the Hasidim. Maybe now I've finally felt what King David felt when he danced before the Lord. During those moments, nothing could have bothered me. If my garments flew up around my waist like King David's did, it wouldn't have mattered. At least to me. The joy would steamroll right on through.

My altered state only lasted all of ten seconds. Maybe less. And then it faded away. But not totally. There's still some background radiation—which I hope to God stays for weeks, months.

Driving back to New York, I ask myself, why did that just happen? Did it have something to do with my frazzled state after Nancy's death? Maybe. Was it because my project is about to end, and I forced myself into the state? Yeah, probably. But even if it was manufactured, it was still real. Farm-bred salmon is better than no salmon at all. Or to put it another way: My year was a controlled experiment, but sometimes experiments produce results precisely because they create extreme circumstances. If Gregor Mendel (a monk, incidentally) had let his pea pods grow willy-nilly, he never would have understood genetics.

Without my year, I wouldn't have been open to that feeling I got on the dance floor. And for that alone, all the craziness and Handy Seats and locusts and snakes might have been worth it.

The end of all things is at hand . . .

—1 PETER 4:7

Day 378. One day to go. I've decided not to go on a Bible binge this last day. I don't want to waste it running around like a *kaparot* chicken. I try to make it a slow day, a day of meditation. I want to try to get a little perspective. Such as:

Did the Bible make me a better person? It's hard to say for sure, but I hope it did. A little, at least. The other day I handed out flyers at a Save Darfur rally, but then got angry at the people who walked by without acknowledging me. I came up with elaborate revenge fantasies in which they read about the rally in the *New York Times* and felt guilty for not taking my flyer, even tracking me down to apologize. In other words, I'm pretending to be a better person, which is a good first step, if C. S. Lewis is to be believed.

I'm more tolerant, especially of religion, if that helps my case. Here's how I know this: When Jasper was born, my Orthodox aunt Kate gave him a bunch of building blocks with Hebrew letters and paintings of biblical scenes. I didn't want Jasper using them because I was worried the blocks would somehow imprint on his brain and eventually convert him to Hasidism. Nowadays I'm not just OK with him playing with his Bible blocks, I like it. I want him to know his religion.

And the Bible itself? What do I think of it after my yearlong immersion?

When I started my project, Elton Richards made that majestic food analogy: He said my quest was like a banquet table, and not everyone would sit with me at my banquet table, but I have a hunger and thirst, so I deserve to nourish it. I loved the way he talked. I decided that by year's end, I would employ an extended food metaphor of my own. I think I have one now. It may not be majestic, but here goes:

There's a phrase called "Cafeteria Christianity." It's a derisive term used by fundamentalist Christians to describe moderate Christians. The idea is that the moderates pick and choose the parts of the Bible they want to follow. They take a nice helping of mercy and compassion. But the ban on homosexuality? They leave that on the countertop.

Fundamentalist Jews don't use the phrase "Cafeteria Judaism," but they have the same critique. You must follow all of the Torah, not just the parts that are palatable.

Their point is, the religious moderates are inconsistent. They're just making the Bible conform to their own values.

The year showed me beyond a doubt that everyone practices cafeteria religion. It's not just moderates. Fundamentalists do it too. They can't heap everything on their plate. Otherwise they'd kick women out of church for saying hello ("the women should keep silence in the churches. For they are not permitted to speak . . ."—1 Corinthians 14:34) and boot out men for talking about the "Tennessee Titans" ("make no mention of the names of other gods . . ."—Exodus 23:13).

But the more important lesson was this: there's nothing wrong with choosing. Cafeterias aren't bad per se. I've had some great meals at cafeterias. I've also had some turkey tetrazzini that gave me the dry heaves for sixteen hours. The key is in choosing the right dishes. You need to pick the nurturing ones (compassion), the healthy ones (love thy neighbor), not the bitter ones. Religious leaders don't know everything about every food, but maybe the good ones can guide you to what is fresh. They can be like a helpful lunch lady who—OK, I've taken the metaphor too far.

Now, this does bring up the problem of authority. Once you acknowledge that we pick and choose from the Bible, doesn't that destroy its credibility? Doesn't that knock the legs out from under it? Why should we put stock in any of the Bible?

"That's the big question," says one of my rabbis, Robbie Harris. I put the question to Robbie as well as every other member of my advisory board. There's no simple or totally satisfying answer. But let me offer two interesting ideas from them:

The first is from the pastor out to pasture, Elton Richards. Here's his metaphor: Try thinking of the Bible as a snapshot of something divine. It may not be a perfect picture. It may have flaws: a thumb on the lens, faded colors in the corners. But it still helps to visualize.

"I need something specific," says Elton. "Beauty is a general thing. It's abstract. I need to see a rose. When I see that Jesus embraced lepers, that's a reason for me to embrace those with AIDS. If he embraced Samaritans, that's a reason for me to fight racism."

The second is from Robbie himself. He says we can't insist that the

Bible marks the end of our relationship with God. Who are we to say that the Bible contained all the wisdom? "If you insist that God revealed himself only at one time, at one particular place, using these discrete words, and never any time other than that—that in itself is a kind of idolatry." His point is: You can commit idolatry on the Bible itself. You can start to worship the words instead of the spirit. You need to "meet God halfway in the woods."

Which brings up another question: Do I believe in a traditional biblical God? Well, not in the sense that the ancient Israelites believed in Him. I could never make the full leap to accepting a God who rolls up His sleeves and fiddles with our lives like a novelist does his characters. I'm still agnostic. But in the words Elton Richards, I'm now a reverent agnostic. Which isn't an oxymoron, I swear. I now believe that whether or not there's a God, there is such a thing as sacredness. Life is sacred. The Sabbath can be a sacred day. Prayer can be a sacred ritual. There is something transcendent, beyond the everyday. It's possible that humans created this sacredness ourselves, but that doesn't take away from its power or importance.

I come away from this year with my own cafeteria religion. I'll be doing things differently than I did thirteen months ago, things both big (resting on the Sabbath) and small (wearing more white clothes). And I'll keep on saying prayers of thanksgiving. I'm not sure whom I'm thanking, but I've become addicted to the act of thanking (see the overlong acknowledgments section).

> *There is . . . a time for every matter under heaven.*
>
> —Ecclesiastes 3:1

Day 381. My favorite book, Ecclesiastes, has these famous lines:

> For everything there is a season, and a time for every matter under heaven; a time to be born, and a time to die; a time to plant and a time to pluck up what is planted.

This is the time for me to uproot my topiary.

I've been anxious about this for weeks. First of all, I'd heard nightmare stories about kids who didn't recognize their fathers postshave. Some of these kids went on extended crying jags. They'd scream about this strange man in their house. The relationship took weeks to recover.

I'm so paranoid about this, I came up with an idea of how to prep Jasper for the day of defoliation. It involved breaking the Second Commandment—you shall not make any images—but I did it anyway. A couple of weeks ago, I went to Staples and printed out a large color photo of my face circa 2005, from the era of smooth cheeks. I attached the photo to a Popsicle stick. Then, every morning, for an hour while I fed him breakfast, I'd hold the photo in front of my face like a mask. I made holes for the eyes and mouth. He seemed a little weirded out.

Now the day is here. I spend the morning inspecting my beard. I go into the living room to get in some last-minute prayers. Julie's in there.

"You OK?" asks Julie.

"Not really."

"Well, you're making me really happy. Try to focus on that."

The shave itself is scheduled for two o'clock on September 18. The publisher sent a photographer over to get before and after shots, so I spend a few minutes staring at the camera and trying not to look too much like a terrorist. Don't want to scare off potential book buyers.

Luckily, the photographer doesn't ask me to smile. This would have been hard. My mood is black for several reasons. First, there's always an immediate postpartum depression after finishing a big project. I felt it when I read the entry on Żywiec in the encyclopedia. I feel unmoored and a little scared. What do I do? I don't have structure. Second, my beard has been with me for so long, it's taken on its own identity, almost become a living organism. I feel like I'm losing a pet rabbit.

And third, I'm not just shaving my beard, I'm amputating a large part of my identity. In a couple of hours, I won't be Jacob anymore. I'll be back to being a regular old, unremarkable New Yorker, one of millions.

It's two o'clock when I take the first snip out of my beard. It's not easy, the logistics of shaving this thing. You can't just put on some cream and whip out the razor. First, I hack away at the beard for forty-five minutes with a big silver pair of scissors. The clumps of hair float down, turning the sink black and making the floor look like a Supercuts franchise. The beard eventually shrinks down to the length of putting-green grass. I sweep up all the tufts and stuff them into a gallon-sized Ziploc bag. Not sure what I'm going to do with this bag of hair. Maybe give away patches with the first one hundred copies of the book.

And now for the razor. Actually, I bought a new razor for the occasion. In this year, a lot has happened in the razor industry. Back when I was shaving regularly, they had a mere three blades. Now these newfangled five-bladed ones have popped up. I lather up, jut out my chin, and put the razor to my neck. I hear that familiar scrape. A stripe of skin appears. And another. After ten minutes, I wash off the rest of the shaving cream, and there it is. My face.

Man, I look weird. I feel naked, vulnerable. My cheeks are tingling, like my face just got out of a yearlong steam bath.

Julie has been watching the last five minutes. "You look like you're fourteen!"

And it's true. Maybe it's an optical illusion—like how a little circle looks even smaller when it's next to a huge circle—but I could pass for an eighth-grader.

Julie grabs my cheeks and pulls me toward her. I kiss her for the first time in two months. Which is lovely. I had forgotten how her lips felt.

The photographer was kind enough to bring champagne. He pops it over our sink and pours some glasses for me, him, and Julie. I'm about to take a sip, when I pause. I say a silent prayer of thanks for the champagne. The prayer feels good, different, unforced. I'm off the clock.

He shall restore what he took by robbery . . .

—Leviticus 6:4

Day 387. It's been a week since the shave. The first day was the worst. I felt unanchored. Too many choices. It reminded me of the overwhelming freedom I experienced on that first day of freshman year at college, but without any of the exhilaration and double the dread.

Oh, and lots of guilt. I felt like I was getting away with all sorts of transgressions. I went to the barber and had my hair washed by a woman.

All the while I was thinking, "Can I really do this? Can I really flip through the *People* magazine while she's trimming my sideburns? Can I really buy a banana on the way home without worrying if it's from a tree that's more than four years old?" It still seemed wrong.

Every day the guilt recedes a little. Every day I get a bit more accustomed to choice. Choice isn't necessarily a bad thing, I tell myself. And at least my year helped narrow my choices.

I'll never be Jacob again. I'll never live with so many restrictions. But a part of my biblical alter ego has carried over. If my Bible self had a footlong beard, what remains is barely a five o'clock shadow, but it's there. I think it'll always be there.

Right now I'm at the post office, Jasper in tow. I told him I was running an errand, and he insisted on coming, since he's somehow gotten the idea that errands are as exciting as the Central Park merry-go-round. We wait fifteen minutes before getting to the front of the line. I slide a brown bubble-wrap package onto the scale. Six dollars to go to Monte Sereno, California. I pay my money. In three days my ex-girlfriend will open her mailbox to find her black leather Bible with its tissue-thin pages and faded gold embossing, the 1,536 pages that have shaped my year.

Jasper and I leave the post office, turn left, and head toward home for a quiet Friday night.

A Note from the Author

All the events in this book are true. Some of the sequences have been re-arranged, and, in certain cases, the names and identifying details have been changed. Unless otherwise specified, the Bible quotations are from the Revised Standard Version.

Notes

INTRODUCTION

Forgive me. I know I used the I'm-as-Jewish-as-the-Olive-Garden-is-Italian line in my last book. But it just happens to be the best description of my ethnicity.

THE PREPARATION

It's nearly impossible to get an accurate count on the number of different Bible editions. "In English, there are more than 3,000 versions of the entire Bible or portions of the Bible," writes Kenneth C. Davis in *Don't Know Much About the Bible*. Kevin Phillips's book *American Theocracy* gives a much higher number: 7,000.

Thanks to professor Julie Galambush for tipping me off to the anesthesia brouhaha.

To be precise: The Protestant Old Testament has 39 books, but the Jewish and Catholic versions have a different count. The Hebrew Bible comes in at 35 books, because several books—like Kings and Chronicles—are not split into two parts. The Catholic Old Testament totals 46 books, since it contains sections not found in the Protestant version, such as Tobit, Judith, and Maccabees.

The term *midrash* has a couple of meanings. It can be used to describe Jewish folklore such as the Nachshon tale. But it also has a wider meaning, namely, the collection of rabbinic sermons and commentaries on the Bible. For more, see the *Encyclopedia Judaica*'s *midrash* entry, which comes right after the entry on Bette Midler.

DAY 2

Other suspects that have been mentioned as the actual forbidden fruit: the fig, pomegranate, grapes, and wheat.

For more on Genesis' fertility themes, see *Who Wrote the Bible?* by Richard Elliott Friedman.

I got concerned that my memory had distorted the meaning of cognitive dissonance. And there are a bunch of definitions nowadays. But I found the original 1959 paper establishing the theory, and it says that when there is a conflict between a person's thoughts and actions, the "the private opinion changes so as to bring it into closer correspondence with the overt behavior." See www.psych classics.yorku.ca/Festinger/index.htm.

D<small>AY</small> 6

My wife's ex-boyfriend's gadget is called a Light Wedge, in case you want to buy one.

Yes, I know the whole "Eskimos have lots of words for snow" is kind of an urban legend. See *Word Myths* by David Wilton, p. 53, which says, "So, how many Eskimo words for snow are there? The answer is either a few or a lot, depending on how you count." Does that clarify it?

The rabbi who talks about coveting Jaguars is Joseph Telushkin, author of *Biblical Literacy,* as referenced in *Don't Know Much About the Bible.*

D<small>AY</small> 23

For an excellent article on Proverbs and spanking, see www.religioustol erance.org/spankin13.htm.

D<small>AY</small> 31

Speaking of calendars, I didn't pay proper attention this year to the intricacies of the biblical calendar. Forgive me. I could have spent a year unraveling the debates on this topic alone. There's the well-known Hebrew calendar, but also the Karaite calendar and the Samaritan calendar.

D<small>AY</small> 40

I still have no idea what that "Don't Look Back" sign at the airport was all about. If you do, let me know.

The polls in question include Gallup and CBS News. Here's a good article on it: www.straightdope.com/columns/061110.html.

D<small>AY</small> 42

The Jubilee year hasn't been observed since the time of the Temple (*The Second Jewish Book of Why,* p. 262). The Sabbath year is still observed in some form, but only in Israel (ibid., p. 320).

D<small>AY</small> 44

I first learned about the "domino" phrase in the book *Serving the Word: Literalism in America from the Pulpit to the Bench,* a very interesting look at fundamentalism.

The history of literalism is actually far more complex and subtle than my thirty-second summary. (I know, shocking!) There's much debate over how literally the ancients took the Bible. Some religious scholars—including Karen Armstrong and Marcus Borg—argue they didn't take it literally at all (see the discussion of *mythos* and *logos* in Day 272). These scholars say the ancients saw the Bible stories as myth—true on a deep metaphorical level, not as hard fact. It wasn't supposed to be reportage like *The Wall Street Journal.* Borg quotes a Georgian aphorism: "It is true, and it is not true."

Most scholars agree that at some point—after the Gutenberg Bible was printed? after the Renaissance?—believers started taking the Bible as factual, literal truth. And it was this literal interpretation of the Bible that spawned the dueling worldviews of modernism and fundamentalism. To complicate matters further, there are many alternatives to modernism and fundamentalism. For instance, geneticist Francis Collins wrote *The Language of God,* about how religion and science can be reconciled.

In Jewish biblical interpretation, the literal meaning of a passage is sometimes called *"pshat"* and the interpretation is called *"derush."* And if you want to get really technical, there are four levels of biblical interpretation in traditional Judaism: *"pshat* (the literal meaning of the text), *remez* (its allusions), *derush* (the homilies that can be derived from it), and *sod* (its mystical secrets)." They spell out the acronym *"pardes,"* which means orchard (from the Lubavitcher website sichosinenglish.org).

I did, in fact, smash an idol. I took a hammer to a faux Oscar statuette that my wife bought as a party favor once. I got out some of my hostility toward celebrity culture. But frankly, it didn't feel like it merited a chapter.

Day 45

Sorry. I used the line about my dad working through the Apocalypse in my previous book. That's the last time in this book that I'll recycle a line from *The Know-It-All*.

Day 46

Actually, in Judaism, life trumps all except for adultery, murder, and idolatry. Traditionally, you should choose to die before committing those. Also, I probably shouldn't say that all rabbis would allow pig's valves, since religion has a way of making a mockery of absolute statements. But I have yet to hear of a rabbi who would ban this.

Day 50

If you want to be nitpicky about the whale/big fish thing: The Book of Jonah says "great fish," though when the story is referenced in Matthew 12:40, the word *whale* is, in fact, used.

Day 64

I should note that Orthodox Jews today say prayers both before and after a meal, as do some Christians.

Day 70

The book with the broad definition of evil tongue is *The 613 Mitzvot* by Ronald L. Eisenberg.

Day 82

The "vapor of vapors" translation is from *Reading the Bible Again for the First Time* by Marcus J. Borg. In fact, I was helped enormously by Borg's brilliant section on the conflict between the conventional wisdom of Proverbs and the more nuanced wisdom of Ecclesiastes and Job.

Day 87

Other Catholic objections to IVF include: (1) it usually involves masturbation; and (2) it sometimes involves discarding fertilized eggs. For more on that see Day 314.

Day 93

The Apocrypha contains such texts as Tobit, Judith, Maccabees, and Ben Sira. In Judaism and Protestant Christianity they aren't considered part of the canon. But in Catholicism they are and go by the name Deuterocanonical works.

Day 110

The two most zealous propolygamy Jewish web pages: www.polygamy.com/

articles/templates/?a=28&z=; and www.come-and-hear.com/editor/america_
4.html.

DAY 117

Later parts of the Bible seem to reject the notion of intergenerational punishment. Most notably, Ezekiel 18:20: "The son shall not suffer for the iniquity of the father, nor the father suffer for the iniquity of the son."

DAY 120

Incidentally, Tamar's second husband, Onan, is most famous for being the originator of the Sin of Onan. I had always thought the Sin of Onan was masturbation. But technically, that's not the case. Onan incurred God's wrath when he stopped midway through intercourse with Tamar and spilled his seed on the ground. Onan didn't want Tamar to get pregnant because, according to custom, the child would be considered his late brother's, not his own. Onan showed disrespect for his dead brother and for God by wasting his seed. So that is the literal Sin of Onan.

DAY 128

For more on whether the commandments actually total ten, I recommend the fascinating book *How to Read the Bible* by Marc Brettler.

DAY 131

The scavenger hunt company is called Watson Adventures. The hunts are great. And I'm not just saying that because I sleep next to the company's vice president.

DAY 140

The expert of all experts on kosher crickets is Natan "the Zoo Rabbi" Slifkin, whose website is zootorah.com. According to him, not all crickets are kosher, just one variety favored by Yemenite Jews.

DAY 153

The Bible says to attach tassels (or fringes) to the four corners of your garment. Where are my garment's corners? During my DIY phase, I usually went with the two corners at the end of my Oxford shirtsleeves and the two corners at the bottom of my shirt front. If I was feeling bold, I'd go with the corners on the shirt collar.

DAY 157

The upright posture quote comes from *The Jewish Book of Why* by Alfred J. Kolatch.

DAY 168

For more on red heifers and the apocalypse, I recommend a great *New Yorker* article, "Letter from Jerusalem: Forcing the End," by Lawrence Wright, July 20, 1998.

I've just skimmed the surface of the debates over Revelation. For an excellent summary of two ways of reading Revelation, I once again recommend Borg's *Reading the Bible Again for the First Time*. He argues strongly that Revelation was not a prediction of events yet to come (the futurist view), but was written as a short-term prophecy about the Roman Empire (the past-historical view). There are also many people who believe in some combination of the two.

DAY 181

To be precise, the documentary hypothesis refers only to the first five books of the Bible, the Books of Moses. But the same idea—multiple authors, multiple editors—applies to other parts of the Bible as well.

For a remarkably in-depth analysis of the Dr. Laura email—including more on the overliteralization of the word *pigskin*—you can read "President Bartlet's Fallacious Diatribe" by Hank Hanegraaff in the *Christian Research Journal,* volume 23, number 3 (2001).

DAY 202

There are several other differences between the Samaritan Bible and the Hebrew Bible. They're pretty technical, but if you're interested, here are two websites: www.lulu.com/content/186110; and web.meson.org/religion/torahcompare.php.

DAY 205

Speaking of the Naked Cowboy, I did a photo shoot for this book in Times Square. The publisher rented a sheep and had me in a white robe and carrying a staff. For forty-five absurd minutes I drew more onlookers than the Naked Cowboy himself. I think that will forever be the zenith of my fame.

I think Gil misspoke when he said "Jacob was buried with Rachel," because Jacob was actually buried with Leah. I'm guessing he meant "Abraham was buried with Sarah."

DAY 223

Actually, the notion of booze-hating Puritans is a bit of an exaggeration. Some did, but others believed it was OK in moderation. In the words of Increase Mather, "Drink is in itself a good creature of God, and to be received with thankfulness."

DAY 229

Regarding the lamb juice: A kosher lamb is drained of its blood, in accordance with the Bible's taboo against eating blood. But I can't imagine there isn't some residual blood left in there, even if it's just a hint.

DAY 233

For more on the oft-forgotten male impurity laws try reading the article on Taharat Hamishpachah at www.kenyon.edu/Depts/Religion/Projects/Reln91/Blood/Judaism/new%20family/purity.htm. Also, in case you really, really want to know: I tried to comply with Leviticus 15:16, which says "And if a man has an emission of semen, he shall bathe his whole body in water, and be unclean until the evening." It wasn't so bad. I have no objections to extra bathing, and Julie didn't take this one personally.

DAY 234

A confession: I cut way back on movies this year, but never successfully eliminated them from my life. I saw this one, plus a whole bunch of Bible-themed films. Also, for a good, basic section on the fifth commandment (Honor your father and mother) see *Don't Know Much About the Bible,* p. 120.

DAY 237

Thanks to the rock-and-roll rabbi Robbie Harris for the insight that the Bible is a "minority report."

Day 243

As is de rigueur with all things relating to *The Da Vinci Code,* the notion that a married Jesus is a more human Jesus is a controversial one. One of my spiritual advisers (who asked to remain unnamed) emailed me: "There is no scandal in supposing that Jesus married and had children. It is a stupid reading of the scriptural text, and it is very doubtful historically, but not troubling theologically. And that Dan Brown supposes that it is reveals that he does not have a clue about Christianity and that he has a very low opinion both of humanity and of the holy estate of marriage. Jesus is a man—that's the point of the holy incarnation of the Second Person of the Trinity."

Day 264

The *New York Times* article on the Reverend Boyd is "Disowning Conservative Politics, Evangelical Pastor Rattles Flock" by Laurie Goodstein, July 30, 2006.

Day 277

The King James version cleans up Ezekiel 23:20. But the New International Version gives a more earthy, and accurate, translation: "There, she lusted after her lovers, whose genitals were like those of donkeys and whose emission was like that of horses."

For more history of cursing try "Almost Before We Spoke, We Swore" by Natalie Angier, September 20, 2005. And "Tarnation Heck!" by William Safire, February 12, 2006. Both in the *New York Times.*

Day 287

See *A Practical Handbook for Ministry* by Wayne E. Oates for more on mentally ill patients who try to pluck out their eyes.

Day 297

Thanks to *Roadside Religion* by Timothy K. Beal for first introducing me to the quote about religious study making the "strange familiar and the familiar strange" (p. 299). It's an interesting book about religious tourist destinations.

Many scholars—including Bart Ehrman, in *Misquoting Jesus*—contend that the Gospel of Mark originally ended with the verse 16:8. Or else, it continued, but the real ending has been lost.

Day 314

The translation of Exodus 21:22 is notoriously difficult. If you translate the Hebrew word for "lose her offspring" as "a miscarriage," the passage seems to bolster the pro-choicers. If you translate it as "premature birth," then it can be used by pro-lifers. For more on this, see www.religioustolerance.org/abo_biblh .htm.

Here are some other websites that deal with abortion and the Bible from both sides:

www.prochoiceactionnetwork-canada.org/articles/bible.html; www.priests forlife.org/brochures/thebible.html; www.elroy.net/ehr/abortion.html; www .jimfeeney.org/pro-life.html.

By the way, here's an etiquette tip: Do not say "Mazal tov" to a Karaite. The phrase *mazal tov* means "good stars" or "good constellations," which they see as violating the Bible's ban on astrology.

DAY 372

The C. S. Lewis quote is from *Surprised by Joy: The Shape of My Early Life* (New York: Harcourt, Brace & World, 1956), p. 192.

DAY 378

For more on women being banned from talking in church, see *Rescuing the Bible from Fundamentalism* by John Shelby Spong.

Selected Bibliography

Armstrong, Karen. *The Battle For God.* New York: Ballantine, 2000.
———. *The Great Transformation.* New York: Knopf, 2006.
———. *A History of God.* New York: Knopf, 1993.

Ballmer, Randall. *Thy Kingdom Come.* New York: Basic Books, 2006.
Barton, John, and John Mudiman, eds. *The Oxford Bible Commentary.* Oxford: Oxford University Press, 2001.
Beal, Timothy K. *Roadside Religion.* Boston: Beacon Press, 2005.
Bell, James Stuart, and Stan Campbell. *The Complete Idiot's Guide to the Bible.* New York: Penguin Group, 2005.
Blackhouse, Robert. *The Kregel Pictorial Guide to the Temple.* Grand Rapids, Mich.: Kregel Publications, 1996.
Blanton, Brad. *Radical Honesty.* Stanley, Va.: Sparrowhawk Publications, 2005.
Bloom, Harold. *Jesus and Yahweh: The Names Divine.* New York: Riverhead Books, 2005.
Bloom, Harold, and David Rosenberg. *The Book of J.* New York: Grove/Atlantic, 1990.
Bock, Darrell. *The Missing Gospels: Unearthing the Truth Behind Alternative Christianities.* Nashville: Thomas Nelson, 2006.
Borg, Marcus J. *Reading the Bible Again for the First Time.* New York: HarperCollins, 2001.
Borowski, Oded. *Daily Life in Biblical Times.* Leiden, The Netherlands: Society of Biblical Literature, 2003.
Boyd, Gregory. *The Myth of a Christian Nation.* Grand Rapids, Mich.: Zondervan, 2005.
Boyer, Pascal. *Religion Explained.* New York: Basic Books, 2001.
Brettler, Marc Zvi. *How to Read the Bible.* Philadelphia: Jewish Publication Society, 2005.
Butler, Trent, Chad Brand, and Archie England, eds. *Holman's Illustrated Bible Dictionary.* Nashville: B&H Publishing Group, 2003.

Carmichael, Calum. *Ideas and the Man: Remembering David Daube.* Frankfurt, Germany: Vittorio Klostermann, 2004.

Carter, Jimmy. *Our Endangered Values*. New York: Simon & Schuster, 2005.
————. *Sources of Strength*. New York: Three Rivers Press, 1997.
Chilton, Bruce. *Rabbi Jesus: An Intimate Biography*. New York: Image, 2002.
Coffin, William Sloane. *Letters to a Young Doubter*. Louisville, Ky.: Westminster John Knox Press, 2005.
Colbert, Don. *What Would Jesus Eat?* Nashville: Thomas Nelson, 1982.
Collins, Francis. *The Language of God*. New York: Free Press, 2006.
Crabb, Larry. *Finding God*. Grand Rapids, Mich.: Zondervan, 1993.
Crapanzano, Vincent. *Serving the Word: Literalism in America from the Pulpit to the Bench*. New York: New Press, 2000.
Cross, Carlene. *Fleeing Fundamentalism: A Minister's Wife Examines Faith*. New York: Algonquin Books, 2006.

Davis, Kenneth C. *Don't Know Much About the Bible*. New York: William Morrow, 1998.
Dawkins, Richard. *The God Delusion*. New York: Houghton Mifflin, 2006.
Dossick, Rabbi Wayne. *Living Judaism*. San Francisco: HarperSanFrancisco, 1995.
Dowley, Tim. *Everyday Life in Bible Times*. Grand Rapids, Mich.: Kregel Publications, 1998.

Ehrman, Bart D. *Misquoting Jesus*. New York: HarperCollins, 2005.
Eisenberg, Ronald L. *The JPS Guide to Jewish Traditions*. Philadelphia: Jewish Publication Society of America, 2004.
————. *The 613 Mitzvot*. Rockville, Md.: Schreiber Publishing, 2005.
Englert, Jonathan. *The Collar*. New York: Houghton Mifflin, 2006.

Finkelstein, Israel, and Neil Asher Silberman. *The Bible Unearthed*. New York: Free Press, 2002.
Fox, Everett. *The Five Books of Moses*. New York: Schocken Books, 1995.
Fox, Robin Lane. *The Unauthorized Version*. New York: Knopf, 1991.
Freedman, David Noel, ed. *The Anchor Bible Dictionary*. New York: Doubleday, 1992.
Friedman, Richard Elliott. *Commentary on the Torah*. San Francisco: HarperSanFrancisco, 2003.
————. *Who Wrote the Bible?* New York: Summit Books, 1987.

Galambush, Julie. *The Reluctant Parting: How the New Testament's Jewish Writers Created a Christian Book*. New York: HarperCollins, 2006.
Geoghegan, Jeffrey, and Michael Homan. *The Bible for Dummies*. Hoboken, N.J.: Wiley, 2003.
Girzone, Joseph. *My Struggle with Faith*. New York: Doubleday, 2006.
Goldberg, Michelle. *Kingdom Coming*. New York: Norton, 2006.
Greenberg, Rabbi Steven. *Wrestling with God & Men*. Madison, Wisc.: University of Wisconsin Press, 2004.

Hahn, Scott. *Letter and Spirit: From Written Text to Living Word in the Liturgy.* New York: Doubleday, 2005.

Harris, Roberta. *The World of the Bible.* London: Thames & Hudson, 1995.

Harris, Sam. *The End of Faith.* New York: Norton, 2004.

———. *Letter to a Christian Nation.* New York: Knopf, 2006.

Hedges, Chris. *American Fascists.* New York: Simon & Schuster, 2006.

Hendricks, Howard G., and William D. Hendricks. *Living by the Book.* Chicago: Moody Press, 1991.

James, William. *The Varieties of Religious Experience.* New York: Modern Library, 2002.

Kelemen, Lawrence. *Permission to Receive.* Southfield, Mich.: Targum Press, 1996.

Kelly, Stuart. *The Book of Lost Books.* New York: Random House, 2006.

Kennedy, D. James. *Why the Ten Commandments Matter.* New York: Time Faith, 2005.

Kierkegaard, Soren. *Fear and Trembling.* New York: Knopf, 1994.

Kolatch, Alfred. *The Jewish Book of Why.* Middle Village, N.Y.: Jonathan David Publishers, 1981.

———. *The Second Jewish Book of Why.* Middle Village, N.Y.: Jonathan David Publishers, 1985.

Kornbluth, Doron. *Jewish Matters.* Southfield, Mich.: Targum Press, 1999.

Kozodoy, Ruth Lurie. *The Book of Jewish Holidays.* Springfield, N.J.: Behrman House, 1981.

Kugel, James L. *The Bible as It Was.* Cambridge, Mass.: Belknap Press of Harvard University Press, 1997.

LaHaye, Tim, and Jerry B. Jenkins. *Left Behind.* Wheaton, Ill.: Tyndale House, 1995.

Levine, Baruch A. *Leviticus: The Traditional Hebrew Text with the New JPS Translation.* Philadelphia: Jewish Publication Society of America, 1989.

Lewis, C. S. *Mere Christianity.* New York: HarperSanFrancisco, 2001.

———. *The Screwtape Letters.* San Francisco: HarperSanFrancisco, 2001.

Lightfoot, Neil R. *How We Got the Bible.* Grand Rapids, Mich.: Baker Books, 2003.

Locks, Gil. *Coming Back to Earth.* New York: L'Chaim Publications, 2004.

MacArthur, John. *What the Bible Says About Parenting.* Nashville: Thomas Nelson, 2000.

Matthews, Victor H. *Manners and Customs in the Bible.* Peabody, Mass.: Hendrickson Publishers, 1991.

McBrien, Richard P. *Catholicism: New Study Edition.* San Francisco: HarperSanFrancisco, 1994.

———. *Lives of the Saints: From Mary and Francis of Assisi to John XXIII and Mother Teresa.* San Francisco: HarperSanFrancisco, 2001.

McClellan, Ruth. *An Incredible Journey*. Lynchburg, Va.: Liberty University, 2006.

McDowell, Josh. *Evidence for Christianity*. Nashville: Thomas Nelson, 2006.

McManis, Cliff. *Christian Living*. The Woodlands, Tex.: Kress Christian Publications, 2006.

Mennonite Confession of Faith. Crockett, Ky.: Rod and Staff Publishers, 1963.

Metzger, Bruce, and Michael D. Coogan, eds. *The Oxford Companion to the Bible*. New York: Oxford University Press, 1993.

Miles, Jack. *God: A Biography*. New York: Knopf, 1995.

Morrow, Jimmy, with Ralph W. Hood. *Handling Serpents*. Macon, Ga.: Mercer University Press, 2005.

Nicholi, Armand M. *The Question of God: C. S. Lewis and Sigmund Freud Debate God, Love, Sex, and the Meaning of Life*. New York: Free Press, 2003.

Nicolson, Adam. *God's Secretaries*. New York: HarperCollins, 2003.

Omartian, Stormie. *A Book of Prayer*. Eugene, Oreg.: Harvest House Publishers, 2006.

Oppenheimer, Mark. *Thirteen and a Day*. New York: Farrar, Straus and Giroux, 2005.

Pagels, Elaine. *Adam, Eve and the Serpent*. New York: Vintage, 1989.

Pakkala, Lorraine. *Yea God!* Trumansburg, N.Y.: Crossing Press, 1980.

Perkins, Bill. *When Good Men Are Tempted*. Grand Rapids, Mich.: Zondervan, 1997.

Phillips, Kevin. *American Theocracy*. New York: Viking Penguin, 2006.

Priolo, Lou. *Teach Them Diligently*. Woodruff, S.C.: Timeless Texts, 1977.

Rousas, John Rushdoony. *The Institutes of Biblical Law*. Nutley, N.J.: Craig Press, 1973.

Rubin, Jordan S. *The Maker's Diet*. New York: Penguin Group, 2004.

Russell, Bertrand. *Why I Am Not a Christian*. New York: Simon & Schuster, 1957.

Ruthven, Malise. *Fundamentalism: The Search for Meaning*. Oxford: Oxford University Press, 2004.

Sarna, Jonathan D. *American Judaism*. New Haven, Conn.: Yale University Press, 2004.

Sarna, Nahum M., ed. *The JPS Torah Commentary: Genesis*. Philadelphia: Jewish Publication Society, 1989.

Shulevitz, Judith. "Bring Back the Sabbath." *New York Times*, March 2, 2003.

———. "What Do Orthodox Jews Think of Abortion, and Why?" *Slate*, August 25, 2000.

Simon, Ethelyn, and Joseph Anderson. *Teach Yourself to Read Hebrew*. Albany, Calif.: EKS Publishing, 2002.

Skolnik, Fred, ed. *Encyclopedia Judaica*. New York: Macmillan, 2006.

Smith, Huston. *The World's Religions*. San Francisco: HarperSanFrancisco, 1991.

Spong, John Shelby. *Rescuing the Bible from Fundamentalism*. San Francisco, HarperSanFrancisco, 1991.

———. *The Sins of Scripture*. San Francisco: HarperSanFrancisco, 2005.

Steinberg, Milton. *As a Driven Leaf*. Springfield, N.J.: Behrman House, 1939.

Steinsaltz, Adin. *The Essential Talmud*. New York: Basic Books, 1984.

Stewart, Matthew. *The Courtier and the Heretic*. New York: Norton, 2006.

Strobel, Lee. *The Case for Faith*. Grand Rapids, Mich.: Zondervan, 2000.

Strong, James. *The New Strong's Exhaustive Concordance of the Bible*. Nashville: Thomas Nelson, 1996.

Telushkin, Joseph. *The Book of Jewish Values: A Day-by-Day Guide to Ethical Living*. New York: Harmony/Bell Tower, 2000.

Tigay, Jefrey H. *The JPS Torah Commentary: Deuteronomy*. Philadelphia: Jewish Publication Society, 1989.

Tillich, Paul. *History of Christian Thought*. New York: Touchstone, 1972.

Turner, Denys. *Faith, Reason and the Existence of God*. Cambridge: Cambridge University Press, 2004.

Twain, Mark. *Letters from Earth*. New York: Perennial, 1991.

Unger, Merrill F. *The New Unger's Bible Handbook*. Chicago: Moody Press, 2005.

United States Catholic Catechism for Adults. Washington, D.C.: USCCB, 2006.

Wallis, Jim. *God's Politics*. New York: HarperCollins, 2005.

Warren, Rick. *The Purpose Driven Life*. Grand Rapids, Mich.: Zondervan, 2002.

Weisman, Charles A. *A Handbook of Bible Law*. Burnsville, Minn.: Weisman Publications, 1991.

Wills, Garry. *What Jesus Meant*. New York: Viking Penguin, 2006.

Woodmorappe, John. *Noah's Ark: A Feasibility Study*. Santee, Calif.: Institute for Creation Research, 1996.

Zacharias, Ravi. *Can Man Live Without God?* Nashville: Thomas Nelson, 1996.

BIBLE BIBLIOGRAPHY

Alter, Robert, trans. *The Five Books of Moses.* New York: Norton, 2004.
American Bible Society. *Good News Bible,* 1993 (GNB).

Doubleday. *The New Jerusalem Bible,* 1990 (NJB).

Fox, Everett, trans. *The Five Books of Moses.* New York: Schocken Books, 1983.

Jewish Publication Society. *Tanakh: The Holy Scriptures,* 1985 (JPS).

Lockman Foundation. *Amplified Bible,* 1954 (AB).

Mesorah Publications. *The Stone Tanach,* 1996.

Oxford University Press. *The Holy Bible: New Revised Standard Version,* 1989 (NRSV).
Oxford University Press. *The New Oxford Annotated Bible,* 2001.

Thomas Nelson. *The Holy Bible: Revised Standard Version,* 1972 (RSV).
Thomas Nelson. *The Holy Bible: New King James Version,* 1982 (NKJV).
Tyndale House. *The Living Bible,* 1976 (TLB).

United States Conference of Catholic Bishops. *The New American Bible,* 2005 (NAB).

World Publishing. *The Holy Bible King James Version,* 1928 (KJV).
World Bible Publishing. *God's Word Bible,* 1998 (GWT).

Zondervan. *Holy Bible: New International Version,* 1989 (NIV).

Acknowledgments

The Bible says to give thanks (Psalms 44:8), so I hope you'll forgive me if I get a little carried away.

Thanks to my editor Marysue Rucci at Simon & Schuster, who is a joy to work with—passionate, generous, and wise.

I'm grateful to my agent Sloan Harris at ICM, who insists on breaking his profession's stereotype by being a complete mensch.

I'm indebted to Rob Weisbach, a brilliant editor and great friend without whom I would not be doing this for a living.

There's an astounding number of people to thank at Simon & Schuster for their unrivaled support: David Rosenthal, the *capo di tutti capi*, as well as Victoria Meyer, Aileen Boyle, Tracey Guest, Julia Prosser, Leah Wasielewski, Jackie Seow, Marcella Berger, Marie Florio, Lisa Healy, and my friendly taskmaster, Ginny Smith.

If this were an awards show, I'm guessing I'd be played off right about now. But I've got plenty more. My spiritual advisory board consisted of the following insightful and kind people: Elton Richards, Andy Cohen, Marsha Marks (the Christian aunt I never had), Julie Galambush, David Bossman, David Cohen, Nathaniel Deutsch (who understood my project better than I did), Roger Bennett, Fay Landis, Rev. Stan Duncan, Robbie Harris, Azriel Hirsch, Oded Borowski, Father Michel Lavoie, Darrell Bock, Dean Hubbard, Bill Berkowitz, Calum Carmichael, Michael Berenbaum, Glen Hoptman, Benyamin Cohen, Joseph Ginzberg, Greg Frier, Eddy Portnoy, and Vincent Crapanzano.

Thanks to all those who read the manuscript and gave me their editorial wisdom, namely: Lizzie Berne DeGear, Peter Griffin, Andrew Lund (who read it twice!), Chad Millman, Brian Frazer, Neely Harris (who used a highlighter), Carolyn Bernstein, Rob Kurson, Albert Kim, Ken Jennings (yes, as in the Ken Jennings of *Jeopardy!*), Shannon Barr, Mark Warren, Elicia Pomeroy (who kindly donated a metaphor), Stephen Friedman, Sam Davidoff, Laura Bittner, Martin Zuckerman, Mark Warren, Uri Grezemkovsky, Paul Mandell, Jennifer Landis, Burt Cohen, and Melanie Davis.

I'm grateful to David Granger of *Esquire*, a visionary editor (who didn't get mad when I slacked off on my *Esquire* duties for three months—maybe four). And to Josie Freedman of ICM, who is the female version of a mensch, whatever that is called, as well as Liz Farrell, Michael McCarthy, and Kristyn Keene.

Thanks to Victor Ozols, a researcher/adviser whose attention to detail is matched by his big vision.

Thanks to former S&S'er Geoff Kloske, who bought the book and gave me good advice on sandals.

Thanks to Ivan Hrazdira, who gave me excellent insights on biblical banking. Laurie Davis, who was invaluable in helping me release debt. Kevin Roose, my slave/intern (I'm telling you, the kid is going places). Justin Balding and Jamie Novogrod for making images. Thomas Wheatley and Buddy Kite for their research. To Ruth Feinberg for her insights into temptation and impurity. And the madcap minds of Jay Reiss and Jeremy Kleiner.

I'm especially grateful to my family, who instilled in me Judeo-Christian values (without the explicit Judeo-Christian parts): my parents, my sister, her husband, Willy, and my grandfather. Also thanks to my aunts Kate and Marti, who may be on opposite ends of the theological spectrum, but who are both wonderful people.

And, of course, thank you to Julie, my *beshert*. And to my sons, Jasper, Zane, and Lucas.

Index

Page numbers in *italics* refer to illustrations.
Page numbers beginning with 335 refer to notes.

as "sanctuary in time," 124–25
bat mitzvah, epiphanic dancing at,
    325–26
Battle for God, The (Armstrong), 277
Baywatch, 216
beard (AJ's), *iv, 2*
    Christian view of, 254–55
    indie record producer phase of,
        108
    as itchy and uneven on day seven,
        28
    professorial phase of, 4
    Rosario Dawson as fan of, 133
    summary of woes ascribed to, 3
    traumatic removal of, 329–31
    "under or over the covers," 106
    unexpected directions taken by,
        88
    unjust demotion in soup kitchen
        caused by, 81–82
    when 60 percent of AJ's face was
        covered by, *150, 180*
beards:
    Amish, 30
    ex-uncle's colloquy on, 223
beds, unclean, avoidance of, 51
being fruitful and multiplying, 3
    avoiding topic of, 18–19
    as Bible's Alpha Rule, 19
    failed attempts at, 18–20, 48–52
    IVF seen as way to go in, 116–18,
        146–47
    Malthusian issue in, 159
    as moral imperative, 117
    uncommon literal interpretation
        of, 19
    see also fertility; pregnancy; twins
Bennett, Roger, 35–36
    AJ advised on surrendering
        control by, 36
Bentley, Wes, 153
Berkowitz, Mr. (Bill), 268
    AJ chided for missing prayers by,
        250
    AJ's alarming lies to, 53–54
    doing commandments loved by,
        250–51
    guided through a properly devout
        day by, 141–44

learning how to separate a mother
    pigeon from her egg with, *184,*
    185–88
offering (potentially) nonkosher
    water to, 140–41
ready-made rituals favored by, 148
on rights vs. responsibilities, 251
shatnez testing demonstrated by,
    23–25, 36
shofar lessons also given by, 206
spiritual questions fielded by,
    24–25, 203
as totally religious (doesn't
    straddle both worlds), 68
bestiality, 91, 135
Bible:
    alcohol-friendly theology sought
        in, 231–33
    apocalypse sections of, 190–92
    atheist's confrontational approach
        to, 97
    authorship issues of, 200–201
    baffling and federally outlawed
        rules of, 8; *see also* Most
        Perplexing Rules; rules, biblical
    circumcision a huge part of, 319
    "clobbered" antigay passages in,
        266–67
    committing idolatry in, 328–29
    December holidays not
        conspicuous in, 121
    dysfunctional father-son stories
        in, 230
    an estimated three thousand
        versions of, 9, 335
    fundamentalism vs. modernism
        on, 67
    as history's most mistranslated
        text, 70–71; *see also*
        mistranslations, biblical
    importance vs. unworthiness of
        humans in, 107–8
    Jubilee year of, 63–65, 262
    living and dying alone not a major
        theme in, 322
    more than seven hundred rules
        found in, 8
    needy aided through financial
        laws of, 63

on hair length, 181

on love recording no wrongs, 273

women in church admonished to keep silent by, 328

coveting, 195, 203, 227

of charity CEOs, 38

a few things worthy of, 26

finer points of, 27, 336

Covington, Dennis, on serpent handlers, 294

cows:

in biblical times, 173

kosher issues when cheese is made from enzyme in stomachs of, 69

purification by one that is red and perfect, 188; *see also* red heifer

unsolved murder as occasion for breaking neck of, 20

cow's milk, goat's milk as replacement of, 173

creationism, 56–63, 200, 277

on age of earth, 58, 107–8

astonishing mental gymnastics of, 60

far-right fundamentalists in, 11

feeling of being less inconsequential taught by, 107–8

meaning of "day" in, 58

moderation in, 63

on racism, 59

Creationist Museum, 44, 56–63, 166, 258

astrophysicist of, 60

awesome lobby of, 57

pop culture monitored at, 61

Crocodile Dundee (movie), 58

Crown Heights:

eighteenth-century life still seen in, 162

experiencing kaparot in, 160–65

subway to Hasidim of, 84

why bottled water is a winner in, 140

see also Hasidic Jews

cud-chewing debate, 59

Daily Life in Biblical Times (Borowski), 198, 302

Daly City, Calif., Karaites living in, 69

dancing:

with Hasidim, 84–86, 214, 326

of King David, uptight wife's ill-fated reaction to, 84, 326

at Natalia's bat mitzvah, 325–26

Daniel, Book of, on God protecting the nearly martyred faithful, 77

Darfur, aid to, 11, 38, 59, 327

Darrow, Clarence, 62

Darwin, Charles:

AJ's unforgettable factoid about, 56

Noah's ark in disconnect with theory of, 67

David, King, 147, 200, 211

Absalom and, 188–89, 230

harps inspired by, 168

Nathan's parable on Bathsheba and Uriah heard by, 195

progeny of, 159

rock hurling learned while shepherding by, 212

wardrobe malfunction during dance of, 84, 326

wives of, 84, 135, 137

David, Larry, 36

David (cousin), 117

David (*Esquire* colleague), 70–71

David (friend), 13, 132

David (Israeli) tithing tried on, 214–15

David (Julie's friend), 197

Da Vinci Code, The (Brown), 256, 340

Davis, Kenneth C., 335

Dawkins, Richard, 98, 305

Dawson, Rosario, interview with, 131, 133

Dead Sea Scrolls, 66

December holidays, Bible's scant guidance on, 121

definitions and etymologies:

of "Bible," 110

of "blasphemy," 281

of "day," 58

of "evil tongue," 99

of "helmet," 108–9

of "Isaac," 19

—*SWC*